COPING

COPING

THE PSYCHOLOGY OF WHAT WORKS

Edited by
C. R. Snyder

New York   Oxford

Oxford University Press

1999

Oxford University Press

Oxford   New York
Athens   Auckland   Bangkok   Bogotá   Buenos Aires   Calcutta
Cape Town   Chennai   Dar es Salaam   Delhi   Florence   Hong Kong   Istanbul
Karachi   Kuala Lumpur   Madrid   Melbourne   Mexico City   Mumbai
Nairobi   Paris   São Paulo   Singapore   Taipei   Tokyo   Toronto   Warsaw

and associated companies in
Berlin   Ibadan

Published by Oxford University Press, Inc.
198 Madison Avenue, New York, New York 10016

Oxford is a registered trademark of Oxford University Press

Library of Congress Cataloging-in-Publication Data
Coping : the psychology of what works / edited by C. R. Snyder.
p.   cm.
Includes bibliographical references and index.
ISBN 0-19-511934-7
1. Adjustment (Psychology)   I. Snyder, C. R.
BF335.C587   1999
155.2'4—dc21   98-30270

9 8 7 6 5 4 3 2 1

Printed in the United States of America
on acid-free paper

To all the people at the home on 1656 Illinois Street,
where coping is a daily adventure . . .

Foreword

Robert Frank

In many ways, the field of psychology stands at yet another critical crossroads. Clinical practitioners find their practices eroded by increasingly aggressive competition with other health professions and reluctance by healthcare payors to fund psychological treatments or assessment. At the same time, psychological researchers are reevaluating the direction of the science enterprise within the profession. Increasingly, there is emphasis on the "psychology of the positive" in contrast to historic models based on psychopathology. A recent president of the American Psychological Association, Martin Seligman, from the University of Pennsylvania, crystallized national attention on the relatively uncharted human emotions. Seligman noted that most research focuses on psychopathology and often ignores positive emotions such as joy or courage (1). Seligman has emphasized the advantage of studying emotions that have been neglected, such as "virtues, courage, or hope." Seligman's plea found an empathetic audience among psychologists and, indeed, among the general public. Now, this volume, *Coping: The Psychology of What Works*, focuses the growing academic and public interests in the spectrum of emotion and how coping affects emotion. In addition, it addresses the importance of coping to both healthy functioning and the so-called "positive emotions," as well as the consequences of deficiencies in coping that lead to the manifestation of psychopathology.

Snyder and his colleagues have previously addressed the broader questions regarding the interface between social and clinical psychology (2,3). In these works, Snyder and colleagues demonstrated the increasing synergies between two previously distinct fields. Clearly, clinical processes are substantially augmented by a distinct understanding of social psychology. In this volume, Snyder has drawn together a remarkably talented pool of authors to articulate the power of coping to psychological health. There is a pleasing synergy in this volume. Arguably, coping processes form the connection between social and clinical psychology. In this work, Snyder and colleagues have created a platform to expand psychology's understanding of human behavior in both deviant and healthy situations.

The growing recognition of the interrelationship between social and clinical psychology parallels changes in medicine. Over the last 100 years, medicine has systematically increased its territorial boundaries. One hundred years ago, medicine was still a relatively untested discipline. Increases in our understanding of the transmission of disease lead to vast improvements in public health. Hospitals were among the first institutions to grasp the importance of sanitary environments and to implement standards of care. With these changes, hospitals became environments of greater health, rather than higher mortality, as had previously been the case. Physicians joined with hospitals in the endorsement of sterile treatment environments. This led to substantial improvements in the efficacy of medicine that were further enhanced by the development of antibiotics and other effective pharmaceuticals. During this period, the profession of medicine, along with hospital administrators, successfully marketed the concept that improved health required the use of hospitals and medical institutions (4). During this epic, medicine grew significantly.

Medicine's greatest growth, however, was the recognition of its newly perceived value to the public. Leaders in medicine and hospital managers quickly recognized the value of their new image. A part of the marketing of medicine, driven initially by improved sanitary conditions, was the expansion of the definition of medicine to cover virtually every aspect of health. With this expansion of boundaries, medicine grew to include many areas previously viewed as social or cultural. Areas such as birth, death, violence, nutrition, dietary standards, and many other aspects of daily life became "medicalized." Many of the areas in which medicine expanded fell within the domain of psychology.

Most recently, escalating healthcare costs—and the recognition that despite escalating cost, there has been limited improvements in the overall health of the population (5)—have resulted in decreased public confidence in the American healthcare delivery system. Over the last decade, a virtual revolution in the delivery of healthcare has resulted from these economic and quality concerns. Changes in healthcare delivery systems have lead to a new emphasis on outcome measures (6). Consumers and healthcare payors are now interested in healthcare outcomes. There has been an increased interest in outcome measures that focus on the "health of the community" as opposed to the health of an individual. "Health of the community" models have altered the practice of medicine. No longer is it efficient to rely on the "medical model" treating a single disease. Rather, healthcare systems must now focus on the effective prevention of disease and securing high levels of health for the entire population served. The altered focus of healthcare systems has also created opportunities and demands for psychology. Now the prevention of disease is essential. Fundamental to the prevention of disease is a comprehensive understanding of coping and its implications for psychological and physical health.

In this volume, Snyder and the participating authors have provided a comprehensive, and timely, review of current conceptualizations of coping, ranging from coping with catastrophic events, to the value of effective coping, to the nature of hope and the relationship of coping to positive emotions. The application of coping to the broader domain of health and basic daily human functioning is timely. As healthcare systems assume responsibility for the health of individuals served, knowledge of the role of coping in health is even more important. Like medicine 100 years ago, the merging of society needs with the profession's contributions creates a unique opportunity.

Of course, applying coping to healthcare systems and suggesting it is a fundamental mechanism in prevention, essential to the overall health of the community, goes beyond the applications described in this text. The applications of coping described are, however, fundamental to understanding the value of the articles included within this text, as well as the magnitude of the potential implications of the text. Snyder has created a tour de force of coping research; the most renowned theoreticians and investigators of coping research grace the pages of this book. As Snyder notes in the last chapter, texts such as this will hopefully move the field to a more prospective, theoretically driven model of coping research. The rampant escalation of correlational studies derived from the advent of coping measurement scales has hopefully run its course. In addition to defining the theory and current research on coping, the text moves the field to the brink of one of the largest issues facing Americans: How can we prevent disease and live gracefully with chronic health conditions that will affect as many as 100 million Americans (7)? By advancing the theory and science of coping, Snyder and his colleagues have positioned the field to contribute to this much larger debate.

References

1. Hall, T. (1998, Tuesday, April 28). Seeking a focus on joy in the field of psychology. *New York Times*, p. B10.
2. Snyder, C. R., & Forsyth, D. R. (Eds.) (1991). *Handbook of social and clinical psychology*. Elmsford, NY: Pergamon Press, Inc.
3. Snyder, C. R., & Ford, C. E. (1987). *Coping with negative life events: Clinical and social psychological perspectives*. New York: Plenum.
4. Stevens, R. (1989). *In Sickness and in wealth: American hospitals in the twentieth century*. New York: Basic Books, Inc. Publishers.
5. Frank, R. G., & VandenBos, G. R. (1994) Health care reform: The 1993–1994 evolution. *American Psychologist*, 94(10), 851–854.
6. Frank, R. G. (in press). Organized delivery systems: Implications for clinical psychology services or We zigged when we should have zagged. *Rehabilitation Psychology*.
7. Hoffman, C., Rice, D., & Sung, H. Y. (1995). Persons with chronic conditions: Their prevalence and costs. *Journal of the American Medical Association*, *276*, 1473–1479.

Preface

The genesis of this volume was the 1987 Snyder and Ford edited volume entitled *Coping with Negative Life Events: Clinical and Social Psychological Perspectives.* That edited volume brought together social and clinical psychologists on a topic that had provided a natural common turf for them—coping. Much to my surprise and delight, that volume proved to be a useful one to the people who do work in this area, at least as judged by the feedback that I received from both applied and research-oriented professionals who had read it. It has been more than a decade since that coping book was published, however, and in the last several years I have been asked about the possibility of a new book on coping, one that bridges the work of clinical and social psychologists, as well as personality psychologists. The present volume provides such an update and overview of coping as we close the present twentieth century. Although this book is by no means exhaustive in terms of covering the many new and exciting developments in the field of coping, it does give the reader a sampling of the advances that have been made.

I want to thank publicly the prominent scholars whose work fills the pages of the present volume. Their thinking has helped to define the progress that has been made on the concept of coping. Although there obviously are many scholars whose work I was not able to include here because of space constraints, I believe that the present writers offer an excellent overview of this burgeoning field. Furthermore, contrary to the horror stories that I have heard about how difficult it is to get the truly prominent scholars to participate in such an edited book project, I had not a single turndown. Indeed, everyone agreed to participate, and I am enormously grateful to these busy people for carving out the time necessary to provide their forward-looking chapters. Likewise, in contrast to the supposed problems that are inevitable in getting such a stable of scholar/writers to adhere to a schedule, the present chapters and their revisions arrived in a timely fashion. Accordingly, a full dose of gratitude is due to the chapter authors.

There are several people who deserve special attention for their help on this book. At various points throughout the project, my assistants Lynne Cobler and Martha Dickinson provided critical technical help. Likewise, my editor at Oxford, Joan Bossert, has been unflagging in her endorsement of the present book idea from start to finish. Furthermore, to my wonderful colleagues and graduate students in the Clinical Psychology Program at the University of Kansas, I thank you for providing a supportive professional "home" where the norms are to care about each other and to foster the very best in people. It is easy to write about coping in such an atmosphere. Lastly, to my family members who always remained remarkably supportive about the interloper who took me away from them (i.e., this, my latest book venture), I extend my appreciation and love.

C. R. S.   Lawrence, Kansas

Contents

Contributors

Glenn Affleck, Professor of Community Medicine and Health Care, University of Connecticut School of Medicine

Roy F. Baumeister, Elsie B. Smith Professor in the Liberal Arts, Case Western Reserve University

Brian T. Bedell, Doctoral Student in Psychology, Department of Psychology, Yale University

Charles S. Carver, Professor, Department of Psychology, University of Miami

Jen Cheavens, Doctoral Student, Graduate Training Program in Clinical Psychology, Department of Psychology, University of Kansas, Lawrence

James P. David, Research Scientist, Department of Psychology, University of Iowa

Jerusha B. Detweiler, Doctoral Student in Psychology, Department of Psychology, Yale University

Beth L. Dinoff, Doctoral Student, Graduate Training Program in Clinical Psychology, Department of Psychology, University of Kansas, Lawrence.

Carol S. Dweck, Professor, Department of Psychology, Columbia University

Jon E. Faber, Doctoral Student, Department of Psychology, Case Western Reserve Univeristy

Robert Franz, Doctoral Student, Graduate Training Program in Clinical Psychology, Department of Psychology, University of Kansas, Lawrence

Jane E. Gillham, Research Associate, Department of Psychology, University of Pennsylvania

Raymond L. Higgins, Professor and Director, Psychological Clinic, Graduate Training Program in Clinical Psychology, Department of Psychology, University of Kansas, Lawrence

Ronnie Janoff-Bulman, Professor, Department of Psychology, University of Massachusetts

Ruth Q. Leibowitz, Doctoral Student, Graduate Training Program in Clinical Psychology, Department of Psychology, University of Kansas, Lawrence

John D. Mayer, Associate Professor, Department of Psychology, University of New Hampshire

Scott T. Michael, Doctoral Student, Graduate Training Program in Clinical Psychology, Department of Psychology, University of Kansas, Lawrence

Christina H. Moon, Undergraduate, Department of Psychology, University of Michigan, Ann Arbor

James W. Pennebaker, Professor, Department of Psychology, University of Texas at Austin

Christopher Peterson, Professor, Department of Psychology, University of Michigan, Ann Arbor

Karen Reivich, Research Associate, Department of Psychology, University of Pennsylvania

Peter Salovey, Professor of Psychology and Epidemiology, Department of Psychology, Yale University

Michael F. Scheier, Professor, Department of Psychology, Carnegie Mellon University

Martin E. P. Seligman, Kogod Professor of Psychology, Department of Psychology, University of Pennsylvania

Andrew J. Shatté, Research Associate, Department of Psychology, University of Pennsylvania

Joshua M. Smyth, Assistant Professor, Department of Psychology, North Dakota State University, Fargo

C. R. Snyder, Professor and Director, Graduate Training Program in Clinical Psychology, Department of Psychology, University of Kansas, Lawrence

Lisa A. Sorich, Doctoral Student in Psychology, Department of Psychology, Columbia University

Annette L. Stanton, Associate Professor and Coordinator, Health and Rehabilitation Specialty, Graduate Training Program in Clinical Psychology, Department of Psychology, University of Kansas, Lawrence

Jerry Suls, Professor, Department of Psychology, University of Iowa

Howard Tennen, Professor of Community Medicine and Health Care, University of Connecticut School of Medicine

Harry M. Wallace, Doctoral Student in Psychology, Department of Psychology, Case Western Reserve University

David Watson, Professor, Department of Psychology, University of Iowa

COPING

1

Coping

Where Have You Been?

C. R. Snyder
Beth L. Dinoff

Getting Out of a Rabbit Trap and Other Acts of Coping

It happened at the edge of dusk on a fall day in 1950. The leaves were still clinging to their branches, and I (CRS) listened to their rustling sounds in the breezes. The nights no longer were scorchers, and my extended family was sitting on the back porch of my grandparents' home. Their house was a two-bedroom, reddish-brown brick house up at the end of Morgan Street in Council Bluffs, Iowa. I loved it there. As usual, the conversation turned to cars, a favorite topic because Grandpa Gus had sold Chevys for over 30 years. Tiring of this car talk, I bolted from the porch. With all the speed that my six-year-old legs could muster, I ran through the tall weeds of a nearby empty lot. Semi-fearless, I was reveling in the sheer fun of breaking loose.

Suddenly, I heard and felt a "TWANG," and instantly hit the ground like a stunned critter. Indeed, I was a wounded animal, but not the one intended. A rabbit trap had snapped closed on the black, canvas Keds sneaker on my right foot. Instead of crying out, however, I was strangely silent. The pain was excruciating, and I was filled then with fear that I can remember to this day. Indeed, it is my first memory of being flooded with negative feelings. My heart was racing but my initial thoughts were that I couldn't let this "get to me." I remember telling myself to "calm down," and "I can take care of this myself." These attitudes were the standard in my family and, I believe, for much of that part of middle America.

What could I do? I looked down, and there wasn't much blood . . . or, was it too dark to get a good look? I knew I had to get those metal teeth off my foot, but I wasn't strong enough to do it with my arms alone. Dragging the trap and its heavy chain behind me, I set out to find a branch to use as

3

a lever. A first stick was not enough, however, and it snapped from the pressure. Finally, I found a big stick and pried open the jaws of the trap.

Free now, I limped into my grandparents' house through the side door. Tiptoeing into the bathroom, I bolted the door and turned on the light, a single bulb hanging down from the center of the ceiling. This place was to be my private emergency room. By now my foot was bleeding, and the dark syrup-like liquid scared me. Grabbing toilet paper, a roll was gone before I could get the bleeding stopped. Rummaging through the medicine cabinet, I found some Band-Aids and placed them on my puncture wounds. It was not pretty, but the bleeding was stopped.

My next challenge was cleaning up the blood, for which I used another full roll of toilet paper. To my horror, however, all of the TP stuck in a big blob when I tried to flush it. I did the only thing I could think of—I stuck my skinny arm in the toilet bowl and pushed it real hard. It worked . . . and after a flush, I watched the water swirl around as the last vestige of the cleanup disappeared.

"Riiiiiiiiiiiick," cried out my Mom, "We gotta' go." Her voice startled me, but I unlocked the bathroom door, stuck my head out, and called back, "Meet you in the Chevy" (sold to us, of course, by Grandpa Gus). Racing to the car, I jumped into the back seat and acted real tired. When we got back to our house on 6th Avenue, I waited till my parents were through the front door, and then scampered to my corner of the small house, announcing with feigned sleepiness, "Night." That evening, I made sure I didn't leave any evidence of blood.

For the next several days I tended to my wounds out of sight of the grownups, and I got through things on my own. Because my right Keds shoe was covered with blood, I had to do something with it. In the early morning as the sun was rising, I snuck over to the nearby train yard, and threw the "evidence" into an open door of a slow moving boxcar. "CLICKEDDY-CLACK, Clickeddy-clack," my old Keds (one torn and blood-ied, the other in just fine shape but no longer of use to me) continued their trip out West.

Until now, I have never told this story. The closest it ever came to "com-ing out" was when my Mom noticed my foot several weeks after the acci-dent, but I mumbled something about getting spiked in a sandlot baseball game, and this explanation worked. Indeed, this event quietly slipped into my little corner of history. Forty-seven years have passed since it happened, and it has remained my secret. Looking back, the chances that the dirty, rusty trap jaws would infect me probably were quite high. But, this is not my point. Rather, this tale is my first memory of coping.

Nothing is particularly special about this story. It does, however, contain many elements that are common to the coping process, including apprais-ing the event as stressful (i.e., stretching one's immediate resources), feeling rather overwhelmed (i.e., stress as a mediator between environment and behavior), and behaviorally responding to specific components of an event (i.e., coping, including with both emotions and events). Indeed, all of us have personal exemplars of coping, both large and small, some acute and others chronic. If you were to make a count of the number of times daily that you are called upon to cope, you would be surprised at the sheer prevalence and complexity of these activities.

Life is filled with experiences that push our repertoire of thinking, feeling, and behaving. We are expected to learn and grow from the events that initiate our coping responses, with the implication that coping is part of the very essence of the human change process. Thus, coping not only is basic for survival, but it also relates to the quality and the ensuing constructive meaning of our own lives. Indeed, a fulfilling life is a tale about coping that works and works well.

In this chapter, we will trace the history of the coping process and will arrive at a definition that encompasses modern thinking and research. Later, in the final chapter of this book, we will pick up on the themes of the talented researchers whose work you will read in the chapters of this book. In addition, our closing chapter will turn toward future coping constructs, as well as theory, research, and applications. For now, let's establish a working definition of coping and explore where we have come from in terms of the existing literature.

What Is Coping?

Although various definitions and classification systems have been proposed for coping (see references 1, 2, and 3), a definition that encompasses many previous views is that coping is a response aimed at diminishing the physical, emotional, and psychological burden that is linked to stressful life events and daily hassles (see 4, 5). Therefore, by this definition, coping strategies are those responses that are effective in reducing an undesirable "load" (i.e., the psychological burden). The effectiveness of the coping strategy rests on its ability to reduce immediate distress, as well as to contribute to more long-term outcomes such as psychological well-being or disease status. During the "rabbit trap" incident, for example, the desirable coping response was to halt the pain, and to do so as efficiently as possible. Not only immediate physical relief was sought, but there was also a conscious interpretation of the consequences of this event.

Coping can be viewed from the perspective of the person doing the coping, and this insider approach will produce a different understanding than the outsider perspective by people who are viewing or judging the coping (4). From the insider perspective, the nature of the stressor may seem much different than from the view of the outsider. We are reminded here of the old joke that major surgery is any operation on oneself, and minor surgery is on another person. As we live our lives and are forced to cope, of course, we apply the unique insider perspective; when we study coping in others, however, we inevitably must take the outsider perspective.

Is coping always a conscious process? Although some researchers (see 6) suggest that responses must be conscious to qualify as coping, this qualification seems unduly restrictive in that we so often may repeatedly respond to a recurring stressor that we lose our awareness of doing so. Although there is theory and research to support this automatic type of coping (see 7, 8, 9), it probably is that case that most instances of coping responses are within our awareness.

If coping is defined as attempts to diminish the physical and psychological load, we see that both problem- and emotion-focused coping may play a part in the response. To this day, it surprises me that I (C.R.S.) can so clearly remember the feeling of being scared when the rabbit trap caught my foot, and yet I also can recall the immediate reaction of needing to get control of my emotions before they literally overwhelmed me. This is called emotion-focused coping. Likewise, I set out to get the trap off and to tend my wounds. This is called problem-focused coping. The history of these emotion- and problem-focused types of coping will be described in the next section (see chapter 5 in this volume for important clarifying points).

Other Times, Other Names

If one were to explore the history of coping as a psychological concept by looking for the term "coping," a misleading conclusion would result. Namely, it was not until 1967 that *Psychological Abstracts* began to utilize a separate category for "coping" (10). For the reader who is interested in learning more about the history of coping, we would recommend the following sources cited in the reference section: 10, 11, 12, 13, 14, 15, 16, 17, 18, 19, 20, 21, 22.

A *PsycINFO* search that we did for research published during the subsequent 16-year period from 1967 to 1983 yielded 3,282 articles directly related to coping. During a more recent three-year period of 1994 to 1997, a literature search on *PsycINFO* revealed 3,760 articles directly related to coping were published. Obviously, a tremendous surge has occurred in our interest, awareness, and understanding of the coping concept. Though coping research has blossomed recently, however, it would be inaccurate to conclude that the examination of psychological coping "came to life" in the 1960s. This follows because coping was masquerading under other names long before that time.

Psychodynamic Roots and Defense Mechanisms

The first major roots of coping in psychology can be traced to the psychodynamic model promulgated by Freud and his disciples. In this well-known model, coping is a defense mechanism that enables one to deal with unconscious sexual and aggressive conflicts. As such, thoughts and feelings that are troublesome to the conscious mind are rendered unconscious, a view that was posed very early in Freud's thinking. In this regard, the term "defense" can be linked to some of Freud's first writings, such as his 1894 "The Neuro-Psychoses of Defense" (23). Some 30 years passed, however, before Freud used the defense term again in the 1920s. When he spoke of defenses, however, Freud emphasized their role in changing the perception of stressful circumstances stemming from one's *internal* environment (19). When he spoke of defenses, Freud's emphasis on one's internal environment may have foreshadowed our current understanding of the role of appraisal in coping.

Historically, it is important to emphasize a difference in opinion that Freud had with one of his principle students, Alfred Adler. More specifically, Adler conceptualized defenses as "safeguards" (24, 25), and posited that these coping strategies serve to protect the self from *external, environmental threats*, whereas Freud suggested that they protected the ego against *internal, instinctual forces*. This fundamental difference reflected the biases of each prodigal thinker—Freud building upon physical determinants and Adler using social/environmental forces as the source of his conceptualization (26).

Since the 1930s, definitions of defenses actually have begun to favor the Adlerian perspective, in that these mechanisms are thought to be the coping devices that people use to handle external threats to the self. In part, this change reflects Anna Freud's 1936 (27) admission that defenses surely must protect one against both *internal* threats (similar to her famous father's position), as well as *external* threats (similar to the position of student-turned rival, Alfred Adler). Subsequent scholars of the defense concept have adopted the dual mechanism related to internal and external threats (see 14, 28).

The coping literature owes an enormous debt to Anna Freud in that it was she who succinctly summarized the original 10 defense mechanisms described by her father in earlier writings (e.g., repression, regression, isolation, reaction formation, undoing, introjection, projection reversal, sublimation, and turning against the self), but she also added important new mechanisms, such as intellectualization, ego restriction, identifying with the aggressor, denial (18). Additionally, it was she who highlighted the important fact that any given person has only a subset of favored defense mechanisms (see 29), a point that is commonly adopted by coping researchers as we enter the twenty-first century.

Based on the historical points raised in this section, one might assume that defense mechanisms are seen as being very similar to coping. On the contrary, there is considerable disagreement about this point. For example, the noted psychodynamic writer Hann (e.g., 14, 30, 31, 42) has suggested that there are important distinctions between these two concepts. Granting that the underlying mental processes of defenses and coping are virtually identical, she has suggested that defense mechanisms have more negative properties in comparison to the actual workings of coping mechanisms. Namely, she argues that defenses inherently attend to issues from the past, that they are rigid in their operation, unconscious, and distorting of reality. On the other hand, coping supposedly is more forward looking, flexible, largely conscious, and attentive to reality. Indeed, more recent writers such as Shelley Taylor and her colleagues (see 33, 34, 35, 36) make similar arguments in distinguishing the positive illusion-based coping processes from defense mechanisms, but Snyder and colleagues have maintained that the similarities in the coping and defense mechanism concepts are fundamental (37, 38, 39, 40). One compromise between these two positions is that defenses can be categorized between being adaptive or maladaptive (14, 30, 31, 32, 41, 42, 43, 44, 45, 46, 47), with the implication that the more adaptive defenses are similar to the coping that is characteristic of positive illusions.

In the rabbit-trap story, we see examples of both defense mechanisms and coping strategies as described in Haan's (30) psychodynamic analysis of these concepts. Our young protagonist was driven to protect his developing image of self, both in his own eyes and for the impression management of significant others. Therefore, he hid his physical, psychological, and emotional injuries from his family. Furthermore, he consciously labored mightily to preserve his sense of individual control over personal threat and harm (coping mechanism). It would not be surprising to find that these coping strategies, once used successfully, will be mastered and become part of the user's coping armamentarium over time.

In summary, it appears that the coping concept in psychology owes its intellectual birthright to the defense mechanism notion. An obvious primary player was Sigmund Freud, but there were two additional costars who deserve major billing—his student turned critic, Alfred Adler, and his daughter turned theory modernizer, Anna Freud. Not only was psychology given a theoretical foundation for understanding coping via defense mechanisms, but this concept and its exemplars also worked their way into the very language and thinking of Western culture. Yet, there is more to this story of coping—a scientific concept that is growing and changing because of the theory and laboratory work of another and more recent cohort of influential psychologists and physicians.

Appraisal/Transactional Processes

Thus far in our description of the elements of coping as a psychological construct, we have purposefully avoided complicating the idea of coping by interweaving it with conceptualizations of stress. As we move forward in the history of coping, however, we next enter a period of time that spans the 1960s to the 1980s (and perhaps even later) where appraisal of the event as stressful is essential to understanding coping efforts and outcomes. It was during this period that writers began using the term "coping" in the social and medical sciences (see 15, 48, 49). Previously, stress was seen as any nonspecific result of mental or somatic demands placed on the body (50). Accordingly, this pattern was stereotyped, initiating supposedly essentially identical neurological and biological changes that allow us to cope with the demands, thereby leaving little room for individual variance.

Richard Lazarus and his colleagues at Berkeley helped to set the intellectual agenda regarding coping via insightful theory and empirical demonstrations. In his 1966 pioneering book entitled *Psychological Stress and the Coping Process* (51), as well as a subsequent book in 1984 (with coauthor Susan Folkman) entitled *Stress, Appraisal, and Coping* (52), Lazarus moved the focus away from the previous psychodynamic defense-related mechanisms, as well as Selye's innate biochemical reactivity, and directed attention toward active appraisal processes. Likewise, he abandoned the previous emphasis on enduring traits, and placed the spotlight on situational determinants by conceptualizing coping as a *cognitive transaction* between the individual and the environment within a specific context (see 21). Lazarus's stress and coping model defined coping as "constantly changing cognitive, behavioral, [and emotional] efforts to manage particular external and/or internal demands that are appraised as taxing or exceeding the resources of the person" (52, p. 141). The significant points to highlight in this definition relate to the fact that it proposes coping as process-related rather than trait-oriented, it is interactive instead of automated, deconstructs coping from outcome, and implies a developmental rather than a mastery model.

The centerpiece of the Lazarus and colleagues approach to understanding coping is the notion of how the person appraises the situation. Appraisal is posited to occur when the perceiver encounters situations that are interpreted as excessive relative to resources (i.e., stressors). In the model detailed by Lazarus and Folkman (52; see also 53), a person utilizes two levels of appraisals in selecting coping responses. The first level is primary appraisal, where an individual evaluates whether the situation is potentially harmful (i.e., personal injury), threatening (i.e., potential for harm), blocking of a goal, creating a void, or presenting a challenge (i.e., a mastery opportunity). In other words, the person determines that something important is or is not at risk in a particular situation. This decision reflects a cognitive evaluation of the particulars of the stressful event and how important it is to the person's well-being. When the event is perceived as harmful or threatening, the individual enters into secondary appraisal, wherein the available resources for coping are examined. For the reader who is interested in theory and empirical support on problem- and emotion-focused coping, we would recommend the following sources in the reference section: 1, 2, 3, 17, 51, 52, 53, 54, 55, 56, 57, 58. To highlight a critical point, the unique and important contribution that this conceptualization made over earlier views of coping is that it clearly demarcated the appraisal process from subsequent coping responses.

Depending on the person's evaluation of these two cognitive appraisal processes, that individual then decides which coping strategies to implement. In keeping with the stress and coping model, two major types of coping are proposed. We introduced these previously in the section in which coping was defined. Problem-focused coping includes efforts that are directed at controlling or changing the sources of the stress (e.g., learning new skills, removing barriers, generating alternative solutions). Emotion-focused coping strategies are attempts at managing emotional responses to the stressor (e.g., wishful thinking, seeking emotional support, social comparison). If coping is defined as attempts to diminish the physical, emotional, and psychological burden of an event, we see that both problem- and emotion-focused coping may play a part in the response (52). To this day, it surprises me (CRS) that I can so clearly remember the feeling of being scared when the rabbit trap caught my foot, and yet I also can recall the immediate reaction of needing to get control of my emotions before they literally overwhelmed me. This is called *emotion-focused coping*. Likewise, I set out to get the trap off and to tend my wound, an effort that would be called *problem-focused coping*.

Use of the coping strategies is not considered to be mutually exclusive and, in fact, may be mutually facilitating. Benefit gained from using a particular coping strategy will depend upon the individual and the demands of the situation. According to the Lazarus and Folkman model, coping efforts are believed to be inherently neutral, that is, they are neither innately adaptive nor maladaptive. Nevertheless, through an onslaught of investigations demonstrating consistent findings, researchers have concluded that specific coping strategies produce superior outcomes when used by the appropriate person undergoing a particular stressor in the right context. For example, with those situations deemed to have the potential for instrumental change and improvement, the person who selects problem-focused coping strategies should lessen the sources of stress and demonstrate positive psychological well-being. With situations determined not to be amenable to change, the person who adopts emotion-focused strategies is likely to encounter more psychologically positive outcomes, such as less depression and anxiety. Furthermore, emotion-focused coping is believed to be particularly beneficial for dealing with health-related problems (52), thus leading to increased compliance with medical regimens and diminished psychological distress when facing setbacks. In contrast, emotion-focused coping relates inversely to measures of psychological adjustment. One important caveat is in order, however, in regard to the supposed negative sequelae of emotion-focused coping. On this point, Stanton and colleagues (59) provide evidence that emotion-focused coping has been confounded with psychopathology in scales used to investigate coping, indicating that many of the previously demonstrated relations between emotion-focused coping and psychological maladjustment may be erroneous.

Lazarus, Folkman, and colleagues also should be credited with introducing a self-report index of coping that was patterned after the face validity of their theoretical ideas. This measure, known as the Ways of Coping checklist (WOC), originally contained 68 items formulated to reflect problem- and emotion-focused coping (55). Respondents were asked to consider these items in response to a given stressor. Later, Lazarus and Folkman

(52) modified the format of the WOC and shortened it to 66 items. Subsequently, there was an explosion of research using the WOC, and it quickly became the gold standard of coping measurement in research designs. This emphasis on using the WOC partly was due to what can be called an "instrument effect," wherein researchers found the WOC to be a handy measure that was applicable for a variety of arenas, including coping with disease, job-related stress, and the loss of a loved one. Additionally, the popularity of the WOC also rested on the intuitive appeal of the primary/secondary appraisal and problem-/emotion-focused coping theoretical foundations.

Type A Behavior Pattern

The Lazarus and Folkman appraisal/transactional model (52) contains many of the biases of traditional cognitively based models in that it proposes that coping choices are tied robustly to physical health and well-being without offering an explanation of physiological mechanisms that mediate and moderate such effects. Interestingly, during this same general time period, a separate group of researchers introduced and explored another construct that was to become highly influential in our understanding of coping responses—Type A Coronary-Prone Behavior pattern. The Type A Coronary-Prone Behavior pattern concept was the brainchild of cardiologists Meyer Friedman and Ray Rosenman (60, 61). It grew out of their perceptive observations that many of their patients exhibited a time urgent, competitive, and hostile style in their interactions with other people. Type A style was seen as a person-environment interaction, with only predisposed people reacting in this perfectionistic demanding style to threatening environments (62). Moreover, these individuals also eventually exhibited an elevated risk for coronary heart disease. Obviously, Type A was construed as a coping style having severe negative physiological and psychological outcomes.

The principal means of measuring Type A was the Structured Interview, which is an orally delivered test that pulls for the respondent's impatience, competitiveness, and hostility (63). Additionally, two self-report indices of Type A, the Jenkins Activity Survey (64) and the Framingham Type A Scale (65) were developed, but they generally did not exhibit relationships between coping and coronary heart disease of the same magnitude as did the Structured Interview (see 66). With researchers using all three of the aforementioned measurement approaches, the amount of research on Type A during these decades was huge, and indeed this term readily worked its way into the lexicon of American language. No doubt, it gave a rather bleak sense of the effects of interacting evidenced by the prototypical hard-charging Caucasian, American, white-collar male. (Unfortunately, the research rarely examined females or members of ethnic minority groups.)

As the 1980s unfolded, however, discontent grew about the predictive capability of the Type A construct. Such unraveling could be seen at a conference that I (CRS) put on in 1988 with my late colleague, B. Kent Houston. Gathering the international experts together to discuss the status of the Type A construct, the participants could find little upon which to agree. Indeed, a subsequent *Time* magazine article covering the conference gave their story the rather derogatory title of "Type A−." Eventually, the focus of this research moved to a more powerful and reliable predictor of coronary heart disease, and what emerged was the hostility component of the Type A Behavior pattern. Heading this transition, Dembrowski and his colleagues suggested that hostility was truly a lethal component of Type A (67, 68). In support of this contention, the present consensus is that hostility not only is related to a higher risk for coronary heart disease, but also all-cause mortality (69, 70). Presently, three indices, the Cook-Medley Hostility Scale (Ho Scale: 71), the Buss-Durkee Hostility Inventory (BDHI: 72 ,73), and the Hostile Automatic Thoughts Scale (74), have continued the tradition of exploring the negative sequelae of coping with hostility.

In summary, this second and more recent phase of the evolution of the coping construct was woven around the appraisal/transactional ideas of Lazarus and his colleagues, as well as the Type A person-situation interaction. This era was one of rampant empirical research as the coping construct became the mainstream fare of scholars in the fields of personality, clinical, and social psychology. Furthermore, this second wave paid little attention or homage to the previous first wave of Freudian and post-Freudian coping ideas related to defense mechanisms.

The Battle of Situations and Personalities: The Emergence of the Individual Differences View

The aforementioned 1960s through 1980s was a time in which situationalist thinking permeated all aspects of psychology, with the topic of coping being no exception. As a general backdrop to this period, behaviorism was flourishing. Among personality, clinical, and social psychologists, the bellwether scholarly situationalist book was Walter Mischel's *Personality and Assessment* (75), which was first published in 1968 and thereafter became the standard required reading for waves of graduates students. In this small, but highly influential volume, Mischel argued that individual differences provided little in the way of predictive variance for understanding a variety of important human behavioral outcomes.

The individual differences thinkers slowly marshaled their retort to the Mischel position. One person who made a cogent counterargument was Seymour Epstein (76), who suggested that individual differences became much more robust in their predictive capabilities when the criterion variable was changed from a single to multiple behaviors. Next, Funder and Ozer (77) pointed out that the vaunted situationalist predictors only on rare occasions outperformed individual differences. Furthermore, Kendrick and Funder (78) noted that the typical correlation of .30 between individual differences and other markers is quite respectable in the context of magnitude of scientific effects. Another professional event that opened the gates to the respectability of individual differences was the appointment of Robert Hogan as the editor of the personality section of the *Journal of Personality and Social Psychology*. During his tenure as editor, the sheer number of articles published in this leading outlet jumped several fold, as did the quality and interest in this approach. For the reader who is interested in a stinging criticism of negative impact of the situationalist perspective, we would invite you to examine the text of Hogan's 1997 Southwestern Psychological Association presidential address (79). For other good overviews of the reemergence of individual differences or personality variables, check the following in the reference section: 80, 81, 82.

In brief, the individual differences approach rests on the assumption that there are important dimensions of personhood along which people can be rated or measured, and that such information is critical for understanding their subsequent coping adventures. For example, perhaps there were early personality characteristics that would enable one to understand how I (CRS) tried to cope with the rabbit trap escapade. The favored family explanation may well be that I am high on a stubbornness dimension. In this regard, theoretical frameworks studying personality and coping strongly promote the impact of individual differences in exposure, reactivity, and availability of coping strategies, as well as the view that these are predictive of psychological well-being and physical health.

Although it is tempting to continue the story of the revitalization of the individual differences approach to the study of coping, this is best left to the concluding chapter where I discuss the trends evidenced in the writings of the chapters of this book. We presently are living through a period where the individual differences approach is the transcendent one, and the strengths and weaknesses of this perspective will be examined in the final chapter. For now, it is important to realize that this view captures the present dominant paradigm for the study of coping.

Who Has Studied Coping?

Having defined and traced the two previous major periods regarding coping, our final issue in this chapter pertains to those people who study this important concept. In the earliest period, that in which coping was studied under the rubric of defenses, the original thinkers such as Freud were psychoanalysts who had retained the biological emphasis of their physician training, and yet had turned to theories about the workings of the human mind in response to internal stressors.

When Freud's original concept of defense as a reaction against internal threats increasingly became supplanted with the views that such defenses helped to handle external threats, it was his analyst and physician-trained pupil, Adler, who charted the direction of the field. In the ensuing years of the defense as coping period, many of the major thinkers were not physicians, but lay analysts by training.

As the second phase of coping research began to unfold in the 1960s, the appraisal/transactional model was developed and studied principally by psychologists, many of whom, such as Richard Lazarus, were the graduates of post-World War II clinical psychology programs (83). Without explicitly noting their lack of adherence to the previous dominant pathology-oriented paradigm, these clinical psychologists opened the way for psychologists from other areas to join the fray. Indeed, it was during the 1970s that an entire new field began to flourish. Called *health psychology*, there were psychologists trained in social and experimental programs who joined their clinical colleagues in order to study the psychological processes related to the promotion and maintenance of physical health. This new field has grown rapidly, and coping literally has become the central focus of its activities. Today, therefore, we see psychologists from various training programs who identify themselves with the study of health and coping. Furthermore, although psychologists are the major players in studying coping, this concept also is examined by scholars trained in epidemiology, psychiatry, social work, sociology, counseling, and communication. As such, the topic of coping is championed by a large and growing group of professionals from various fields.

Coping in Perspective

Perhaps it is best to close this introductory chapter with an observation about the fundamental importance of coping. It is through the coping processes that we are able to survive the many challenges that life brings and to flourish as people. Indeed, suppose that you were able to select one and only one asset for your soon-to-be-born offspring. What would that asset be? If all the possibilities were described, coping skills surely would be at the very top of such a wish list. Coping is a precious gift, and the following pages give us a glimpse of the many forms that it may take.

References

1. Lazarus, R. S., & Launier, R. (1978). Stress-related transactions between person and environment. In L. A. Pervin & M. Lewis (Eds.), *Perspectives in interactional psychology* (pp. 287–327). New York: Plenum.
2. Moos, R. H., & Billings, A. G. (1982). Conceptualizing and measuring coping resources and processes. In L. Goldberger & S. Breznitz (Eds.), *Handbook of stress* (pp. 212–230). New York: Macmillan.
3. Pearlin, L. I., & Schooler, C. (1978). The structure of coping. *Journal of Health and Social Behavior, 19*, 2–21.
4. Snyder, C. R., Ford, C. E., & Harris, R. N. (1987). The effects of theoretical perspective on the analysis of coping with negative life events. In C. R.

Snyder & C. E. Ford (Eds.), *Coping with negative life events: Clinical and social psychological perspectives* (pp. 3–13). New York: Plenum.

5. Houston, B. K. (1987). Stress and coping. In C. R. Snyder & C. E. Ford (Eds.), *Coping with negative life events: Clinical and social psychological perspectives* (pp. 373–399). New York: Plenum.

6. Stone, A. A., & Neale, J. M. (1984). New measure of daily coping: Development and preliminary results. *Journal of Personality and Social Psychology, 46,* 892–906.

7. Erdelyi, M. H. (1979). Let's not sweep repression under the rug: Toward a cognitive psychology of repression. In J. F. Kihlstrom & F. J. Evans (Eds.), *Functional disorders of memory* (pp. 355–402). New York: Wiley.

8. Snyder, C. R. (1985). Collaborative companions: The relationship of self-deception and excuse-making. In M. Martin (Ed.), *Essays in self-deception* (pp. 35–51). Lawrence, KS: Regents Press of Kansas.

9. Snyder, C. R., Higgins, R. L., & Stucky, R. (1983). *Excuses: Masquerades in search of grace.* New York: Wiley-Interscience.

10. Popplestone, J. A., & McPherson, M. W. (1988). *Dictionary of concepts in general psychology.* New York: Greenwood Press.

11. Barone, D. F., Maddux, J. E., & Snyder, C. R. (1997). *Social cognitive psychology: History and current domains.* New York: Plenum.

12. Cramer, P. (1990). *The development of defense mechanisms: Theory, research, and assessment.* New York: Springer-Verlag.

13. Endler, N. S., & Parker, J. D. A. (1995). Assessing a patient's ability to cope. In J. N. Butcher (Ed.), *Practical considerations in clinical personality assessment* (pp. 329–352). New York: Oxford University Press.

14. Haan, N. (1977). *Coping and defending: Processes of self-environment organization.* New York: Academic Press.

15. Lazarus, R. S. (1993). Coping theory and research: Past, present, and future. *Psychosomatic Medicine, 55,* 234–247.

16. Lazarus, R. S., Averill, J. R., & Opton, E. M. (1974). The psychology of coping: Issues of research and assessment. In G. V. Coelho, D. A. Hamburg, & J. E. Adams (Eds.), *Coping and adaptation* (pp. 47–68). New York: Basic Books.

17. Parker, J. D. A., & Endler, N. S. (1992). Coping with coping assessment: A critical review. *European Journal of Psychology, 6,* 321–344.

18. Parker, J. D. A., & Endler, N. S. (1996). Coping and defense: A historical overview. In M. Zeidner & N. S. Endler (Eds.), *Handbook of coping: Theory, research, and applications* (pp. 3–23). New York, Wiley.

19. Snyder, C. R. (1988). From defenses to self-protection: An evolutionary perspective. *Journal of Social and Clinical Psychology, 6,* 155–158.

20. Snyder, C. R., & Ford, C. E. (Eds.) (1987). *Coping with negative life events: Clinical and social psychological perspectives.* New York: Plenum.

21. Suls, J., David, J. P., & Harvey, J. H. (1996). Personality and coping: Three generations of research. *Journal of Personality, 64,* 711–735.

22. Vaillant, G. E. (1986). *Empirical studies of ego mechanisms of defense.* Washington, DC: American Psychiatric Press.

23. Freud, S. (1964). The neuro-psychoses of defense. In J. Strachey (Ed. & Translator), *The standard edition of the complete psychological works*

of Sigmund Freud (Vol. 3, pp. 45–61). London: Hogarth. (Originally published in 1894.)

24. Adler, A. (1929). *Problems of neuroses: A book of case histories.* London: Kegan Paul, Trench, Treubner.

25. Ansbacher, H. L., & Ansbacher, R. R. (1967). *The individual psychology of Alfred Adler.* New York: Harper & Row. (Originally published in 1956.)

26. Snyder, C. R., & Smith, T. W. (1982). Symptoms as self-handicapping strategies: The virtues of old wine in a new bottle. In G. Weary & H. Mirels (Eds.), *Integrations of clinical and social psychology* (pp. 104–127). New York: Oxford University Press.

27. Freud, A. (1948). *The ego and the mechanisms of defense.* London: Hogarth Press. (Originally published in 1936.)

28. Vaillant, G. E. (1994). Ego mechanisms of defense and personality psychopathology. *Journal of Abnormal Psychology, 103,* 44–50.

29. Waeldner, R. (1960). *Basic theory of psychoanalysis.* New York: International Universities Press.

30. Haan, N. (1963). Proposed model of ego functioning: Coping and defense mechanisms in relationship to IQ change. *Psychological Monographs, 77,* 1–27.

31. Haan, N. (1965). Coping and defense mechanisms related to personality inventories. *Journal of Consulting Psychology, 29,* 373–378.

32. Kroebner, T. C. (1963). The coping functions of the ego mechanisms. In R. W. White (Ed.), *The study of lives: Essays on personality in honor of Henry A. Murray* (pp. 178–189). New York: Atherton Press.

33. Taylor, S. E. (1989). *Positive illusions: Creative self-deception and the healthy mind.* New York: Basic Books.

34. Taylor, S. E., & Brown, J. D. (1988). Illusion and well-being: A social psychological perspective on mental health. *Psychological Bulletin, 103,* 193–210.

35. Taylor, S. E., & Brown, J. D. (1994a). Positive illusions and well-being revisited: Separating fact from fiction. *Psychological Bulletin, 116,* 21–27.

36. Taylor, S. E., & Brown, J. D. (1994b). "Illusion" of mental health does explain positive illusion. *American Psychologist, 49,* 972–973.

37. Snyder, C. R. (1989). Reality negotiation: From excuses to hope and beyond. *Journal of Social and Clinical Psychology, 8,* 130–157.

38. Snyder, C. R., & Higgins, R. L. (1988). Excuses: Their effective role in the negotiation of reality. *Psychological Bulletin, 104,* 23–35.

39. Snyder, C. R., & Higgins, R. L. (1997). Reality negotiation: Governing one's self and being governed by others. *General Psychology Review, 4,* 336–350.

40. Snyder, C. R., Irving, L. M., Sigmon, S., & Holleran, S. (1992). Reality negotiation and valence/linkage self theories: Psychic showdown at the "I'm OK" corral. In L. Montrada, S-H Filipp, & M. L. Lerner (Eds.), *Life crises and experiences of loss in adulthood* (pp. 275–297). Hillsdale, NJ: Erlbaum.

41. Bond, M., Gardiner, S. T., Christian, J., & Sigel, J. J. (1983). An empirical examination of defense mechanisms. *Archives of General Psychiatry, 40,* 333–338.

42. Haan, N. (1982). Assessment of coping, defense, and stress. In L. Gold-berger & S. Bresnitz (Eds.), *Handbook of stress: Theoretical and clinical aspects* (pp. 254–269). New York: Free Press.

43. Haan, N. (1992). The assessment of coping, defense, and stress. In L. Goldberger & S. Bresnitz (Eds.), *Handbook of stress: Theoretical and clinical aspects* (2nd ed., pp. 258–273). New York: Free Press.

44. Menninger, K. A. (1954). Regulatory devices of the ego under major stress. *International Journal of Psychoanalysis, 35*, 412–420.

45. Perry, J. C., & Cooper, S. H. (1989). What do cross-sectional measures of defense mechanisms predict. In G. E. Vaillant (Ed.), *Empirical studies of ego mechanisms of defense* (pp. 47–59). Washington, DC: American Psychiatric Press.

46. Vaillant, G. E. (1971). Theoretical hierarchy of adaptive ego mechanisms. *Archives of General Psychiatry, 24*, 107–118.

47. Vaillant, G. E. (1977). *Adaptation to life*. Boston: Little, Brown.

48. Roth, S., & Cohen, L. J. (1986). Approach, avoidance, and coping with stress. *American Psychologist, 41*, 813–819.

49. White, R. W. (1974). Strategies of adaptation: An attempt at systematic description. In G. V. Coelho, D. A. Hamburg, & J. E. Adams (Eds.), *Coping and adaptation* (pp. 47–68). New York: Basic Books.

50. Selye, H. (1976). *The stress of life* (revised edition). New York: McGraw-Hill.

51. Lazarus, R. S. (1966). *Psychological stress and the coping process*. New York: McGraw-Hill.

52. Lazarus, R. S., & Folkman, S. (1984). *Stress, appraisal, and coping*. New York: Springer.

53. Folkman, S., & Lazarus, R. S. (1985). If it changes it must be a process: A study of emotion and coping during three stages of a college examination. *Journal of Personality and Social Psychology, 48*, 150–170.

54. Coyne, J. C., & Lazarus, R. S. (1980). Cognitive style, stress perception, and coping. In I. L. Kutash & L. B. Schlesinger (Eds.), *Handbook of stress and anxiety: Contemporary knowledge, theory, and treatment* (pp. 144–158). San Francisco: Jossey-Bass.

55. Folkman, S., & Lazarus, R. S. (1980). An analysis of coping in a middle-aged community sample. *Journal of Health and Social Behavior, 21*, 219–239.

56. Lazarus, R. S. (1981). The stress and the coping paradigm. In C. Eisdorfer, D. Cohen, A. Kleinman, & P. Maxim (Eds.), *Models for clinical psychopathology* (pp. 177–214). New York: Spectrum.

57. Prochaska, J. O., & DiClimente, C. C. (1985). Common processes of self-change in smoking, weight control, and psychological distress. In S. Shiffman & T. A. Wills (Eds.), *Coping and substance use* (pp. 345–363). New York: Academic Press.

58. Rothbaum, F., Weisz, J. R., & Snyder, S. S. (1982). Changing the world and changing the self: A two-process model of perceived control. *Journal of Personality and Social Psychology, 42*, 5–37.

59. Stanton, A. L., Danoff-Burg, S., Cameron, C. L., & Ellis, A. P. (1994). Coping through emotional approach: Problems of conceptualization and confounding. *Journal of Personality and Social Psychology, 66*, 350–362.

60. Friedman, M., & Rosenman, R. H. (1959). Association of specific overt behavior pattern with blood and cardiovascular findings. *Journal of American Medical Association, 169*, 1286–1296.
61. Friedman, M., & Rosenman, R. H. (1974). *Type A behavior and your health*. New York: Knopf.
62. Rhodewalt, F., & Smith, T. W. (1991). Current issues in Type A behavior, coronary proneness, and coronary heart disease. In C. R. Snyder & D. R. Forsyth (Eds.), *Handbook of social and clinical psychology: The health perspective* (pp. 197–220). Elmsford, NY: Pergamon.
63. Rosenman, R. H. (1978). The interview method of assessment of the coronary-prone behavior pattern. In T. M. Dembroski, S. M. Weiss, J. L. Shields, S. G. Haynes, & M. Feinleib (Eds.), *Coronary-prone behavior*. New York: Springer-Verlag.
64. Jenkins, C. D., Zyanski, S., & Rosenman, R. H. (1971). Progress toward validation of a computer-scored test of the Type A coronary-prone behavior pattern. *Psychosomatic Medicine, 33*, 193–202.
65. Haynes, S. G., & Feinleib, M. (1982). Type A behavior and the incidence of coronary heart disease in the Framingham study. *Advances in Cardiology, 29*, 85–95.
66. Houston, B. K., & Snyder, C. R. (Eds.) (1988). *Type A behavior pattern: Research, theory, and intervention*. New York: Wiley.
67. Dembrowski, T. M., & MacDougall, J. M. (1985). Beyond global Type A: Relationships of paralinguistic attributes, hostility, and anger-in to coronary heart disease. In T. Field, P. McCabe, & N. Schneiderman (Eds.), *Stress and coping* (pp. 223–241). Hillsdale, NJ: Erlbaum.
68. Dembrowski, T. M., MacDougall, J. M., Williams, R. B., Haney, T. L., & Blumenthal, J. A. (1985). Components of Type A, hostility, and anger-in: Relationship to angiographic findings. *Psychosomatic Medicine, 47*, 219–233.
69. Miller, T. Q., Smith, T. W., Turner, C. W., Guijarro, M. L., & Hallet, A. J. (1996). A meta-analytic review of research on hostility and physical health. *Psychological Bulletin, 119*, 322–348.
70. Siegman, A. W., & Smith, T. W. (Eds.) (1994). *Anger, hostility and the heart*. Hillsdale, NJ: Erlbaum.
71. Cook, W. W., & Medley, D. M. (1954). Proposed Hostility and Pharisiac-Virtue scales for the MMPI. *Journal of Applied Psychology, 38*, 414–418.
72. Buss, A. H. (1961). *The psychology of aggression*. New York: Wiley.
73. Buss, A. H., & Durkee, A. (1957). An inventory for assessing different kinds of hostility. *Journal of Counseling Psychology, 21*, 343–349.
74. Snyder, C. R., Crowson, J. J., Jr., Houston, B. K., Kurylo, M., & Poirier, J. (1997). Assessing hostile automatic thoughts: Development and validation of the HAT Scale. *Cognitive Therapy and Research, 4*, 477–492.
75. Mischel, W. (1968). *Personality and assessment*. New York: Wiley.
76. Epstein, S. (1979). The stability of behavior. On predicting most of the people much of the time. *Journal of Personality and Social Psychology, 37*, 1097–1126.
77. Funder, D., & Ozer, D. (1983). Behavior as a function of the situation. *Journal of Personality and Social Psychology, 44*, 107–112.

78. Kendrick, D. T., & Funder, D. C. (1988). Profiting from controversy: Lessons from the person-situation debate. *American Psychologist, 43,* 23–34.
79. Hogan, R. (1997). Personality matters. *Journal of Social and Clinical Psychology, 17,* 1–10.
80. Angleitner, A. (1991). Personality psychology: Trends and developments. *European Journal of Personality, 5,* 185–197.
81. Endler, N. S., & Parker, J. D. A. (1992). Interactionism revisited: The continuing crisis in the personality area. *European Journal of Personality, 6,* 177–198.
82. Wiggins, J. S., & Pincus, A. L. (1992). Personality: Structure and assessment. *Annual Review of Psychology, 43,* 473–504.
83. Lazarus, R. S. (1998). *Fifty years of the research and theory of R. S. Lazarus: An analysis of historical and perennial issues.* Mahwah, NJ: Erlbaum.

2

Reality Negotiation and Coping

The Social Construction of Adaptive Outcomes

Raymond L. Higgins
Ruth Q. Leibowitz

O ur goal in this chapter is to provide an overview of the development and current status of the reality-negotiation construct, to relate the construct to coping processes, and to suggest that it has important implications for conceptualizations of social support and the mechanisms through which social support is related to coping. Following brief definitional, historical, and measurement sections, we will provide a compendium of reality-negotiation strategies before moving on to relate the reality-negotiation construct more specifically to the issue of coping with adversity. A discussion of selected issues related to coping with chronic illness and disability will serve as the vehicle for linking the reality-negotiation construct to some evolving notions about the underlying nature of social support. Finally, we will offer some brief thoughts about the limitations of reality negotiation as an adaptive process, as well as a caveat concerning negotiating the "reality" of the findings that emerge from our scientific enterprise.

Reality Negotiation Defined

In 1988, Snyder and Higgins (1, 2) introduced the term "reality negotiation" to describe a process whereby individuals pursue self-serving interpretations of outcomes in order to avoid revising their self-theories in the face of challenging discrepant information. The context of this coinage was an examination of the effectiveness of excuse tactics for lessening the self-threatening implications of negative outcomes. Accordingly, the emphasis was on preserving positive self-definitions. More recent explications of reality negotiation have expanded the construct to incorporate processes aimed at preserving or enhancing not only positive self-theories (3), but also *negative* ones (4, 5).

Based on the idea that self-theories are rooted in the acts that people author, the reality-negotiation construct proposes that people continually appraise the value or valence of self-relevant outcomes as well as the extent to which they may be causally linked to the outcomes (6, 7, 8). For heuristic purposes, this valence-linkage framework may be conceptualized as a two-dimensional, orthogonal matrix where "valence of outcome" (ranging from positive to negative) forms the y axis and "linkage to outcome" (ranging from none to total) forms the x axis.

As illustrated in Figure 2.1, an individual's operative self-theory may be mapped onto this valence-linkage matrix according to the propensity to see the self as causally linked (or not) to either positive or negative outcomes. The individual depicted in Figure 2.1 illustrates the positive regression line slope associated with a prototypical positive self-theory. Such an individual tends to associate the self with increasingly positive outcomes and to disassociate the self from increasingly negative outcomes. Conversely, Figure 2.2 illustrates the negative regression line slope associated with a prototypical negative self-theory. In this instance, the individual tends to associate the self with negatively valenced outcomes and to disassociate the self from positive outcomes. The individual who suffers from depression, for example, may assume that she is responsible for awkward interpersonal encounters, while crediting others for those interactions that go well.

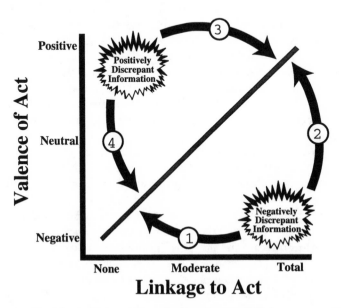

Figure 2.1. Positive self-theory on valence-of-act and linkage-to-act dimensions and the associated reality negotiation processes.

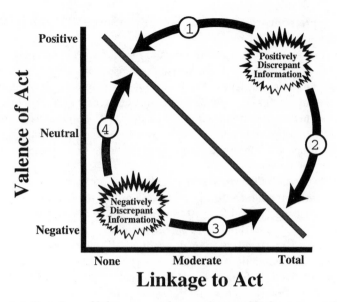

Figure 2.2. Negative self-theory on valence-of-act and linkage-to-act dimensions and the associated reality negotiation processes.

In effect, the reality negotiation process is aimed at sustaining one's self-theory and targets the perceived negativity/positivity of outcomes and/or the individual's perceived causal linkage to such outcomes. For example, people with positive self-theories who are linked to a reproachful act may attempt to decrease the perceived negativity of the act (see arrow 2, Fig. 2.1), to decrease their perceived causal link to the act (see arrow 1, Fig. 2.1), or both. By the same token, people with negative self-theories who confront the prospect of having done something praiseworthy may try to decrease the perceived positivity of the act (see arrow 2, Fig. 2.2), to decrease their perceived agency in producing the outcome (see arrow 1, Fig. 2.2), or both.

By logical extension, it is also possible that those with positive self-theories who are not clearly linked to a desirable outcome might want either to increase their linkage (arrow 3, Fig. 2.1), or to decrease the outcome's perceived positivity (arrow 4, Fig. 2.1). People with negative self-theories might wish to increase their perceived responsibility for negative outcomes to which they are only weakly connected (see arrow 3, Fig. 2.2), or to increase the perceived positivity of outcomes which they have not authored (see arrow 4, Fig. 2.2). Although of theoretical interest, these particular permutations of the valence-linkage matrix take us beyond our focus in this chapter and will not be elaborated further (however, see 4, 5).

Reality Negotiation in Historical Context

The reality-negotiation construct is firmly embedded within the social constructivist tradition (4). Certainly, the idea that reality is negotiated (or created) rather than merely discerned is a contemporary paraphrasing of constructivist philosophies dating back to Kant (9) and Hegel (10). Moreover, the notion that people interact with the social environment to secure views of reality that preserve their "self-theories" clearly implies that the "self" is a product of social interaction. In this sense, the "self-theory" construct borrows from such early expressions of the self-constructive process as Cooley's (11) "symbolic interactionism," Mead's (12) "looking glass self," and Piaget's (13) "schemas."

The inception of the reality-negotiation construct was stimulated by a simple awareness that excuse attributions for negative acts are effective only if both the proffering individual *and* the target audience accept the attributions as plausible (1, 2, 14). As we conceived it, this requirement necessitates a process of *negotiation* that might involve exchanges between the person and *actual* others, or between the person and his or her *mental representations* of the relevant external audience(s). In this latter regard, we coined the term "revolving self-images" (15, p. 38) to capture the idea that one consequence of the socialization process is that people's self-image concerns inevitably come to reflect the values of their role-models and caregivers. Even in the absence of witnesses, therefore, internal appraisal processes involve a fusion of internal and external audience concerns.

Fundamental to our early work on excuses was the assumption that they are used to preserve one's positive sense of self and being in control by lessening the negative personal implications of "bad" acts by either reducing their perceived negativity (valence) or by decreasing the individual's perceived responsibility (linkage) for them (15). This assumption was based on the works of writers like William James (16), Gordon Allport (17), Carl Rogers (18), and Abraham Maslow (19), all of whom stressed the importance of self-esteem maintenance as a fundamental human motive (see also, 20, 21, 22, 23). Moreover, we found empirical support for the self-esteem motive in the growing literature documenting the self-serving nature of causal attributions for positive and negative outcomes (24, 25, 26).

By 1988, our definition of the responsibility-diminishing aspect of excuses (which we now regarded as a subset of reality-negotiation tactics) denoted them as shifts of causal attributions for negative outcomes from "sources that are relatively more central to the person's sense of self to sources that are relatively less central" (1, p. 23). This definition explicitly incorporated a (causal) linkage dimension (i.e., from none to total). The positive valence dimension of the above-mentioned valence-linkage matrix was first introduced by Snyder (3), when he presented the construct of "hoping" as the flip side of excuse-making. Whereas excuses were thought to weaken causal linkages to negative outcomes and/or to decrease the perceived negativity of bad outcomes, hoping was conceived as a process of increasing causal linkages to *positive* outcomes (see chapter 10 in this volume). The valence-linkage matrix was introduced to contrast the excusing and hoping processes, and the reality-negotiation construct was expanded from one that focused primarily on self-esteem maintenance to one that also emphasized self-esteem enhancement.

Subsequent accretions to the reality-negotiation construct have fleshed out a developmental role for the valence-linkage matrix in addition to its role in efforts to maintain or enhance established self-theories. The acquisition of a sense of personal (causal) agency and a capacity to make value judgments concerning one's actions are seen as crucial to the socialization process and they provide the necessary foundation for the formation of such self-related schemata as the "self-theory" (4, 5, 6, 7, 8, 27). As Epstein (28) has argued, for example, the self "develops out of the desire of the child to gain approval and avoid disapproval" (p. 86). In a very real sense, the linkage-to-act and valence-of-act cognitive schemata serve in a manner analogous to the navigational Global Positioning System by enabling people to determine their psychological latitude and longitude and to ascertain how best to negotiate from where they are to where they want—or perceive they need—to be.

Individual Differences in Reality Negotiation

Many measures may be construed as indices of reality-negotiation tendencies. Given our stance that the phenomenon is ubiquitous, the relevant question is not "Does she or doesn't she?" Rather, the issue is one of differences in style or in the self-theory arenas that are most vigorously safeguarded. Indeed, a bit of reflection leads to the conclusion that virtually any measure involving reference to standards of performance, values, causal attributions, or perceived control potentially relates to differences in reality negotiation. Furthermore, this is true whether it is the individual who is assessed or a group or person with whom the individual identifies. Snyder, Lassegard, and Ford (29), for example, showed that people try to sever their ties to groups that perform poorly, a process termed "CORFing" (cutting off reflected failure). Conversely, others have studied a phenomenon called "BIRGing" (basking in reflected glory) whereby people affiliate themselves with others' success (30, 31). We will argue below that people often have a stake in other's positive self-theories and actively collude in helping to preserve them.

Despite the plethora of possibilities, a few individual difference measures stand out as having been clearly associated with reality-negotiation tendencies. Measures of excuse-making, for example, relate directly to the use of linkage-weakening tactics. A notable example here is the Self-Handicapping Scale (see 32 for review) in both the original (32, 33) and short forms (34).

Measures of self-esteem serve as a somewhat global evaluation metric for what we refer to as one's self-theory, and also pertain to differences in reality negotiation. High versus low levels of self-esteem predict contrasting use of downward social comparison (a valence-shifting tactic; 35), differences in the use of self-enhancement (linkage-shifting) strategies (36, 37), and differences in excuse-making behavior (38). High versus low uncertainty about one's self-esteem also has been associated with self-handicapping differences (39).

Somewhat related to the findings for self-esteem are indications that varying levels of depression are accompanied by differences in reality negotiation. Most notable here is the evidence that people who score high on measures of depression are particularly prone to making internalizing (linkage-increasing) rather than externalizing (linkage-weakening) attributions for negative events (for review, see 40). Moreover, it appears that attributing failure to characterologic causes is more typical of depression than is attributing failure to personal behaviors (41). Both types of attribution are to "internal" sources, but dispositions are more likely than specific behaviors to be "central" to one's sense of self (see also 42).

In our discussion placing the reality-negotiation construct into historical context, we observed that the full (bipolar) linkage-valence matrix was first elaborated by Snyder (3) in introducing his concept of "hope." Since then, Snyder and his colleagues have developed scales designed to measure both trait (43) and state levels of hope (44). These measures are conceived as tapping individuals' motivation and perceived capacity for achieving (linking to) desired goals, and have demonstrated substantial correlations with a variety of indices related to self-presentation, coping, and health (for reviews, see 4, pp. 266–268; 27; 45).

To date, the only theory-derived individual difference measure specifically designed to assess reality-negotiation proclivities is the *Linkage Into Valenced Elements Scale* (LIVE; 46). The LIVE Scale contains 32 items selected to equally represent eight important life arenas (i.e., appearance, health, intelligence, school, job, leisure, personality, and relationships). Half of the items within each arena refer to positive (e.g., "superior intellectual abilities") and half to negative characteristics (e.g., "very poor academic performance"). Subjects respond using 9-point rating scales (1 = "not at all linked to cause" to 9 = "totally linked to cause"). The LIVE Scale yields a subscale score for each life arena and an average score.

At present, there is no published research employing the 32-item LIVE Scale so its validity and psychometric properties are open to question. Samuelson (47), however, tested an earlier, 80-item version with college students. Several of her findings relate to the construct validity of this expanded LIVE Scale. In particular, she found support for the notion that one's self-theory biases one's perceptions of "reality." Students with high (positive) average LIVE scores ranked themselves higher on the School and Intelligence subscales than their actual grade point averages would warrant, whereas students with low average LIVE scores were unrealistically self-disparaging. Samuelson also demonstrated that the expanded LIVE Scale correlated positively with scores from the (trait) Hope Scale (43). As noted above, Snyder (27) regards hope as a goal-directed, self-enhancing, motivational state characterized by efforts to link one's self to positive outcomes.

In its present state of development the LIVE Scale has a number of limitations as well as potential strengths. A strength is that it provides self-theory appraisals across separate life domains, thus allowing for comparisons that may be of interest in both research and clinical work. Assessment of multiple domains may also allow for greater sensitivity to developmental issues, given that responses to the various life arenas may shift over time depending on such factors as age, cultural standards, social roles, and personal history.

A conceptual limitation of the LIVE Scale is that it affords no means for assessing the importance the individual attaches to the eight life arenas or their perceived linkages to the associated items. For example, two individuals may express strong causal linkage to an outcome (e.g., "poor academic performance"), but the meaning of this linkage may differ according to how important academic performance is to their self-theories. It is also possible that an individual would express little causal linkage to items that are perceived as unimportant. The present wording of the LIVE Scale obscures whether claims of little linkage are based on an item's lack of relevance or on the individual's lack of perceived causality. The addition to the scale of a means for subjects to record the importance of the scale elements might be worthwhile for the information it would provide, particularly within clinical contexts.

Reality-Negotiation Tactics: An Overview

In the following sections, we will provide a brief overview of reality-negotiation strategies as they pertain to the challenge of maintaining a positive sense of self in the face of adverse information. Although our earlier remarks have acknowledged an important role for reality negotiation in the service of maintaining negative self-theories, our emphasis in the remaining portions of this chapter will be on maintaining and promoting positive self-theories. We refer the reader who is interested in those strategies aimed at preserving negative self-theories to Barone, Maddux, and Snyder (4), and Snyder and Higgins (5).

Reality Negotiation as an Automatic Process

Within our constructivist framework, reality negotiation is often essentially automatic and "unconscious" in the sense of not being within active awareness (1, 14, 48). Self-schemas that are activated within particular contexts render certain kinds of information more expected, searched for, and recognized (49, 50), as well as subsequently recalled (51). So long as no schema-discrepant information is detected, there is little to raise the activity into the more effort-costly arena of conscious processing. Even ambiguous information is unlikely to stir the individual out of an automatic processing mode, judging from findings that such information is likely to be interpreted as confirming rather than disconfirming expectations (52, 53).

Conscious (and motivated) processing is likely to arise, however, when unexpected or schema-discrepant information is salient enough to require active awareness for purposes of comprehension and response. The extent to which conscious effort-after-meaning is elicited will likely depend upon the degree to which the information is unexpected (54, 55) or schema-discrepant, and upon the availability of existing knowledge structures to handle it (56). The presence of an external audience to the schema-discrepant information or outcome may also serve to push reality negotiation into the conscious realm (1, 2, 14).

Negotiating Linkages to Preserve Positive Self-Theories

As we noted above, excuses are variously designed either to decrease the perceived negativity of bad outcomes or to shift causal attributions for them away from the individual's core sense of self. In their various manifestations (e.g., accounts, rationalizations, justifications), then, excuses encompass the array of those reality-negotiation tactics that are aimed at weakening linkages to negative outcomes (see arrow 1, Fig. 2.1). Denial, which is arguably the most primitive of linkage-focused excuses, aims to completely disrupt the individual's connection to outcomes. As our definition of excuses implies, however, their focus is often aimed more at shifting causal attributions to more peripheral (to the core self) origins than at completely severing them. Such excuses appear more likely than denials to be effective in eliciting both positive internal and external audience response (57, 58). One need look no further than the 1997–98 Murrah Federal Building bombing trials in Denver to see the impact of jurors' perceptions that Terry Nichols lacked the *intention* to kill.

Many *linkage-transforming* (as opposed to linkage-severing) excuses can be understood within Kelley's (59, 60) theory of attribution. Consistency-lowering excuses, for example, cite lack of effort (25, 61), lack of intentionality (62, 63), unforeseeable consequences, or evidence of other positive acts to elevate the distinctiveness of a negative outcome. In doing so, they undermine disposition-based causal attributions. During the Terry Nichols trial, for example, much was made of the fact that despite his involvement in conspiring to build the bomb that blew up the Murrah Federal Building, he appeared to be a "good family man." On the other hand, in the previously tried case of Timothy McVeigh, little evidence came forth to broaden his image beyond that of a government-hating extremist.

Within Kelley's attribution framework, consensus-raising excuses serve to undermine dispositional causal attributions by emphasizing the importance of situational factors (e.g., task difficulty, bad luck) over which neither the individual *nor anyone else* could be expected to have control. By implicating situational elements, such excuses weaken (but do not sever) the individual's unique causal link to the outcome (25, 26, 64, 65).

Kelley's attribution principles may also apply to anticipatory (before-the-fact) contexts. For example, a person may lower consistency prior to an evaluation by announcing that he or she is going to "blow it off," or raise consensus by claiming that an upcoming task is too difficult and, therefore, unfair (66, 67). Perhaps the most recognized anticipatory excuses are collectively known as "self-handicapping" strategies (68, 69). By gaining a handicap (e.g., drinking alcohol, failing to prepare) or claiming a preexisting illness or fatigue, the individual capitalizes on Kelley's (60) "discounting" principle. This principle states that when an outcome is associated with more than one possible cause, the attribution of causality to any one of them is weakened. Handicaps, therefore, create attributional confusion (for reviews, see 70, 71). Theoretically, they may also capitalize on Kelley's (60) principle of "augmentation." In the event of a positive performance, attributions to ability are augmented because the success occurred despite the presence of a handicap.

Although many potentially handicapping conditions may be temporary (e.g., intoxication, fatigue), others such as test anxiety (67), hypochondriasis (72), or shyness (73) may constitute dispositional characteristics of the individual. Although it may seem counterproductive to focus causal attributions on seemingly negative dispositional characteristics to preserve one's positive self-theories, doing so may actually be quite effective—if the targeted disposition is less central to the core sense of self than the threatened self-attribute. Threats to one's fundamental sense of competence or ability, for example, may be thwarted by citing one's performance anxiety. Such *incorporated* excuses are not without drawbacks (14). By removing the excusing condition from public scrutiny and framing it within a medical model, however, the effectiveness of the excuse may be enhanced (1, 2, 14, 70, 74).

Negotiating Valences to Preserve Positive Self-Theories

The essential thrust of valence-shifting strategies is to negotiate a more positive view of image-threatening outcomes or acts (see arrow 2, Fig. 2.1). One such strategy is to undermine the credibility of the source of threatening information, whether that source is a person (75, 76), a personality test (77), or a performance test (78, 79). If an individual's negative act involves a "victim," intimating that the victim got what he or she deserved may lessen the act's perceived negativity (80, 81), as might resorting to exonerative moral reasoning to suggest that an apparently negative act actually serves a loftier purpose (e.g., "spare the rod and spoil the child"). Other strategies for working alchemy on negative outcomes or acts include minimization (e.g., "it's not as bad as it looks"; 8), or using positive language to redefine the negative acts or the intentions which produced them (e.g., "lies" become "white lies," physical abuse or neglect becomes "tough love").

As we will argue in our later section on reality negotiation in the context of coping with illness and disability, another form of valence-shifting tactic frequently becomes paramount in the individual's ongoing adjustment. Illness or disability may or may not threaten a person's self-theory of being a "good" person, but it will typically threaten his or her sense of being in control. Just as wrapping a bad act within the garb of higher purpose may decrease its negative valence and, therefore, lessen its harmful impact on the individual's positive self-theories, there is good evidence that finding hidden benefits or "meaning" in one's illness or disability is beneficial to adjustment. We turn our attention now to a generalized consideration of reality negotiation as a coping process before focusing more specifically on reality-negotiation processes in the increasingly studied arena of health-related challenges.

Reality Negotiation as Coping

We have heretofore presented reality negotiation as fundamental to people's efforts to sustain their self-theories in the face of disconfirming information. The logic of this suggests that, to some extent, the individual's self-theories are *illusional* in that they are more positive (or negative) than is warranted.

A substantial literature attests to the adaptive advantages of having positive self-illusions (see for reviews, 82, 83). These advantages include the effects of perceived control on affect (84, 85), health (86, 87), task persistence (88, 89), performance (90), and psychological well-being (91, 92). Such relations speak to the limitations of traditional "psychological health = accurate self-perception" formulations (93, 94), and highlight the coping role of mechanisms that promote positive self-illusions. Although there are times when people wish to appraise the self accurately (95, 96) or consistent with existing beliefs, a dominant motive emerging from the literature on self-evaluation is self-enhancement (97).

There also appears to be a coping function for reality-negotiation mechanisms that support *negative* self-illusions. Brown and McGill (98), for example, demonstrated that ostensibly desirable life changes were associated with increased illness among subjects with low self-esteem, but with decreased illness for high self-esteem subjects. They attributed the adverse consequences for low self-esteem subjects to the identity disruption associated with reconciling their negative self-concepts to the "favorable" outcomes.

The idea that the stressfulness of an event is more related to the degree to which it demands personal redefinition than to its consensual negativity finds indirect support in the research of Swann and his associates. These authors report studies indicating that subjects with negative self-views preferentially seek out negative feedback in a variety of contexts (99, 100 study 1), are more committed to spouses who affirm their negative self-views (101), and respond to positive (self-discrepant) feedback by seeking self-verifying (negative) information (100 study 2).

In a related arena, Hammen, Marks, Mayol, and DeMayo (102) found that when interpersonal goals were central to their self-concepts, subjects were more likely to become depressed following negative relationship events than following achievement failures. The opposite tendency was found when subjects' self-definitions included strong achievement themes. Such findings point to the importance of self-consistency or self-verification in people's efforts to maintain predictability and control in their lives.

How does a reality-negotiation perspective reconcile our apparently contradictory positions concerning the importance of self-enhancement and self-consistency? We conclude that reality negotiation, as a form of "secondary control" (103), aids in coping, *not because the resulting products are inherently self-enhancing or self-verifying, but rather because the individual experiences a degree of control over the self-definitional implications of the person—data transaction.* Clearly, however, the individual's sense of predictability and control are maximal when those self-definitional implications affirm the basic tenets of the existing self-theory. Even for those persons whose self-theories are dominated by negative themes, information which confirms them appears to be cognitively preferable, despite the fact that it may occasion temporary states of negative affectivity (104).

Although the bulk of the preceding remarks has emphasized the role of reality negotiation in promoting self-theory stability, we do not mean to imply that ideally it leads to psychological stasis. Indeed, the term, "negotiation," implies an ongoing process. The central point is that even if aspects of the self-concept will or must eventually change, the individual may perceive him or herself as sitting in the "driver's seat" with respect to the rate and nature of the assimilation of new information, attitudes, or beliefs. As noted by Snyder and Higgins (1), "The regnant negotiated reality is not an end-state, but is constantly evolving in reaction to the never-ending flow of challenging events across the life span" (p. 32).

To the extent that reality-negotiation processes enable people to control the pace and direction of self-theory change, they play an important role in helping them sustain a continuous and integrated sense of "self." Early in the eighteenth century, the philosopher Hume (105) held that our experience of ourselves as having an enduring personal identity was an illusion based on our inability to notice change when it occurs gradually over time. In addition to requiring some self-consistency, however, people also must adapt to changing circumstances, including changing individual aptitudes.

In other words, they must grow, develop, and age. The self-constructive reality-negotiation process rests squarely at the nexus of the dialectic between the opposing needs for permanence and transformation.

Personal Control versus Social Control

Previous writings on reality negotiation have explicitly recognized the role of external audiences, but have tended to emphasize the individual's control of the process. Two recent discourses, however, have directed more attention to social influences. In doing so, they have yielded a more dynamically interactive vision of how reality is negotiated. Snyder and Higgins (5; see also 4) have argued that society's interest in sustaining its members' commitment to prosocial goals leads it to actively abet the individual's efforts to sustain self-theories *that serve the larger social interest.* The quid pro quo for this bit of assistance is society's exertion of far-reaching control over the individual. Currently, such normative social influences (106) can easily be seen in the area of health-related behaviors like smoking, where the zeitgeist (not to mention legislation) increasingly serves to ostracize smokers and to reward those who quit.

Perhaps more interesting still are areas where societal subgroups compete to define society's value structure related to particular behaviors or beliefs and use a currency of distinctive social support assets to foster allegiance to their viewpoint. A timely example is the struggle between "pro-life" and "pro-choice" advocates who offer adoption and family planning resources, respectively, to those who adhere to their value (valence) framework. The critical point is that, through dispensing or withholding rewards, social groups work to shape the individual's goal choices, actions, and, ultimately, self-theories. This social control is intrinsically connected to the availability of material and coping resources which, as suggested above, are provided to those who affiliate themselves with approved goal and value structures.

Collaborative Companions

Audience involvement in the reality-negotiation process can be viewed as both an obstacle and an aid to the individual (1, 2, 5, 14, 74). Audiences often complicate matters by curtailing people's ability to engage biased perceptions, interpretations, or recall, and by forcing them to articulate their rendering of reality for the audience's consideration and possible amendment. Such negotiations unfold in a give-and-take process, wherein the goal is to arrive at a compromise that both the individual and the outside audience can accept (1). Although there are contexts in which such negotiations are distinctly adversarial (e.g., court proceedings), more often others collaborate with the individual to arrive at mutually beneficial outcomes. Indeed, we believe that it is at the level of person-to-person or, on occasion, person-to-group interaction that mutual self-interests converge to yield the advantages that are associated with social support and close relationships (107, 108, 109).

We suggested above that the self is largely constructed through the reflected appraisals of others (i.e., our notion of revolving self-images; see also 110). It follows logically that the coping advantages conferred by social support often result from the active collaboration of close or intimate others who have an investment in the individual's outcomes. Memberships in groups, including dyads, provide people with frames of reference from which to evaluate "reality," as well as standards of performance. Such memberships themselves are a part of the reality-negotiation enterprise, as is seen in evidence that individuals actively affiliate or disaffiliate from groups depending on how the group's outcomes are valued or reflect on the self (e.g., see our earlier discussion of BIRGing and CORFing). Also, it goes without saying that this is not a unidirectional transaction. Just as we link ourselves to groups or individuals that serve our self-definitional interests, they link (or unlink) themselves to us and, in so doing, accrue (or forsake) a stake in *our* outcomes. This is probably nowhere more true than in the arena of close or intimate relationships where the partners may develop a truly reciprocal economy of "grace."

Close personal relationships would appear to be particularly well positioned to play a role in people's reality negotiations and related coping efforts. Closeness may promote less "defensive" (i.e., more honestly self-disclosive) negotiation efforts and, consequently, more opportunity for impactful feedback (111). In providing an arena for open self-expression, such relationships may be unique in their ability to foster the type of self-theory change that leads to greater integration, growth, and maturation (112, 113, 114). It is also possible, however, that some close relationships might be particularly likely to inhibit integrative change. For example, to the extent that relational partners have a need to view reality in similar ways (perhaps because their welfare is intertwined and their outcomes are shared), their mutually supportive collaboration toward self-serving interpretations could sustain dysfunctional self-theories. A particularly dramatic example of maladaptive mutual reality negotiation would be the occurrence of "shared psychotic disorder" or *Folie à Deux* (115, pp. 305–306), the hallmark of which is the sharing of a belief system that is considered (by others) to be delusional. A major question that emerges from these considerations is: What are the dynamics of the collusive reality-negotiation patterns that we recognize as social support, and what are the determinants of when such collusion translates into improved as opposed to impaired coping? In the following section we will highlight some of the reality-negotiation dynamics that attend efforts to cope with serious illness and disability. Our primary focus, however, will be on outlining some recent speculations regarding the determinants of which coping strategies "work" within the affected individual's social matrix, and the coercive nature of "social support."

Reality Negotiation and Social Support in Coping With Illness and Disability

Reality-negotiation dynamics have previously been related to health benefits in several contexts. With regard to linkage-shifting processes, for example, Seligman and his colleagues have reported findings that excuse-related patterns of causal attributions for negative experiences were related to greater longevity and better immune system functioning (116), as well as to improved long-term health outcomes (117, 118). In their analysis of coping among cancer victims, Taylor, Wood, and Lichtman (119) identified a number of valence-shifting processes among their subjects, including making downward social comparisons, finding benefits in their illness, and tailoring standards of adjustment to make their own adjustment appear superior. More recently, Higgins and Snyder (6) provided a review of the use of both valence- and linkage-shifting reality-negotiation dynamics in coping with health threats.

In this section we will examine the role of reality negotiation in peoples' adjustment to enduring health challenges. Rather than attempting a comprehensive overview, however, we will selectively focus on a limited subset of both linkage- and valence-shifting strategies in order to illustrate some recent speculations concerning the relationship between reality negotiation and social support in the coping process. In doing so, we will look beyond the individual's role and attempt to convey a more systemic vision of reality negotiation in the coping process.

Linkage: Conceptual Expansions

When individuals are faced with illness or adversity, a frequent and early response is a search for cause (120, 121). Superficially at least, the causes people discover may often appear at odds with our premise that positive adjustment is typically promoted by preferentially linking oneself to positive outcomes. Bulman and Wortman (122), for example, found that spinal cord injury patients who engaged in *self-blame* for their injuries tended to show *better* adjustment. Similar findings linking self-blame to adjustment have been reported in breast cancer (123) and renal failure patients (124). We believe a reality-negotiation perspective may help reconcile such findings with other literature that suggests that self-blame has only a modest (125) or even a negative or indifferent relationship to adjustment following illness or disability (126, 127, 128). Specifically, we will suggest that in addition to serving the individual reality negotiator's need to understand, causal attributions play an important role in maintaining the individual's connectedness to the social environment. Moreover, there is evidence that the importance of the role of causal attributions in sustaining this social connectedness shifts across time.

Higgins and Snyder (6) argued that self-blame in cases of illness or injury may often serve to preserve the individual's sense of control. By blaming themselves for their accidents, for example, Bulman and Wortman's (122) spinal cord patients may have reaffirmed their linkage to this valued self-concept as well as to a worldview in which what happens to people makes sense (80). Applying a reality-negotiation perspective, however, also leads to a recognition that the "victims" of illness or disability must continue to function within a social matrix. Among other things, ill or disabled individuals may be particularly dependent upon others for material and emotional support. Accordingly, in the process of negotiating a consensual view of one's health dilemma, the individual must deal with the audience's emotional need to distance itself from a similar fate. Especially to the extent that the person's difficulties are serious, external audiences are likely to experience vicarious threat (129, 130) and to engage in victim derogation or other defensive attributional distortions in order to preserve their belief that they can avoid a similar fate (131).

In some instances, then, self-blame may not only affirm the health sufferers' sense of control, it may also be a particularly easy "sell" because it upholds fellow travelers' coveted assumptions about their own (positive) destinies. There are, however, other facets of self-blame to consider. According to the literature on social reactions to victimization, for example, self-blame is likely to be a two-edged sword. Although it may help preserve one's own sense of control and assuage others' vicarious discomfort, it may also serve to disrupt the sufferer's ties to important social support resources. A consistent finding in the literature has been that sufferers who are seen as responsible for the onset of their conditions are likely to experience more negative social reactions than those who are not seen as responsible (132). Indeed, it may be that this double-edged quality of self-blame partially accounts for the fact that studies have identified an inconsistent relationship between self-blame and adaptation (122, 126, 128) as well as the fact that, over time, initial causation appears to fade in relevance to the sufferer. In fact, this latter observation led Schulz and Decker (125) to suggest that the coping relevance of causal linkage to the onset of disability decreases over time *as the importance of such factors as friends and the availability of resources increase in salience.*

Shifting patterns and relationships are to be expected within a reality-negotiation framework that recognizes a developmental progression in the process of adaptation. Indeed, a number of models of adaptation have looked at illness and disability acceptance in terms of stages (120, 133, 134, 135). None of them speaks of negotiations that are static. In general, however, we suggest that first causes and the nature of the individual's linkage to them fade in relevance as the individual transitions from negotiating a relationship with the initial trauma (or diagnosis) to negotiating a relationship with the ongoing demands of living. From the perspective of the survival of the "self," perhaps no task is more crucial to this enterprise than the negotiation or scripting of a new self-narrative (136) that not only supports a positive self-theory, *but also sustains the individual's ties to the community.* Frequently, the outcome of this effort hinges on the question of "meaning."

Valence: Conceptual Expansions

Broadly conceptualized, reality-negotiation processes are forms of "secondary" control (103), where the distinction drawn is between changing one's view of the challenge (secondary control) and changing the challenge itself (primary control). Once a leg has been lost to amputation, it remains lost regardless of who or what led to the amputation: The individual still must negotiate multiple personal and social meanings of this situation. Indeed, the exercise of such secondary control is particularly relevant to disabilities and chronic illnesses over which the individual has little or no physical control but, nevertheless, has many cognitive and emotional options.

One type of cognitive reframing, benefit-finding, has been closely linked to better adjustment (see chapter 13 in this volume). When asked if their disability had brought purpose or meaning to their lives, for example, 64% of one sample of persons with spinal cord injury answered affirmatively (125). Benefit-finding also has been found to aid in coping with myocardial infarction (137, 138), amputation (139), breast cancer (119, 120, 140), and rheumatoid arthritis (141). Benefits commonly mentioned include realizing what is most important in life, improved relationships with loved ones, renewed spirituality, and new opportunities for self-exploration.

The idea that finding positive reframes for negative outcomes can lead to emotional benefits has a long tradition. The Greek stoic philosopher, Epictetus (c. 60–c. 120 AD), for example, wrote that men are disturbed by their views of things rather than by the things themselves. More recently, this line of thought has been actively carried on in cognitive theories of depression (142) and anxiety (143). As we have emphasized above, however, the reality-negotiation enterprise is inherently a social one, especially when outcomes of importance to external audiences are at issue. While the occasion of a serious illness or disability may understandably stimulate the affected individual to attempt to forge a relationship to his or her "new" self through the discovery or creation of new meanings (135), it also necessitates the negotiation of a new set of relationships and understandings with the social environment.

Asymmetries in the exchange of social support resources between chronically ill or disabled individuals and their social networks have long posed difficulties for economic models of social support (143). Models based on reciprocity predict that ill and disabled individuals, those presumably least capable of reciprocation, should be more bereft of social support than appears to be the case (144). As Stroebe and Stroebe (145) point out, such findings have led some to propose modifications in exchange theories designed to salvage an equity viewpoint (144, 146), and others to frame re-

lationships with the ill, elderly, and disabled as being governed by principles other than equity (147).

A reality-negotiation perspective does not supplant such modifications.
Rather, it suggests a way of thinking about how "equity" is defined within
particular relationships. More to the point with regard to our focus on coping, it suggests that those (ostensibly *individual*) coping strategies that aid
adaptation via maintaining access to social support resources are those that
also address the needs of the support providers and, therefore, form a sort
of currency of exchange. According to this view, coping efforts which do
not address the needs of support providers should be met with a withdrawal
of support resources. In fact, similar arguments have been made by Silver
and her associates (129) who suggested that helpers whose ministrations
are unrewarded by the subject's improvement react negatively and with-
draw. As intimated above, considerations such as these have implications
for possible expansions in the range of exchange resources to be considered
as currency in equity-based theories of social support. They also raise questions concerning the extent to which the selection of effective coping strategies is an individual versus a negotiated communal enterprise, and how
specific coping efforts evolve.

In our preceding discussion of the negotiation of causal linkages we suggested that a sufferer's "self-blame" may often serve to preserve the audience's illusion of control. The thesis we develop here leads to similar conclusions concerning the role of benefit-finding (negotiating valences).
Specifically, we are suggesting that the finding of meaning, spiritual en-
lightenment, or renewed purpose through suffering not only meets the emotional needs of the afflicted individual, but also services a powerful social
and cultural imperative. Terror management theory (148, 149), for example,
holds that an essential function of culture is to provide its members with a
worldview that reduces anxiety about death by creating a sense of purpose,
meaning, and permanence. To the extent that exposure to individuals suffering from serious illness or disability raises awareness of one's own mortality or vulnerability, it should also motivate efforts to seek relief from the
resulting discomfort. Our reality-negotiation framework suggests that, toward this end, the sufferer and relevant audiences embark on a series of
transactions, one goal of which is a more positive (or more benign) view of
the sufferer's reality. Not coincidentally, those resolutions which emerge
as indicative of "model" coping are also those which reflect our culture's
worldview that transcendent truth is revealed through suffering (136).
Prominent individuals who appear to embody that view are widely hailed
as cultural heroes (e.g., Christopher Reeve, Jim Valvano).

Adaptive Reality Negotiation: Limiting Considerations

In an article on "the optimal margin of illusion," Baumeister (150) argued
persuasively that illusory beliefs, when indulged to just the right degree,

are beneficial. Either too much or too little illusion, however, may be mal-adaptive. It is, of course, the goal of the reality-negotiation enterprise to locate that "golden" mean. In this section, we will once again use the context of coping with illness and disability to illustrate Baumeister's premise, and to suggest the manner in which the optimal *balance* of illusion is often struck.

In our remarks concerning negotiating valences, we argued that finding meaning in tribulation is often beneficial because it addresses both the sufferer's and audience's emotional needs. By reducing the vicarious threat inherent in their disorders, we averred, such benefit-finding also preserves sufferers' ties to social support resources. There is, however, an important caveat to consider. Namely, sufferers who show too little distress may be likely to experience a diminution of social support resources. Based on findings such as those of Silver and her colleagues (129), Schreurs and de Ridder (151) concluded that both "good" and "bad" copers are likely to receive reduced social support. For good copers, they speculate, the reduction results from insufficient communication of need. For bad copers, the reduction results from overwhelming vicarious threat and feelings of helplessness at being able to adequately respond to the individual's suffering. It is, therefore, the "balanced" coper who is likely to receive the optimal level of support.

Another vision of how an optimistic (positive illusional) take on the reality of one's illness or disorder may lead to diminished social support (i.e., corrective social feedback) is provided by Ersek (152) in a discussion of reality negotiation within nursing settings. Ersek speaks of the tensions that may develop between nurses and their seriously ill patients when the patients hold what Ersek characterizes as unrealistically hopeful beliefs. Significantly, Ersek sees such mismatches and the resulting emotional alienation as potentially threatening to the nurses' ability to continue providing quality services to such patients. Moreover, to counter these potential negative effects, Ersek points to the importance of providing *institutional support* for the nurses' views so they may continue to function effectively. Despite Ersek's appearing to suggest that it is primarily the patients' views of their illnesses that are illusional or negotiated, she provides an important "insiders" perspective on one aspect of the reality negotiation that occurs within these vital health settings.

In his article on the optimal level of illusion, Baumeister (150) suggested that the primary liability associated with having an overly positive margin of illusion is increased vulnerability to disconfirmation. Although Baumeister did not specifically address health-related issues, it is easy to construct scenarios in which overly illusional beliefs expose one to adverse and even potentially fatal disconfirmations. For example, one consequence of an overly positive construction of the reality of one's situation may be that it undermines motivation to engage in important health-promoting activities. One occasionally hears of extreme cases where people suffer or die because of beliefs that deny the reality of physical illness or promote magical thinking about recovery. More commonplace are difficulties associated with getting people to engage in health-promoting activities at the level of either prevention (e.g., exercising properly, quitting smoking) or treatment (e.g., compliance with treatment recommendations). These and other behaviors may often result from an illusion of "unique invulnerability" (153), and the disconfirming feedback, rather than emanating from the social environment, may be the occurrence or exacerbation of health problems.

Summary and Conclusions

Dating from our early work on excuse theory (15) when our thoughts about reality negotiation as a more encompassing process were forming, it has been commonplace within our circle to joke about how difficult it has become to take things, including our own behavior, at face value. Our growing awareness of the pervasiveness of and need for self-illusional processes, along with the need for social relatedness, has seemed to dictate a skeptic's stance. For the present authors, this skeptical view has extended into the realm of the scientific method itself. Even on this hallowed turf, one can discern the workings of the human need to negotiate an illusional vision of reality.

In a book with far-reaching (but much ignored) implications, McClure (154) argued that social scientists often succumb to the illusion that their research paradigms reveal "truth," whereas in reality they are subtly biased toward preformed conclusions. An interesting example of this is the repeated finding of significant, clinician-rated antidepressant drug effects in double-blind trials of new medications. The illusory and self-serving belief is that double-blind designs protect against rater bias. The reality, however, is that active drugs are typically easily discriminable from placebos, and the identified drug effects are often inflated due to rater bias and allegiance effects (155).

Here at the close of this chapter, it is interesting to extend McClure's cautionary view to our own domain and to speculate that many of the research areas we have surveyed may, themselves, be subject to illusional influences. In studies of the nature of "good" coping, for example, to what extent are physician- and patient-rated indices of positive adaptation influenced by the give-and-take process of physicians and patients negotiating a relationship to one another? Tennen, Affleck, Allen, McGrade, and Ratzan (156), in only one of many possible examples, reported that insulin-dependent children who attributed the onset of their disorders to internal, variable, and specific factors were rated by their physicians as coping better than children who made external, stable, and global attributions. Is it possible that such findings partially reflect the end-result of reality-negotiation sequences in which the children and their physicians arrive at a mutual understanding, wherein taking responsibility for one's disorder (and meeting the physicians' needs by complying with treatment recommendations) comes to be recognized as "good" coping? In our own section above on the limiting considerations in adaptive reality negotiation, we cite failure to comply with treatment recommendations as a potentially fatal complication of overly positive self-illusions. This is despite empirical evidence that adherence to medical recommendations in cases of chronic health problems is only weakly associated with improved health outcomes (157). Again, is it possible that the value that (we) health professionals place on patients' actively adhering to treatment recommendations derives from (our) the professional's needs to feel efficacious? Although research paradigms often foster the illusion that the outcomes of queries are determined by the "subjects," we are left wondering about the extent to which the findings actually reflect the outcomes of dynamically interacting systems aimed at negotiating mutually agreeable realities.

In this chapter we have provided an overview of the reality-negotiation construct and some of the processes related to it. Reality negotiation is fundamental to virtually all human enterprises where individual interests are involved and outcomes depend on our ability to symbolize. Given this potential scope, our illustrations have been, by necessity, highly selected and limited. Our use of problems related to illness and disability as illustrations in no way defines this as the primary or only domain of interest. Rather, our use of a problem area that eventually touches all of us may afford the reader a more personal glimpse of the diversity of issues that attend our efforts to make our way in this life. With reference to the impossibility of making something be what it is not, it has often been said that you can't make silk purses from sows' ears. While this may literally be so, our capacity to negotiate how we perceive things tells us that, so long as the interests of the individual and interested others converge and they approach the enterprise with a common purpose, nobody will know the difference.

References

1. Snyder, C. R., & Higgins, R. L. (1988). Excuses: Their effective role in the negotiation of reality. *Psychological Bulletin, 104,* 23–35.
2. Snyder, C. R., & Higgins, R. L. (1988). Excuse attributions: Do they work? In S. L. Zelen (Ed.), *Self-representation: The second attribution-personality theory conference* (pp. 50–122). New York: Springer-Verlag.
3. Snyder, C. R. (1989). Reality negotiation: From excuses to hope and beyond. *Journal of Social and Clinical Psychology, 8,* 130–157.
4. Barone, D. F., Maddux, J. E., & Snyder, C. R. (1997). *Social cognitive psychology: History and current domains.* New York: Plenum Press.
5. Snyder, C. R., & Higgins, R. L. (1997). Reality negotiation: Governing one's self and being governed by others. *General Psychology Review, 1,* 336–350.

6. Higgins, R. L., & Snyder, C. R. (1991). Reality negotiation and excuse-making. In C. R. Snyder & D. R. Forsyth (Eds.), *Handbook of social and clinical psychology: The health perspective* (pp. 79–95). Elmsford, NY: Pergamon.

7. Snyder, C. R., & Higgins, R. L. (1990). Reality negotiation and excuse-making: President Reagan's March 4, 1987 Iran arms scandal speech and other literature. In M. J. Cody & M. L. McLauglin (Eds.), *Psychology of tactical communication* (pp. 207–228). Clevedon, England: Multilingual Matters.

8. Snyder, C. R., Irving, L. R., Sigmon, S. T., & Holleran, S. (1992). Reality negotiation and valence/linkage self theories: Psychic showdown at the "I'm OK" corral and beyond. In L. Montrada, S-H. Filipp, & M. J. Lerner (Eds.), *Life crises and experiences of loss in adulthood* (pp. 275–297). Hillsdale, NJ: Erlbaum.

9. Kant, I. (1965). *Critique of pure reason* (unabridged ed.; N. K. Smith, Trans.). New York: St. Martin's Press. (Original work published 1781)

10. Hegel, G. W. (1967). *The phenomenology of mind* (J. B. Baillie, Trans.). New York: Harper & Row. (Original work published 1807.)

11. Cooley, C. H. (1902). *Human nature and the social order.* New York: Scribner.

12. Mead, G. H. (1934). *Mind, self, and society.* Chicago: University of Chicago Press.

13. Piaget, J. (1963). *The origins of intelligence in children* (M. Cook, Trans.). New York: Norton. (Original work published in 1936)

14. Higgins, R. L., & Snyder, C. R. (1989). Excuses gone awry: An analysis of self-defeating excuses. In R. C. Curtis (Ed.), *Self-defeating behaviors: Experimental research, clinical impressions, and practical implications* (pp. 99–130). New York: Plenum.

15. Snyder, C. R., Higgins, R. L., & Stucky, R. J. (1983). *Excuses: Masquerades in search of grace.* New York: Wiley-Interscience.

16. James, W. (1890). *The principles of psychology* (Vols. 1 & 2). New York: Holt.

17. Allport, G. W. (1937). *Personality: A psychological interpretation.* New York: Holt.

18. Rogers, C. R. (1951). *Client-centered therapy: Its current practice, implications, and theory.* Boston: Houghton Mifflin.

19. Maslow, A. (1968). *Toward a psychology of being* (2nd ed.). New York: Van Nostrand.

20. Epstein, S. (1973) The self-concept revisited: Or a theory of a theory. *American Psychologist, 28,* 404–416.

21. Wells, L. E., & Marwell, G. (1976). *Self-esteem: Its conceptualization and measurement.* Beverly Hills, CA: Sage Publications.

22. Wylie, R. C. (1974). *The self-concept: A review of methodological and measuring instruments* (Vol. 1, rev. ed.). Lincoln: University of Nebraska Press.

23. Wylie, R. C. (1979). *The self-concept: Theory and research on selected topics* (Vol. 2, rev. ed.). Lincoln: University of Nebraska Press.

24. Arkin, R. M., Cooper, H., & Kolditz, T. (1980). A statistical review of the literature concerning the self-serving attribution bias in interpersonal influence situations. *Journal of Personality, 48,* 435–448.

25. Miller, D. T. (1976). Ego involvement and attribution for success and failure. *Journal of Personality and Social Psychology, 34*, 901–906.
26. Zuckerman, M. (1979). Attribution of success and failure revisited, or: The motivational bias is alive and well in attribution theory. *Journal of Personality, 47*, 245–287.
27. Snyder, C. R. (1994). *The psychology of hope: You can get there from here.* New York: Free Press.
28. Epstein, S. (1980). The self-concept: A review and the proposal of an integrated theory of personality. In E. Staub (Ed.), *Personality: Basic issues and current research* (pp. 82–132). Englewood Cliffs, NJ: Prentice-Hall.
29. Snyder, C. R., Lassegard, M., & Ford, C. E. (1986). Distancing after group success and failure: Basking in reflected glory and cutting off reflected failure. *Journal of Personality and Social Psychology, 51*, 382–388.
30. Cialdini, R. B., Borden, R. J., Thorne, A., Walker, M. R., Freeman, S., & Sloan, L. R. (1976). Basking in reflected glory: Three (football) field studies. *Journal of Personality and Social Psychology, 39*, 406–415.
31. Cialdini, R. B., Finch, J. F., & DeNicholas, M. E. (1990). Strategic self-presentation: The indirect route. In M. J. Cody & M. L. McLaughlin (Eds.), *The psychology of tactical communication* (pp. 194–206). Clevedon, England: Multilingual Matters.
32. Rhodewalt, F. (1990). Self-handicappers: Individual differences in the preference for anticipatory self-protective acts. In R. L. Higgins, C. R. Snyder, & S. Berglas, *Self-handicapping: The paradox that isn't* (pp. 69–106). New York: Plenum.
33. Jones, E. E., & Rhodewalt, F. (1982). *The Self-Handicapping Scale.* (Available from Rhodewalt at the Department of Psychology, University of Utah.)
34. Strube, M. J. (1985). An analysis of the Self-Handicapping Scale. *Basic and Applied Social Psychology, 7*, 211–224.
35. Aspinwall, L. G., & Taylor, S. E. (1993). Effects of social comparison direction, threat, and self-esteem on affect, self-evaluation, and expected success. *Journal of Personality and Social Psychology, 64*, 708–722.
36. Baumeister, R. F., Tice, D. M., & Hutton, D. G. (1989). Self-presentational motivations and personality differences in self-esteem. *Journal of Personality, 57*, 547–579.
37. Schütz, A. (in press). Autobiographical narratives of good and bad deeds: Defensive and favorable self-description moderated by trait self-esteem. *Journal of Social and Clinical Psychology.*
38. Tice, D. M., & Baumeister, R. F. (1984, May). *Self-handicapping, self-esteem, and self-presentation.* Paper presented at the meeting of the Midwestern Psychological Association, Chicago.
39. Harris, R. N., & Snyder, C. R. (1986). The role of uncertain self-esteem in self-handicapping. *Journal of Personality and Social Psychology, 51*, 451–458.
40. Burns, M. O., & Seligman, M. E. P. (1991). Explanatory style, helplessness, and depression. In C. R. Snyder & D. R. Forsyth (Eds.), *Handbook of social and clinical psychology: The health perspective* (pp. 267–284). Elmsford, NY: Pergamon Press.

41. Anderson, C. A., Miller, R. S., Riger, A. L., Dill, J. C., & Sedikides, C. (1994). Behavioral and characterological attributional styles as predictors of depression and loneliness: Review, refinement, and test. *Journal of Personality and Social Psychology, 66*, 549–558.

42. Janoff-Bulman, R. (1979). Characterological versus behavioral self-blame: Inquiries into depression and rape. *Journal of Personality and Social Psychology, 37*, 1798–1809.

43. Snyder, C. R., Harris, C., Anderson, J. R., Holleran, S. A., Irving, L. M., Sigmon, S. T., Yoshinobu, L., Gibb, J., Langelle, C., & Harney, P. (1991). The will and the ways: Development and validation of an individual-differences measure of hope. *Journal of Personality and Social Psychology, 60*, 570–585.

44. Snyder, C. R., Sympson, S. C., Ybasco, F. C., Borders, T. F., Babyak, M. A., & Higgins, R. L. (1996). Development and validation of the State Hope Scale. *Journal of Personality and Social Psychology, 70*, 321–335.

45. Snyder, C. R., Irving, L. R., & Anderson, J. R. (1991). Hope and health. In C. R. Snyder & D. R. Forsyth (Eds.), *Handbook of social and clinical psychology: The health perspective* (pp. 285–305). Elmsford, NY: Pergamon Press.

46. Snyder, C. R., & Samuelson, B. E. A. (1998). *Development and validation of the LIVE Scale: Linkage into valenced elements.* Unpublished manuscript. University of Kansas.

47. Samuelson, B. E. A. (1996). *Measuring linkage into valenced elements: The LIVE scale.* Unpublished master's thesis. University of Kansas.

48. Snyder, C. R. (1985). Collaborative companions: The relationship of self-deception and excuse-making. In M. Martin (Ed.), *Essays in self-deception* (pp. 35–51). Lawrence, KS: Regents Press of Kansas.

49. Bargh, J. A., & Pratto, F. (1986). Individual construct accessibility and perceptual selection. *Journal of Experimental Social Psychology, 22*, 293–311.

50. Markus, H. M., & Wurf, E. (1987). The dynamic self-concept: A social psychological perspective. *Annual Review of Psychology, 38*, 299–337.

51. Higgins, E. T., King, G. A., & Mavin, G. H. (1982). Individual construct accessibility and subjective impressions and recall. *Journal of Personality and Social Psychology, 43*, 35–47.

52. Higgins, E. T. (1989). Knowledge accessibility and activation: Subjectivity and suffering from unconscious sources. In J. S. Uleman & J. A. Bargh (Eds.), *Unintended thought: Limits of awareness, intention, and control* (pp. 75–123). New York: Guilford.

53. Jones, R. A. (1990). Expectations and delay in seeking medical care. *Journal of Social Issues, 46*, 81–95.

54. Hastie, R. (1984). Causes and effects of causal attribution. *Journal of Personality and Social Psychology, 46*, 44–56.

55. Pyszczynski, T. A., & Greenberg, J. (1981). Role of disconfirmed expectancies in the instigation of attributional processing. *Journal of Personality and Social Psychology, 40*, 31–38.

56. Bargh, J. A. (1996). Automaticity in social psychology. In E. T. Higgins, & A. W. Kruglanski (Eds.), *Social psychology: Handbook of basic principles* (pp. 169–183). New York: Guilford.

57. Mehlman, R. C., & Snyder, C. R. (1985). Excuse theory: A test of the self-protective role of attribution. *Journal of Personality and Social Psychology, 49*, 994–1001.
58. Weiner, B., Amirkhan, J. Folkes, V. S., & Verette, J. A. (1987). An attributional analysis of excuse giving: Studies of a naive theory of emotion. *Journal of Personality and Social Psychology, 31*, 415–421.
59. Kelley, H. H. (1967). Attribution theory in social psychology. In D. Levine (Ed.), *Nebraska Symposium on Motivation* (Vol. 15, pp. 192–238). Lincoln: University of Nebraska Press.
60. Kelley, H. H. (1971). *Attribution in social interaction*. New York: General Learning Press.
61. Lazarus, R. S., Deese, J., & Osler, S. F. (1952). The effects of psychological stress upon performance. *Psychological Bulletin, 49*, 293–317.
62. Rotenberg, K. (1980). Children's use of intentionality in judgments of character and disposition. *Child Development, 51*, 282–284.
63. Shaw, M. E., & Reitan, H. T. (1969). Attribution of responsibility as a basis for sanctioning behavior. *British Journal of Social and Clinical Psychology, 8*, 217–226.
64. Davis, W. L., & Davis, D. E. (1972). Internal-external control and attribution of responsibility for success and failure. *Journal of Personality, 40*, 123–136.
65. Larson, J. R. (1977). Evidence for a self-serving bias in the attribution of causality. *Journal of Personality, 45*, 430–441.
66. Frankel, A., & Snyder, M. L. (1978). Poor performance following unsolvable problems: Learned helplessness or egotism? *Journal of Personality and Social Psychology, 36*, 1415–1423.
67. Smith, T. W., Snyder, C. R., & Handelsman, M. M. (1982). On the self-serving function of an academic wooden leg: Test anxiety as a self-handicapping strategy. *Journal of Personality and Social Psychology, 42*, 314–321.
68. Berglas, S., & Jones, E. E. (1978). Drug choice as a self-handicapping strategy in response to noncontingent success. *Journal of Personality and Social Psychology, 36*, 405–417.
69. Jones, E. E., & Berglas, S. (1978). Control attributions about the self through self-handicapping strategies: The appeal of alcohol and the role of underachievement. *Personality and Social Psychology Bulletin, 4*, 200–206.
70. Higgins, R. L., Snyder, C. R., & Berglas, S. (1990). *Self-handicapping: The paradox that isn't*. New York: Plenum.
71. Snyder, C. R., & Smith, T. W. (1982). Symptoms as self-handicapping strategies: The virtues of old wine in a new bottle. In G. Weary & H. L. Mirels (Eds.), *Integrations of clinical and social psychology* (pp. 104–127). New York: Oxford University Press.
72. Smith, T. W., Snyder, C. R., & Perkins, S. C. (1983). The self-serving function of hypochondriacal complaints: Physical symptoms as self-handicapping strategies. *Journal of Personality and Social Psychology, 44*, 787–797.
73. Snyder, C. R., Smith, T. W., Augelli, R. W., & Ingram, R. E. (1983). On the self-serving function of social anxiety: Shyness as a self-handi-

capping strategy. *Journal of Personality and Social Psychology, 48,* 970–980.

74. Snyder, C. R., & Higgins, R. L. (1988). From making to being the excuse: An analysis of deception and verbal/nonverbal issues. *Journal of Nonverbal Behavior, 12,* 237–252.

75. Aronson, E., & Worchel, P. (1966). Similarity vs. liking as determinants of interpersonal attractiveness. *Psychonomic Science, 5,* 157–158.

76. Jones, S. (1973). Self and interpersonal evaluations: Esteem theories versus consistency theories. *Psychological Bulletin, 79,* 185–199.

77. Snyder, C. R., & Shenkel, R. J. (1976). Effects of "favorability," modality, and relevance on acceptance of general personality interpretations prior to and after receiving diagnostic feedback. *Journal of Consulting and Clinical Psychology, 44,* 34–41.

78. Clair, M. S., & Snyder, C. R. (1979). Effects of instructor-delivered sequential evaluative feedback upon students' subsequent classroom-related performance and instructor ratings. *Journal of Educational Psychology, 71,* 50–57.

79. Snyder, C. R., & Clair, M. (1976). Effects of expected and obtained grades in teacher evaluation and attribution of performance. *Journal of Educational Psychology, 68,* 75–82.

80. Lerner, M. J. (1980). *The belief in a just world: A fundamental delusion.* New York: Plenum.

81. Lerner, M. J., & Miller, D. (1978). Just world research and the attribution process: Looking back and ahead. *Psychological Bulletin, 85,* 1030–1051.

82. Brown, J. D. (1991). Accuracy and bias in self-knowledge. In C. R. Snyder & D. R. Forsyth (Eds.), *Handbook of social and clinical psychology: The health perspective* (pp. 158–178). Elmsford, NY: Pergamon Press.

83. Taylor, S. E., & Brown, J. (1988). Illusion and well-being: A social psychological perspective on mental health. *Psychological Bulletin, 103,* 193–210.

84. Dunn, D. S., & Wilson, T. D. (1990). When the stakes are high: A limit to the illusion-of-control effect. *Social Cognition, 8,* 305–323.

85. Golin, S., Terrell, T., & Johnson, B. (1977). Depression and the illusion of control. *Journal of Abnormal Psychology, 86,* 440–442.

86. Langer, E. J., & Rodin, J. (1976). The effects of choice and enhanced personal responsibility for the aged: A field experiment in an institutional setting. *Journal of Personality and Social Psychology,* 191–198.

87. Schulz, R. (1976). Effects of control and predictability on the physical and psychological well-being of the institutionalized aged. *Journal of Personality and Social Psychology, 33,* 563–573.

88. Bandura, A. (1989). Self-regulation of motivation and action through internal standards and goal systems. In L. Pervin (Ed.), *Goal concepts in personality and social psychology* (pp. 19–86). Hillsdale, NJ: Erlbaum.

89. Felson, R. B. (1984). The effect of self-appraisals of ability on academic performance. *Journal of Personality and Social Psychology, 47,* 944–952.

90. Dweck, C. S., & Leggett, E. L. (1988). A social-cognitive approach to personality and motivation. *Psychological Review, 95,* 256–273.

91. Alloy, L. B., & Abramson, L. Y. (1988). Depressive realism: Four theoretical perspectives. In L. B. Alloy (Ed.), *Cognitive processes in depression* (pp. 223–265). New York: Guilford.

92. Roth, D. L., & Ingram, R. E. (1985). Factors in the Self-Deception Questionnaire: Associations with depression. *Journal of Personality and Social Psychology, 48,* 243–251.

93. Jahoda, M. (1958). *Current concepts of positive mental health.* New York: Basic Books.

94. Maslow, A. (1950). Self-actualizing people: A study of psychological health. *Personality,* Symposium No. 1, 11–34.

95. Trope, Y. (1986). Identification and inferential processes in dispositional attribution. *Psychological Review, 93,* 239–257.

96. Trope, Y. (1986). Self-enhancement and self-assessment in achievement behavior. In R. M. Sorrentino & E. T. Higgins (Eds.), *Handbook of motivation and cognition: Foundations of social behavior* (Vol. 2, pp. 350–378). New York: Guilford.

97. Sedikides, C. (1993). Assessment, enhancement, and verification determinants of the self-verification process. *Journal of Personality and Social Psychology, 65,* 317–338.

98. Brown, J. D., & McGill, K. L. (1989). The cost of good fortune: When positive life events produce negative health consequences. *Journal of Personality and Social Psychology, 57,* 1103–1110.

99. Swann, W. B., Jr., Wenzlaff, R. M., Krull, D. S., & Pelham, B. W. (1992). Allure of negative feedback: Self-verification strivings among depressed persons. *Journal of Abnormal Psychology, 101,* 293–306.

100. Swann, W. B., Jr., Wenzlaff, R. M., & Tafarodi, R. W. (1992). Depression and the search for negative evaluations: More evidence on the role of self-verification strivings. *Journal of Abnormal Psychology, 101,* 314–317.

101. Swann, W. B., Jr., Hixon, J. G., & De La Ronde, C. (1992). Embracing the bitter "truth": Negative self-concepts and marital commitment. *Psychological Science, 3,* 118–121.

102. Hammen, C. L., Marks, T., Mayol, A., & DeMayo, A. R. (1985). Depressive self-schemas, life stress, and vulnerability to depression. *Journal of Abnormal Psychology, 94,* 308–319.

103. Rothbaum, F., Weisz, J., & Snyder, S. (1982). Changing the world and changing the self: A two-process model of perceived control. *Journal of Personality and Social Psychology, 42,* 5–37.

104. Swann, W. B., Jr., Griffin, J. J., Jr., Predmore, S. C., & Gaines, B. (1987). The cognitive-affective crossfire: When self-consistency confronts self-enhancement. *Journal of Personality and Social Psychology, 52,* 881–889.

105. Hume, D. (1911). *A treatise on human understanding.* London: J. M. Dent and Sons. (Original work published 1738)

106. Deutsch, M., & Gerard, H. B. (1955). A study of normative and informational social influence upon individual judgment. *Journal of Abnormal and Social Psychology, 51,* 629–635.

107. Cohen, S. (1988). Psychosocial models of the role of social support in the etiology of physical disease. *Health Psychology, 7,* 269–297.

108. Myers, D. G., & Diener, E. (1995). Who is happy? *Psychological Science, 6*, 10–19.
109. Schwarzer, R., & Leppin, A. (1992). Social support and mental health: A conceptual and empirical overview. In L. Montada, S. H. Filipp, & M. J. Lerner (Eds.), *Life crises and experiences of loss in adult life* (pp. 435–458). Hillsdale, NJ: Erlbaum.
110. Markus, H. M., & Cross, S. (1990). The interpersonal self. In L. A. Pervin (Ed.), *Handbook of personality: Theory and research* (pp. 576–608). New York: Guilford.
111. Reis, H. T., & Patrick, B. C. (1996). Attachment and intimacy: Component processes. In E. T. Higgins & A. W. Kruglanski (Eds.), *Social psychology: Handbook of basic principles.* (523–563). New York: Guilford.
112. Pennebaker, J. W., & Beall, S. K. (1986). Confronting a traumatic event: Toward an understanding of inhibition and disease. *Journal of Abnormal Psychology, 95*, 274–281.
113. Pennebaker, J. W., Colder, M., & Sharp, L. K. (1990). Accelerating the coping process. *Journal of Personality and Social Psychology, 58*, 528–537.
114. Pennebaker, J. W., Kiecolt-Glaser, J. K., & Glaser, R. (1988). Disclosure of traumas and immune function: Health implications for psychotherapy. *Journal of Consulting and Clinical Psychology, 56*, 239–245.
115. American Psychiatric Association. (1994). *Diagnostic and statistical manual of mental disorders* (4th ed.). Washington, DC: Author.
116. Seligman, M. E. P. (1986, August). *Explanatory style: Depression, Lyndon Baines Johnson and the Baseball Hall of Fame.* Paper presented at the 94th Annual Convention of the American Psychological Association, Washington, DC.
117. Elder, G., Bettes, B. A., & Seligman, M. E. P. (1982). Unpublished data. Cornell University. [Cited on p. 368 of Peterson, C., & Seligman, M. E. P. (1984). Causal explanations as a risk factor for depression: Theory and evidence. *Psychological Review, 91*, 347–374.]
118. Peterson, C., Seligman, M. E. P., & Viallant, G. E. (1988). Pessimistic explanatory style is a risk factor for physical illness: A thirty-five-year longitudinal study. *Journal of Personality and Social Psychology, 55*, 23–27.
119. Taylor, S. E., Wood, J. V., & Lichtman, R. R. (1983). Selective evaluation as a response to victimization. *Journal of Social Issues, 39*, 19–40.
120. Taylor, S. E. (1983). Adjustment to threatening events: A theory of cognitive adaptation. *American Psychologist, 38*, 1161–1173.
121. Wong, P. & Weiner, B. (1981). When people ask "why" questions, and the heuristics of attributional search. *Journal of Personality and Social Psychology, 40*, 650–663.
122. Bulman, R. J., & Wortman, C. B. (1977). Attributions of blame and coping in the "real world": Severe accident victims react to their lot. *Journal of Personality and Social Psychology, 35*, 351–363.
123. Timko, C., & Janoff-Bulman, R. (1985). Attributions, vulnerability and psychological adjustment: The case of breast cancer. *Health Psychology, 4*, 521–546.

124. Witenberg, S. H., Blanchard, E. B., Suls, J., Tennen, H., McCoy, G., & McGoldrick, M. D. (1983). Perceptions of control and causality as predictors of compliance and coping in hemodialysis. *Basic and Applied Social Psychology, 4*, 319–336.
125. Schulz, R., & Decker, S. (1985). Long-term adjustment to physical disability: The role of social support, perceived control and self-blame. *Journal of Personality and Social Psychology, 48*, 1162–1172.
126. Heinemann, A. W., Bulka, M., & Smetak, S. (1988). Attributions and disability acceptance following traumatic injury: A replication and extension. *Rehabilitation Psychology, 33*, 195–206.
127. Nielson, W. R., & MacDonald, M. R. (1988). Attributions of blame and coping following spinal cord injury: Is self-blame adaptive? *Journal of Social and Clinical Psychology, 7,* 163–175.
128. Richards, J. S., Elliott, T. R., Shewchuk, R. M., & Fine, P. R. (1997). Attribution of responsibility for onset of spinal cord injury and psychosocial outcomes in the first year post-injury. *Rehabilitation Psychology, 42*(2), 115–124.
129. Silver, R. C., Wortman, C. B., & Crofton, C. (1990). The role of coping in support provision: The self-representational dilemma of victims of life crises. In B. R. Sarason, I. G. Sarason, & G. R. Pierce (Eds.), *Social support: An interactional view* (pp. 397–426). New York: Wiley.
130. Walster, E. (1966). Assignment of responsibility for an accident. *Journal of Personality and Social Psychology, 3*, 73–79.
131. Shaver, K. G. (1970). Defensive attribution: Effects of severity and relevance on the responsibility assigned for an accident. *Journal of Personality and Social Psychology, 14*, 101–113.
132. Herbert, T. B., & Dunkel-Schetter, C. (1992). Negative social reactions to victims: An overview of responses and their determinants. In L. Montada, S-H. Filipp, & M. J. Lerner (Eds.), *Life crises and experiences of loss in adulthood* (pp. 497–518). Hillsdale, NJ: Erlbaum.
133. Charmaz, K. (1995). The body, identity, and self: Adapting to impairment. *The Sociological Quarterly, 36*, 657–680.
134. Janoff-Bullman, R. & Schwartzberg, S. S. (1991). Toward a general model of personal change. In C. R. Snyder & D. R. Forsyth (Eds.), *Handbook of social and clinical psychology* (pp 488–508). Elmsford, NY: Pergamon.
135. Wright, B. A. (1983). *Physical disability: A psychosocial approach* (2nd ed.). New York: Harper and Row.
136. Frank, A. W. (1993). The rhetoric of self-change: Illness experience as narrative. *The Sociological Quarterly, 34*, 39–52.
137. Affleck, G., Tennen, H., Croog, S., & Levine, S. (1987). Causal attribution, perceived benefits, and morbidity after a heart attack: An 8-year study. *Journal of Consulting and Clinical Psychology, 55*(1), 29–35.
138. Affleck, G., Tennen, H., Croog, S., & Levine, S. (1987). Causal attribution, perceived control, and recovery from a heart attack. *Journal of Social and Clinical Psychology, 5*, 339–355.
139. Dunn, D. S. (1996). Well-being following amputation: Salutary effects of positive meaning, optimism, and control. *Rehabilitation Psychology, 41*, 285–302.

140. Taylor, S. E., Lichtman, R. R., & Wood, J. V. (1984). Attributions, beliefs about control, and adjustment to breast cancer. *Journal of Personality and Social Psychology, 46,* 489–502.
141. Tennen, H., Affleck, G., Urrows, S., Higgins, P., & Mendola, R. (1992). Perceiving control, construing benefits, and daily processes in rheumatoid arthritis. *Canadian Journal of Behavioral Science, 24,* 186–203
142. Beck, A. T., Rush, A. J., Shaw, B. F., & Emery, G. (1979). *Cognitive therapy of depression.* New York: Guilford Press.
143. Beck, A. T., & Emery, G. (1985). *Anxiety disorders and phobias: A cognitive perspective.* New York: Basic Books.
144. Antonucci, T. C., Jackson, J. S. (1990). The role of reciprocity in social support. In B. R. Sarason, I. G. Sarason, & G. R. Pierce (Eds.), *Social support: An interactional view* (pp. 173–189). New York: Wiley.
145. Stroebe, W., & Stroebe, M. (1996). The social psychology of social support. In E. T. Higgins & A. W. Kruglanski (Eds.), *Social Psychology: Handbook of basic principles* (pp. 597–621). New York: Guilford Press.
146. Coleman, J. S. (1988). Social capital in the creation of human capital. *American Journal of Sociology, 94,* S95–S120.
147. Clark, M. S., & Mills, J. (1979). Interpersonal attraction in exchange and communal relationships. *Journal of Personality and Social Psychology, 37,* 12–24.
148. Greenberg, J., Pyszczynski, T., & Solomon, S. (1986). The causes and consequences of the need for self-esteem: A terror management theory. In R. F. Baumeister (Ed.), *Public self and private self* (pp. 189–207). New York: Springer-Verlag.
149. Solomon, S., Greenberg, J., & Pyszczynski, T. (1991). Terror management theory of self-esteem. In C. R. Snyder & D. R. Forsyth (Eds.), *Handbook of social and clinical psychology: The health perspective* (pp. 21–40). Elmsford, NY: Pergamon Press.
150. Baumeister, R. F. (1989). The optimal margin of illusion. *Journal of Social and Clinical Psychology, 8,* 176–189.
151. Schreurs, K. M. G., & de Ridder, D. T. D. (1997). Integration of coping and social support perspectives: Implications for the study of adaptation to chronic diseases. *Clinical Psychology Review, 17,* 89–112.
152. Ersek, M. (1992). Examining the process and dilemmas of reality negotiation. *IMAGE: Journal of Nursing Scholarship, 24,* 19–25.
153. Burger, J. M., & Burns, L. (1988). The illusion of unique invulnerability and the use of effective contraception. *Personality and Social Psychology Bulletin, 14,* 264–270.
154. McClure, J. (1991). *Explanations, accounts, and illusions: A critical analysis.* Cambridge: Cambridge University Press.
155. Greenberg, R. P., Bornstein, R. F., Greenberg, M. D., & Fisher, S. (1992). A meta-analysis of antidepressant outcome under "blinder" conditions. *Journal of Consulting and Clinical Psychology, 60,* 664–669.
156. Tennen, H., Affleck, G., Allen, D. A., McGrade, B. J., & Ratzan, S. (1984). Causal attributions and coping with insulin-dependent diabetes. *Basic and Applied Social Psychology, 5,* 131–142.

157. Hays, R. D., Kravitz, R. L., Mazel, R. M., Sherbourne, C. D., DiMatteo, R. R., Rogers, W. H., & Greenfield, S. (1994). The impact of patient adherence on health outcomes for patients with chronic disease in the Medical Outcomes Study. *Journal of Behavioral Medicine, 17,* 347–360.

3

Coping and Ego Depletion

Recovery after the Coping Process

Roy F. Baumeister
Jon E. Faber
Harry M. Wallace

In this chapter, we combine a new approach to the self with a traditional, standard idea about coping in order to understand the coping process. The central idea is that many operations of the self involve the consumption of a limited resource. This resource is used in volition (e.g., choice, responsible decision-making, and active responses) and self-control. Stress makes severe demands on this resource, because people must engage in active responding and must regulate themselves so as to adapt to difficult circumstances. One major consequence of stress is that the resource becomes depleted. This will impair the person's functioning across a broad spectrum of activities. For the person to recover, therefore, this resource must be replenished. Although it has been recognized previously that coping with stress consumes resources (e.g., 1, 2, 3, 4), our analysis differs in that it offers more in-depth insight into the nature of this resource.

Another important distinction of the present model is that the depletion of resources results from the individual's responses and coping efforts, rather than from the stress itself. In a sense, then, our focus is on how the person *recovers from coping* rather than on how the person copes with stress. A stressful event will demand coping responses, and these will deplete the person's resources. Having coped with the trauma, however, the person may suffer from the adverse depleting effects of the coping process. The person will not be back to normal until this recovery from coping is complete.

It should be acknowledged that the links between this ego depletion model and recovery from coping are somewhat speculative at present. We are suggesting previously unexplored links between separate and fairly well-established literatures.

Nature of Ego Depletion

It is first necessary to summarize recent evidence about the resource that the self expends in volitional activities. Much of this evidence is fairly recent, but it offers a way to understand the self that departs from the previous information-processing views that have dominated recent thinking about the self.

The present research paradigm began with a basic question about the nature of self-regulation. Carver and Scheier (5, 6) provided an influential model of self-regulation based on feedback-loop theory (from 7). Their acronym TOTE referred to test (i.e., comparing the self against relevant standards), operate (change the self so as to bring it up to standard), test (another comparison), and exit (cease the regulatory process if the self has reached the standard). Their analysis focused on self-awareness and standards, although they were vague about the nature of the specific operations used by the self to reduce discrepancies.

An analysis of self-control failure by Baumeister, Heatherton, and Tice (8) led to a tentative conclusion that self-regulatory operations often operate like a strength. That is to say, many cases of changing the self so as to conform better to ideal standards involve overriding impulses to act in an undesirable manner. Because these impulses have a certain strength, the self must have an equal or greater strength in order to overcome them. Baumeister et al. (8) noted that many patterns of self-control failure have implicated some form of strength. (We use the term *self-control* to refer to all active efforts to alter the self, and it corresponds to the "operate" phase in a self-regulatory feedback loop.)

Direct tests of the strength model were undertaken by Muraven, Tice, and Baumeister (9). The design of these studies involved the person's engaging in two consecutive (but otherwise unrelated) acts of self-control. If self-control involves strength, then that strength presumably would be expended in the first act of self-control, leaving it fatigued (so to speak). As a result, self-regulatory performance on the second task should be impaired. In contrast, if self-control operated on a schema-like information-processing model, then the initial act of self-control should have an effect similar to priming a schema, and self-control on the second task would be facilitated. A third view of self-control would compare it to a skill, which remains constant from one trial to the next (although in the long run skill is gradually improved), so no change would be predicted.

The series of studies by Muraven et al. (9) supported the strength model. In one study, people who engaged in affect regulation by trying either to amplify or to stifle their emotional reactions to an upsetting film later showed decrements in physical stamina, as compared to people who watched the same film but did not try to alter their emotions. In a second study, people who engaged in a thought suppression task of trying not to think about a white bear (from 10) later gave up faster on unsolvable anagrams than people who had not tried to control their thoughts. Thus, apparently the initial effort to control thoughts (or emotions) depleted some resource that was then unavailable to help them persist in the face of discouraging failure. In a third study, the thought suppression task impaired people's ability to control their emotions, as measured by how well people could refrain from laughing or smiling in response to a funny video.

A similar test using impulse control was conducted by Baumeister, Bratslavsky, Muraven, and Tice (11). In this experiment, food-deprived people were seated next to attractive, delicious chocolates and cookies but were given instructions to eat only the radishes available in a nearby bowl. Later, these people gave up faster on unsolvable geometric figure puzzles than did people in either of the two control groups: those who ate the tempting foods, and those who were not tempted. Thus, resisting temptation depleted some strength or resource that was then unavailable for helping them to keep trying at the difficult puzzle.

These and similar findings suggest that self-regulatory operations involve a psychological resource that is in some manner limited. These results indicate that the same resource is used in a wide assortment of self-control operations, including affect regulation, thought control, task persistence, physical stamina, and impulse control (in this case, resisting temptation). These results also indicate that this resource is quite limited: After only a few minutes of exertion, people show substantial decrements on other, seemingly unrelated tasks.

The next question in our program of research was whether the self uses the same resource for anything else beyond self-control. Baumeister (72) proposed that the self's *executive function* encompasses all of its active, volitional activities, including choice and responsible decision-making as well as self-control. To see whether these other activities would consume this same psychological resource, Baumeister, Bratslavsky et al. (11) borrowed a choice procedure from cognitive dissonance research (12). Subjects agreed to make a counterattitudinal speech under either high or low choice conditions. Instead of measuring the attitudinal consequences of this act as has been done in many past studies, however, the researchers put them to work on the same unsolvable geometric puzzle that had revealed decrements following the radish-chocolate procedure. Sure enough, people who had engaged in a choice process gave up faster on the puzzles. In another study, we showed that an initial exertion of self-control made people more passive in a subsequent decision-making situation. Thus, acts of volition undermine subsequent self-control, and vice versa, indicating that both volition and self-control draw on the same, common resource. Hence, the term *ego depletion*: Some resource that is used for all these activities becomes depleted following initial exertion.

The broad implication of this line of work is that the self is built upon a very limited psychological resource that is used in a wide variety of volitional activities, including choice, active (instead of passive) responding, and self-control. In recent years, psychologists have distinguished between automatic and controlled processes and have shown that a great many behaviors are mediated by these automatic responses (13). The present research on ego depletion suggests an important reason for the pervasive automaticity in human behavior. Automatic responses, by definition, do not require the self to engage in active, volitional responding, and so automatic responses do not consume this precious resource of the self and hence do not cause ego depletion. In contrast, the self is the controller of controlled responses and expends its resources in such responses. Because this resource is quite limited, the self must conserve it by doing as many things as possible with automatic responses.

Stress, Coping, and Ego Depletion

In this section, we explain why we think that ego depletion is central to the problem of coping with stress and trauma. The notion that coping has something to do with resources is quite familiar. One of the first to propose it was Selye (4). He described a "general adaptation syndrome" in which the body's adaptation to noxious agents takes its toll. The aftereffects of such adaptation can involve increased vulnerability and exhaustion, "as though something were lost, or used up, during the work of adaptation" (4, p. 82). That loss of "something," we would argue, is analogous to the ego depletion in our model.

More recent work has frequently invoked the notion that coping consumes resources. Antonovsky (14) proposed that there are generalized resources that help people (some more than others) to resist the adverse effects of stress. Wheaton (15) distinguished between personal and environmental resources. Lazarus and Folkman (3) explained that resources precede and influence coping, and changes in these resources mediate the effects of stress. Hammer and Marting (16) listed five different types or domains of coping resources. Hobfall (17) articulated the central motivational importance of conserving resources, in that the potential or actual loss of valued resources is central to what people find stressful or threatening. The similarity in these allusions to resources in coping may be more apparent than real, because various researchers have had quite different things in mind when they discuss such resources: spiritual faith, a social network, money, personal energy, an emotional sense of security.

Contrary to these previous views, our analysis is focused on a particular kind of resource: the one used by the self in volitional responding. As we explained in the preceding section, there appears to be some limited but important psychological resource that people use when actively controlling their own responses, making choices and decisions, or initiating behavior.

It is clear that coping can make demands on this resource, and in fact there are several different ways that this can happen. An important distinction is often made between active and passive coping (e.g., 18), although the terms are somewhat misleading. Active coping refers to altering the objective outcomes. Passive coping refers to subjective adaptation when one cannot alter the outcome itself. Thus, if one's bedroom window is broken one wintry night, active coping might entail replacing the glass, whereas passive coping could involve putting on one's winter coat and huddling under the covers all night, or learning to tolerate sleeping in a cold room. Although passive coping may be passive with respect to the stressor, it often requires active exertion of control over oneself, and so it may draw on the person's volitional resources just as much as active coping. In fact, it may sometimes require more total exertion, insofar as the problem may persist. To pursue the window example, the active coping of repairing the window resolves the problem, whereas the passive coping of huddling under the covers dictates facing the same problem the next night (because the window is still broken).

A comparable distinction was made in an influential work by Rothbaum, Weisz, and Snyder (19) with regard to primary and secondary control. Although these terms also may be misleading, primary control refers to altering the environment or situation to suit the self, whereas secondary control involves altering the self to suit the situation. Both of these approaches to coping require the expenditure of the self's volitional resource, and, as such, both may be draining. Hence, although either coping approach may be an effective way of responding to a problem, in both instances the person may require some time to replenish the depleted resource.

Some situations clearly are more stressful and demanding than others. A well-known line of work by Brady (20) showed that pairs of monkeys differed in stress-related outcomes such as ulcers, even though both endured the same threat (of electric shock) and the same total punishment (because shock was yoked). The monkey who had responsibility for repeatedly pressing the button in order to prevent the shock was far more likely to die of ulcers than the monkey without such responsibility.

In following up this work, Weiss (21, 22, 23) identified several key variables that increase the stressfulness of the situation. These included a situational demand for many responses, even if each response was relatively easy (such as pressing a button). Thus, simply having to perform a great many active behaviors can be harmful. Second, uncertainty contributed to stress: animals who received no success feedback and thus had to cope with seemingly constant threat suffered far more than those whose punishment contingencies were identical but who received clearer feedback about the success of their efforts. Third, having to choose the lesser of two evils constituted a highly stressful choice, as compared to situations in which one option would yield a wholly positive outcome. This third finding was obtained by making the feedback itself unpleasant, in the form of loud, aversive noise, so that the animal's choice was between receiving the shock or receiving the loud noise upon successfully preventing the shock.

Extrapolating from these animal studies to human beings, one may suggest that people experience considerable stress when many responses under uncertain, ambiguous conditions are required in order to deal with threat, or when there is no clearly positive, desirable option available. Such situations may be regarded as the operational definition of hard choices, and such choices are presumably especially draining of the individual's psychological, volitional resource. Thus, even when the threat can be objectively defeated, active coping responses may take a severe toll on the individual.

Meanwhile, situations that permit no objective or primary control can also be quite hard on the person. Seligman's (24) work on learned helplessness indicated the debilitating effects of exposure to aversive, threatening situations, where there is no option for altering the outcome to suit the self. Glass and Singer (2; also 25) showed that working under conditions of uncontrollable, unpredictable stress (aversive noise) takes a toll on individuals and thereafter leaves them in a vulnerable state. Cohen (1) verified that unpredictable and uncontrollable stresses are highly threatening, make greater demands on the person, and produce aftereffects that are not attributable to mood or arousal. Compas (26) showed that children who assess a situation as concrete and unchangeable show a variety of deficits, including discouragement, diminished effort, and deteriorating performance.

In our view, these effects of responding to an uncontrollable, aversive situation occur in substantial part because the person exerts control over the self. An impulse to respond to failure or injustice by fighting for success must be stifled if the cause is hopeless. Negative emotions such as frustration, anger, and depression must be overcome, and so the demands for affect regulation can be severe. Thoughts must also be controlled, such as when one stops oneself from ruminating about the aversive situation and one's thwarted efforts (e.g., 27). One may also alter further performance attempts, such as setting more appropriate goals or withholding effort so as to prevent further disappointments (e.g., 28, 29, 30). Thus, coping requires regulating or controlling the self (see also 31, 32).

All of these responses involve self-regulatory operations on the self, and so they may drain the volitional resource just as much as do those active responses aimed at rectifying the situation or warding off threat. Indeed, these self-regulatory responses may eventually be all the more draining, because they do not objectively solve the problem but leave the person having to perform these accommodations repeatedly. For example, the difficulty of adapting oneself to a new physical handicap such as accident-related paralysis may derive in part because the person must accommodate the self in multiple, ongoing ways to the new limitations and must repeatedly adjust the self, both pragmatically and emotionally, to them (see 33, 34, 35). Sherrod, Hage, Halpern, and Moore (36) showed that the aftereffects of noise stress had a linear relation to the degree of control the person had had over the noise, such that the greatest decrements were found among people who had suffered through the most uncontrollable noise. Thus, putting up with uncontrollable, aversive situations can be more draining than having primary, direct control over them.

The notion that coping with stress depletes some psychological resource is particularly relevant to any evidence that people show deficits after, as opposed to merely during, the exposure to stress. There is considerable evidence that people show deficits in the aftermath of coping with stress (see 1, 37, for reviews). A seminal study by Glass, Singer, and Friedman (25), for example, exposed people to uncontrollable, unpredictable noise and then measured subsequent frustration tolerance (persistence on unsolvable problems) and proofreading performance in a quiet, stress-free environment. People who had been exposed to the uncontrollable, unpredictable noise performed worse on those subsequent tasks than did the people who had been exposed to the same amount of noise but in a predictable and hence less stressful manner. Similar effects have been found following a learned helplessness treatment (38).

Hence, we propose that the self's volitional resources are expended in the process of coping with stress. They are least drained in situations that allow simple, direct, and unambiguous exertion of control over the stress. When control is difficult to exert, however, such as because there is no clearly superior option, or feedback is ambiguous, or many responses are required, the self must expend considerable volition. Meanwhile, when the situation cannot be controlled and is aversive, the person must exert control over the self in order to adapt to the situation, such as by regulating emotional responses and thoughts. These efforts too can deplete the self.

Consequences of Stress and Coping

In the previous section, we argued that responding to stress and trauma would consume the self's volitional resources, leaving them depleted. In this section, we describe the likely consequences of this process of depletion.

Our own research has suggested where to look for such effects. Ego depletion consumes the resources that the self uses for volition, including self-control, controlled processes, active response, initiative, and decision-making. If coping with stress consumes that same resource, then decrements in those spheres should be expected. Indeed, evidence supports these latter speculations. The debilitation of self-control following stress, for example, has been well established for addictive and impulsive behaviors. Thus, in a smoking cessation clinic, Wewers (73) found that higher levels of life stress following the completion of the program were correlated with higher relapse rates. Cohen and Lichtenstein (39) reported that self-reports of high stress led to higher relapse rates among people who had successfully quit smoking. Hull, Young, and Jouriles (40) showed comparable results in alcoholism relapse following successful detoxification, although the link between high life stress and relapse was confined to people who were high in dispositional self-awareness (presumably because people who blame their troubles on others do not return to alcohol to escape aversive self-awareness). Hodgins, el Guebaly, and Armstrong (41) likewise found high stress predicted relapse among alcoholics. Marlatt and Gordon (42) drew the same conclusion about heroin addiction.

The findings linking stress to addictive relapse employ correlational methods, because it would not be ethical to manipulate stress so as to cause addictive relapse in research participants. Still, some evidence points toward the conclusion that the stress causes the relapse, rather than the reverse. Doherty, Kinnunen, Militello, and Garvey (43) found that stress at time 1 predicts relapse at time 2. Even in laboratory studies, limited stressors produce more indulgence in conflictual behaviors. On this latter point, Schachter, Silverstein, Kozlowski, Herman, and Liebling (44) showed that painful electric shocks caused smokers to smoke more (and smoking was measured after the shocks had ended). Payne, Schare, Levis, and Colletti (45) demonstrated that having an escape option reduced the effect of stress on increased smoking.

Dietary failure and binge eating also seem to be linked to stress (for review, see 46; also 8). These findings are particularly relevant because stress does not appear to increase eating among nondieters, which rules out the alternative explanation that stress simply makes people hungry. Rather, it appears that stress weakens the inner restraints that dieters have against eating, and so only dieters eat more (e.g., 47, 48).

These studies have examined the effects of stresses in general on particular forms of self-control, but other studies have worked the other way by studying how specific, major stresses produce a variety of effects. Again, self-control and volition seem to deteriorate in the aftermath of trauma. Kaiser, Sattler, Bellack, and Dersin (49) discovered that the aftereffects of Hurricane Hugo included several patterns indicating loss of self-control or volition: crying easily, difficulty concentrating, moodiness, uncontrolled arousal (including sleeping disruptions), and increases in smoking and drinking. Similar patterns were observed by Taimen and Tuominen (50) among survivors of an Estonia shipwreck. Some of these survivors also showed signs of heightened verbal aggressiveness. Indeed, aggressive actions in general form a further category of impulsive behaviors that increase when stress undermines inner restraints and controls (see 37 for review).

Thus, decrements in self-control have been well established in the aftermath of stress. Other signs that the self's executive function has been impaired are less well researched, but we regard these as promising arenas for further research. One that has received some attention is passivity. Seligman (24) described how exposure to uncontrollable outcomes can produce learned helplessness, although among human beings these effects appear to be complex and dependent on a host of other factors. Learned helplessness is characterized by a failure to learn subsequent contingencies and a failure to exert control subsequently when control is available.

Most of Seligman's (24) examples and illustrations involve uncontrollable stress. In principle, learned helplessness could arise from experiencing noncontingent success experiences, because those also would demonstrate that outcomes are not contingent. Yet research has had far less success demonstrating helplessness following success than failure, which suggests that the stressful aspect of failure may play an important role. We think it is plausible that ego depletion accounts for some of the effects that have been demonstrated by researchers working in the area of learned helplessness. Noncontingent failure experiences are often felt as uncontrollable stress, and as such they require the person to regulate the self so as to adapt to the aversive conditions (e.g., regulating affect). The strain of adapting oneself to such aversive conditions could deplete the self's volitional resources, resulting in greater passivity afterward. Thus, we would predict many of the same effects found with learned helplessness, but the mediating process may be more a matter of depleted self resources than of the generalized perception of noncontingency.

A priority for further research is to examine possible negative effects that come from having control or making choices. Indeed, one might think that people would always prefer to have more control, but there seem to be limits. An important paper by Burger (51) showed that many situations cause people to relinquish or avoid control, and moreover many people prefer to avoid control even under optimal circumstances. A possible reason is that exerting control is costly to the self, and so people only want to exert control under circumstances where it can do them the most good.

Extreme forms of relinquishing control can be found in sexual masochism, in which people desire to be rendered dramatically helpless, to the point of being tied up or subjected to the arbitrary commands of a dominant partner. Evidence suggests that these practices appeal most widely to people who have considerable control and responsibility in their ordinary lives, so that the helplessness functions as an escape (see 52, 53, for review; also 54). One possible interpretation is that the regular exertion of control and responsibility is depleting, so these individuals desire their private lives to incorporate some activities in which they are dramatically relieved of further control and responsibility. Whether depleting experiences of coping with particular stresses can contribute to these desires remains a worthy question for further research.

Additional evidence of ego depletion can be found in studies of stress and burnout. Burnout is a state of emotional, physical, and mental exhaustion that occurs in people who invest too much of themselves in an activity or cause and then encounter major stress through that activity (55). People who were once driven to make a difference in their world or their careers feel a loss of intensity, idealism, and emotional investment, and they often find themselves struggling to find meaning in their life and activities (56). Symptoms of burnout include a variety of executive function deficits, including loss of will, substance abuse and addiction, absence from or lateness to work, and feelings of helplessness (57, 58).

Altogether, then, there is an assortment of evidence fitting the view that coping with stress produces deficits in the self's executive function. Because some of the findings are subject to multiple interpretations, we cannot assert that our theoretical view is proven to the exclusion of all rival theories. Further work is needed. Nonetheless, it appears that one plausible consequence of stress is the depletion of the resources that the self uses for self-control, responsible choice, and other volition.

Replenishing the Resource

Thus far we have argued that coping with stress or trauma consumes the self's volitional resources, and as a result, a variety of activities and functions normally performed by the self may suffer. Hence, the aftereffects of stress and trauma may persist for a while after the person has coped with the stress or trauma itself. The person will not be back to normal until s/he has recovered from the coping process, in the sense of replenishing the resources that were expended in the trauma.

We would compare volition to the physical exertion of one's limbs, with strength as the focus of the analogy. Rest appears to be central to the recovery of the self's volitional strength. A variety of evidence from past work attests to the importance of sleep (e.g., 59, 60, 61). When people are deprived of sleep over several days, they show decrements in self-control and related executive functions of the self: They engage in impulsive behavior, have difficulty controlling their emotions, find it hard to concentrate, and perform worse at various work tasks, all of which suggest decrements in impulse control, affect regulation, thought control, and performance regulation—the four main spheres of self-regulation (see 8).

Another sign of the replenishing effects of rest is that most major self-control breakdowns occur late in the day, after the person has gone the longest without sleep while presumably continuing to engage in self-control and decision-making. For example, dieters mainly break their diets in the evenings (62, 63). Likewise, bulimics are most likely to binge late in the day, when they are tired (64). Most impulse crimes, particularly acts of violence, also occur late at night (after 1:00 A.M.; 65). Alcohol and drug abuse problems, including addictive relapses, occur most frequently late in the day too, as do sex acts that the person will later regret, although these latter findings are particularly confounded with greater opportunity (e.g., more bars are open later in the day, which contributes to the increased availability of alcohol and of potentially regretted sex partners).

We think that sleep is probably the major way to replenish the ego after the depleting effects of everyday decision-making, self-control, and other volition. Ordinary rest, however, may be inadequate to replenish the self after the large expenditure of resources required for coping with severe stress or serious trauma. Major coping is probably far more depleting than ordinary volition. To pursue the analogy, the muscle is likely to be injured rather than merely tired.

When a muscle is pulled or a bone is broken, it is often necessary for the person to immobilize it for a period of time in order for it to recover. If this analogy is indeed applicable to the self that has been severely drained from coping, then something akin to an "ego cast" would be desirable. Just as a cast immobilizes an injured limb to allow for complete, uninterrupted rest, an "ego cast" would allow the self to remain substantially inert, in order for it to replenish the volitional resources that have been consumed.

In extreme cases of severe physical injury, neurosurgeons may purposefully send the patient into a lengthy (drug-induced) coma so as to allow the body to repair itself. The analogue for severe ego depletion may be a long period of rest and recovery, such as an extended vacation.

Hence, recovery from stress (and from coping) may require the person to find a way to live without making serious demands on the self for a period of time. Automatic, habitual activities make the least demands on the self, because by definition the self does not have to exert control. If people can operate on the basis of very familiar patterns and habits, the self can recover its resources better, because it will not have to expend any more of them by confronting novel situations and exerting volitional control. If you see a friend or colleague seem to operate on "automatic pilot" (that is, habit and routine) in the aftermath of stress, you might consider that this is a highly adaptive way of allowing the self to recover. The nexus of habit is a form of an ego cast.

Likewise, recovery from stress and coping would be facilitated by a relative absence of demands for self-control. Earlier, we cited evidence that people indulge their impulses (such as smoking and drinking) more than usual in the aftermath of stress. Although this often is seen in a negative light, the reluctance to exert self-control may have a more adaptive side, in that it too may constitute an ego cast. To be sure, others may deplore this pattern because failure to exert self-control can create additional or secondary problems, which can create further difficulties in the future. For example, someone who has been victimized in a crime may subsequently take to alcohol or substance abuse, and although the lack of self-control may help the self recover from the victimization (and from the expenditure of volitional resources in coping with it), the substance abuse may evolve into another problem. C. R. Snyder (29) has labeled these as "Faustian bargains," because they resemble the mythological Faust's deal with the devil: Rewards are garnered in the short run, but in the long run the cost proves excessive.

Still, a decrease in self-control after stress may be adaptive or, at least, necessary for the sake of the depleted self. Some indulgence in various forms of impulsive, proscribed behaviors may be acceptable if it is merely temporary and does not do lasting harm—because it may help the self recover.

Of course, avoiding temptation may be a more salutary strategy than impulsive indulgence of sparing the self from having to exert self-control. In the aftermath of stress and coping, it may be ideal to be in some circumstance where one is not exposed to cues or opportunities that set off the impulses that one needs to control. A temptation-free zone may be a better form of an ego cast than a zone of total indulgence.

By the same token, affect regulation, thought control, and performance pressure all require further expenditures of the self's resources, and so ideally they too would be excluded from an ego cast. For example, in the aftermath of coping with severe stress, people may find that they overreact emotionally. Although these strong emotional reactions may be unpleasant and awkward for other people, they may again be understood as a way of sparing the self from having to exert control, and so in a sense they are better than forcing the person to control his or her emotions. Again, the notion of an ego cast would be best served by avoiding emotionally reactive circumstances and events, so the need for control does not arise. The same goes for avoiding performance pressures, because the need to perform at a high level of efficacy invokes self-control and thus may drain the already depleted self further.

Ego casts may not be useful for everyone. People who are accustomed to a style of coping that involves high activity and the reassertion of control may find it quite difficult to comply with a requirement for relinquishing control and volition. In plainer terms, people who are known as "control freaks" may be temperamentally unsuited to being passive and doing nothing. Therefore, when research does reach the point of testing whether the "ego cast" form of passivity helps replenish the self, it would be useful to attend to individual differences.

A crucial theoretical question is whether the self's volitional resource can be replenished by anything other than rest. At present we do not have a clear answer to this question, but there is one likely candidate: positive emotion. In a pair of recent, unpublished studies conducted by Karen Dale in collaboration with Baumeister and Tice, inducing positive mood offsets the effects of ego depletion. These effects were measured by performance on solvable anagrams (Study 1) and persistence on unsolvable anagrams (Study 2), both of which have been confirmed in prior work as sensitive to the deleterious effects of ego depletion. These deleterious effects were replicated among participants in neutral and bad moods, but among people who were put in a good mood, performance and persistence were as good as in the control condition. (Moreover, there was no independent benefit of positive mood in terms of improved performance or longer persistence.)

Further evidence is needed, but these findings suggest an important function for good moods, which is to replenish the self's depleted resources and improve volition. Emotion researchers have postulated many functions for negative affect in terms of initiating behavior (such as the notion that fear improves one's chances for survival by motivating one to flee from danger), but it is much harder to cite functions for most positive emotions.

A potentially valuable source of converging evidence is Snyder's (30, 66, 67) work on hope. Snyder defines hope in terms of agency and pathways, yet hope is also marked by positive affect and is colloquially familiar as a positive emotional resource (e.g., as the opposite of despair or hope-lessness). Agency directly involves volition. Pathways, as explained by Snyder, involve planning ways to reach one's goals, and planning is itself an important self-regulatory operation. Moreover, if goals are elusive or obstacles are encountered, self-regulation may be needed to construct multiple pathways and to adjust them in the face of obstacles, so volition and self-regulation can be particularly important. Circumstances such as stress and trauma would be particularly relevant to such disruptions of goal-directed behavior, and so the link between hope and self-regulation may become especially important under such circumstances.

If positive emotion does indeed help replenish the depleted self, the implications for coping would be enormous. As we have emphasized, a crucial and easily neglected aspect of stress and trauma is that the self becomes depleted by its own coping efforts, and so the person does not get back to normal for a possibly long time after the trauma (even if coping has been successful). Positive affect might speed this recovery in important ways because it would help the self regain its power to exert volition and self-control. The cultivation of positive emotional experiences would then take a central place to help people recover from stress.

It must be noted that instilling positive affect in the aftermath or stress or trauma may not be easy. The person may be suffering from considerable negative affect, which might make it more difficult to have positive emotions at the same time. Alternatively, the person may have become emotionally numb in response to the negative affect from the stress or trauma, and on this point, Janoff-Bulman (68) has suggested that denial is highly adaptive in response to trauma because it helps shut down the emotional system. In a similar vein, Baumeister (69) concluded that research findings depict suicidal individuals as people who have essentially shut down their emotional systems in response to the personal misfortunes that they have recently experienced. Emotional numbness would, of course, make it more difficult to experience positive emotions (70).

A further difficulty with instilling positive affect is that ego depletion would impair the person's capacity for affect regulation. Many people are able to pull themselves out of a bad mood and into a good mood, and many others can at least cooperate with external forces so as to allow themselves to be cheered up. Either path requires affect regulation, however, and a depleted self would have less capacity for engaging in affect regulation (because it is a form of self-control that draws on the same resource that has been depleted). Hence, it should be more difficult than usual to generate a good mood or pleasant emotional state.

Nonetheless, if a good mood can be instilled, it may help to replenish the self's volitional resource. Combined with rest and the "ego cast," positive affect may be a potent force for healing and recovery. The combination would suggest enabling someone to be essentially passive, which is to say free from having to make decisions or exert self-control, while simultaneously being bombarded with cues and other stimuli that can induce positive emotion. We hasten to add that this is not the strategy we are recommending for coping directly with an ongoing threat—rather, it is what may be optimal for recovering from the depleting aftereffects of direct coping.

Why Does Social Support Work?

It is well established that social support is a valuable, powerful, and multifaceted aid to coping. People who have good social support recover from stress and trauma better than people who do not. Yet the precise mechanism by which social support helps people cope and recover is not entirely clear. Quite possibly there are multiple ways. We offer some speculative remarks to suggest that ego depletion provides potential insights into the beneficial effects of social support.

The benefits of social support are typically divided into two main categories: practical, material help and emotional support. For our purposes, each of these may be further subdivided, but in any case we think that both forms of social support can contribute in powerful, important ways to helping people recover from stress or trauma.

Practical, material help can serve as the "ego cast" par excellence. Such help involves directly helping the person cope with the stressful situation and deal with his or her everyday affairs in the aftermath of the trauma or stressor. Clearly, either of these can take considerable weight off the person's own executive function. Helping the person cope with the stress (e.g., assisting a flood victim to clean and dry her belongings) will obviate the need for the person to respond to the threatening, unusual demands of the difficult situation. This may be especially helpful insofar as such stresses involve many problematic choices and often require extensive, even constant activity in response to the damage. Meanwhile, helping the person deal with everyday demands (e.g., bringing groceries to someone who has suffered a major personal loss) can free the person from having to make ordinary decisions which, to a depleted self, can seem much more difficult and draining than they normally would. In both cases, the victim's self is allowed to remain inert and psychologically immobile, which enables it to rest.

As we have proposed, serious rest may often be crucial in enabling the person to recover from a serious case of depletion. Even deciding what to eat for lunch could conceivably put a small strain on the executive function. When other people take over such seemingly minor decisions, they allow the self to avoid even small exertions. In that way, they allow the damaged self to rest and recover.

The other dimension to social support is emotional support. Here again we propose to distinguish two aspects. One of these involves direct efforts to cheer the person up. For example, friends may smile, tell jokes, administer alcohol, distract the person, and do other things to help someone feel better.

These efforts form an important aspect of an "ego cast." As we have said, some of the major demands of coping involve regulating one's own affective state, for one cannot persist in feeling anxiety or grief indefinitely, but a depleted self may find itself unable to accomplish the seemingly huge task of making oneself feel better. Insofar as other people take over this function of affect regulation, the victim's own self is spared the effort. (In some cases, to be sure, people may exert themselves to allow themselves to be cheered up. Still, it is easier to let someone cheer you up than it is to cheer yourself up unassisted, and so again the self is spared the worst exertions.)

Moreover, the ego-cast aspect of social affect regulation applies simply because other people take over the job of trying to cheer the victim up. If they are successful in generating positive affect, the second form of replenishment—positive affect itself—may begin to operate and heal the person. We proposed that positive affect may help restore the executive function to its full power and resources, and so if social support does succeed in generating positive emotions, recovery may be facilitated. (Simply bringing the negative affect to an end may not be sufficient for this, however, even though calming the person down is undoubtedly a first goal of emotional support. The cessation of anxiety or other misery is clearly a desirable step, but if people can help the victim actually begin to feel positive emotions, the executive function should benefit much more.)

The second aspect of emotional support involves simply being present and implicitly reassuring the victim that he or she still has social ties. Undoubtedly, feeling that others care about you can be a comforting, uplifting experience. Baumeister and Leary (71) proposed that people are characterized by a powerful and basic need to belong and that the emotional system is closely linked to social belongingness. If that is correct, then receiving interpersonal reassurances and affirmations from others would be a potentially strong source of positive affect. This positive affect may well have its salutory effect on restoring the self's executive function to its full strength.

Conclusion and Summary

In this chapter we have argued that a very important aspect of the self, namely its executive function, operates on the basis of a limited resource that is depleted when the person makes choices, exerts self-control, or performs any other act of volition. We have proposed that this scarce and precious psychological resource is often strained to its maximum capacity when the person encounters stress or trauma.

As a result, the aftermath of coping often will find the person in a state of severe depletion. This state would be marked by severe decrements in all areas involving the executive function, such as (again) choice, responsible decision, self-control, and active initiative. We have suggested, further, that this state may derive not from the stress or trauma itself (although it is likely that people will tend to interpret it that way), but rather from the individual's own coping efforts, which exhausts the self's capacity to carry out its normal functions.

Recovery from stress therefore also may carry an element of recovering from one's own coping—that is, recovering from the depleting effects of one's coping efforts, including dealing with the pragmatic problems presented by the stress and managing one's own feelings and thoughts during the difficult period. After the threat has been addressed and seemingly vanquished, people may expect the victim to return to normal, but a major depletion of the self's resources may produce weakness and vulnerability that lasts well beyond that point.

We have proposed two things that facilitate recovery from ego depletion. One is simply rest—not physical rest per se, but rather a rest of the self's executive function, such as would be produced by not making choices or engaging in self-regulation. To be sure, it may be impossible to achieve a complete "ego cast" in the sense of finding a situation that would allow someone to avoid using the self for any form of volition for an extended period of time. Still, the less volition the person has to exert, the faster the self will recover. Social support may help people recover by taking over some of these volitional tasks, such as by helping the person make choices and exerting initiative on behalf of the victim.

The other facilitator is positive affect, although as we have noted, the research evidence for this part of the theory is quite preliminary. Nevertheless, some work does encourage us to think that pleasant emotional states may help restore the self to its full strength and resources. If people can manage to achieve such positive states in the aftermath of stress or trauma, they may recover better. Social support may prove helpful on this score, insofar as people help take over the self's affect regulation efforts (thereby sparing the victim from having to cheer himself or herself) and induce positive affect directly by affirming their concern for the victim.

Although research on ego depletion is relatively recent, it may provide a helpful new way of understanding the role of the self in stress and coping. Even successful coping can take a severe toll on the individual, insofar as the self becomes drained by its efforts to exert control. Full recovery may require that the self go through a psychological recharging process.

References

1. Cohen, S. (1980). Aftereffects of stress on human performance and social behavior: A review of research and theory. *Psychological Bulletin, 88*, 82–108.
2. Glass, D. C., & Singer, J. E. (1972). *Urban stress: Experiments on noise and social stressors*. New York: Academic Press.
3. Lazarus, R. S., & Folkman, S. (1984). *Stress, appraisal, and coping*. New York: Springer.
4. Selye, H. (1956/1976). *The stress of life* (Rev. ed.). New York: McGraw-Hill.

5. Carver, C. S., & Scheier, M. F. (1981). *Attention and self-regulation: A control-therapy approach to human behavior.* New York: Springer-Verlag.
6. Carver, C. S., & Scheier, M. F. (1982). Control theory: A useful conceptual framework for personality-social, clinical, and health psychology. *Psychological Bulletin, 92,* 111–135.
7. Powers, W. T. (1973). *Behavior: The control of perception.* Chicago: Aldine.
8. Baumeister, R. F., Heatherton, T. F., & Tice, D. M. (1994). *Losing control: How and why people fail at self-regulation.* San Diego: Academic Press.
9. Muraven, M., Tice, D. M., & Baumeister, R. F. (1998). Self-control as limited resource: Regulatory depletion patterns. *Journal of Personality and Social Psychology, 74,* 774–789.
10. Wegner, D. M., Schneider, D. J., Carter, S. R., & White, T. L. (1987). Paradoxical effects of thought suppression. *Journal of Personality and Social Psychology, 53,* 5–13.
11. Baumeister, R. F., Bratslavsky, E., Muraven, M., & Tice, D. M. (1998). Ego depletion: Is the active self a limited resource? *Journal of Personality and Social Psychology, 74,* 1252–1265.
12. Linder, D. E., Cooper, J., & Jones, E. E. (1967). Decision freedom as a determinant of the role of incentive magnitude in attitude change. *Journal of Personality and Social Psychology, 6,* 245–254.
13. Bargh, J. A. (1996). Automaticity in social psychology. In E. T. Higgins & A. W. Kruglanski (Eds.), *Social psychology: Handbook of basic principles* (pp. 169–183). New York: Guilford Press.
14. Antonovsky, A. (1979). *Health, stress, and coping.* San Francisco: Jossey-Bass.
15. Wheaton, R. B. (1983). Stress, personal coping resources, and psychiatric symptoms: An investigation of interactive models. *Journal of Health and Social Behavior, 24,* 208–229.
16. Hammer, A. L., & Marting, M. S. (1985). *Manual for the coping resources inventory.* Palo Alto, CA: Consulting Psychologists Press.
17. Hobfall, S. E. (1989). Conservation of resources: A new attempt at conceptualizing stress. *American Psychologist, 44,* 513–524.
18. Bongard, S. (1995). Mental effort during active and passive coping: A dual-task analysis. *Psychophysiology, 32,* 242–248.
19. Rothbaum, F., Weisz, J. R., & Snyder, S. S. (1982). Changing the world and changing the self: A two-process model of perceived control. *Journal of Personality and Social Psychology, 42,* 5–37.
20. Brady, J. V. (1958). Ulcers in "executive" monkeys. *Scientific American, 199,* 95–100.
21. Weiss, J. M. (1971a). Effects of coping behavior in different warning signal conditions on stress pathology in rats. *Journal of Comparative and Physiological Psychology, 77,* 1–13.
22. Weiss, J. M. (1971b). Effects of coping behavior with and without a feedback signal on stress pathology in rats. *Journal of Comparative and Physiological Psychology, 77,* 22–30.
23. Weiss, J. M. (1971c). Effects of punishing the coping response (conflict)

on stress pathology in rats. *Journal of Comparative and Physiological Psychology, 77,* 14–21.
24. Seligman, M. E. P. (1975). *Helplessness: On depression, development, and death.* San Francisco: Freeman.
25. Glass, D. C., Singer, J. E., & Friedman, L. N. (1969). Psychic cost of adaption to an environmental stressor. *Journal of Personality and Social Psychology, 12,* 200–210.
26. Compas, B. E. (1987). Coping with stress during childhood and adolescence. *Psychological Bulletin, 101,* 393–403.
27. Pyszczynski, T., & Greenberg, J. (1987). Self-regulatory perseveration and the depressive self-focusing style: A self-awareness theory of reactive depression. *Psychological Bulletin, 101,* 122–138.
28. Frankel, A., & Snyder, M. L. (1978). Poor performance following unsolvable problems: Learned helplessness or egotism? *Journal of Personality and Social Psychology, 36,* 1415–1423.
29. Snyder, C. R. (1984). Excuses. *Psychology Today, 18,* 50–55.
30. Snyder, C. R. (1994). *The psychology of hope: You can get there from here.* New York: Free Press.
31. Hockey, G. R. J. (1993). Cognitive-energetical control mechanisms in the management of work demands and psychological health. In A. D. Baddeley & L. Weiskrantz (Eds.), *Attention: Selection, awareness, and control: A tribute to Donald Broadbent* (pp. 328–345). Oxford, England: Clarendon Press/Oxford University Press.
32. Taylor, S. E., & Pham, L. B. (1996). Mental simulation, motivation, and action. In P. M. Gollwitzer & J. A. Bargh (Eds.), *The psychology of action: Linking cognition and motivation to behavior* (pp. 219–235). New York: Guilford Press.
33. Brickman, P., Coates, D., & Janoff-Bulman, R. (1978). Lottery winners and accident victims: Is happiness relative? *Journal of Personality and Social Psychology, 36,* 917–927.
34. Bulman, R. J., & Wortman, C. B. (1977). Attributions of blame and coping in the "real world": Severe accident victims react to their lot. *Journal of Personality and Social Psychology, 35,* 351–363.
35. Snyder, C. R. (1998). A case for hope in pain, loss, and suffering. In J. Harvey, J. Omarzu, & E. Miller (Eds.), *Perspectives on loss: A sourcebook.* (pp. 63–79) Washington, DC: Taylor & Francis.
36. Sherrod, D. R., Hage, J. N., Halpern, P. L., & Moore, B. S. (1977). Effects of personal causation and perceived control on responses to an aversive environment: The more control, the better. *Journal of Experimental Social Psychology, 13,* 14–27.
37. Muraven, M., & Baumeister, R. F. (1998). *Self-regulation and depletion of limited resources: Does self-control resemble a muscle.* Manuscript submitted for publication.
38. Cohen, S., Rothbart, M., & Phillips, S. (1976). Locus of control and the generality of learned helplessness in humans. *Journal of Personality and Social Psychology, 34,* 1049–1056.
39. Cohen, S., & Lichtenstein, E. (1990). Perceived stress, quitting smoking, and smoking relapse. *Health Psychology, 9,* 466–478.
40. Hull, J. G., Young, R. D., & Jouriles, E. (1986). Applications of the self-

awareness model of alcohol consumption: Predicting patterns of use and abuse. *Journal of Personality and Social Psychology, 51,* 790–796.

41. Hodgins, D. C., el Guebaly, N., & Armstrong, S. (1995). Prospective and retrospective reports of mood states before relapse to substance use. *Journal of Consulting and Clinical Psychology, 63,* 400–407.

42. Marlatt, G. A. (1985). Relapse prevention: Theoretical rationale and overview of the model. In G. A. Marlatt & J. R. Gordon (Eds.), *Relapse prevention: Maintenance strategies in the treatment of addictive behaviors.* (pp. 3–70) New York: Guilford Press.

43. Doherty, K., Kinnunen, T., Militello, F. S., & Garvey, A. J. (1995). Urges to smoke during the first month of abstinence: Relationship to relapse and predictors. *Psychopharmacology, 119,* 171–178.

44. Schachter, S., Silverstein, B., Kozlowski, L.T., Perlick, D., Herman, C.P., & Liebling, B. (1977). Studies of the interaction of psychological and pharmacological determinants of smoking. *Journal of Experimental Psychology: General, 106,* 3–40.

45. Payne, T. J., Schare, M. L., Levis, D. J., & Colletti, G. (1991). Exposure to smoking-relevant cues: Effects on desire to smoke and topographical components of smoking behavior. *Addictive Behaviors, 16,* 467–479.

46. Heatherton, T. F., & Baumeister, R. F. (1991). Binge eating as escape from self-awareness. *Psychological Bulletin, 110,* 86–108.

47. Heatherton, T. F., Polivy, J., Herman, C. P., & Baumeister, R. F. (1993). Self-awareness, task failure, and disinhibition: How attentional focus affects eating. *Journal of Personality, 61,* 49–61.

48. Wadden, T. A., & Letizia, K. A. (1992). Predictors of attrition and weight loss in patients treated by moderate and severe caloric restriction. In T. A. Wadden & T. B. VanItallie (Eds.), *Treatment of the seriously obese patient.* (pp. 383–410) New York: Guilford Press.

49. Kaiser, C. F., Sattler, D. N., Bellack, D. R., & Dersin, J. (1996). A conservation of resources approach to a natural disaster: Sense of coherence and psychological distress. *Journal of Social Behavior and Personality, 11,* 459–476.

50. Taimen, T. J. & Tuominen, T. (1996). Psychological responses to a marine disaster during a recoil phase: Experiences from the Estonia shipwreck. *British Journal of Medical Psychology, 69,* 147–153.

51. Burger, J. M. (1989). Negative reactions to increases in perceived personal control. *Journal of Personality and Social Psychology, 56,* 246–256.

52. Baumeister, R. F. (1988). Masochism as escape from self. *Journal of Sex Research, 25,* 28–59.

53. Baumeister, R. F. (1989). *Masochism and the self.* Hillsdale, NJ: Lawrence Erlbaum.

54. Janus, S., Bess, B., & Saltus, C. (1977). *A sexual profile of men in power.* Englewood Cliffs, NJ: Prentice-Hall.

55. Pines, A. M., Aronson, E., & Kafry, D. (1981). *Burnout: From tedium to personal growth.* New York: Free Press.

56. Perlman, B., & Hartman, E. A. (1982). Burnout: Summary and future research. *Human Relations, 35,* 283–305.

57. Farber, B. A. (1983). Introduction: A critical perspective on burnout.

In B. A. Farber (Ed.), *Stress and burnout in the human service professions.* (pp. 1–20) New York: Pergamon Press.

58. Maslach, C. (1982). Understanding burnout: Definitional issues in analyzing a complex phenomenon. In W. S. Paine (Ed.), *Job stress and burnout: Research, theory, and intervention perspectives* (pp. 29–40). Beverly Hills, CA: Sage.

59. Marks, P. A., & Monroe, L. J. (1976). Correlates of adolescent poor sleepers. *Journal of Abnormal Psychology, 85,* 243–246.

60. Mikulincer, M., Babkoff, H., Caspy, T., & Sing, H. C. (1989). The effects of 72 hours of sleep loss on psychological variables. *British Journal of Psychology, 80,* 145–162.

61. Monroe, L. J. (1967). Psychological and physiological differences between good and poor sleepers. *Journal of Abnormal Psychology, 72,* 255–264.

62. Grilo, C. M., Shiffman, S., & Wing, R. R. (1989). Relapse crises and coping among dieters. *Journal of Consulting and Clinical Psychology, 57,* 488–495.

63. Stunkard, A. J., Grace, W. J., & Wolff, H. G. (1955). The night-eating syndrome: A pattern of food intake among certain obese patients. *American Journal of Medicine, 53,* 78–86.

64. Johnson, C., & Larson, R. (1982). Bulimia: An analysis of moods and behavior. *Psychosomatic Medicine, 44,* 341–351.

65. Gottfredson, M. R., & Hirschi, T. (1990). *A general theory of crime.* Stanford, CA: Stanford University Press.

66. Snyder, C. R. (1995). Conceptualizing, measuring, and nurturing hope. *Journal of Counseling and Development, 73,* 355–360.

67. Snyder C. R., Harris, C., Anderson, J. R., Holleran, S. A., Irving, L. M., Sigmon, S. T., Yoshinobu, L., Gibb, J., Langelle, C., & Harney, P. (1991). The will and the ways: Development and validation of an individual-differences measure of hope. *Journal of Personality and Social Psychology, 60,* 570–585.

68. Janoff-Bulman, R. (1992). *Shattered assumptions: Towards a new psychology of trauma.* New York: Free Press.

69. Baumeister, R. F. (1990). Suicide as escape from self. *Psychological Review, 97,* 90–113.

70. Williams, J. M., & Broadbent, K. (1986). Autobiographical memory in suicide attempters. *Journal of Abnormal Psychology, 95,* 144–149.

71. Baumeister, R. F., & Leary, M. R. (1995). The need to belong: Desire for interpersonal attachments as a fundamental human motivation. *Psychological Bulletin, 17,* 497–529.

72. Baumeister, R. F. (1998). The self. In D. Gilbert, S. Fiske, & G. Lindzey (Eds.), *Handbook of social psychology* (4th edition) pp. 680–740. New York: McGraw-Hill.

73. Wewers, M. E. (1988). The role of postcessation factors in tobacco abstinence: Stressful events and coping responses. *Addictive Behaviors, 13,* 297–302.

4

Sharing One's Story

Translating Emotional Experiences into Words as a Coping Tool

Joshua M. Smyth
James W. Pennebaker

The Basic Paradigm and Results

Within the domains of psychosomatic medicine and health psychology there are two major treatment approaches that have been found to benefit health: Relaxation and talk therapies. Relaxation approaches, including hypnosis, biofeedback, meditation, yoga, and the relaxation response, have consistently been found to improve mood, immune function, and physical health (1, 2, 3). Similarly, basically all forms of talk therapy—from psychoanalysis to cognitive/behavioral therapies—have been shown to reduce psychological distress and promote both physical and mental well-being (4, 5). Most therapies include the labeling of the problem and a discussion of its causes and consequences as part of the therapeutic process. Participating in therapy also presupposes that the individual recognizes a problem exists and discusses it with another. We will argue that the act of disclosure itself is a powerful therapeutic agent that may account for much of the healing process.

When people put their emotional upheavals into words their physical and mental health seems to improve markedly. Systematic investigation of this phenomenon started over a decade ago, when college students were asked to write their deepest thoughts and feelings about traumatic experiences as part of a psychology laboratory experiment. Much more happened than just their writing about traumatic experiences, however. The writing exercise often changed their lives. There was something remarkable about their expressing themselves in words.

The basic technique was quite straightforward. Students were brought into the laboratory and told that they would be participating in a study, wherein they would write about an assigned topic for four consecutive days for 15 minutes each day. They were assured that their writing would be anonymous and that they would not receive any feedback on it. As far as they knew, the purpose of the project was to learn more about writing and psychology. The only rules about the writing assignment were that once they began writing, they were to continue to do so without stopping and to disregard spelling, grammar, and sentence structure. Participants then were randomly assigned to either an experimental or a control group.

Those who, by a flip of the coin, ended up in the experimental group were asked to spend each session writing about one or more traumatic experiences in their lives. In the words of the experimenter:

> For the next four days, I would like for you to write your very deepest thoughts and feelings about the most traumatic experience of your entire life. In your writing, I'd like you to really let go and explore your very deepest emotions and thoughts. You might tie your topic to your relationships with others, including parents, lovers, friends, or relatives, to your past, your present, or your future, or to who you have been, who you would like to be, or who you are now. You may write about the same general issues or experiences on all days of writing or on different traumas each day. All of your writing will be completely confidential.

Those who were assigned to the control group were asked to write about nonemotional topics for 15 minutes on all four days of the study. Examples of their assigned writing topics included describing the laboratory room in which they were seated or their living room. One group, then, was encouraged to delve into their thoughts and emotions, and the other was to describe objects and events dispassionately.

The first writing study conducted yielded astounding results (6). Most striking was that beginning college students immediately took to the task of writing. Those in the experimental group averaged writing 340 words during each 15-minute session. Although many cried, the vast majority reported that they found the writing to be extremely valuable and meaningful. Indeed, 98% of the experimental participants said that, if given the choice, they would participate in the study again. Most surprising was the nature of the writing itself. The students, who tended to come from upper-middle-class backgrounds, described a painful array of tragic and depressing stories. Rape, family violence, suicide attempts, drug problems, and other horrors were common topics. Indeed, approximately half of the people wrote about experiences that any clinician would agree were truly traumatic.

Even the ways the participants wrote were remarkable. The same students who would turn in sloppy, poorly constructed, appallingly spelled term papers or essay exams would write eloquently about their own personal tragedies. When given the opportunity in the study, the participants intuitively knew how to put together their life experiences into remarkably coherent narratives with few spelling or grammatical errors.

What made this first experiment so compelling, however, was not just the narratives themselves. Rather, the primary interest was how the writing exercise influenced physical health. During the school year, students' illness visits to the university health center in the months before and after the experiment were followed. Amazingly, those who had written about their thoughts and feelings drastically reduced their doctor visit rates after the study in comparison to the control participants who had written about trivial topics (6). Confronting traumatic experiences had a salutary effect on physical health.

Over the last decade, more than two dozen studies from multiple laboratories around the world have confirmed and extended these basic findings. Researchers have relied on a variety of physical and mental health measures to evaluate the effect of writing: (a) those pertaining to health reports and visits to health care providers; (b) mood and well-being measures; (c) employment and academic functioning (e.g., reemployment and academic achievement); (d) immunological outcomes; and (e) short-term effects (i.e., pre- post-writing changes). While more complete reviews may be found elsewhere (7, 8), studies from each category are discussed below. The health reports are considered first.

Pennebaker and Beall showed that college students who disclosed about traumatic topics had significantly fewer visits to health services, compared to control subjects, for the six months after writing (6). Greenberg and Stone found a decrease in physician visits for college students who wrote about deeply traumatic events as compared to subjects who wrote about relatively mild traumatic events or superficial topics (9). Richards, Pennebaker, and Beall found that among 95 maximum security prison inmates, those assigned to write about past traumas showed a drop in illness visits after writing (compared to those assigned to write about neutral topics; 10).

Some studies have asked participants to write about current problems instead of past traumas. Pennebaker and colleagues have had college freshmen write their deepest thoughts and feelings about coming to college, while control subjects wrote about neutral topics (11, 12, 13). Once again, these studies found that experimental subjects had improved physical health (fewer visits to health care providers) relative to control subjects for the two to four months following writing. In sum, these self-report symptom studies have revealed salutary effects on reported physical health from writing about past or current stressful events.

Studies examining psychological well-being have provided more complex results. Distress, negative moods, and depression have been reduced in several disclosure studies (9, 14, 15, 16, 17, 18). Several studies, however, have failed to find hypothesized improvements in self-reported mood and well-being (6, 13, 19, 20). Although these equivocal results exist, a meta-analysis of psychological well-being measures across a number of written disclosure studies found an overall significant positive effect (8). The inconsistent results between studies may be due to measurement or procedural differences between studies. Alternatively, moderating variables may influence the magnitude of the effect of written disclosure on psychological well-being (8).

Some studies have examined outcomes related to participants functioning in their profession, either as employee or college student. Francis and Pennebaker found that university employees writing about upsetting experiences showed a reduction in absentee rates relative to control subjects for the two months subsequent to writing (21). Spera, Buhrfeind, and Pennebaker found that 63 recently unemployed professionals assigned to write about the thoughts and emotions surrounding their (unexpected) job loss were reemployed more quickly than those who wrote about nontraumatic topics (18). Interestingly, this difference in reemployment did not appear to be due to differences in the effort put forth (e.g., number of resumes sent out or applications for jobs). Pennebaker and colleagues also found that college students assigned to the experimental group were superior to control subjects on measures of academic achievement (such as grade point average), even after controlling for proxies of academic ability (previous grades and SAT scores; 11, 12).

Other studies have examined effects of written disclosure on the immune system. Pennebaker, Kiecolt-Glaser, and Glaser showed that students assigned to the experimental condition exhibited improved immune function relative to control subjects after the last day of writing (19). Francis and Pennebaker found that experimental subjects (university employees) writing once a week for four weeks about upsetting topics had improved liver enzyme function relative to control subjects for the two months subsequent to writing (21). Esterling, Antoni, Kumar, and Schneiderman found that college students selected for being high-disclosers (as shown by the use of emotion in written essays) had better immune function than did those students whose essays conveyed less emotion (22). Esterling and colleagues subsequently reported that college students who wrote about traumatic topics had significantly better cellular immune control over a latent herpes virus (Epstein-Barr) than did students assigned to write about neutral topics (23). Finally, Petrie and colleagues assigned participants testing negative to Hepatitis B antibodies to write about traumatic or neutral events immediately prior to receiving their first Hepatitis B vaccine (with booster injections at one and four months). Participants writing about traumatic topics showed significantly higher antibody levels against Hepatitis B at four- and six-month follow-up periods (indicating superior immune control over the latent virus; 20). Overall, therefore, individuals who write about traumatic events show reliable improvements in immunological function when compared to individuals writing about neutral topics (8).

Participants also show a strong short-term reaction to the writing procedure. Experimental participants show marked increases on measures on autonomic arousal, such as blood pressure and skin conductance, during writing. During the procedure, participants writing about traumas also have a distinct shift to more negative affect; no changes in affect are observed for participants writing about innocuous topics (8). This is interesting because the effect of the writing task several weeks later is the opposite: Participants who wrote about traumas typically have more positive affect and less negative affect than participants assigned to write about neutral topics. In the absence of intervening coping strategies, this is contrary to the prediction of stress and coping theory, which would suggest that the short-term stress produced by writing about past trauma would result in negative long-term mood and health outcomes. The negative physiological and affective state produced by writing must reverse or be alleviated at some point following writing, yet prior to measurement of health outcomes. Clearly, additional information on factors contributing to this shift is important to understanding the manner in which writing about stressful events produces health benefits.

Factors Related to Effectiveness of Story Sharing

This accumulated evidence points to the important role that sharing one's story plays in influencing our health and well-being. It is important, however, to examine the parameters of such autobiographical storytelling. For example, is this effect generalizable across settings, populations, and topics? What other factors may be related to the benefit of sharing one's story?

Writing versus Talking about Traumas

Several studies have compared writing alone versus talking either into a tape recorder (23) or to a therapist (24, 25). Although these studies find similar long-term biological, mood, and cognitive effects, there is some evidence that writing produces more immediate (short-term) distress. Talking and writing about stressful experiences are both clearly superior to writing about neutral topics.

Topic of Disclosure

Whereas two studies have found that health effects only occur among individuals who write about particularly traumatic experiences (9, 26), most studies have found that disclosure is more broadly beneficial. Choice of topic, however, may selectively influence the outcome. For beginning college students, for example, writing about emotional issues related to beginning college influences grades more than writing about traumatic experiences (6, 8, 12).

Length of Time over which Writing Is Spaced

Participants in various experiments have been asked to write for one to five days, typically on consecutive days, but ranging to sessions separated by a week. The length of each writing session has varied from 15 to 30 minutes. Smyth's meta-analysis suggested that the more days over which the experiment lapses is related to stronger effects, but that the length of the individual sessions was not related to the effectiveness of writing (8). That is, writing once each week over a month may be more effective than writing four times within a single week. Interestingly, participants' self-reports of the value of writing do not distinguish shorter from longer writing sessions.

Actual or Implied Social Factors

Unlike psychotherapy or speaking to one's friends and family, the writing paradigm does not provide feedback to the participant. Rather, after individuals write about their own experiences, they are asked to place their essays into an anonymous-looking box with the promise that their writing will not be linked to their name. In one study comparing the effects of having students either write on paper that would be handed in to the experimenter or write on a "magic pad" (wherein the writing disappears when the person lifts the plastic writing cover), no autonomic or self-report differences were found (27).

Individual Differences

No consistent personality or individual difference measures have distinguished those persons who do or do not benefit from such writing. Several commonly examined variables are unrelated to outcomes, including age, anxiety (or negative affectivity), and measures of inhibition or constraint. One intriguing study preselected participants on hostility and found that those high-hostile participants benefited more from writing than did those who were low in hostility (28). Additionally, the recent meta-analysis by Smyth suggests that males may benefit from written disclosure more than females (although both benefit overall; 8).

Educational, Linguistic, or Cultural Effects

Writing about stressful events has been studied in groups of varying education, in several languages, and multiple countries. Within the United States, writing about stressful events has produced similar benefits for senior professionals with advanced degrees and maximum security prisoners with little education. Differences among college students' ethnicity or native language have not been related to outcomes. Additionally, the writing paradigm has consistently produced positive results among French-speaking Belgians (16), Spanish-speaking residents of Mexico City (29), multiple samples of adults and students in The Netherlands (17), and medical students in New Zealand (20).

The Clinical Benefit of Emotional Writing

One advantage of meta-analysis over traditional narrative reviews is that it allows an estimate of the size of an effect. Thirteen experimental studies, comprising over 800 individuals, were included in the recent meta-analysis by Smyth (8). It is important to note that all of the participants in these studies were psychologically and physically healthy, a point returned to below. The binomial effect size display (BESD) is a method to show the practical importance of an effect size, and is presented as the difference in outcome rates between experimental and control groups (30). In terms of a BESD, the effect of writing is a 23% improvement in those assigned to write about stressful events over those assigned to write about neutral topics. For example, in a population that might normally have a 61% chance of catching a cold during winter, individuals who wrote about stressful events (i.e., experimental participants) would have a 38% chance of getting sick. Similarly, experimental (relative to control) participants are 23% more likely to find reemployment after layoffs.

When trying to evaluate clinical relevance, it may be helpful to compare this writing task to other psychological, behavioral, or educational treatments. (For ease in comparison, all effect size estimates have been translated into BESD.) In their landmark meta-analysis of psychotherapy outcomes, Smith and Glass report an average 32% improvement for those receiving psychotherapy over those who do not (31); an overall effect size that is comparable, albeit somewhat larger, to that achieved by writing about stressful events (a 23% improvement). Recent analyses of psychological, behavioral, or educational interventions have reported similar or smaller effect sizes than the writing task. Wells-Parker and colleagues examined the effects of remediation with drinking/driving offenders and found that individuals receiving remediation (e.g., drug/alcohol counseling) had 8–9% lower recidivism rates than individuals not receiving remediation (32). A meta-analysis of the effects of psychosocial interventions with adult cancer patients found a range of improvement from 9% to 14% across various outcome measures, again somewhat lower than the improvement produced by writing (33). Finally, Lipsey and Wilson examined effect sizes from 302 meta-analyses of behavioral and educational interventions, and reported very similar average improvements for experiments that randomly assigned participants into experimental conditions (23%)—the same procedure used in most written expression experiments (34). While it is not possible to strictly compare effect sizes between studies when the same outcomes are not used, these comparisons support the view that the effect produced by writing about stressful events is clinically significant and similar to a variety of other psychological interventions.

Overall, the effects of written disclosure appear clinically relevant and generalizable across age, gender, race/ethnicity, social class, and a variety of other demographic variables. At this time an important caveat must be sounded: To this point, studies have been conducted with participants that were both psychologically and physically healthy. The potential utility of telling one's story through autobiographical writing in clinical samples has yet to be carefully demonstrated.

There is some evidence that writing may not be effective in samples with disordered cognitive processing or relatively severe depression, at least in the absence of additional intervention. A recent study by Stroebe and Stroebe on recently bereaved older adults failed to find benefits from writing (35). Similarly, Gidron and colleagues found that in a group of 14 posttraumatic stress disorder (PTSD) patients, the half assigned to write and orally expand about their traumas seemed to get worse (compared to controls; 36). The authors suggest that writing may not benefit PTSD patients in the absence of cognitive and/or coping skills training. Although generalizations from this study are limited by several factors (small sample size, confounding of oral elaboration with written disclosure), it does sound a cautionary note for additional research prior to the use of written disclosure in psychiatric (or other at-risk) populations.

Several investigators have begun to explore the potential of telling one's story in samples of individuals with chronic illness. Lumley and colleagues examined the effects of emotional disclosure of stressful events on pain, joint condition, and physical and affective dysfunction in a sample of rheumatoid arthritis patients (37). At three months after disclosure, participants who had disclosed about past trauma had less affective disturbance and better physical function than those who disclosed neutral topics (37). To our knowledge, this is the first demonstration that telling one's story may be helpful to medical patients as well as healthy individuals.

An ongoing study attempts to replicate and extend this provocative finding. Smyth and colleagues are evaluating written disclosure as a supplemental treatment for community-dwelling adults with mild to moderate asthma or rheumatoid arthritis (RA; 38). Participants were randomly assigned to write about either the "most stressful event" in their life, or neutral topics, for 20 minutes on three consecutive days. Spirometry (to evaluate pulmonary function) was conducted on asthmatics one week prior to writing (baseline), and at two, eight, and 16 weeks post-writing. RA patients had a clinical examination by a rheumatologist at the same intervals. (All health assessments were made without awareness of experimental condition in both groups.) Written disclosure (compared to the control condition) in asthmatics was associated with significant improvement in pulmonary function. Written disclosure (compared to the control condition) in RA patients led to improvement in physician-assessed stiffness and fatigue, and seems to reduce pain report over time. These results provide preliminary support for the potential of written disclosure as a supplemental treatment for asthma and RA, and perhaps other chronic conditions as well (38).

Why Does Writing or Talking about Emotional Experiences Influence Health?

This has been the central question that has guided our research over the last several years. One possibility is that by writing about emotional experiences, people simply become more health conscious and change their behaviors accordingly. Very little evidence supports this explanation. As indicated by the Smyth meta-analysis, most experiments find that after writing about emotional topics, participants continue to smoke, exercise, diet, and socialize in rates unchanged from before writing, and in ways similar to those in the control condition (8).

A second idea conceptualized writing as allowing individuals to confront upsetting topics, reducing the constraints or inhibitions associated with not talking about the event. Drawing on existing animal and psychophysiological literatures, it was asserted that active inhibition was a form of physiological work. This inhibitory work is reflected in autonomic and central nervous system arousal. The autonomic arousal arising from inhibition can be viewed as a chronic low-level stressor on the organism. This prolonged stress response could then cause or exacerbate psychosomatic processes, increasing the risk of illness and other stress-related problems. Just as constraining thoughts, feelings, or behaviors linked to a stressful or traumatic event is stressful, disclosing thoughts and feelings about these experiences should, in theory, reduce the stress of inhibition.

Findings in support of this inhibition model of psychosomatics are growing. Individuals who conceal their gay status (39), traumatic experiences in their past (40), or who are considered inhibited or shy by others (41) have more health problems than those less inhibited. Although inhibition seems related to long-term health problems, there is less support for theory that disclosure through writing reduces inhibition and should therefore improve health. Greenberg and Stone found that individuals benefited equally from writing about traumas that they had previously disclosed as well as traumas that they had kept secret (9). Changes in self-reports of how inhibited a participant feels before and after writing have not consistently related to the benefits of written disclosure. At this point, the role of inhibition/disinhibition in producing health benefits from writing about stressful events is not fully understood.

It is interesting to note that traditional research on catharsis or the venting of emotions has failed to support the clinical value of emotional expression in the absence of cognitive processing (42). Attempts to separate the relative contributions of emotion and language, specifically to determine the degree to which language is necessary for physical and mental health improvement, have been made. A recent innovative experiment sought to learn if the disclosure of a trauma through dance or bodily movement would bring about health improvements in ways comparable to writing (43). In the study, students were asked to either express a traumatic experience using bodily movement, to express an experience using movement and then write about it, or to exercise in a prescribed manner for three days, 10 minutes per day. Whereas the two movement expression groups reported that they felt happier and mentally healthier in the months after the study, only the movement plus writing group evidenced significant improvements in physical health and grade point average. It seems the mere expression of a trauma is not sufficient to bring about long-term physiological changes. Health gains appear to require the translation of experiences into language.

A third broad explanation for the effects of writing is that the act of converting emotions and images into words changes the way the person organizes and thinks about the trauma. Further, part of the distress caused by the trauma lies not just in the events but in the person's emotional reactions to them. By integrating thoughts and feelings, then, the person can more easily construct a coherent narrative of the experience. Once formed, the event can now be summarized, stored, and forgotten more efficiently.

Research on how people respond to traumatic events has often noted differences between memories for ordinary events and memories for traumatic events. Memories for traumatic events seem resistant to change, and are more emotional and perceptual than declarative in nature (44). Such memories often are first experienced as sensory fragments of the original experience. Visual, olfactory, auditory, and even kinesthetic sensations, in addition to intense feelings corresponding to the sensations at the time of the traumatic event, are typically reported (45).

Memories for traumatic events are also encoded differently, likely from restricted attentional focus and/or altered hippocampal memory function as a result of extreme arousal (46). When an individual is under stress, endogenous stress hormones are secreted that will influence the consolidation of a memory ("storage"). Emotion-laden material, stored in a state of high arousal, is more readily recalled during later states of similarly heightened arousal ("state-dependent memory"). Individuals who are particularly traumatized by an event appear to have lost some discriminatory function of memory recall: memory traces related to the traumatic memory are accessed too easily, thus cuing the remembering of the traumatic event inappropriately ("intrusions"). Perhaps most notably, the traumatic memory is recalled spontaneously, even when it is not relevant to their current experience (47).

There is also evidence that if an individual is upset about a traumatic event, memories are not integrated into a personal narrative (autobiographical memory). This results in the memory being stored as sensory perceptions, obsessional ruminations, or behavioral reenactment (45, 48). McFarlane and others have argued that it is these intrusive and distressing symptoms, avoidance, and hyperarousal, not the traumatic memory itself, that can cause the observed psychological and biological dysfunction (49).

One goal in treating individuals with particularly traumatic memories is to facilitate the processing of the memory (50). Foa and Riggs note that, as traumatic memories are more disorganized than other memories, treatments aimed at organizing memory should be particularly effective (more organized memories being easier to integrate into existing memory; 51). DiSavino and colleagues examined victims' narratives about their personal trauma during exposure treatment and found that decreasing disorganization over time was associated with improvement (52). Along these same lines, van der Kolk and Fisler report that traumatized individuals initially had no narrative memories of traumatic events, and formed a narrative memory only as they became aware of more elements of the traumatic experience (53). This suggests that the organization of stressful memories, particularly narrative structure, may be a critical factor in the beneficial effects of writing about stressful events.

One problem with processing, organizing, and integrating traumatic memories seems to be that they initially lack any verbal component and therefore cannot be effectively communicated or organized. Rauch and colleagues found that during the provocation of traumatic memories, there was a decrease in activation of Broca's area, the area most involved in the transduction of subjective experience into speech and language. Concurrently, there was an increase of activation in areas of the right hemisphere that are thought to process intense emotions and visual images (54). This provides some support for a neuropsychological basis underlying the apparent lack of linguistic and organizational properties of traumatic memories. The lack of a linguistic representation seems to be the primary impediment to the development of narrative memory and the assimilation of traumatic memories.

Emotional writing about traumatic or stressful events may be beneficial because it is effective at forcing the recoding of the traumatic memory into narrative language. While this transduction process will initially increase distress, it may allow a modification of the fear structure associated with the trauma, in turn facilitating the integration of the traumatic memory. Integrated memories should no longer cause intrusive reexperiencing, a change that will allow the attenuation of conditioned fear responses. The chronic hyperarousal associated with intrusion and fear responses should be eliminated, ultimately leading to reductions in psychological and physiological symptomatology.

Although the theoretical explanation that writing produces a restructuring of memories through narrative formation seems plausible, it needs to be explored in the context of writing about past trauma. One of our first systematic approaches to understanding the potential cognitive processes underlying the benefits of writing was to examine the essays themselves. Independent raters initially compared the writing samples of people whose health subsequently improved after the experiment with those whose health remained unchanged. Essays from those who improved were judged to be more self-reflective, emotionally open, and thoughtful. Not being content with clinical evaluations, we decided to subject the essays to computer text analyses to learn if language use could predict improvements in health among people who had written about emotional topics.

To achieve this goal, Pennebaker and Francis developed a computer program that could measure emotional and cognitive categories of word usage (13). The result was a computer program called LIWC (Linguistic Inquiry and Word Count) that analyzed essays in text format. LIWC was developed by having groups of judges evaluate the degree to which over 2,000 words or word stems were related to each of several dozen categories. Although there are now over 70 word categories in the most recent version of the LIWC program (actually SLIWC—the Second LIWC), only four were of primary interest. Two of the categories were emotion dimensions and the other two were cognitive. The emotion categories included negative emotion words (e.g., sad, angry) and positive emotion words (e.g., happy, laugh). The two cognitive categories, causal and insight words, were intended to capture the degree to which participants were actively thinking in their writing. The causal words (e.g., because, reason) were included because they implied people were attempting to put together causes and reasons for the events and emotions that they were describing. The insight words (e.g., understand, realize) reflected the degree to which individuals were specifically referring to cognitive processes associated with thinking. For each essay that a person wrote, we were able to quickly compute the percentage of total words that these and other linguistic categories represented.

The beauty of the LIWC program is that it allowed us to go back to previous writing studies and link word usage among individuals in the experimental conditions with various health and behavioral outcomes. To date, the most extensive reanalysis of data concerns six writing studies: two studies involving college students writing about traumas where blood immune measures were collected, two studies where first-year college students wrote about their deepest thoughts and feelings about coming to college, one study by maximum security prisoners in a state penitentiary, and one study using professionals who had unexpectedly been laid off from their jobs after over 20 years of employment.

Analyzing the use of negative and positive emotion words, Pennebaker, Mayne, and Francis uncovered two important findings (55). First, the more that people used positive emotion words, the more their health improved. Negative emotion word use also predicted health changes but in an unexpected way. Individuals who used a moderate number of negative emotions in their writing about upsetting topics evidenced the greatest drops in physician visits in the months after writing. That is, those people who used a very high rate of negative emotion words and those who used very few were the most likely to have continuing health problems after participating in the study. In many ways, these findings are consistent with other literatures. Individuals who tend to use very few negative emotion words are undoubtedly most likely to be characterized as repressive copers—people who have been defined as poor at being able to identify and label their emotional states (56). Those who overuse negative emotion words may well be the classic high neurotic or high negative affect individuals (57). These individuals are people who ponder their negative emotions in exhaustive detail and who may simply be in a recursive loop of complaining without attaining closure. Indeed, this may be exacerbated by the inability of these individuals to develop a story or narrative.

Although the findings concerning emotion word use were intriguing, it paled in comparison to the robust results surrounding the cognitive word categories. Remember that in written disclosure studies, people typically wrote for 3–5 days, 15–30 minutes per day. As they wrote, they gradually changed what they said and how they said it. The LIWC analyses showed strong and consistent effects for changes in insight and causal words over the course of writing. Specifically, people whose health improved, who got higher grades, and who found jobs after writing went from using relatively few causal and insight words to using a high rate of them by the last day of writing. In reading the essays of people who showed this pattern of language use, it became apparent that they were constructing a story over time. Building a narrative, then, seemed to be critical in reaching understanding. Interestingly, those people who started the study with a coherent story that explained some past experience did not benefit from writing (58). This is very consistent with the aforementioned view from the traumatic stress literature.

These findings are also consistent with current views on narrative and psychotherapy in suggesting that it is critical for clients to confront their anxieties and problems by creating a story to explain and understand past and current life concerns. The story can be in the form of an autobiography or even a third-person narrative. Interestingly, our data indicate that merely having a story may not be sufficient to assure good health. A story that may have been constructed when the person was young or in the midst of a trauma may be insufficient later in life when new information is discovered or broader perspectives are adopted. In written disclosure studies, as in narrative therapies, then, the act of constructing the stories is associated with mental and physical health improvement. A constructed story, then, is a type of knowledge that helps to organize the emotional effects of an experience as well as the experience itself.

Within the psychological literature, there is a broadly accepted belief that humans—and perhaps most organisms with at least a moderately complex nervous system—seek to understand the worlds around them. If we feel pain or hear a strange noise, we try to learn the cause of it. Once we understand how and why an event has occurred, we are more prepared to deal with it should it happen again. By definition, then, we will be far more motivated to learn about events that have unwanted or, on the contrary, very desired consequences than about common or predictable events that don't affect us. Similarly, events with large and significant personal consequences will be examined to a greater degree than relatively superficial events (59).

Over the course of a normal day, we are constantly surveying and analyzing our worlds. The person in the car behind us honks his horn while we sit at a red light. Automatically, we ask questions such as, "Is the person honking at me?" "Is the light green?" "Do I know this person?" As soon as we come to some understanding as to the meaning of the honking horn, we adjust our behavior (we go if the light is green, wave if it is a friend) or return to our private world if the honk was not relevant to us. As soon as this brief episode is over, we will probably put it out of our mind forever.

Whereas the search for the meaning of a honking horn is a brief, relatively automatic process, major life events are far more difficult to comprehend. If our lover leaves us, a close friend dies, or we face a significant career setback, we generally mull the event over in our mind trying to understand the causes and consequences of it. To complicate matters, a major life event usually consists of many events and experiences. If our lover has gone, it will affect our relationships with others, our finances, how we view ourselves, and even our daily eating, sleeping, talking, and sexual habits. In trying to understand this experience, we will naturally attempt to ask ourselves why this happened and how we can cope with it. To the degree that the event is unresolved, we will think, dream, obsess, and talk about it for days, weeks, or years.

Exactly what constitutes meaning or understanding is far less clear. Philosophers, psychologists, poets, and novelists have noted that a single event can have completely different meaning for different individuals. Following the death of a very close friend, some may find meaning in religion ("God has a plan"), others in understanding the cause of the death ("he smoked, what can you expect?"), yet others in exploring the implications for their own lives ("he would have wanted me to change my life"). Simple analyses relying on a single causal explanation may be useful in explaining some aspects of the death but will probably not be helpful in all aspects. We may have a straightforward explanation on why the friend died, but we still must deal with a change in our friendship network, our daily routine of talking with our friend, and so on. The beauty of a narrative is that it allows us to tie all of the changes in our life into a broad comprehensive story. That is, in the same story we can talk both about the cause of the event and its many implications. Much as in any story, there can be overarching themes, plots, and subplots—many of them arranged logically and/or hierarchically. Through this process, then, the many facets of the presumed single event are organized into a more coherent whole (59).

Drawing on research on conversation and language, Leslie Clark points out that conveying a story to another person requires that the speech act be coherent (60). Linguistic coherence subsumes several characteristics, including structure, use of causal explanation, repetition of themes, and an appreciation of the listener's perspective. Referring to the work of Labov and Fanshel (61), Clark emphasizes that conversations virtually demand the conveying of stories or narratives that require an ordered sequence of events.

Once a complex event is put into a story format, it is simplified. The mind doesn't need to work as hard to bring structure and meaning to it. As the story is told over and over again, it becomes shorter with some of the finer detail gradually leveled. The information that is recalled in the story is that which is congruent with the story. Whereas the data (or raw experience) was initially used to create the story, once the story is fixed in the person's mind, only story-relevant data are conjured. Furthermore, as time passes, we have the tendency to fill in gaps in our story to make the story more cohesive and complete. The net effect of constructing a good narrative is that our recollection of emotional events is efficient—in that we have a relatively short, compact story—and undoubtedly biased. One fact about this process emerges clearly: For reasons we are just beginning to understand, sharing one's story through writing promotes good physical and mental health.

How Can We Use Writing about Emotional Experiences as a Coping Tool?

The evidence outlined in this chapter clearly supports the salutary effects of writing about stressful or traumatic experiences. How, then, can one best use writing as a coping tool? It is most important for individuals to create environments within which they are comfortable writing about troubling topics. Our suggestions for helping individuals effectively utilize writing as a coping tool are outlined below:

- Find a location where there will be no disturbances (from others, the phone, etc.).
- Set aside about 30 minutes each day: 20 minutes for writing, with a few minutes afterward to compose yourself if necessary.
- Write for three or four days, usually consecutively.
- Explore your deepest thoughts and feelings about any experiences or topics that are weighing heavily upon you.
- Explore how this topic is related to a variety of issues in your life: your childhood, your relationships, who you are, who you would like to be, and so forth.
- Write continuously, without regard for spelling or grammar.
- Remember that the writing is for you, not someone else.

It appears best not to try to impose too much structure on the writer. For example, giving the writer particular words to try to use seems to disrupt the writing. On the other hand, it seems important to explore both the positive and negative aspects of the selected topic. Finally, the writer should try to bring his or her experiences together into a coherent narrative.

Is writing in this fashion somehow special, or would it be sufficient to keep a diary? We are not aware of any research that directly addresses this commonly asked question, but suspect that the lack of structure in diary-keeping may impede the beneficial process. It is important to recall that either merely listing stressful events or expressing emotions without the associated cognitions does not appear helpful (6). Rather, benefits seem to arise from the writing process, facilitating the integration of cognitive and emotional components of stressful experiences into a more coherent narrative (6, 55). To the extent that keeping a diary achieves this goal we expect that it should be helpful, but are not certain that this process is common to diary writing.

Using writing as a coping tool for individuals who are particularly over-whelmed by a traumatic experience may not be advisable. Recall that writing in recently bereaved older adults and in Vietnam veterans suffering from PTSD failed to produce benefit (35, 36). It may be that individuals in these groups were not able to successfully integrate emotional and cognitive components of their traumatic experience, perhaps due to particularly intense grief or disordered cognitive processing. It is not yet clear, however, if writing would be helpful if accompanied by additional coping skills training or therapeutic intervention (36), or if there are critical times where writing may be beneficial to such individuals (i.e., at different periods post-trauma). Additional research exploring the effects of writing in severely traumatized individuals is clearly needed.

More encouraging is the potential utility of writing as a coping mechanism in chronic physical conditions. Domínguez and colleagues (29), for example, have started to use writing to help clarify the psychological variables that increase a patient's risk of developing a chronic pain disorder. Individuals with chronic pain who had limitations in their ability to express and communicate emotional states had the highest distress and suffering. Preliminary data suggest that using writing in pain patients seems to improve their chances of clinical improvement, and may reduce the likelihood of developing a chronic condition (29). Smyth and colleagues (38) also present preliminary data suggesting that writing seems to be a useful adjunct in at least some chronic illnesses. Again we must emphasize that, regardless of the benefit of writing as a coping tool, it should not replace medical treatment. Furthermore, we suggest that individuals who do incorporate writing as a coping tool keep their primary care physician informed, particularly if writing leads to changes in how they care for themselves (e.g., their activities or medication use).

It is interesting to note that the overwhelming majority of individuals with chronic asthma or rheumatoid arthritis that participated in our study wrote about topics other than their illness when asked to write about the most stressful aspects of their lives (38). The few who do write about their illness are primarily individuals writing about the limitations imposed by their illness on their vocational activities (e.g., a plumber whose arthritis limits the number or length of days he can work). It is intriguing that writing about topics other than their illness still produced improvements in objective indicators of their illness. Although the nonspecific, broad benefit of writing has been previously noted (9), we as yet do not understand the underlying mechanisms of such improvements.

Overall, we have consistently been amazed at the readiness of people to disclose through writing and the powerful effects this process has on health. We are excited by the potential of sharing one's story through writing, as a coping mechanism—both in healthy individuals and as a supplemental treatment for chronic illness. The power of a coherent narrative is just beginning to be understood; it may represent a fundamental link between the experience of stressful events and subsequent health. We may find the most important relationship is that between being able to tell a good story and good health.

References

1. Eppley, K. R., Abrams, A. I., & Shear, J. (1989). Differential effects of relaxation techniques on trait anxiety. *Journal of Clinical Psychology, 45*, 957–974.
2. Linden, W., & Chambers, L. (1994). Clinical effectiveness of non-drug treatment for hypertension: A meta-analysis. *Annals of Behavioral Medicine, 16*, 35–45.
3. van Rood, Y. R., Bogaards, M., Goulmy, E., & Van Houwelingen, H. C. (1993). The effects of stress and relaxation on the in vitro immune response in man: A meta-analysis. *Journal of Behavioral Medicine, 16*, 163–181.
4. Mumford, E., Schlesinger, H. J., & Glass, G. V. (1983). Reducing medical costs through mental health treatment: Research problems and recommendations. In A. Broskowski, E. Marks, & S. H. Budman (Eds.), *Linking health and mental health* (pp 257–273). Beverly Hills, CA: Sage.
5. Smith, M. L., Glass, G. V., & Miller, R. L. (1980). *The benefits of psychotherapy*. Baltimore: Johns Hopkins University Press.
6. Pennebaker, J. W., & Beall, S. K. (1986). Confronting a traumatic event: Toward an understanding of inhibition and disease. *Journal of Abnormal Psychology, 95*, 274–281.
7. Pennebaker, J. W. (1993). Putting stress into words: Health, linguistic, and therapeutic implications. *Behaviour Research and Therapy, 31*, 539–548.
8. Smyth, J. M. (1998). Written emotional expression: Effect sizes, outcome types, and moderating variables. *Journal of Consulting and Clinical Psychology, 66*, 174–184.
9. Greenberg, M. A., & Stone, A. A. (1992). Writing about disclosed versus undisclosed traumas: Immediate and long-term effects on mood and health. *Journal of Personality and Social Psychology, 63*, 75–84.
10. Richards, J. M., Pennebaker, J. W., & Beal, W. E. (1995). *The effects of criminal offense and disclosure of trauma on anxiety and illness in prison inmates.* Paper presented at the Midwest Psychological Association, Chicago and currently submitted for publication.
11. Pennebaker, J. W. (1991, Jan/Feb). Writing your wrongs. *American Health, 10*, 64–67.
12. Pennebaker, J. W., Colder, M., & Sharp, L. K. (1990). Accelerating the coping process. *Journal of Personality and Social Psychology, 58*, 528–537.
13. Pennebaker, J. W. & Francis, M. E. (1996). Cognitive, emotional, and language processes in disclosure. *Cognition and Emotion, 10*, 601–626.
14. Greenberg, M. A., Stone, A. A., & Wortman, C. B. (1996). Health and psychological effects of emotional disclosure: A test of the inhibition-confrontation approach. *Journal of Personality and Social Psychology, 71*, 588–602.

15. Murray, E., & Segal, D. (1994). Emotional processing in vocal and written expression of feelings about traumatic experiences. *Journal of Traumatic Stress, 7,* 391–405.
16. Rime, B. (1995). Mental rumination, social sharing, and the recovery from emotional exposure. In J. W. Pennebaker (Ed.), *Emotion, disclosure, and health.* Washington, DC: American Psychological Association.
17. Schoutrop, M. J. A., Lange, A., Brosschot, J., & Everaerd, W. (1996). *The effects of writing assignments on reprocessing traumatic events: Three experimental studies.* Paper presented at The (Non) Expression of Emotions and Health and Disease Conference, Tilburg, The Netherlands.
18. Spera, S. P., Buhrfeind, E. D., & Pennebaker, J. W. (1994). Expressive writing and coping with job loss. *Academy of Management Journal, 37,* 722–733.
19. Pennebaker, J. W., Kiecolt-Glaser, J., & Glaser, R. (1988). Disclosure of traumas and immune function: Health implications for psychotherapy. *Journal of Consulting and Clinical Psychology, 52,* 781–793.
20. Petrie, K. J., Booth, R., Pennebaker, J. W., Davison, K. P., & Thomas, M. (1995). Disclosure of trauma and immune response to Hepatitis B vaccination program. *Journal of Consulting and Clinical Psychology, 63,* 787–792.
21. Francis, M. E., & Pennebaker, J. W. (1992). Putting stress into words: Writing about personal upheavals and health. *American Journal of Health Promotion, 6,* 280–287.
22. Esterling, B., Antoni, M., Kumar, M., & Schneiderman, N. (1990). Emotional repression, stress disclosure responses, and Epstein-Barr capsid antigen titers. *Psychosomatic Medicine, 52,* 397–410.
23. Esterling, B. A., Antoni, M. H., Fletcher, M. A., Margulies, S., & Schneiderman, N. (1994). Emotional disclosure through writing or speaking modulates latent Epstein-Barr virus reactivation. *Journal of Consulting and Clinical Psychology, 62,* 130–140.
24. Murray, E. J., Lamnin, A. D., & Carver, C. S. (1989). Emotional expression in written essays and psychotherapy. *Journal of Social and Clinical Psychology, 8,* 414–429.
25. Donnelly, D. A., & Murray, E. J. (1991). Cognitive and emotional changes in written essays and therapy interviews. *Journal of Social and Clinical Psychology, 10,* 334–350.
26. Lutgendorf, S. K., Antoni, M. H., Kumar, M., & Schneiderman, N. (1994). Changes in cognitive coping strategies predict EBV-antibody titer change following a stressor disclosure induction. *Journal of Psychosomatic Research, 38,* 63–78.
27. Czajka, J. A. (1987). *Behavioral inhibition and short term physiological responses.* Unpublished master's thesis. Southern Methodist University.
28. Christensen, A., Edwards, D., Wiebe, J., Benotsch, E., McKelby, J., Andrews, M., & Lubaroff, D. (1996). Effect of verbal self-disclosure on natural killer cell activity: Moderating influences of cynical hostility. *Psychosomatic Medicine, 58,* 150–155.
29. Domínguez, B., Valderrama, P., Meza, M. A., Perez, S. L., Silva, A., Martinez, G., Mendez, V. M., & Olvera, Y. (1995). The roles of emo-

tional reversal and disclosure in clinical practice. In J. W. Pennebaker (Ed.), *Emotion, disclosure, and health*. Washington, DC: American Psychological Association.

30. Rosenthal, R., & Rubin, D. (1982). A simple, general purpose display of magnitude of experimental effect. *Journal of Educational Psychology, 74,* 166–199.

31. Smith, M., & Glass, G. (1977). Meta-analysis of psychotherapy outcome studies. *American Psychologist, 32,* 752–760.

32. Wells-Parker, E., Bangert-Drowns, R., McMillen, R., & Williams, M. (1995). Final results from a meta-analysis of remedial interventions with drunk-driving offenders. *Addiction, 90,* 907–926.

33. Meyer, T., & Mark, M. (1995). Effects of psychosocial interventions with adult cancer patients: a meta-analysis of randomized experiments. *Health Psychology, 14,* 101–108.

34. Lipsey, M., & Wilson, D. (1993). The efficacy of psychological, educational, and behavioral treatment. Confirmation from meta-analysis. *American Psychologist, 48,* 1181–1209.

35. Stroebe, M., & Stroebe, W. (1996). *Writing assignments and grief.* Paper presented at The (Non) Expression of Emotions and Health and Disease Conference, Tilburg, The Netherlands.

36. Gidron, Y., Peri, T., Connolly, J. F., & Shalev, A. Y. (1996). Written disclosure in posttraumatic stress disorder: Is it beneficial for the patient? *Journal of Nervous & Mental Disease, 184,* 505–507.

37. Lumley, M. A., Kelley, J. E., & Leisen, J. C. C. (1997). Health effects of emotional disclosure in rheumatoid arthritis patients. *Health Psychology, 16,* 331–340.

38. Smyth, J. M., Shertzer, E., Hurewitz, A., Kaell, A., & Stone, A. A. (1998). *Written disclosure about stressful life events produces health benefits in adult asthmatics and rheumatoid arthritics: Preliminary results from an ongoing study.* Paper presented at the 1998 Annual Meeting of the American Psychosomatic Society, March 11–14, 1998 in Clearwater Beach, FL.

39. Coles, S. W., Kemeny, M. W., Taylor, S. E., & Visscher, B. R. (in press). Elevated health risk among men who conceal their homosexuality. *Health Psychology.*

40. Pennebaker, J. W. (1993). Mechanisms of social constraint. In D. M. Wegner & J. W. Pennebaker (Eds.), *Handbook of mental control* (pp. 200–219). Englewood Cliffs: Prentice Hall.

41. Kagan, J., Reznick, J. S., & Snidman, N. (1988). Biological bases of childhood shyness. *Science, 240,* 167–171.

42. Lewis, W. A., & Bucher, A. M. (1992). Anger, catharsis, the reformulated frustration-aggression hypothesis, and health consequences. *Psychotherapy, 29,* 385–392.

43. Krantz, A., & Pennebaker, J. W. (1995). Bodily versus written expression of traumatic experience. Manuscript submitted for publication.

44. Terr, L. (1994). *Unchained memories.* New York: Basic Books.

45. van der Kolk, B., & van der Hart, O. (1991). The intrusive past: The flexibility of memory and the engraving of trauma. *American Imago, 48,* 425–454.

46. van der Kolk, B. (1994). The body keeps the score: Memory and the evolving psychobiology of posttraumatic stress. *Harvard Review of Psychiatry, 1,* 253–265.

47. Pitman, R. K., & Orr, S. P. (1990). The black hole of trauma. *Biological Psychiatry, 27,* 469–471.

48. Janet, P. (1917). *Les nervoses.* Paris: E. Flammarion.

49. McFarlane, A. (1992). Avoidance and intrusion in posttraumatic stress disorder. *Journal of Nervous and Mental Disease, 180,* 439–445.

50. Foa, E., Roghbaum, B., & Molnar, C. (1995). Cognitive-behavioral treatment of posttraumatic stress disorder. In Friedman, Charney, & Deutch (Eds.), *Neurobiological and clinical consequences of stress: From normal adaption to posttraumatic stress disorder.* (pp. 483–494). Philadelphia: Lippincott-Raven.

51. Foa, E., & Riggs, D. (1993). Posttraumatic stress disorder in rape victims. In Oldham, Riba, & Tasman (Eds.), *American Psychiatric Press Review of Psychiatry, 12,* 273–303. Washington, DC.

52. DeSavino, P., Turk, E., Massie, E., Riggs, D., Penkower, D., Molnar, C., & Foa, E. (1993). *The content of traumatic memories: Evaluating treatment efficacy by analysis of verbatim descriptions of the rape scene.* Paper presented at the 27th Annual Meeting of the Association for the Advancement of Behavior Therapy, Atlanta, Georgia.

53. van der Kolk, B., & Fisler, R. (1995). Dissociation and the fragmentary nature of traumatic memories: Review and experimental confirmation. *Journal of Traumatic Stress, 8,* 505–525.

54. Rauch, S., van der Kolk, B., Fisler, R., Alpert, N., Orr, S., Savage, C., Fischman, A., Jenike, M., & Pitman, R. (1996). A symptom provocation study of posttraumatic stress disorder using positron emission tomography and script driven imagery. *Archives of General Psychiatry, 53,* 380–387.

55. Pennebaker, J. W., Mayne, T. J., & Francis, M. E. (1997). Linguistic predictors of adaptive bereavement. *Journal of Personality and Social Psychology, 72,* 863–871.

56. Weinberger, D., Schwartz, G. E., & Davidson, R. J. (1979). Low-anxious, high-anxious, and repressive coping styles: Psychometric patterns and behavioral and physiological responses to stress. *Journal of Abnormal Psychology, 88,* 369–380.

57. Watson, D., & Clark, L. A. (1984). Negative affectivity: The disposition to experience aversive emotional states. *Psychological Bulletin, 96,* 465–490.

58. Gergen, K. J., & Gergen, M. M. (1988). Narrative and the self as relationship. In L. Berkowitz (Ed.), *Advances in experimental social psychology (Vol. 21)* (pp.17–56). New York: Academic Press.

59. Kohler, W. (1947). *Gestalt psychology.* New York: Liveright.

60. Clark, L. (1993). Stress and the cognitive-conversational benefits of social interaction. *Journal of Social and Clinical Personality, 12,* 25–55.

61. Labov, W., & Fanshel, D. (1977). *Therapeutic discourse.* New York: Academic Press.

5

Focusing on Emotion

An Adaptive Coping Strategy?

Annette L. Stanton
Robert Franz

Students of emotion long have emphasized its disorganizing and dysfunctional qualities, with intense or negative emotions viewed as being particularly dangerous or undesirable (1, 2). In psychology, for example, a central metaphor for emotion is its portrayal as an irrational force which inexorably drives behavior (3). Traditional conceptualizations of emotion "emphasize how irrational and stressful features of emotional arousal make it difficult to maintain competent functioning" (4, p. 270). The literature on stress and coping has paralleled this focus, portraying emotion-oriented coping processes as maladaptive (5).

Comprising perhaps the most important recent development in the field of emotion (6), functionalist approaches represent a countervailing view to the previous perspective (e.g., 7, 8, 9). Theorists and researchers in a number of areas now are directing attention toward the fundamentally adaptive nature of emotion and its expression (e.g., 2, 9, 10, 11, 12, 13, 14). These researchers are exploring how emotions can "organize social communication and interaction, personality processes, goal-achievement, and cognitive processing from an early age" (4, p. 270). Functionalists regard emotion as a major organizing force (7), emphasizing its intra- and interpersonal regulatory effects (8).

Adaptive roles of emotion in coping processes also are beginning to garner attention. These are the focus of this chapter. To this end, we will first review literature in several areas outside coping research that points to the potential utility of processing and expressing emotions. This review is intended to be illustrative rather than comprehensive. Second, we argue that the coping literature has lagged behind developments in other areas in its narrow focus on the dysfunctional aspects of emotion-oriented coping and its concomitant lack of consideration of the functionality of emotion. We offer explanations for this focus on negative consequences of emotion-oriented mechanisms in the coping literature and go on to discuss research and theory that bear on potentially adaptive functions of coping through emotional approach (i.e., active processing and expression of emotion). Finally, we address theoretical, empirical, and applied directions for work on this construct.

Converging Lines of Evidence on the Utility of Emotion

Although no universally accepted definition of emotion exists, most researchers agree that emotions are comprised of experiential (affect and appraisal), physiological, and behavioral (or action readiness) components (13, 15, 16) and are expressed via separate systems that are weakly, but positively, correlated: verbal report of feelings, overt behavior, and expressive physiology (17). In the array of conceptualizations of emotion, Levenson's (16) functionalist view suits our purposes:

> Emotions are short-lived psychological-physiological phenomena that represent efficient modes of adaptation to changing environmental demands. Psychologically, emotions alter attention, shift certain behaviors upward in response hierarchies, and activate relevant associative networks in memory. Physiologically, emotions rapidly organize the responses of different biological systems including facial expression, muscular tonus, voice, autonomic nervous system activity, and endocrine activity to produce a bodily milieu that is optimal for effective response. Emotions serve to establish our position vis-à-vis our environment, pulling us toward certain people, objects, actions, and ideas, and pushing us away from others. Emotions also function as a repository for innate and learned influences, possessing certain invariant features along with others that show considerable variation across individuals, groups, and cultures. (p. 123)

The genesis of emotions in specific encounters and the relation between emotion and cognition are subject to debate (see 18 for a review). Our focus here is not on how emotion arises, but rather on the potential utility of emotional processing and expression when one confronts taxing circumstances. First, we briefly review theoretical and empirical developments from the areas of personality psychology, psychotherapy, and experimental work on emotional expression that highlight the benefits of emotional approach.

Research in Personality

Although researchers interested in personality dispositions and processes often have focused on emotional dysregulation (e.g., neuroticism, 19; negative affectivity, 20), some are attending to adaptive emotion-directed personality attributes. Three theoretical constructs exemplify a functionalist view of emotion in personality research: emotional competence (21), emotional intelligence (22), and emotional creativity (23). Most important in the present context, all three constructs reflect the view that an ability to approach one's emotional life plays a primary role in *healthy* intrapersonal and interpersonal functioning.

Emotional Competence.   The construct of emotional competence originated in Saarni's thoughtful analysis of the skills that children must develop in order to use their emotional experience successfully in service of interpersonal goals. On this point, Saarni (24) defined emotional competence as "the demonstration of self-efficacy in the context of emotion-eliciting social transactions" (p. 38). Emotional competence refers to the ability to use one's own emotional responses, as well as those of other people, as cues for action and effective interpersonal coping. In Saarni's view, emotionally competent individuals are aware of and sensitive to their feelings, tolerant of negative emotional experience, and able to express emotion strategically and flexibly (in genuine or modified form depending on one's goals and the emotional context).

According to Saarni (21), the following 11 specific skills comprise emotional competence: (a) awareness of one's emotional state, including the possibility that one is experiencing multiple emotions and, at more mature levels, awareness that one might not be consciously aware of all feelings; (b) ability to discern others' emotions based on situational and expressive cues that have some degree of cultural consensus; (c) ability to use the vocabulary of emotion; (d) capacity for empathic involvement in others' emotional experience; (e) ability to realize that inner emotional state need not correspond to outer expression, both in oneself and others; (f) awareness of cultural display rules; (g) ability to take into account unique personal information about individuals and apply it when inferring their emotional states; (h) understanding that one's emotionally expressive behavior may affect another and taking this into account in self-presentation; (i) capacity for coping adaptively with aversive or distressing emotions by using self-regulatory strategies; (j) awareness that the structure and nature of relationships is in part defined by the degree of emotional immediacy or genuineness of expressive display and by the degree of reciprocity or symmetry within the relationship; and (k) capacity for emotional self-efficacy (viewing oneself as feeling the way one wants to feel overall).

Clearly, the emotional competence construct is firmly grounded in the functionalist approach. Further, Saarni (25) has posited that most individuals have at least rudimentary ability in the first six skills, but that the other skills may not be as well developed. Saarni (24) also emphasized the natural interdependence of these skills in normal development and hypothesized that programs aimed at developing competence in certain skills should have beneficial effects on others. She cautioned, however, that interventions promoting emotional competence will carry little advantage for those individuals residing in emotionally thwarting environments.

Emotional Intelligence.   Emotional intelligence is another construct that emphasizes the adaptive value of emotional experience and expression (e.g., 22, 26; see chapter 7 in this volume). Salovey and Mayer (22) integrated a diverse literature on emotion with the work of researchers who posited the existence of multiple intelligences (e.g, personal intelligences, 27; social intelligence, 28) and contended that "the adaptive use of emotion-laden information is a significant aspect of what is meant by anyone's definition of intelligence, yet it is not studied systematically by investigators" (26, p. 22).

Emotional intelligence is defined as a subset of social intelligence and is comprised of four psychological processes: (a) the ability to perceive, appraise, and express emotion accurately; (b) the ability to access and/or generate feelings when they facilitate thought; (c) the ability to understand and use emotional knowledge effectively; and (d) the ability to regulate emotions adaptively and reflectively in ways that promote emotional and intellectual growth (26; see chapter 7 in this volume). Thus, emotionally intelligent individuals presumably are geared toward success in a number of ways (26, 29). For example, they may thrive in interpersonally oriented careers such as social work, teaching, and human relations, and may develop satisfying intimate relationships.

Emotional Creativity.   A third illustration of adaptive emotional dispositions is the construct of emotional creativity, which involves the creation of emotional responses that are novel with respect to the individual or the individual's group, effective in enhancing the individual's well-being, and authentic, reflecting something of the individual's unique self (30). According to Averill and Thomas-Knowles (23), emotionally creative individuals display facility in integrating and expressing emotions symbolically, form complex appraisals of situations, and deeply explore emotional meanings. Such creativity supposedly renders individuals more able to understand their own emotions and to communicate effectively with others.

Averill and Nunley (30) described steps to facilitate the development of emotional creativity. These include making a commitment to become emotionally creative, gathering knowledge regarding the nature of emotions (e.g., dispelling "myths of emotion," such as the notion that we are "overcome" by emotion or that emotions are impossible to control), increasing self-awareness, setting goals regarding an emotional life, and practicing new emotional responses.

Clinical Approaches to the Resolution of Stressful Experiences

Many approaches to psychotherapy share an assumption that strong, negative emotions should be targeted for eradication over the course of therapy.

The methods by which practitioners would rid their clients of such emotions vary as a function of specific theoretical orientations. Historically, practitioners have used the three methods of emotional discharge, insight, and control to deal with emotionality in therapy (2). Other clinical theorists, however, have emphasized the utility of emotional experience. Here, we describe illustrative clinical approaches that implicitly or explicitly hold a functionalist view of emotion and that conceptualize emotional engagement, understanding, and expression as assets in the pursuit of positive change.

Relatively early approaches to psychotherapy that emphasized the fundamentally adaptive nature of emotions are Rogers' client-centered therapy (31, 32) and Perls's gestalt therapy (33, 34). Both are discovery-oriented approaches, with individuals assumed to be motivated toward personal growth. Dysfunction purportedly results from efforts to control or eliminate unwanted emotions (33). A critical pathway for facilitating growth is to help clients gain an accurate awareness of their inner experience, accept and express their feelings and needs, and use them as guides to action. Perls (33) noted that, "it is only through the recognition of your emotions that you can be aware, as a biological organism, either of what you are up against in the environment, or of what special opportunities are at the moment presented" (pp. 98–99). The nature of the therapeutic relationship itself is an essential vehicle for growth in client-centered therapy, and a variety of techniques aimed at promoting emotional awareness and expression are used in gestalt therapy.

A recent clinical approach that illustrates a functionalist view of emotion is that of Mahoney (2). Mahoney's developmental constructivist approach values intense emotions as primitive and powerful knowing processes. In this view, strong, negative emotions are natural expressions of individual realities, even though discomfort and disorganization may accompany them. As such, emotional experience is critical to facilitating the adaptive reorganization of tacit assumptions regarding the self and the world. Mahoney (2) asserted that, "emotions are not the problems; our estranged relationships with our emotionality (and that of our companions) are more fundamentally problematic than the emotions themselves" (p. 177). Mahoney went on to offer two fundamental points regarding the role of emotion in therapy and personal development. First, he suggested that clients are unlikely to develop satisfying relationships with themselves or others "unless they can come to acknowledge, respect, and explore the range and power of their feelings" (p. 177). Second, emotional involvement is crucial to effecting change in core personal meanings. Although opposed to "technolatry," Mahoney described several techniques that promote emotional exploration and therefore facilitate the change process. Among these are therapeutic writing, personal narrative reconstruction, embodiment exercises, role playing, and resolution rituals.

The process-experiential approach developed by Greenberg and Safran (e.g., 12, 35, 36) also exemplifies a functionalist view. In their conceptualization, internal organizing processes referred to as emotion schemes are of central importance. Involving appraisals of situations in relation to one's needs and concerns, emotion schemes integrate cognition, affect, motivation, and relational action. These operate outside of conscious awareness to produce felt meanings and action tendencies. The therapy relies on "methods by which clients in therapy can access emotionally relevant schemes, can more adequately symbolize their experience, and can reprocess important experiences relevant to dysfunctional schemes" (35, p. 12). The therapist attempts to create conditions whereby the client can reexperience concrete, single experiences fully so that relevant, problematic emotion schemes are made available for reorganization. The complete processing of a specific emotional experience leads to a shift in the nature of the experience, promoting emergence of new, adaptive response tendencies (12). Four modes of engagement are critical at different points in therapy, and they include attending/awareness, experiential search, active expression, and interpersonal learning (35). These modes foster changes in perception, the creation of novel solutions, and a feeling of being supported and understood; together, these are responsible for positive change.

Therapeutic approaches that promote emotional processing and expression also have undergone empirical tests and been demonstrated to be effective in controlled trials with individuals confronting stressful or traumatic experiences (e.g., cancer, sexual assault). These interventions have fostered enhanced psychological adjustment (37, 38), improved immunocompetence (39), and longer survival (40, 41) in groups with malignant melanoma or metastatic breast cancer. Because these therapeutic approaches included multiple components, it is impossible to specify those responsible for the positive effects. Active processing and expression of emotions, however, were important facets of these treatments.

Experimental Research in Emotional Processing and Expression

For more than a decade, Pennebaker and his colleagues have investigated the health benefits of talking and writing about one's deepest thoughts and feelings regarding stressful experiences. This research (summarized in 42, 43, 44; see also chapter 4 in this volume) has demonstrated consistently that individuals randomly assigned to write or talk about deeply personal topics reap health benefits compared to control participants who discuss more superficial topics. The positive effects of emotionally expressive writing have emerged across a variety of stressors, ranging from transition to college (45) to experiences during the Holocaust (46). Researchers in other labs have replicated and extended Pennebaker's findings (e.g., 47, 48, 49). Further, Smyth's (50) recent meta-analysis of 13 studies of written emotional expression revealed an overall effect size of $d = .47$, representing an improvement of 23% in experimental groups compared with controls. This effect size is similar to that produced by many other psychological interventions (50). Significant beneficial effects of emotionally expressive writing emerged on self-reported health, psychological well-being, physiological functioning (e.g., immune function), and general functioning (e.g., grade point average, reemployment after layoff).

Emotional Approach Coping in Stress and Coping Theory and Research

As the material in the preceding section demonstrates, converging lines of evidence from personality psychology, the psychotherapy literature, and experimental investigation of emotional expression point to the adaptive potential of approaching emotion. These bodies of work stand in marked contrast to the conceptualization of emotion-oriented coping processes in the stress and coping literature, in which emotion-oriented forms of coping often are portrayed as dysfunctional. Indeed, some definitions of coping reflect an implicit assumption that actively approaching emotion through processing or expression is maladaptive. For example, Pearlin and Schooler (51), pioneers in the study of coping, initially defined coping as "any response to external life-strains that serves to prevent, avoid, or control emotional distress" (p. 3). Moreover, as illustrated in the quotations below, emotion-focused coping consistently has been associated with poor adaptational outcomes in the empirical literature on coping:

> A consistent body of research points to reliance on avoidance coping processes (primarily emotional discharge) as an important risk factor that predicts distress among both adults and their children (52, p. 249).

> EMOT [emotion-oriented] coping should be considered a risk factor for eating disturbance (53, p. 55).

> Emotion-focused coping, by contrast, has consistently proven to be associated with negative adaptation (54, p. 186).

In this section, we attempt to explain how emotion-focused coping mechanisms in general, and emotional approach strategies in particular, have gained a bad reputation in coping research. We then propose a new conceptualization of emotional approach coping and describe associated research. We follow with a discussion of putative moderators and mediators of emotional approach coping on outcomes in stressful encounters, as well as speculation on the developmental trajectory of emotional approach.

The Bad Reputation of Emotion-Focused Coping

The distinction between emotion-focused and problem-focused coping is central to coping theory (55, 56). Although both involve efforts to manage demands appraised as taxing one's resources, emotion-focused coping is aimed at regulating emotion surrounding the stressful encounter, whereas problem-focused coping involves direct efforts to modify the problem at hand (56). How can we explain the repeatedly demonstrated empirical association of emotion-focused coping with untoward outcomes (e.g., 53, 55, 57, 58)? Stanton et al. (5) identified three problems in the conceptualization and operationalization of emotion-focused coping that may account for this finding.

First, consider the following items, all of which are included on published scales to assess coping strategies:

"I let my feelings out" versus "I blame myself for being too emotional about the situation."
"I avoid being with people" versus "I get sympathy and understanding from someone."
"I learn to live with it" versus "I say to myself 'this isn't real.' "

Although all of these strategies might be undertaken to facilitate a common goal of regulating emotion in a stressful encounter, it is clear that some emotion-focused strategies facilitate approach toward the stressor whereas others promote avoidance. Indeed, some forms of emotion-focused coping are inversely correlated (59). When these conceptually distinct aspects of emotion-focused coping are aggregated within single scales, any obtained association of emotion-focused coping with poor adaptational outcomes results in interpretational ambiguity. The association may be driven to a greater extent, for example, by endorsement of avoidance-oriented strategies than of approach-oriented mechanisms. Indeed, hierarchical factor analyses of coping scales have revealed that approach and avoidance represent higher-order factors that subsume the problem- and emotion-focused coping distinction (60, 61). Both conceptually and operationally, it is essential to disaggregate emotion-focused coping into its component parts, and particularly to separate its approach- and avoidance-oriented dimensions.

Now consider these published emotion-focused coping items, which illustrate a second problem:

"I get upset and let my emotions out."
"I take it out on other people when I feel anxious or depressed."
"I become very tense."
"I feel anxious about not being able to cope."
"I focus on my general inadequacies."

Lazarus and Folkman (56) advanced the distinction between coping and adaptational outcomes, arguing that coping is neither inherently maladaptive nor adaptive. The above items, however, confound coping efforts with distress-laden and self-deprecatory content, thereby illustrating a second problem in the emotion-focused coping literature. Such redundancy in measurement may account in part for the obtained associations between emotion-focused coping and distress or psychopathology. This is not to suggest that we should avoid assessing aspects of coping that engender distress, but rather that we should ensure that any relation obtained between coping and distress is not a function of redundant items.

A third flaw in the relevant literature is the notable absence of measures to assess approach-oriented emotion-focused strategies. For example, the often-used Ways of Coping questionnaire (56) contains only two items that tap emotional expression. Other published scales that contain emotional approach content (e.g., 60, 62, 63, 64) often are confounded with distress or contain interpersonal content (and thus are included on scales of social support seeking). These problems in the extant coping literature lead us to believe that coping through actively processing and expressing emotion (i.e., coping through emotional approach) has not been offered a fair test with regard to its association with adjustment to stressful experiences.

Coping through Emotional Approach:
Revising the Bad Reputation

In order to examine problems in the conceptualization and measurement of emotion-focused coping, Stanton et al. (5) performed two studies. The first followed the method of Dohrenwend, Dohrenwend, Dodson, and Shrout (65), who investigated the confounding of measures of stressful life events and psychological symptoms. Our goal was to assess the confounding of extant and author-constructed measures of emotion-focused coping with psychopathological content, as judged by experts. A randomly selected sample ($n = 400$) of Ph.D. level psychologists with specializations in clinical psychology was generated from the American Psychological Association membership. A questionnaire sent to this sample requested that respondents ($n = 194$; response rate $= 48.5\%$) rate items from four published emotion-focused coping subscales (60, 62, 63, 64), as well as author-constructed emotion-focused coping items, on the extent to which each item reflected negative psychological symptoms. Author-constructed items were designed to tap coping through acknowledging, understanding, and expressing emotions and to include no mention of extent of distress experienced. Respondents also rated two anchor subscales used by Dohrenwend et al. (65), one to reflect unequivocal symptoms of psychopathology and the other to be free of psychopathological content.

Results suggested that items on emotion-focused coping scales indeed are contaminated by psychopathological content. Although the four published emotion-focused scales were rated as being less maladaptive than a symptom-laden anchor scale, experienced clinicians rated all four scales as being more indicative of pathological functioning and less indicative of healthy functioning than a neutral anchor subscale and the author-constructed scale. A majority of published items, but none of the author-constructed items, were rated as symptomatic of psychopathology.

These findings suggested that published emotion-focused scales are contaminated with negative symptomatology. It was not clear, however, to what extent this confounding accounted for the association between emotion-focused coping and poor adjustment, nor had it been determined whether coping through emotional processing and expression, when it is unconfounded with distress, promotes positive adjustment in stressful situations. These questions were addressed in a second study (5, Study 2). In an initial session, 191 undergraduate participants completed measures assessing strategies for coping with a self-identified current most stressful situation, as well as standardized measures of psychological distress and well-being. Other relevant coping (i.e., seeking social support) and personality (e.g., neuroticism) measures also were included. Measures of coping included the same items administered in the previous study. One month later, subjects returned to complete the adjustment measures a second time.

Results from an initial factor analysis of the coping items revealed two coherent factors, one comprised of confounded items and the other of unconfounded items. Confounded items included those that merged coping and distress (e.g., "Get upset, and am really aware of it"), that reflected only distress (e.g., "Become very tense"), and that indicated self-deprecation (e.g., "Blame myself for not knowing what to do"). As expected, relations between contaminated items and adjustment indices became considerably weaker when initial adjustment during a stressful encounter was controlled than when it was not. Thus, these items revealed low discriminant validity with distress indices.

Analyses with unconfounded coping items, which primarily tapped coping through emotional processing and expression, revealed intriguing interaction effects between sex and coping on adjustment. These relations remained significant when Time 1 adjustment was controlled. Specifically, females who used emotional approach coping during stressful encounters became less depressed and more satisfied with their lives over time, whereas males who coped through emotional approach became more depressed and less satisfied with their lives. Additional analyses demonstrated that these relations between coping and adjustment were not epiphenomena of the relations of neuroticism, dispositional emotional expressiveness, or coping through seeking social support with adjustment. Situational context did moderate the relations, however. With depression as a dependent variable, the previously obtained sex by coping interaction held for relatively uncontrollable and for interpersonal situations, but not for controllable and achievement-oriented situations. Emotional approach coping did not predict depression for either sex in controllable and achievement-oriented situations.

General conclusions emerging from these two studies were that (a) a number of items on current measures designed to assess emotion-focused coping are confounded with measures of distress and psychopathology; (b) the inclusion of these contaminated items on coping scales produces at least partially spurious relations, suggesting that emotion-focused coping is associated with maladjustment; and (c) to the contrary, specific emotion-focused coping strategies, involving active efforts to acknowledge, under-

stand, and express emotion, appear adaptive in managing stressful encounters, at least under particular conditions.

These promising results led us to believe that the construction of a measure designed to tap coping through emotional processing and expression
was warranted. Thus, we conducted an initial Emotional Approach Coping
Scale construction study (66). Items designed to tap coping through emotional approach were embedded in the COPE (62), a coping measure of
demonstrated reliability and validity, and administered to 400 undergraduates, along with dispositional instructions (i.e., how one usually copes
with stressful situations). Factor analyses revealed two distinct factors: one
reflecting coping through emotional processing (e.g., "I take time to figure
out what I'm really feeling"; "I realize that my feelings are valid and important") and the other indicating coping through emotional expression
(e.g., "I take time to express my emotions"; "I let my feelings come out
freely"). These factors were distinct from other coping factors (e.g.,
problem-focused coping, avoidance, seeking social support), and they were
more highly correlated with coping strategies oriented toward approaching
stressors (e.g., problem-focused coping) than avoiding them (e.g., mental
disengagement). In addition, they were internally consistent and moderately reliable over a four-week period ($n = 141$). Further, they were uncor-
related with social desirability and neuroticism (except that neuroticism
was correlated negatively with emotional processing for females). As expected, the emotional expression coping subscale was correlated with measures of dispositional emotional expressiveness and family expression.
Women reported using significantly more emotional processing and expression in response to stressors than did men.

Interesting gender differences in the relations of the coping scales with
other measures also emerged in this study. Relative to women who were
low on emotional approach, women who used more emotional approach
coping (either processing or expression or both) had (a) higher levels of
instrumentality and hope, a construct reflecting a sense of goal-directed
determination and ability to generate plans for achieving goals (see chapter
10 in this volume); (b) higher self-esteem; (c) lower trait anxiety and neuroticism; (d) lower likelihood of silencing their feelings and thoughts in
intimate relationships, a cognitive schema related to depression in women
(67); (e) higher life satisfaction; and (f) lower depression. By contrast, hope,
self-esteem, anxiety, and silencing the self were not related significantly to
emotional approach coping in men. Men high on emotional approach were
significantly more likely than women to report ruminating when feeling
depressed. From these results, we might speculate that young women use
emotional approach coping as a vehicle for clarifying and pursuing goals
in stressful situations, whereas for young men, emotional approach coping
more resembles the kind of rumination over negative affect that has been
demonstrated by Nolen-Hoeksema and colleagues to contribute to depression (e.g., 68). Thus, a more voluntary and effortful approach to emotion
may be taken by women, whereas young men's emotional approach may

be more involuntary and unbidden. Related to these findings, Compas and colleagues (69) have suggested that this distinction between effortful and less voluntary coping has been neglected in the literature and carries important implications for coping efficacy.

We went on to develop a situation-specific version of the emotional approach coping scales and attempted to replicate the relations of emotional approach coping and adjustment. Undergraduates coping with self-nominated stressful situations completed measures of coping and adjustment during the beginning of the semester and one month later. Findings supported the psychometric adequacy of the emotional processing and expression coping scales. Further, partial correlations controlling for initial level of distress revealed that emotional processing (but not emotional expression) was related to distress in opposite directions for women and men. As expected, women who used more emotional processing to cope with a stressful experience became less distressed over time, whereas men became more distressed. When sex, the emotional approach scales, and their interactions were entered as predictors of distress, however, only the interaction of emotional processing and expression was significant. Participants who were low on both processing and expression had the largest increase in distress over time. In the context of low processing, low expression was detrimental and high expression was useful. In the context of high processing, high expression was detrimental and low expression was useful. Although other interpretations are possible, perhaps emotional expression is effective only when one has processed one's feelings fully (and hence reports low processing). Further, these findings suggest that young adults who evidence poverty in emotional approach are those most prone to distress as they undergo stressful experiences. Clearly, further investigation is warranted of the conditions under which emotional approach coping is successful.

For Whom and Under What Conditions Is Emotional-Approach Coping Effective?

What conditions moderate the utility of emotional approach coping? Because we do not yet have a sufficient empirical base to offer more specific speculation, in general we will discuss emotional approach coping as an integrated construct rather than addressing its processing and expression components in this section. We suggest that individual difference characteristics, contextual attributes, and their interaction may moderate the utility of emotional approach.

Characteristics of the Individual.   From the preceding discussion, gender appears to be a prime candidate as a moderator of the relation between emotional approach coping and adaptive outcomes in stressful situations. Results from investigations with undergraduates suggest that emotional approach coping may be useful for women and detrimental for men. Why might this be? As the data suggested, women more than men may find emotional approach useful as a vehicle for clarifying goals and as a catalyst for action in stressful situations. Men's emotional approach, on the other hand, may take on a more ruminative character. Developmental research reveals that, from infancy, girls are exposed by caretakers to a wider range of emotion (through facial and verbal display) than are boys (70). Greater emotional facility may result, which may be reinforced by the ensuing social context (e.g., 71).

It is important to consider the limitations of the research thus far. The data supporting gender as a moderator of the coping-adjustment relation has been gleaned from studies with undergraduates only. Indeed, in a longitudinal investigation of married couples coping with infertility who were undergoing alternate insemination by husband, different findings emerged (72). In this latter study, husbands and wives completed coping assessments prior to an insemination attempt (Time 1) and were followed through receipt of pregnancy test results (Time 2). We were interested in couples who received a negative pregnancy result. Both men and women in these couples reported significant increases in depressive symptoms at Time 2. Controlling for Time 1 depressive symptoms, both men and women who used emotional approach coping at study entry reported less depression at Time 2 than did those low in emotional approach. Moreover, a significant interaction emerged on women's depressive symptoms. When women were high on emotional approach at Time 1, they had relatively low depression at Time 2, regardless of their partners' coping. When women were low on emotional approach, their partners' coping was more influential. If their partners engaged in emotional approach, the women had relatively low depression. If their partners also were low on emotional approach, women became more depressed at Time 2, with predicted scores suggesting moderate to severe depressive symptoms.

These findings suggest that emotional approach coping can benefit both women and men, and that one partner's use of emotional approach can compensate for the other's paucity of use of this strategy. How can we account for the discrepancy between these findings and those from undergraduate samples? Perhaps it is a function of a developmental process, with men becoming more comfortable with or skilled at emotional approach as they age, particularly with intimate partners. Important contextual attributes also may be relevant. Infertility is a dyadic stressor, and often partners serve as each other's primary or sole confidantes throughout the process. Absence of external social constraint may render emotional approach more adaptive for men. Certainly, mechanisms for gender effects and other individual differences characteristics associated with the efficacy of emotional approach coping within specific contexts require continued study.

Characteristics of the Context. Just as researchers have demonstrated that emotion-focused strategies in general receive greater use and display greater effectiveness in uncontrollable than in controllable contexts, evidence also has emerged for the benefits of emotional approach in contexts of relatively low control, as well as in interpersonal relative to achievement-oriented contexts (5, 72). Further, although emotional processing and expression can assume both interpersonal and intrapersonal (e.g., artistic expression, journal writing) outlets, it also is likely that emotional approach coping may be ineffective, or even detrimental, under conditions of social constraint (see 73).

At this time, we know relatively little about the most productive contexts for emotional approach. This topic deserves investigation, however, especially in light of the contention that "Physical and mental health come from neither emotional inhibition nor exhibition per se, but from flexibility" (74, p. 102). Many theorists have argued that a sign of emotional dysregulation is its situationally inappropriate character (75, 76). Theoretically, the productive contexts for emotional approach should depend on the adaptive functions served, a topic we address in a subsequent section.

Person by Situation Interactions.   The person-environment fit influences the adaptiveness of emotional approach coping. What is the consequence of entering a context that calls for emotional approach when one's preferred strategy is to avoid emotion, or conversely, of being required to dampen emotion when one typically welcomes it? We attempted to test this question in a sample of undergraduates who reported having a parent living with one of several physical or psychological disorders (e.g., cancer, heart disease, alcoholism, depression) (66). Participants first completed emotional approach coping scales with reference to this experience. They then were assigned randomly to talk with an interviewer about either their emotions or the facts regarding their parents' disorder. Participants completed two similar interview sessions separated by 48 hours in which they were instructed to talk for five minutes about the disorder. Heart rate and skin conductance were assessed throughout each interview, and negative affect was assessed at the end of each session. Baseline or first-session initial values on measures were used as covariates in analyses.

Consonant with the findings of Mendolia and Kleck (77), we expected that those assigned to talk about their emotions regarding their stressful experience would show greater habituation and thus less arousal and negative affect during a second exposure to the interview, as compared with those focusing on the facts. As hypothesized, results revealed that participants who were assigned to talk about their emotional reactions had significantly lower heart rates during the second interview session, and they reported lower negative affect after the second interview, than did those who focused on the facts. No between-groups differences emerged during the first interview. Significant preexisting coping by imposed coping interactions qualified the main effects. For both skin conductance and heart rate, participants who were high in self-reported emotional expression experienced lower arousal at the second session when assigned to talk about their emotions, whereas those low on emotional expression evidenced lower arousal when assigned to talk about facts. More specifically, participants high on emotional expression assigned to express their emotions had significantly lower arousal than those in other conditions. Means were in the expected direction for negative affect, although differences were not significant.

These results support the efficacy of matching preexisting coping strategies with situational contingencies. Although external validity is limited by the very brief intervention and short-term follow-up, one easily can imagine naturalistic contexts that might impose specific coping demands. For example, intimate partners might hold strong preferences for their partners' coping in particular stressful contexts, or therapists might promote emotional expression in response to trauma. The match between individual preferences and situational contingencies may be a powerful influence on the adaptive consequences of coping.

Mechanisms for the Effectiveness of Emotional Approach Coping

Although mechanisms for the effectiveness of emotional approach coping have received little empirical attention, several are suggested by the extant literature. Coping through emotional approach may (a) promote habituation to the stressor; (b) serve a signaling function to the individual; (c) engender cognitive reappraisal; (d) direct action; and (e) regulate the social environment.

Habituation to the Stressor.   Reviewing research on exposure-based therapy with anxious and phobic individuals, Foa and Kozak (78) noted that "the activation of affect, its reduction during exposure sessions [i.e., within-session habituation], and its decrease across sessions [i.e., between-session habituation], appear positively related to treatment outcome, denoting evocation and modification of fear memories during therapy" (p. 23). Within-session habituation provides incompatible information to be incorporated into problematic emotional memory structures, weakens links between stimulus and response elements, and provides interoceptive information that evoking stimuli need not be associated with aversive physiological responses. It also provides information incongruent with the belief that fear decreases only through escape or avoidance. Between-session habituation also provides information that is incongruent with the extant emotional memory structure. For example, following a traumatic experience, safety and danger signals often become confused, leading to a lack of perceived predictability and controllability that culminates in exaggerated estimates of the probability of negative outcomes (79). Over time, repeated exposure has the effect of reducing the perceived probability of feared consequences, as safety signals once again become associated with safety rather than fear (80). Clearly, cognitive mechanisms underlie the utility of habituation in Foa's view. Is such cognitive transformation necessary for positive change, is mere habituation of physiological arousal sufficient, or are these processes inextricably interwoven in humans? This question requires investigation.

Signaling Functions of Emotional Approach.   Many theorists suggest that emotion serves as a signaling function for the organism (10, 74, 81). According to Frijda (81), "emotions can be understood to represent a process of relevance signaling" (p. 113). They render the situation salient to the individual, calling one's attention to relevant goals and concerns (10, 75, 81). In their behavioral self-regulation theory, for example, Carver and Scheier (82, 83) contended that emotions signal the extent of discrepancy between an individual's progress toward a goal and her or his expected rate of progress. Thus, emotions provide information about our goals and progress toward them. Certainly, emotions need only be experienced and not necessarily processed in detail or expressed to serve a basic signaling function. However, we would suggest that adaptive processing and expression may enhance awareness of one's central concerns, facilitating specification of impediments to goals and motivating action to address them.

Cognitive Reappraisal.   Coping through emotional approach may promote adaptive cognitive reappraisal of the stressor. Processing and expressing emotion may produce elaboration of the cognitive-affective structure regarding a stressful encounter, introducing elements incompatible with the original structure. For example, through actively approaching emotion, the individual may realize that negative emotion does indeed subside (78), that the situation and associated emotions are not as threatening as initially conceived, and that some benefit can be gleaned from adversity (e.g., 84). In an analysis of six written emotional disclosure experiments, Pennebaker et al. (44) found that use of words associated with insightful and causal thinking was associated with improved health. Although emotional approach coping certainly does not guarantee adaptive cognitive restructuring, we suspect that this new learning is more likely in those who actively approach emotions than in those who shun them.

Direction of Action.   According to Greenberg (85), "if people are organized to avoid their feelings, they rob themselves of information that helps them to orient themselves in the environment and aids problem solving" (p. 502). By contrast, emotional approach provides valuable data that enable individuals to act effectively in order to maintain or alter their relations with the environment (e.g., 10, 13, 81, 86). Additionally, emotions may be conceptualized as action programs (e.g., 17) that serve the individual by providing a general behavioral impetus. For example, anger may serve "progress toward goals in the face of obstacles," and sadness may promote "the relinquishing of desired objects and goals, preventing wasted effort and eliciting nurturance from others" (76, p. 73). It must be noted, however, that although emotions foster action tendencies, the action selected is not specific, but rather depends on individual and contextual factors (10, 74).

Regulation of the Social Environment.   Emotional approach serves a signaling function not only for the individual, but also potentially for others in the social environment (6, 9). One's emotional expression provides information to others regarding one's concerns and prompts social reaction, be it empathic comfort or harsh rejection. It is clear that the responsiveness of the social environment to one's emotional approach will influence its adaptive consequences. For example, Lepore et al. (73) found that initial thought intrusion (assumed to be an indicant of cognitive processing) was associated with a decrease in depression over time in mothers who had lost an infant to sudden infant death syndrome when the environment was not socially constraining, whereas intrusive thoughts were associated with increased depression under conditions of social constraint. Also, a rich understanding of one's emotions allows one to "niche pick" (9), that is, to choose a maximally satisfying emotional environment.

Summary.   Clearly, several mechanisms potentially underlie the adaptive consequences of emotional approach coping. We suggest that these pathways to positive resolution of stressful circumstances are more likely to be available to those who approach emotion than to those who avoid it. However, consideration of these mechanisms points to the likelihood that, just as emotional approach may organize attention and action productively, it also carries the potential for misdirection, perhaps resulting in maladaptive cognitive processes (e.g., rumination) or action tendencies (e.g., violent aggression). As we have discussed, moderators of the effectiveness of emotional approach coping require attention. Examination of the developmental trajectory of emotional approach also may provide clues to how it might be used adaptively or go awry.

Development of Emotional Approach Coping

A rich body of literature is accruing to illuminate developmental processes of emotion regulation. Biologically based approach and withdrawal processes that may underlie positive and negative emotions and affective style or temperament have been the focus of many researchers (e.g, 86, 87, 88, 89). Environmental influences on relevant biological developments also are possible, in light of evidence in humans and other animals that interactions between mothers and infants can affect neural substrates of emotion (6). As we briefly describe here, socialization practices also affect processing and expression of emotion.

Children acquire basic skills relevant to understanding emotion early in life (e.g., 90, 91). For example, children develop intersubjectivity around 9 months of age (92). This can been seen in "social referencing" (93), in which infants attempt to interpret emotionally ambiguous situations by looking at the responses of their caregivers. After 15 months, self-conscious processes emerge that allow children to experience basic emotional states fully and to begin to produce more complex, self-referent emotional states (94). By 28 months, children have developed a functionalist "theory of emotion": they talk about events and actions that lead to emotions and the actions performed as a result of them (7). By age 6, children are sensitive to the cognitive antecedents and consequences of emotion; they elaborate this basic knowledge throughout the school years (95).

Burgeoning developmental research documents children's expectations regarding the interpersonal consequences of expressing negative emotions and characteristics of the child that influence expression, such as age and sex (e.g., 96, 97, 98, 99, 100). Children clearly understand that emotional displays are not always appropriate, and as early as age 6 they can describe specific circumstances in which negative emotional displays are acceptable (101). Children see fathers as generally less receptive than mothers to these displays (except anger), and peers are expected to be less receptive than parents, although this varies with the child's age (98, 100). Relative to girls, boys expect parents and peers to offer less support and understanding in response to negative emotional displays, especially sadness (97, 98, 100). Boys also are more likely than girls to endorse rules such as "one should not express emotion," and girls are more likely to endorse rules such as "one should always show their feelings" and to report that they will feel worse if they do not express emotions (99, 100).

These expectations play an important role in emotional expression during childhood. Saarni (102) characterized children as shrewd decision makers who take potential consequences into account when choosing whether to express (in genuine or modified form) or suppress their emotions. Boys generally tend to regulate emotional displays more than girls (99), with sadness particularly subject to control (97). In response to both positive and negative interpersonal feedback, girls display more emotion than boys (96). Boys report being less likely to display sadness, pain, and fear than girls, but they do not differ in reported anger expression (97, 99, 103), perhaps because of strong cross-situational constraints placed on anger displays (104). Consistent with findings in the adult literature (e.g., 70), girls tend to use verbal modes to express emotions, whereas boys more frequently express emotions through behavior (99).

With its focus on contextual factors and its acknowledgment of gender-related factors as important to emotional expression, this literature bears directly on the moderator variables described earlier. Children's emotional lives are molded by an array of environmental processes, with family contexts being particularly influential (25, 105). We should note that the literature reported here primarily relies on samples of children of European descent. Cultural variation in display rules may carry consequences for the use and utility of emotional approach.

Coping through Emotional Approach: Directions
for Theory, Research, and Application

Implications for Theory

We believe that the work presented in this chapter supports the inclusion of the emotional approach constructs in current stress and coping theories. Coping through cognitive processing and expression of emotion represent theoretically and empirically distinct constructs, both of which fall under the rubric of approach-oriented coping strategies. They also reflect emotion-focused strategies as traditionally conceptualized. At least in some cases, however, it appears that emotional approach strategies may facilitate goal clarification and pursuit. Thus, it is not surprising that emotional approach coping correlates positively with problem-focused coping and negatively with some emotion-focused strategies (e.g., avoidance-oriented coping) (66).

This leads us to propose the more far-reaching theoretical implication that a focus on the broad conceptual categories of problem-focused and emotion-focused coping often is not useful. We base this suggestion on several points. First, emotion-focused strategies represent a diverse set of processes, some of which are inversely intercorrelated and are associated in opposite directions with adaptive outcomes. Second, in our reading of the coping literature, we have observed that the broader term "emotion-focused coping" often is used in scientific manuscripts to describe a smaller set of strategies (e.g., avoidance-oriented coping). Such characterization may promote a misleading conclusion that all emotion-focused strategies are helpful or harmful, depending on the nature of the findings presented. Third, there is evidence that the approach-avoidance coping distinction subsumes the problem- and emotion-focused categories (e.g., 60, 61). This approach-avoidance continuum also reflects a fundamental motivational construct in humans and other animals (82, 83, 88) and thus maps easily onto broader theories of functioning. Consequently, we suggest that coping theorists and researchers consider discontinuing use of the broad problem- versus emotion-focused categories. At minimum, coping researchers should carefully scrutinize the differential utilities of higher-order conceptualizations of coping and use precise language in describing the coping processes they study.

Also with regard to theory, we suggest that coping theorists and researchers, especially those interested in emotional approach and avoidance, can benefit from theory and research in other areas. Important relevant work is being conducted by researchers in personality, emotion and motivation, developmental psychology, and biological psychology. Theory and findings from these areas regarding antecedents and consequences of emotional approach and suppression can inform researchers interested in emotional approach specifically and in coping theory more broadly. In turn, coping research may offer to other areas data on the management of emotion under conditions of adversity.

Implications for Research

Several clear implications arise from the initial studies on emotional approach coping. First, it is important that researchers clearly distinguish among the various forms of emotion-focused coping in research. Second, some researchers have concluded that emotion-focused coping is associated with poorer adaptive outcomes. At least in part, this results from the use of coping measures that are contaminated with distress-laden content. Researchers should examine their assessment devices carefully to ensure that this confounding is minimized. Third, coping research has done much more to illuminate forms of coping that are related to maladjustment than those that facilitate adaptive functioning (106). Emotional approach coping is a candidate as a facilitative strategy under some conditions, and we hope that researchers devote more attention to coping that enhances adaptive functioning (see also Aspinwall & Taylor, 107, on proactive coping). Fourth, we believe that the work on emotional approach described in this chapter suggests that intensive study of single coping mechanisms is a valuable addition to the coping literature, which heretofore primarily has examined the relative efficacy of multiple strategies.

A fifth point refers to the distinction between emotional processing and expression. Through much of this chapter we have referred to emotional approach as a unified construct. However, we have preliminary evidence that, although they are correlated, emotional processing and expression are distinct constructs that may have differential relations with adaptive status. For example, emotional processing seemed more important than emotional expression for predicting adjustment differences in female and male undergraduates (66). On the other hand, emotional expression appeared more important in a longitudinal study of breast cancer patients (108). Women who coped through expressing emotion at medical treatment termination subsequently had fewer unscheduled medical visits for cancer-related symptoms, better perceived health, lower distress, more vigor, and less fear of cancer recurrence over the next three months than did women low in emotional expression. Emotional processing was associated with only one dependent variable. Women high on emotional processing demonstrated an increase in distress over time. Clearly, emotional processing and expression need to be examined separately with regard to their adaptive value.

We have far to go in the study of emotional approach coping. Knowing that someone attempts to understand and express emotions tells us little about the precise cognitive processes involved in this analysis, how these processes work for discrete emotions, and the efficacy of various modes of emotional expression. Thus far, we have relied on self-report assessment of emotional approach with fairly general items (see 109 for a critique of self-report coping assessment). Lending confidence to the utility of self-reported emotional approach are our findings that undergraduates' reports of emotional approach coping correlate significantly with their parents' assessments of the undergraduates' coping (110), and that self-reported emotional approach successfully predicts important outcomes in longitudinal and experimental studies of groups undergoing stressful experiences (66, 72, 108). Other assessment methods such as direct observation and thought sampling, however, may provide a richer portrait of emotional approach coping. Further, experimental induction of emotional approach, as conducted in Pennebaker's and others' work, will enhance understanding of this coping strategy. We also need to know more about the conditions under which emotional approach coping aids or hinders adjustment to stressors. Smyth's (50) meta-analytic finding of significant within-group variance in outcomes for research participants engaged in emotionally expressive writing argues for the examination of moderators of the effectiveness of emotional expression and processing. Finally, developmental antecedents of emotional approach coping and mechanisms by which emotional approach produces its effects require study.

Implications for Clinical Application

The construct of emotional approach carries clinical implications in two respects. First, therapists can foster clients' skills in emotional processing and expression. At least three lines of evidence suggest the promise of interventions designed to promote emotional processing and expression in those who confront stressful experiences: (a) the documented effectiveness of therapeutic interventions that include these components (e.g., 38, 41, 111); (b) experiments that reveal the utility of emotional disclosure (see 43, 50); and (c) evidence that emotional suppression and avoidance-oriented coping have negative consequences for psychological and physical health (e.g., 112, 113, 114, 115, 116). Continued tests of the efficacy of emotional approach coping skills interventions are warranted.

We recognize that emotional approach coping surely is not for everyone in all circumstances. According to Lazarus and Folkman (56), coping strategies that are inconsistent with one's values "are likely to be used reluctantly or without conviction and are likely to fail" (p. 189). For example, imposed emotional approach may engender distress rather than relief in those who characteristically cope through avoidance. Initial high distress upon exposure to emotions associated with stressors eventually may promote therapeutic improvement (117). However, such anticipated or experienced distress may render individuals who avoid emotion reluctant to engage or persist in emotionally evocative therapies. For some individuals, interventions to promote acceptance of one's emotional experiences (see 118 for a review) may be a useful precursor to emotionally evocative approaches, and use of techniques such as emotionally evocative writing initially may be more acceptable to some clients than direct, interpersonal approaches. Certainly, appropriate timing of interventions and guarantee of a safe, supportive environment for emotional approach also are important.

Second, in addition to facilitating emotional approach coping skills in clients, therapists themselves may benefit from emotional approach in their work with clients. A client's emotions can provide the attentive therapist with a wealth of information regarding the client's motivations, beliefs, goals, and perceptions of self, others, and the world (119). The therapist who is committed and equipped to understand a client's emotions (or paucity thereof) can formulate valuable hypotheses about central concerns for the client and about the most productive therapeutic directions. In addition, the fundamental importance of therapist empathy in promoting successful change (120) highlights the utility of the therapist's emotional approach. Without the ability to understand and express (through the provision of feedback) their clients' emotions, therapists lose an important vehicle for catalyzing positive change.

Conclusion

Although nascent, the emotional approach coping construct represents a promising addition to the stress and coping domain, carrying theoretical, empirical, and applied implications. We hope that this chapter stimulates researchers and clinicians to consider emotional approach coping in their own work and to continue critical evaluation of its potential.

References

1. Campos, J. J., & Barrett, K. C. (1984). Toward a new understanding of emotions and their development. In C. Izard, J. Kagan, & R. Zajonc (Eds.), *Emotions, cognition, and behavior* (pp. 229–263). Cambridge: Cambridge University Press.
2. Mahoney, M. J. (1991). *Human change processes: The scientific foundations of psychotherapy.* New York: Basic Books.
3. Averill, J. R. (1990). Inner feelings, works of the flesh, the beast within, diseases of the mind, driving force, and putting on a show: Six metaphors of emotion and their theoretical extensions. In D. E. Leary (Ed.), *Metaphors in the history of psychology* (pp. 104–132). New York: Cambridge University Press.
4. Thompson, R. A. (1991). Emotional regulation and emotional development. *Educational Psychology Review, 3,* 269–307.
5. Stanton, A. L., Danoff-Burg, S., Cameron, C. L., & Ellis, A. P. (1994). Coping through emotional approach: Problems of conceptualization and confounding. *Journal of Personality and Social Psychology, 66,* 350–362.
6. Campos, J. J., Mumme, D. L., Kermoian, R., & Campos, R. G. (1994). A functionalist perspective on the nature of emotion. *Monographs of the Society for Research in Child Development, 59,* 284–303.

7. Bretherton, I., Fritz, J., Zahn-Waxler, C., & Ridgeway, D. (1986). Learning to talk about emotions: A functionalist perspective. *Child Development, 57,* 529–548.
8. Campos, J. J., Campos, R. G., & Barrett, K. (1989). Emergent themes in the study of emotional development and emotion regulation. *Developmental Psychology, 25,* 393–402.
9. Thompson, R. A. (1994). Emotion regulation: A theme in search of definition. *Monographs of the Society for Research in Child Development, 59,* 25–52.
10. Clore, G. C. (1994). Why emotions are felt. In P. Ekman & R. J. Davidson (Eds.), *The nature of emotion: Fundamental questions* (pp. 103–111). New York: Oxford University Press.
11. Ekman, P. (1994). All emotions are basic. In P. Ekman & R. J. Davidson (Eds.), *The nature of emotion: Fundamental questions* (pp. 15–19). New York: Oxford University Press.
12. Greenberg, L. S., & Safran, J. D. (1987). *Emotion in psychotherapy: Affect, cognition, and the process of change.* New York: Guilford.
13. Izard, C. E. (1993). Organizational and motivational fucntions of discrete emotions. In M. Lewis & J. Haviland (Eds.), *Handbook of emotions* (pp. 631–641). New York: Guilford.
14. Smith, C. A. (1991). The self, appraisal, and coping. In C. R. Snyder & D. R. Forsyth (Eds.), *Handbook of social and clinical psychology: The health perspective* (pp. 116–137). Elmsford, NY: Pergamon.
15. Frijda, N. H. (1993). Moods, emotion episodes, and emotions. In M. Lewis & J. M. Haviland (Eds.), *Handbook of emotions* (pp. 381–403). New York: Guilford.
16. Levenson, R. W. (1994). Human emotion: A functional view. In P. Ekman & R. J. Davidson (Eds.), *The nature of emotion: Fundamental questions* (pp. 123–126). New York: Oxford University Press.
17. Lang, P. J. (1984). Cognition in emotion: Concept and action. In C. Izard, J. Kagan, & R. Zajonc (Eds.), *Emotions, cognition, and behavior* (pp. 192–226). Cambridge: Cambridge University Press.
18. Lewis, M., Sullivan, M. W., Michalson, L. (1984). The cognitive-emotional fugue. In C. Izard, J. Kagan, & R. Zajonc (Eds.), *Emotions, cognition, and behavior* (pp. 264–288). Cambridge: Cambridge University Press.
19. McCrae, R. R., & Costa, P. T. (1987). Validation of the five-factor model of personality across instruments and observers. *Journal of Personality and Social Psychology, 52,* 81–90.
20. Watson, D., & Clark, L. A. (1984). Negative affectivity: The disposition to experience aversive emotional states. *Psychological Bulletin, 96,* 465–490.
21. Saarni, C. (1990). Emotional competence: How emotions and relationships become integrated. In R. Thompson (Ed.), *Nebraska symposium on motivation: Socioemotional development* (Vol. 36, pp. 115–182). Lincoln: University of Nebraska Press.
22. Salovey, P., & Mayer, J. D. (1990). Emotional intelligence. *Imagination, Cognition, and Personality, 9,* 185–211.
23. Averill, J. R., & Thomas-Knowles, C. (1991). Emotional creativity. In

K. T. Strongman (Ed.), *International Review of Studies on Emotion* (Vol. 1, pp. 269–299). New York: Wiley.

24. Saarni, C. (1997). Emotional competence and self-regulation in childhood. In P. Salovey & D. Sluyter (Eds.), *Emotional development and emotional intelligence: Educational implications* (pp. 35–66). New York: Basic Books.

25. Saarni, C. (1993). Socialization of emotion. In M. Lewis & J. Haviland (Eds.), *Handbook of emotions* (pp. 435–446). New York: Guilford.

26. Mayer, J. D., & Salovey, P. (1997). What is emotional intelligence? In P. Salovey & D. Sluyter (Eds.), *Emotional development and emotional intelligence: Educational implications* (pp. 3–31). New York: Basic Books.

27. Gardner, H. (1983). *Frames of mind: The theory of multiple intelligences* (10th Anniversary Edition). New York: Basic Books.

28. Sternberg, R. J., & Smith, C. A. (1985). Social intelligence and decoding skills in nonverbal communication. *Social Cognition, 3,* 323–340.

29. Mayer, J. D., & Gehrer, G. (1996). Emotional intelligence and the identification of emotion. *Intelligence, 22,* 89–113.

30. Averill, J. R., & Nunley, E. P. (1992). *Voyages of the heart: Living an emotionally creative life.* New York: Free Press.

31. Rogers, C. R. (1959). A theory of therapy, personality and interpersonal relationships, as developed in the client-centered framework. In S. Koch (Ed.), *Psychology: A study of science* (Vol. 3). New York: McGraw-Hill.

32. Rogers, C. R. (1961). *On becoming a person.* Boston: Houghton Mifflin.

33. Perls, F. S. (1969). *Gestalt therapy verbatim.* Lafayette, CA: Real People.

34. Perls, F. S., Hefferline, R., & Goodman, P. (1951). *Gestalt therapy.* New York: Dell.

35. Greenberg, L. S., Rice, L. N., & Elliott, R. (1993). *Facilitating emotional change: The moment-by-moment process.* New York: Guilford.

36. Safran, J. D., & Greenberg, L. S. (1991). *Emotion, psychotherapy, and change.* New York: Guilford.

37. Fawzy, F. I., Cousins, N., Fawzy, N. W., Kemeny, M. E., Elashoff, R., & Morton, D. (1990). A structured psychiatric intervention for cancer patients, I. Changes over time in methods of coping and affective disturbance. *Archives of General Psychiatry, 47,* 720–725.

38. Spiegel, D., Bloom, J. R., & Yalom, I. (1981). Group support for patients with metastatic cancer: a randomized outcome study. *Archives of General Psychiatry, 38,* 527–533.

39. Fawzy, F. I., Kemeny, M. E., Fawzy, N. W., Elashoff, R., Morton, D., Cousins, N., & Fahey, J. L. (1990). A structured psychiatric intervention for cancer patients, II. Changes over time in immunological measures. *Archives of General Psychiatry, 47,* 729–735.

40. Fawzy, F. I., Fawzy, N. W., Hyun, C. S., Elashoff, R., Guthrie, D., Fahey, J. L., & Morton, D. L. (1993). Malignant melanoma: Effects of an early structured psychiatric intervention, coping, and affective state on recurrence and survival 6 years later. *Archives of General Psychiatry, 50,* 681–689.

41. Spiegel, D., Bloom, J. R., Kraemer, H. C., & Gottheil, E. (1989). Effect of psychosocial treatment on survival of patients with metastatic breast cancer. *Lancet, ii,* 888–890.
42. Pennebaker, J. W. (1989). Confession, inhibition, and disease. In L. Berkowitz (Ed.), *Advances in experimental social psychology* (Vol. 22, pp. 211–244). New York: Academic Press.
43. Pennebaker, J. W. (1993). Putting stress into words: Health, linguistic, and therapeutic implications. *Behaviour Research and Therapy, 31,* 539–548.
44. Pennebaker, J. W., Mayne, T. J., & Francis, M. E. (1997). Linguistic predictors of adaptive bereavement. *Journal of Personality and Social Psychology, 72,* 863–871.
45. Pennebaker, J. W., Colder, M., & Sharp, L. K. (1990). Accelerating the coping process. *Journal of Personality and Social Psychology, 58,* 528–537.
46. Pennebaker, J. W., Barger, S., & Tiebout, J. (1989). Disclosure of traumas and health among Holocaust survivors. *Psychosomatic Medicine, 51,* 577–589.
47. Greenberg, M. A., & Stone, A. A. (1992). Emotional disclosure about traumas and its relation to health: Effects of previous disclosure and trauma severity. *Journal of Personality and Social Psychology, 63,* 75–84.
48. Esterling, B. A., Antoni, M. H., Fletcher, M. A., Margulies, S., & Schneiderman, N. (1994). Emotional disclosure through writing or speaking modulates latent Epstein-Barr virus reactivation. *Journal of Consulting and Clinical Psychology, 62,* 130–140.
49. Donnelly, D. A., & Murray, E. J. (1991). Cognitive and emotional changes in written essays and therapy interviews. *Journal of Social and Clinical Psychology, 10,* 334–350.
50. Smyth, J. M. (1998). Written emotional expression: Effect sizes, outcome types, and moderating variables. *Journal of Consulting and Clinical Psychology, 66,* 174–184.
51. Pearlin, L. I., & Schooler, C. (1978). The structure of coping. *Journal of Health and Social Behavior, 29,* 2–21.
52. Moos, R. H., & Schaefer, J. A. (1993). Coping resources and processes: Current concepts and measures. In L. Goldberger & S. Breznitz (Eds.), *Handbook of stress: Theoretical and clinical aspects* (2nd ed.. (pp. 234–257). New York: Free Press.
53. Koff, E., & Sangani, P. (1997). Effects of coping style and negative body image on eating disturbance. *International Journal of Eating Disorders, 22,* 51–56.
54. Kohn, P. M. (1996). On coping adaptively with daily hassles. In M. Zeidner & N. S. Endler (Eds.), *Handbook of coping: Theory, research, applications* (pp. 181–201). New York: Wiley.
55. Endler, N. S., & Parker, J. D. A. (1990). Multidimensional assessment of coping: A critical evaluation. *Journal of Personality and Social Psychology, 58,* 844–854.
56. Lazarus, R. S., & Folkman, S. (1984). *Stress, appraisal, and coping.* New York: Springer.
57. Felton, B. J., Revenson, T. A., & Hinrichsen, G. A. (1984). Coping and

adjustment in chronically ill adults. *Social Science and Medicine, 18,* 889–898.
58. Moos, R. H., Brennan, P. L., Fondacaro, M. R., & Moos, B. S. (1990). Approach and avoidance coping responses among older problem and nonproblem drinkers. *Journal of Aging, 5,* 31–40.
59. Scheier, M. F., Weintraub, J. K., & Carver, C. S. (1986). Coping with stress: Divergent strategies of optimists and pessimists. *Journal of Personality and Social Psychology, 51,* 1257–1264.
60. Tobin, D. L., Holroyd, K. A., Reynolds, R. V., & Wigal, J. K. (1989). The hierarchical factor structure of the Coping Strategies Inventory. *Cognitive Therapy and Research, 13,* 343–361.
61. Wills, T. A. (1997). Modes and families of coping: An analysis of downward comparison in the structure of other cognitive and behavioral mechanisms. In B. P. Buunk & F. X. Gibbons (Eds.), *Health, coping, and well-being: Perspectives from social comparison theory* (pp. 167–193). Mahwah, NJ: Erlbaum.
62. Carver, C. S., Scheier, M. F., & Weintraub, J. K. (1989). Assessing coping strategies: A theoretically based approach. *Journal of Personality and Social Psychology, 56,* 267–283.
63. Endler, N. S., & Parker, J. D. A. (1990). *CISS: Coping Inventory for Stressful Situations Manual.* Toronto: Multi-Health Systems.
64. Moos, R. H. (1988). *Coping Responses Inventory Manual.* Palo Alto, CA: Stanford University and Department of Veterans Affairs Medical Centers.
65. Dohrenwend, B. S., Dohrenwend, B. P., Dodson, M., & Shrout, P. E. (1984). Symptoms, hassles, social supports, and life events: Problem of confounded measures. *Journal of Abnormal Psychology, 93,* 222–230.
66. Stanton, A. L., Kirk, S. B., Cameron, C. L., & Danoff-Burg, S. (1998). Coping through emotional approach: Scale construction and validation. Manuscript in preparation.
67. Jack, D. C., & Dill, D. (1992). The Silencing the Self Scale: Schemas of intimacy associated with depression in women. *Psychology of Women Quarterly, 16,* 97–106.
68. Nolen-Hoeksema, S., Parker, L. E., & Larson, J. (1994). Ruminative coping with depressed mood following loss. *Journal of Personality and Social Psychology, 67,* 92–104.
69. Compas, B. E., Connor, J., Osowiecki, D., & Welch, A. (1997). Effortful and involuntary responses to stress: Implications for coping with chronic stress. In B. H. Gottlieb (Ed.), *Coping with chronic stress* (pp. 105–130). New York: Plenum.
70. Brody, L. R. (1993). On understanding gender differences in the expression of emotion: Gender roles, socialization, and language. In S. L. Ablon, D. Brown, E. J. Khantzian, & J. E. Mack (Eds.), *Human feelings: Explorations in affect development and meaning* (pp. 87–121). Hillsdale, NJ: Analytic Press.
71. Grossman, M., & Wood, W. (1993). Sex differences in intensity of emotional experience: A social role interpretation. *Journal of Personality and Social Psychology, 64,* 1010–1022.
72. Berghuis, J. P., & Stanton, A. L. (August, 1994). *Infertile couples' coping*

and adjustment across an artificial insemination attempt. In T. A. Revenson & N. P. Bolger (Chairs), Stress, coping, and support processes in the context of marriage. Symposium conducted at the annual meeting of the American Psychological Association, Los Angeles.

73. Lepore, S. J., Silver, R. C., Wortman, C. B., & Wayment, H. A. (1996). Social constraints, intrusive thoughts, and depressive symptoms among bereaved mothers. *Journal of Personality and Social Psychology, 70,* 271–282.

74. Averill, J. R. (1994). Emotions are many splendored things. In P. Ekman & R. J. Davidson (Eds.), *The nature of emotion: Fundamental questions* (pp. 99–102). New York: Oxford University Press.

75. Clark, L. A., & Watson, D. (1994). Distinguishing functional from dysfunctional affective responses. In P. Ekman & R. J. Davidson (Eds.), *The nature of emotion: Fundamental questions* (pp. 131–136). New York: Oxford University Press.

76. Cole, P. M., Michel, M. K., & Teti, L. O. (1994). The development of emotion regulation and dysregulation: A clinical perspective. *Monographs of the Society for Research in Child Development, 59,* 73–100.

77. Mendolia, M., & Kleck, R. E. (1993). Effects of talking about a stressful event on arousal: Does what we talk about make a difference? *Journal of Personality and Social Psychology, 64,* 283–292.

78. Foa, E. B., & Kozak, M. J. (1986). Emotional processing of fear: Exposure to corrective information. *Psychological Bulletin, 99,* 20–35.

79. Foa, E. B., Steketee, G., & Rothbaum, B. O. (1989). Behavioral/cognitive conceptualizations of post-traumatic stress disorder. *Behavior Therapy, 20,* 155–176.

80. Foa, E. B., & Kozak, M. J. (1985). Treatment of anxiety disorders: Implications for psychopathology. In A. Tuma & J. Maser (Eds.), *Anxiety and the anxiety disorders* (pp. 421–452). Hillsdale, N. J.: Erlbaum.

81. Frijda, N. H. (1994). Emotions are functional, most of the time. In P. Ekman & R. J. Davidson (Eds.), *The nature of emotion: Fundamental questions* (pp. 112–122). New York: Oxford University Press.

82. Carver, C. S., & Scheier, M. F. (1990). Origins and functions of positive and negative affect: A control process view. *Psychological Review, 97,* 19–35.

83. Carver, C. S., & Scheier, M. F. (1998). *On the self-regulation of behavior.* New York: Cambridge University Press.

84. Affleck, G., & Tennen, H. (1996). Construing benefits from adversity: Adaptational significance and dispositional underpinnings. *Journal of Personality, 64,* 899–922.

85. Greenberg, L. S. (1993). Emotion and change processes in psychotherapy. In M. Lewis & J. M. Haviland (Eds.), *Handbook of emotions* (pp. 499–508). New York: Guilford.

86. Lang, P. J. (1995). The emotion probe: Studies of motivation and attention. *American Psychologist, 50,* 372–385.

87. Davidson, R. J. (1993). The neuropsychology of emotion and affective style. In M. Lewis & J. M. Haviland (Eds.), *Handbook of emotions* (pp. 143–154). New York: Guilford.

88. Fox, N. A. (1991). If it's not left, it's right: Electroencephalograph asym-

metry and the development of emotion. *American Psychologist, 46,* 863–872.

89. Kagan, J., & Snidman, N. (1991). Temperamental factors in human development. *American Psychologist, 46,* 856–862.

90. Izard, C. E., Kagan, J., & Zajonc, R. B. (Eds.). (1984). *Emotions, cognition, and behavior.* Cambridge: Cambridge University Press.

91. Saarni, C., & Harris, P. L. (Eds.). (1989). *Children's understanding of emotion.* Cambridge: Cambridge University Press.

92. Bretherton, I. (1984). Social referencing and the interfacing of minds. *Merrill-Palmer Quarterly, 30,* 419–427.

93. Campos, J. J., & Stenberg, C. R. (1981). Perception, appraisal and emotion: The onset of social referencing. In M. Lamb & L. Sherrod (Eds.), *Infant social cognition* (pp. 273–314). Hillsdale, NJ: Erlbaum.

94. Lewis, M. (1993). The emergence of human emotions. In M. Lewis & J. Haviland (Eds.), *Handbook of emotions* (pp. 223–236). New York: Guilford.

95. Harris, P. L., & Saarni, C. (1989). Children's understanding of emotion: An introduction. In C. Saarni & P. Harris (Eds.), *Children's understanding of emotion* (pp. 3–24). Cambridge: Cambridge University Press.

96. Casey, R. J. (1993). Children's emotional experience: Relations among expression, self-report, and understanding. *Developmental Psychology, 29,* 119–129.

97. Fuchs, D., & Thelen, M. H. (1988). Children's expected interpersonal consequences of communicating their affective state and reported likelihood of expression. *Child Development, 59,* 1314–1322.

98. Zeman, J., & Garber, J. (1996). Display rules for anger, sadness, and pain: It depends on who is watching. *Child Development, 67,* 957–973.

99. Zeman, J., & Shipman, K. (1996). Children's expression of negative affect: Reasons and methods. *Developmental Psychology, 32,* 842–849.

100. Zeman, J., & Shipman, K. (1997). Social-contextual influences on expectancies for managing anger and sadness: The transition from middle childhood to adolescence. *Developmental Psychology, 33,* 917–924.

101. Saarni, C. (1979). Children's understanding of display rules for expressive behavior. *Developmental Psychology, 15,* 424–429.

102. Saarni, C. (1989). Children's understanding of strategic control of emotional expression in social transactions. In C. Saarni & P. Harris (Eds.), *Children's understanding of emotion* (pp. 181–208). Cambridge: Cambridge University Press.

103. Terwogt, M. M., & Olthof, T. (1989). Awareness and self-regulation of emotion in young children. In C. Saarni & P. Harris (Eds.), *Children's understanding of emotion* (pp. 209–237). Cambridge: Cambridge University Press.

104. Lemerise, E. A., & Dodge, K. A. (1993). The development of anger and hostile interactions. In M. Lewis & J. Haviland (Eds.), *Handbook of emotions* (pp. 537–546). New York: Guilford.

105. Halberstadt, A. G. (1991). Toward an ecology of expressiveness: Fam-

ily socialization in particular and a model in general. In R. Feldman & B. Rimé (Eds.), *Fundamentals of nonverbal behavior* (pp. 106–160). Cambridge: Cambridge University Press.

106. Carver, C. S., & Scheier, M. F. (1994). Situational coping and coping dispositions in a stressful transaction. *Journal of Personality and Social Psychology, 66,* 184–195.

107. Aspinwall, L. G, & Taylor, S. E. (1997). A stitch in time: Self-regulation and proactive coping. *Psychological Bulletin, 121,* 417–436.

108. Stanton, A. L., Danoff-Burg, S., Cameron, C., Collins, C., Bishop, M., Kirk, S., Dinoff, B., Leibowitz, R., & Twillman, R. (November, 1997). *Effects of coping through emotional processing and expression on quality of life in breast cancer patients.* Paper presented at the Department of Defense Breast Cancer Research Program Meeting, Washington, DC.

109. Coyne, J. C., & Gottlieb, B. H. (1996). The mismeasure of coping by checklist. *Journal of Personality, 64,* 959–991.

110. Stanton, A. L., Cameron, C. L., & Danoff-Burg, S. (1998). Convergence of coping assessments in young adults and their parents. Manuscript in preparation.

111. McQueeney, D. A., Stanton, A. L., & Sigmon, S. (1997). Efficacy of emotion-focused and problem-focused group therapies for women with fertility problems. *Journal of Behavioral Medicine, 20,* 313–331.

112. Epping-Jordan, J. E., Compas, B. E., & Howell, D. C. (1994). Predictors of cancer progression in young adult men and women: Avoidance, intrusive thoughts, and psychological symptoms. *Health Psychology, 13,* 539–547.

113. Gross, J. J., & Levenson, R. W. (1993). Emotional suppression: Physiology, self-report, and expressive behavior. *Journal of Personality and Social Psychology, 64,* 970–986.

114. Gross, J. J., & Levenson, R. W. (1997). Hiding feelings: The acute effects of inhibiting negative and positive emotion. *Journal of Abnormal Psychology, 106,* 95–103.

115. Hayes, S. C., Wilson, K. G., Gifford, E. V., Follette, V. M., & Strosahl, K. (1996). Experiential avoidance and behavioral disorders: A functional dimensional approach to diagnosis and treatment. *Journal of Consulting and Clinical Psychology, 64,* 1152–1168.

116. Stanton, A. L., & Snider, P. R. (1993). Coping with a breast cancer diagnosis: A prospective study. *Health Psychology, 12,* 16–23.

117. Jaycox, L. H., Foa, E. B., & Morrel, A. R. (1998). Influence of emotional engagement and habituation on exposure therapy for PTSD. *Journal of Consulting and Clinical Psychology, 66,* 185–192.

118. Hayes, S. C., Jacobson, N. S., Follette, V. M., & Dougher, M. J. (Eds.). (1994). *Acceptance and change: Content and context in psychotherapy.* Reno, NV: Context Press.

119. Lazarus, R. S. (1993). From psychological stress to the emotions: A history of changing outlooks. *Annual Review of Psychology, 44,* 1–21.

120. Goldstein, A. P., & Higginbotham, H. N. (1991). Relationship-enhancement methods. In F. Kanfer & A. Goldstein (Eds.), *Helping people change: A textbook of methods* (pp. 20–69). Elmsford, NY: Pergamon.

6

Personality, Affectivity, and Coping

David Watson
James P. David
Jerry Suls

The Dispositional Basis of Coping

A fundamental premise of coping research is that coping strategies (e.g., planning, social support seeking, denial) are differentially effective in reducing stress and, therefore, give rise to striking individual differences in key adaptational outcomes (such as reported levels of depression, anxiety, and/or physical symptoms). For instance, because avoidance- and denial-based strategies fail to resolve the underlying problems that are generating stress, they can be expected to lead to greater long-term distress than more active, problem-focused approaches (1).

We do not challenge this assumption that coping strategies are differentially associated with distress and dysfunction; indeed, we later will present evidence demonstrating that specific types of coping are differentially related to symptoms of depression and anxiety. However, we do question the meaning and interpretation of these findings. Our central thesis in this chapter is that commonly studied coping strategies reflect broader and more basic dispositional tendencies within the individual. We will argue, moreover, that two general dimensions of temperament—Neuroticism (or Negative Emotionality) and Extraversion (or Positive Emotionality)—are crucially important in influencing both (a) the coping strategy that an individual chooses and (b) the level of distress that he or she experiences. Consequently, these two general temperamental factors represent important "third variables" that can account—in large part—for the observed relations between coping and outcome. These broad temperamental factors, therefore, should become a more central focus of the coping literature.

The Resurgence of Traits in Coping

Although situational approaches to coping dominated research for 20 years (2), there has been a strong reemergence of interest in the role that personality traits play in coping and adaptation (see 3–5). In accord with this renewed emphasis on personological influences, several researchers have developed dispositional measures of coping (6–7). Whereas traditional, situation-specific instruments (such as the Ways of Coping; 8) ask people to indicate how they responded to a particular stressful event, these newer dispositional measures assess what people *typically* do in response to stressful events. This assessment approach obviously assumes that coping is—at least in part—dispositionally driven, and that coping behavior displays the two classic properties of a trait; that is, coping is assumed to be (a) substantially stable over time and (b) broadly consistent across different situations and contexts.

Unfortunately, however, the developers of these instruments generally failed to subject this assumption to a rigorous empirical test; that is, they failed to assess coping strategies over time (which would provide evidence regarding temporal stability) and across multiple types of stressors (which would yield evidence relevant to cross-situational consistency). Consequently, even though these dispositional measures became widely used in the literature, it was unclear whether they were based on a sound rationale. Recently, however, sufficient evidence has accumulated to establish that coping behavior does display significant levels of cross-situational consistency and temporal stability. For instance, in a one-month retrospective assessment, David (9) found that individuals were highly consistent (with *r*s ranging from .42 to .55) in their use of coping strategies across three different types of stressful events. A second study (9) of coping efforts across 14 successive days found that individuals tended to rely on the same adaptational strategies when responding to different types of stressful events. Hence, there is not only substantial temporal stability, but also cross-situational consistency in coping strategy use. On the basis of this and other evidence, *it now is clear that coping behavior displays the classic trait characteristics of stability and consistency, and that a dispositional view of coping strategy use is warranted.*

Coping in Relation to General Traits of Personality

Understanding the Links between Coping and General Traits of Personality

Why do coping behaviors show these traitlike properties of stability and consistency? At one level, these data may indicate that many of the strategies assessed in popular coping inventories (e.g., venting, denial) represent interesting trait dimensions. As we suggested earlier, however, at least part of the answer is that these coping strategies reflect broader and more basic dispositional tendencies within the individual. In this regard, there is no reason to believe that coping responses differ fundamentally from other types of responses (see 3, 5). In fact, as it typically is defined, "coping" simply reflects how individuals respond to a particular class of events (i.e., stressors). Because people show consistency in their responses across different events (10–11), they should respond to stress in ways that relate systematically to the ways in which they respond to other experiences.

For instance, extraverts are highly motivated to interact with others and actually spend more time socializing than do introverts (12–13). Consequently, one would predict that extraverts are more likely than introverts to turn to others for support during times of stress. Similarly, conscientious individuals generally act in a cautious, meticulous, and highly organized manner (13–14); accordingly, one would expect that these individuals develop careful and precise plans (i.e., engage in problem-focused coping) to help them adapt to stressful life events.

Note, moreover, that general traits likely have important implications for the types of adaptational resources that are available to an individual. For instance, people who generally are friendly and agreeable likely will have more extensive social networks available to them during times of stress; this, in turn, makes social support seeking a much more viable coping strategy.

The Big Three and the Big Five

In the last decade, personality researchers have made enormous strides toward developing a systematic, consensual structure of personality, at least at the general factor level (see 13). This robust and well-validated structure provides a useful organizing framework for understanding coping strategies and their relation to adaptational outcomes.

This consensual taxonomy is based on two closely related structural traditions—the Big Three and the Big Five. The Big Three structure grew out of the seminal work of Hans Eysenck. Starting in the late 1940s, Eysenck conducted an extensive series of structural analyses that initially identified two broad factors: Neuroticism and Extraversion (15). Subsequent analyses led to the isolation of a third superfactor that was labeled "Psychoticism" (16); despite its name, however, it is better characterized as a dimension of disinhibition (i.e., undercontrolled behavior) versus constraint (i.e., overcontrolled behavior). Several highly similar three-dimensional models have since been proposed, including those of Tellegen (17), Gough (18), and Watson and Clark (19). All posit three general traits of Neuroticism (or Negative Emotionality), Extraversion (or Positive Emotionality), and Constraint (vs. Disinhibition).

The Big Five model originated in Allport and Odbert's (20) groundbreaking attempt to compile an exhaustive set of trait-related terms in the English language (see 21–22). Allport and Odbert eventually settled on a list of 4,504 terms that clearly described traits of personality. Cattell (23, 24) reduced this list to 35 bipolar scales and initially identified from 12 to 15 factors in peer ratings of these scales. Subsequent researchers, however, have consistently reported that five robust factors—Neuroticism (vs. Emotional Stability), Extraversion (or Surgency), Conscientiousness (or Dependability), Agreeableness, and Openness to Experience (or Imagination, Intellect, or Culture)—are sufficient to describe the structure underlying these traits (25–27).

Despite their differing origins, the Big Three and the Big Five actually define highly similar structures with the latter representing an expansion of the former. Both models share the common "Big Two" of Neuroticism and Extraversion; moreover, the third Big Three dimension is a complex combination of Conscientiousness and Agreeableness (13, 21). Although we will concentrate on the more differentiated Big Five structure in this chapter, interested readers easily can translate our results into Big Three terms.

Affect and the Big Five

To understand how these Big Five traits relate to coping and adaptational outcomes, it is important to consider first how they correlate with basic dimensions of affective experience. Factor analyses of self-rated mood repeatedly have identified two general dimensions: Negative Affect (i.e., the extent to which one is experiencing negative mood states such as fear, sadness, and anger) and Positive Affect (i.e., the extent to which one is experiencing positive mood states such as joy, interest, and enthusiasm). These largely independent superfactors emerge robustly across a very wide range of assessment conditions (28–29), and so provide a basic taxonomic scheme for affect that parallels the role of the Big Three and Big Five in personality.

Note, moreover, that self-rated affect displays a well-articulated hierarchical structure (30, 31). Just as the Big Five traits can be subdivided into narrower components or facets (13–14), the "Big Two" dimensions of affect each can be decomposed into several correlated—yet ultimately distinctive—mood states. Watson and Clark (32) recently created the "Expanded Form" of the Positive and Negative Affect Schedule (PANAS-X) to assess key components of this hierarchical structure. The PANAS-X contains 10 item scales that assess the higher-order dimensions of general Negative Affect (e.g., *distressed*) and Positive Affect (e.g., *active*). In addition, however, it assesses a larger number of lower-order affective states, including four specific negative affects [Fear, Sadness, Guilt, and Hostility] and three facets of positive affect [Joviality, Self-Assurance, and Attentiveness].

To clarify the underlying nature of the Big Five, it is instructive to examine how they correlate with positive and negative affect. Table 6.1 reports relevant data from a sample of several hundred undergraduates. The Big Five traits were assessed using the domain scales from the Revised NEO Personality Inventory (NEO PI-R; 14). The participants also completed a trait form of the PANAS-X in which they rated the extent to which they "generally" experienced each affect descriptor.

These data closely replicate previous findings in this area (12) and demonstrate strong and systematic associations between personality and affectivity. Most notably, they reveal a striking symmetry between the Big Two traits of personality and the Big Two dimensions of affect. On the one hand, Neuroticism clearly is strongly and broadly related to negative emotionality. Consistent with previous results in this area, it is strongly related to general Negative Affect and with the specific negative affects; it also shows more moderate negative correlations with the positive affects that are somewhat higher than those typically reported in this literature (see 12). Based on Neuroticism's consistently strong links with the negative affects, many researchers have argued that "Negative Emotionality" perhaps would be a more fitting label for this dimension (see 12, 17).

Conversely, Extraversion is strongly and broadly related to positive emotional experience. Consistent with the data of Watson and Clark (12), it shows particularly strong associations with general Positive Affect and Joviality, indicating that extraverts describe themselves as active, cheerful, lively, and enthusiastic. Note, moreover, that extraversion is more moderately related to Self-Assurance and Attentiveness. Paralleling the situation with Neuroticism, data such as these have led to the suggestion that "Positive Emotionality" would be a very apt label for this trait (12, 17).

In contrast, the three remaining traits fail to show these same broad relations with experienced affect (12). Consistent with earlier work in this area, Conscientiousness is moderately correlated with general Positive Af-

Table 6.1 Correlations between Trait Affectivity and the Big Five Personality Traits

Affect Scale	N	E	C	A	O
Negative Affect Scales					
General Negative Affect	**.66**	−.32	−.26	−.32	−.16
Fear	**.52**	−.21	−.15	−.19	−.14
Sadness	**.58**	−.40	−.26	−.20	.00
Guilt	**.63**	−.36	−.33	−.17	−.06
Hostility	**.55**	−.33	−.29	−.54	−.13
Positive Affect Scales					
General Positive Affect	−.48	**.64**	**.49**	.17	.18
Joviality	−.46	**.70**	.30	.29	.13
Self-Assurance	−.44	**.54**	.25	−.13	.21
Attentiveness	−.38	**.41**	**.63**	.14	.09

Note: N = 348. N = Neuroticism; E = Extraversion; C = Conscientiousness; A = Agreeableness; O = Openness. Correlations of ∣.40∣ or greater are shown in boldface. Correlations of ∣.11∣ and greater are significant at $p <$ .05, two-tailed.

fect. Analyses at the lower-order level, however, indicate that this effect is confined primarily to Attentiveness. In other words, conscientious individuals describe themselves as being alert, attentive, and determined, but do not report substantially elevated levels of cheerfulness, enthusiasm, or confidence. Similarly, Agreeableness has a strong negative correlation with Hostility, but otherwise is weakly related to affect. Finally, replicating earlier findings, Openness essentially is unrelated to self-rated affect.

These data have extremely important implications for our subsequent consideration of coping. Coping strategies are used to predict important adaptational outcomes that frequently have a substantial affective component (e.g., levels of depression or anxiety). The data in Table 6.1 indicate that Neuroticism/Negative Emotionality and Extraversion/ Positive Emotionality can be expected to correlate strongly with these same adaptational outcomes. Indeed, because general distress and Negative Affect are important components of most types of psychological disorder (33), Neuroticism/ Negative Emotionality is very broadly related to psychopathology; among other things, it is a strong predictor of both depression and the anxiety disorders (34–35). Extraversion/Positive Emotionality is not as broadly related to psychopathology, but does show a more specific (negative) association with depressed mood and symptomatology (35–36).

These findings further suggest that Neuroticism/Negative Emotionality and Extraversion/Positive Emotionality are potentially important "third variables" that may represent competing explanations for the observed relations between coping and adaptational outcomes. That is, if coping strategies are significantly related to Neuroticism/Negative Emotionality or Extraversion/Positive Emotionality, then their ability to predict important outcomes simply may reflect the hidden influence of these broader, affect-laden traits. Thus, it obviously would be more parsimonious to focus simply on these general traits (see 5, 37).

Note, however, that there is another possibility here. In this regard, Bolger (38–39) has argued that coping strategies may *mediate* the effects of Neuroticism/Negative Emotionality on distress and dissatisfaction. In other words, those who are high on this trait may be distressed and dissatisfied precisely because they engage in maladaptive forms of coping. More generally, a mediational model leads to the prediction that once the variance that overlaps with coping is eliminated, Neuroticism/Negative Emotionality no longer would be significantly related to important adaptational outcomes. In a subsequent section, we will evaluate the merits of these competing explanations.

Neuroticism/Negative Emotionality and Coping

Before we can test these competing explanations, however, we first must examine whether—and how—coping relates to the general traits comprising the Big Five model. It hardly is surprising that interest in this area has focused primarily on the Neuroticism/Negative Emotionality dimension.

Research has demonstrated significant links between this trait and virtually every stage in the stress-coping-disorder nexus. First, prospective studies have shown that Neuroticism/Negative Emotionality scores predict the subsequent occurrence of stressful events, even when these events are objectively defined (40–42). It therefore appears that individuals who are high in negative emotionality actively create problems for themselves (for discussions, see 5, 13, 43).

Second, high Neuroticism/Negative Emotionality scorers tend toward negativistic environmental appraisals, so that they are likely to interpret relatively innocuous events as threats (44–45). Because of this, Neuroticism/Negative Emotionality scores are correlated with subjective measures of perceived stress at a level that cannot be explained entirely by differential life experiences (44, 46).

Third, by their own admission, high scorers on this dimension overreact to minor hassles and disturbances (13). In fact, many commonly used measures of the trait contain items directly related to the issue of stress overreactivity (e.g., "I sometimes get too upset by minor setbacks," "I can get very upset when little things don't go my way"). Moreover, recent evidence indicates that this self-perception is accurate; several naturalistic diary studies have found that high Neuroticism/Negative Emotionality scorers display greater elevations in Negative Affect following the occurrence of everyday problems, even after controlling for baseline levels of affect (39, 43, 47).

Finally, as noted earlier, Neuroticism/Negative Emotionality is substantially correlated with many of the criteria that traditionally are used to gauge coping effectiveness, including symptoms of depression and anxiety, somatic complaints, and general Negative Affect (33, 35). Taken together, these data clearly establish that high Neuroticism/Negative Emotionality scorers *must* be doing something wrong when reacting to stress.

Viewed in this larger context, it is not surprising that high Neuroticism/Negative Emotionality scorers tend to use passive, emotion-focused forms of coping (3, 48). For instance, studies using the Ways of Coping have reported that Neuroticism/Negative Emotionality is positively correlated with wishful thinking, self-blame, escape/avoidance, and emotion-focused coping; to a lesser extent, it also is related to the decreased use of problem-focused coping, positive reappraisal, and support seeking (38, 49). Such results have been reported in college students, community residents, and adult caregivers (7, 37) with a variety of different coping instruments.

Coping and the Big Five

Beyond Neuroticism/Negative Emotionality, the available data are much more sparse. Among the remaining traits, Extraversion/Positive Emotionality has received the greatest attention in this literature. Several studies have shown that Extraversion/Positive Emotionality is positively related to active, problem-focused forms of coping, such as positive reappraisal and social support seeking; conversely, extraverts generally are less likely to use emotion-focused coping strategies (50).

Three previous studies have examined coping strategies in relation to the complete Big Five model. First, Vickers, Kolar, and Hervig (51) examined coping styles in a large sample of military personnel who were adapting to the stress of basic training. As one would expect, Neuroticism/Negative Emotionality was related to passive, emotion-focused coping. Extraversion/Positive Emotionality was positively correlated with active, problem-focused forms of coping, such as positive reappraisal, problem solving, and support seeking. In contrast, Agreeableness and Openness both appeared to be much less relevant to this domain and were only weakly related to coping. The most interesting findings, however, concerned Conscientiousness, a trait that previously had been ignored in this literature. Vickers et al. (51) found that Conscientiousness was a moderately strong predictor of problem solving, positive reappraisal, and support seeking. Overall, Conscientiousness and Neuroticism/Negative Emotionality were the two strongest predictors of coping. Hooker et al. (49) subsequently replicated most of these findings on a small sample of Alzheimer's caregivers.

Watson and Hubbard (5) examined the Big Five in relation to the dispositional version of the COPE (7). Neuroticism/Negative Emotionality and Conscientiousness were again the two strongest predictors of coping. As expected, the former was broadly associated with passive, emotion-focused coping. Specifically, high-trait scorers reported that they typically responded to stress by giving up attempts to reach their goals (Behavioral Disengagement), daydreaming or otherwise attempting to take their mind off their problems (Mental Disengagement), expressing their negative feelings openly to others (Venting of Emotions, Social Support Seeking-Emotional), and pretending that their problems weren't real (Denial); in addition, they were not particularly likely to accept what had occurred (Acceptance) or to learn something beneficial from their experience (Positive Reinterpretation and Growth).

Conversely, Conscientiousness again was related to active, problem-focused response strategies. Conscientious individuals reported that they devised careful strategies (Planning) to eliminate the problems they faced (Active Coping), and that they dropped other activities to concentrate more fully on effective problem solving (Suppression of Competing Activities); furthermore, they noted that they were persistent and did not give up their efforts at goal attainment (Behavioral Disengagement), and that they did not turn to alcohol, drugs, or diversionary activities to take their minds off their problems (Alcohol-Drug Disengagement, Mental Disengagement).

In contrast, the three remaining traits were more modestly related to coping. Not surprisingly, extraverts were interpersonally oriented and turned to others in times of stress (Seeking Social Support-Emotional, Seeking Social Support-Instrumental); they also tried to see something beneficial and positive in their experience (Positive Reinterpretation and Growth).

Finally, individuals who were high in Openness reported that they were disinclined to turn to religion as a source of comfort (Turning to Religion), whereas agreeable individuals were unlikely to turn to alcohol or drugs as a means of distraction (Alcohol-Drug Disengagement). We subsequently sought to replicate these findings in a second sample of more than 300 undergraduates. As in Watson and Hubbard (5), these participants completed the dispositional form of the COPE and a measure of the Big Five (the NEO PI-R). Consistent with the results of Watson and Hubbard (5) and other studies in this area, Neuroticism/Negative Emotionality and Conscientiousness were broadly related to passive and active forms of coping, respectively. As expected, Extraversion/Positive Emotionality was correlated with social support seeking and active forms of coping (such as positive reappraisal). Finally, Agreeableness and Openness again failed to show any strong, well-defined correlates.

On the basis of these accumulating data, one can conclude that (a) Neuroticism/Negative Emotionality is broadly related to passive, emotion-focused forms of coping; (b) Conscientiousness is substantially correlated with active, problem-focused strategies; (c) Extraversion/Positive Emotionality is associated with social support seeking and positive reappraisal; and (d) Agreeableness and Openness are only weakly linked to coping.

Personality, Coping, and Adaptational Outcomes

The Mood and Anxiety Symptom Questionnaire

The data that we have reviewed clearly establish substantial links between commonly assessed coping strategies and the basic traits of personality. Most notably, Neuroticism/Negative Emotionality—and, to a lesser extent, Extraversion/Positive Emotionality—is moderately to strongly correlated with various forms of coping. These data, therefore, are consistent with the argument that these two personality dimensions represent potentially important third variables that are partly—perhaps even completely—responsible for the observed relations between coping and adaptational outcomes. Of course, they are entirely consistent with a mediational model as well. To assess the relative merits of these competing explanations, we need now to examine how these two classes of predictors relate to important adaptational outcomes.

To measure current psychological functioning, we assessed undergraduates on the 62-item short form of the Mood and Anxiety Symptom Questionnaire (MASQ; 52); respondents indicated to what extent they had experienced each symptom "during the past week, including today." The MASQ was constructed to test key aspects of the tripartite model of depression and anxiety proposed by Clark and Watson (34). In brief, the tripartite model classifies symptoms as either *nonspecific* (i.e., common to both syndromes) or *specific* (i.e., uniquely characteristic of either depression or anxiety). Accordingly, the MASQ contains two anxiety scales and two depression scales. One member of each scale pair was designed to assess the nonspecific general distress symptoms traditionally associated with the syndrome, whereas the other was constructed to tap its unique symptom cluster. Thus, the General Distress: Anxious Symptoms Scale (GD: Anxiety) includes several indicators of anxious mood, as well as other anxiety symptoms that were expected to overlap heavily with depression (e.g., inability to relax). In contrast, Anxious Arousal includes various manifestations of somatic arousal (e.g., feeling dizzy or lightheaded, shortness of breath, dry mouth).

Similarly, the General Distress: Depressive Symptoms Scale (GD: Depression) contains several items tapping depressed mood along with other nonspecific symptoms of mood disorder (e.g., feelings of disappointment and failure, self-blame). In contrast, Anhedonic Depression has items reflecting anhedonia, disinterest, and low energy and reverse-keyed items assessing positive emotional experiences (e.g., had a lot of energy).

Evaluating Relationships among Traits, Coping, and Symptomatology

Table 6.2 presents correlations between these MASQ scales and (a) the Big Five traits (assessed using the NEO PI-R), (b) trait affectivity (assessed using trait versions of the general negative and positive affect scales of the PANAS-X), and (c) coping (assessed using the dispositional version of the COPE). The most noteworthy aspect of these data is that they demonstrate that Neuroticism/Negative Emotionality and Extraversion/Positive Emotionality both are powerful predictors of current distress and dysfunction. The Neuroticism/Negative Emotionality markers displayed moderate to strong associations with all four MASQ scales. Furthermore, our Extraversion/Positive Emotionality markers were strongly negatively correlated with Anhedonic Depression, moderately related to GD: Depression, and essentially unrelated to anxiety. These patterns are consistent with previous research and theory (35) that Extraversion/Positive Emotionality is unrelated to anxiety and shows a more specific (negative) relation with depression. Finally, Conscientiousness was moderately correlated with both indexes of depression; beyond that, the three remaining traits were weakly linked to symptoms. In terms of predicting distress and dysfunction, it therefore appears that we can subdivide these traits into a dominant "Big Two" (i.e., Neuroticism/Negative Emotionality and Extraversion/Positive Emotionality) and a lesser "Little Three" (Conscientiousness, Agreeableness, and Openness). We will revisit this issue shortly.

Table 6.2 also demonstrates that several coping strategies were moderately related to current symptomatology. Note, moreover, that these correlations offer an interesting parallel to those observed earlier with the gen-

Table 6.2 Correlations between the Symptom Scales and Measures of Personality, Affectivity, and Coping

Scale	Anxious Arousal	GD: Anxiety	GD: Depression	Anhedonic Depression
Personality/Affectivity Scales				
Neuroticism	**.36**	**.50**	**.66**	**.59**
Trait Negative Affect	**.49**	**.62**	**.65**	**.51**
Extraversion	−.12	−.11	−**.30**	−**.53**
Trait Positive Affect	−.13	−.14	−**.43**	−**.70**
Conscientiousness	−.22	−.20	−**.38**	−**.38**
Agreeableness	−.24	−.19	−.19	−.25
Openness	−.04	−.05	.00	−.12
COPE Scales				
Behavioral Disengagement	**.42**	**.36**	**.47**	**.39**
Denial	**.32**	**.30**	**.30**	.28
Focus on and Venting of Emotion	.15	.26	**.30**	.12
Mental Disengagement	.19	.20	.27	.23
Positive Reinterpretation and Growth	−.14	−.17	−**.34**	−**.44**
Active Coping	−.16	−.10	−.27	−**.37**
Planning	−.19	−.15	−.26	−**.32**
Suppression of Competing Activities	−.05	.01	−.10	−.18
Alcohol-Drug Disengagement	**.34**	.28	.26	.26
Seeking Social Support— Emotional	−.03	.07	−.01	−.21
Seeking Social Support— Instrumental	−.07	.02	−.11	−.27
Acceptance	−.06	−.14	−.11	−.08
Restraint Coping	−.01	−.03	−.04	−.06
Turning to Religion	.10	.10	.00	−.07

Note: $N = 348$. GD = General Distress. Correlations of |.30| and greater are shown in boldface. Correlations of |.11| and greater are significant at $p < .05$, two-tailed.

eral traits. One reasonable interpretation is that, because coping scales share considerable amounts of overlapping variance with the personality markers, this overlap may account for the significant associations between coping and symptom levels. For example, paralleling the pattern observed with Neuroticism/Negative Emotionality, scales assessing passive, emotion-focused coping, such as Behavioral Disengagement, tended to show similar, moderate correlations with both depression and anxiety. In contrast—and paralleling the pattern observed with Extraversion/Positive Emotionality—

measures of active, problem-focused coping, such as Planning or Positive reinterpretation, tended to be weakly linked to anxiety and more moderately associated with depression. Finally, it is interesting to note that several of the COPE scales (Suppression of Competing Activities, Acceptance, Restraint Coping, Turning to Religion) essentially were unrelated to current symptomatology.

Taken together with the studies reviewed earlier, the results in Table 6.2 establish that these two classes of predictors (i.e., general traits and coping strategies) represent overlapping—and potentially competing—explanations in the prediction of adaptational outcomes. For instance, Table 6.2 indicates that both of our Neuroticism/Negative Emotionality markers were significant predictors of anxiety. Moreover, the coping strategies of Behavioral Disengagement and Denial also were significantly linked to anxiety. Finally, both of these coping strategies were moderately correlated with Neuroticism/Negative Emotionality in these data. Clearly, these scales contain a substantial amount of overlapping variance that may be largely responsible for their significant associations with anxiety.

Establishing the Unique Contributions of Traits and Coping

To assess the unique predictive contributions of each class of predictors, we conducted three series of multiple regressions. The first series was designed to determine the relative contribution of the "Big Two" versus "Little Three" traits. Throughout this chapter, we have emphasized that Neuroticism/Negative Emotionality and Extraversion/Positive Emotionality are potentially important third variables that may be largely—perhaps even completely—responsible for the observed associations between coping and outcome. Note, however, that we have failed to clarify the role of the three remaining Big Five traits in this context. This leads to an obvious question: Are the traits of Conscientiousness, Agreeableness, and Openness important in the prediction of depression and anxiety?

To examine this issue, we conducted a series of two-step hierarchical multiple regressions using each of the MASQ scales as a criterion in a separate analysis. These results strikingly demonstrated the enormous power of Neuroticism/Negative Emotionality and Extraversion/Positive Emotionality in the prediction of current distress and symptomatology; specifically, markers of these traits accounted for between 24% to 60% of the variance in the MASQ scales. In sharp contrast, the Little Three traits accounted for less than 2% of the criterion variance in every case. On the basis of these findings, we eliminated Conscientiousness, Agreeableness, and Openness from the subsequent series of regressions.

A second series of regressions tested the mediational model that has been articulated by Bolger (38) and others. As discussed previously, this model asserts that the general traits influence outcomes *indirectly*, with coping strategies representing more proximal, *direct* influences. Put another way, individuals who are high on Neuroticism/Negative Emotional-ity—or low in Extraversion/Positive Emotionality—are distressed and dis-satisfied precisely because they tend to engage in passive forms of coping, rather than using active, problem-focused coping strategies. The media-tional model therefore predicts that once the variance attributable to coping is eliminated, Neuroticism/Negative Emotionality and Extraversion/Posi-tive Emotionality no longer will be significantly related to current levels of distress.

The mediational model was tested via a series of three-step hierarchical regression analyses (53), again using each of the MASQ scales as a separate criterion. Following the logic of the previous series, the relevant COPE scales i.e., all of those correlating |.20| or greater with the criterion. were entered as a single block in Step 1. In order to assess the separate contri-butions of Neuroticism/Negative Emotionality and Extraversion/Positive Emotionality, we entered markers of the former as a block in Step 2, fol-lowed by markers of the latter in Step 3.

Two aspects of these results were noteworthy. First, the COPE scales jointly demonstrated substantial power in the prediction of depression and anxiety; across the four criteria, the combined coping strategies accounted for between 21% and 34% of the variance in the MASQ scales.

Second, these results clearly refute a strong version of the mediational model. That is, even after controlling for the effects of multiple coping strat-egies, Neuroticism/Negative Emotionality added substantial incremental power in all four analyses. Across the four MASQ scales, Neuroticism/ Negative Emotionality contributed an additional 9% to to 22% of the cri-terion variance, with a mean value of roughly 17%. In fact, the Neuroticism/ Negative Emotionality markers actually accounted for slightly more vari-ance in the GD: Anxiety scale than did the COPE scales entered previously. As expected, the Extraversion/Positive Emotionality markers also con-tributed substantially (an additional 14%) to the prediction of Anhedonic Depression. On the basis of these findings, we must reject the hypothesis that coping fully mediates the relation between these general traits and outcome, and that the trait-outcome association is entirely indirect. At the same time, however, we acknowledge that these data are entirely con-sistent with a weaker form of the mediational model in which the general traits are posited to have both (a) direct and (b) indirect influences on out-come.

A final series of regressions tested the competing hypothesis that the predictive power of these coping strategies is illusory, and that it simply reflects the hidden influence of these broader, more basic traits. This hy-pothesis generates the straightforward prediction that once the variance attributable to Neuroticism/Negative Emotionality and Extraversion/Posi-tive Emotionality is eliminated, the predictive power of the coping strate-gies will essentially vanish. To test this hypothesis, we conducted another series of regressions, again using each of the MASQ scales as a separate criterion with the Neuroticism/Negative Emotionality markers entered first, followed by the Extraversion/Positive Emotionality scales, and then the relevant COPE scales.

These analyses again demonstrated the enormous predictive power of Neuroticism/Negative Emotionality: Across the four criteria, it contributed between 24% and 51% of the criterion variance, with a mean value of approximately 38%. As in the earlier analyses, Extraversion/Positive Emotionality added substantially only to the prediction of Anhedonic Depression (an additional 23%). In these analyses, however, it is the COPE scales that are the most interesting. After controlling for general individual differences, the combined COPE scales made statistically significant—but quite modest—incremental contributions to three of the four MASQ scales, accounting for roughly 3% of the criterion variance in each case. Together with the earlier results, these findings indicate that in comparison to the general traits, coping scales are relatively weak predictors of current distress; moreover, they clearly add little information beyond that already obtainable from measures of Neuroticism/Negative Emotionality and Extraversion/Positive Emotionality.

The single exception to this pattern involved Anxious Arousal, a scale that contains prominent *somatic* manifestations of anxiety (e.g., shortness of breath, dry mouth, feeling dizzy and lightheaded). Here, the combined COPE scales contributed nearly 9% incremental variance. Furthermore, an inspection of the final model indicated that two specific coping strategies—Alcohol-Drug Disengagement and Behavioral Disengagement—contributed significantly to the overall prediction of Anxious Arousal. Of course, these results require replication before they can be interpreted with any confidence. Nevertheless, they tentatively suggest that coping strategies ultimately may prove most interesting in the prediction of *nonaffective* outcomes.

Implications and Conclusions

The Importance of Neuroticism/Negative Emotionality and Extraversion/Positive Emotionality in Understanding Distress and Dysfunction

The accumulating data clearly establish that the general traits of Neuroticism/Negative Emotionality and Extraversion/Positive Emotionality are enormously important predictors of current distress and dysfunction. The findings regarding Neuroticism/Negative Emotionality are particularly striking. Elevated scores on this trait have been linked to a diverse array of psychopathology, including substance use disorders (54–55), somatoform disorders (56), eating disorders (57), personality disorders (58–59), and schizophrenia (60). In the face of this overwhelming evidence, Widiger and Costa (58) recently concluded that Neuroticism/Negative Emotionality "is an almost ubiquitously elevated trait within clinical populations" (p. 81).

As we have seen, Neuroticism/Negative Emotionality shows an especially strong link to depression and anxiety, syndromes that contain a particularly large component of subjective distress (see also 33, 35–36). The data we presented here were entirely cross-sectional, but it is important to note that substantial associations also have been demonstrated prospectively. For instance, Watson and Clark (36) correlated Neuroticism/Negative Emotionality with MASQ scores assessed approximately 10 weeks later. Consistent with the data shown in Table 6.2, Neuroticism/Negative Emotionality was significantly related to all of the MASQ scales, with correlations ranging from .30 (with Anhedonic Depression) to .49 (with GD: Depression). More striking results were reported by Watson and Walker (61), who also found substantial correlations in a sample in which the MASQ was administered six years after assessing Neuroticism/Negative Emotionality.

Other evidence indicates that depression, anxiety, and Neuroticism/Negative Emotionality all may reflect a single underlying diathesis. Jardine, Martin, and Henderson (62) investigated self-reported anxious and depressive symptoms in a large, community based sample of Australian twins. Their analyses indicated that the observed phenotypic covariation between the two types of symptoms was largely due to a single common genetic factor (see also 63). Moreover, subsequent analyses in this same sample revealed that this common genetic factor also was shared with Neuroticism/Negative Emotionality, thereby linking all three phenomena to a single genetic diathesis that apparently represents an underlying vulnerability to subjective distress and negative emotionality.

It is noteworthy that this same basic pattern subsequently has been observed at the diagnostic level. Specifically, analyses consistently have demonstrated that major depression and generalized anxiety disorder are genetically indistinguishable, with a genetic correlation that approaches +1.00 (64–65). Furthermore, replicating results at the symptom level, Kendler, Neale, Kessler, Heath, and Eaves (66) found that this common genetic diathesis was strongly linked to individual differences in Neuroticism/Negative Emotionality. On the basis of these data, Kendler and his colleagues have suggested that this shared genetic factor represents a general tendency to cope poorly with stress and, therefore, to experience frequent and intense episodes of distress and Negative Affect (67–68). Clearly, the Neuroticism/Negative Emotionality dimension must play a key role in any comprehensive understanding of stress, coping, and adaptational outcome.

In comparison, Extraversion/Positive Emotionality appears to have less pervasive implications for research on distress and dysfunction. Nevertheless, diminished levels of Extraversion/Positive Emotionality have been implicated in a variety of disorders, including agoraphobia and posttraumatic stress disorder (55), social phobia (13, 69), eating disorders (57), substance use (55), and schizophrenia (60).

Moreover, as we demonstrated here (see Table 6.2), Extraversion/Positive Emotionality is particularly strongly linked to depression. Indeed, as with Neuroticism/Negative Emotionality, Extraversion/Positive Emotionality has been shown to be a substantial predictor of subsequent depressive symptomatology in prospective, longitudinal designs. For instance, Watson and Clark (36) found that it correlated −.38 with MASQ Anhedonic Depression scores that were assessed 10 weeks later; Watson and Walker (61) reported a corresponding correlation of −.29 across a time span of slightly more than six years.

Furthermore, as in the case of Neuroticism/Negative Emotionality, it appears that Extraversion/Positive Emotionality may share a common underlying diathesis with some forms of mood disorder. In this regard, Depue and his colleagues have argued that (a) individual differences in Extraversion/Positive Emotionality and (b) certain types of mood disorder (such as melancholic depression and bipolar disorder) both reflect variations in an underlying Behavioral Facilitation System (see 70–72). The Behavioral Facilitation System is an appetitive system of behavioral approach that directs organisms toward situations and experiences that may potentially yield pleasure and reward (70, 73). Fowles (73) describes it as "a reward-seeking or approach system that responds to positive incentives by activating behavior" (p. 418). Its adaptive function is to ensure that organisms obtain the resources (e.g., food and water, warmth and shelter, the assistance of others, sexual partners) that are necessary for the survival of both the individual and the species. Because individuals with mood disorder (especially those with melancholic depression) fail to receive sufficient signals of pleasure or reward, however, they show diminished levels of approach behavior and Behavioral Facilitation System activity.

The accumulating evidence indicates that the ascending dopamine system—which arises from cell groups located in the ventral tegmental area of the midbrain and has projections throughout the cortex (72, 74)—mediates various approach-related behaviors within the Behavioral Facilitation System, including heightened appetitive motivation, enhanced behavioral approach to incentive stimuli, and increased engagement with the environment (e.g., 70, 72, 75–77). Moreover, Depue et al. (71) found that various measures of dopaminergic activity were strongly correlated with individual differences in Extraversion/Positive Emotionality, but were unrelated to Neuroticism/Negative Emotionality. Interestingly, Depue et al. (71) noted that "many of the behavioral and hormonal effects of dopamine activation are significantly influenced by genetic variation in dopamine cell number, including those dopamine cell groups in the ventral tegmental area" (p. 486), implicating interindividual variation in the number of dopamine neurons as a possible source for individual differences in Extraversion/Positive Emotionality. This evidence confirms the wisdom of Meehl's (78) conjecture that "some persons [are] born with more cerebral 'joy-juice' than others" (p. 299), as well as the old "Wild West" maxim (quoted by Meehl, 78, p. 298) that "some men are just born three drinks behind."

The Importance of Neuroticism/Negative Emotionality and Extraversion/Positive Emotionality in Research on Adaptation and Coping

In light of the evidence we have reviewed, we believe that the general traits of Neuroticism/Negative Emotionality and Extraversion/Positive Emotionality need to become a more central focus of the coping literature. We have seen, for example, that Neuroticism/Negative Emotionality is significantly related to the initial occurrence of stress, in that it is associated with both (a) the actual frequency of negative life events and (b) negativistic, threat-oriented appraisals of the environment. Moreover, we have amply demonstrated that both Neuroticism/Negative Emotionality and Extraversion/Positive Emotionality are strong predictors of important adaptational outcomes, such as symptoms of depression and anxiety. Furthermore, because these general traits also are systematically related to commonly assessed coping strategies, they represent potentially important third variables that may partly—perhaps even completely—account for the observed relations between coping and outcome.

We would argue, therefore, that these general traits should be routinely assessed in research on stress, coping, and adaptational outcome (see 5, 13, for discussions of the measurement of these traits). Note, moreover, that the simultaneous assessment of both general traits and coping strategies would encourage the development of more complex conceptual models; it also would help to clarify the nature of the links between personality and coping. For instance, as we suggested earlier, our own data are consistent with a weak form of the mediational model in which traits are posited to have both direct and indirect (via coping) influences on outcome. Along these same lines, Bolger (38) reported results indicating that Neuroticism/Negative Emotionality appeared to cause people to cope ineffectively, thereby leading to elevated levels of distress; these findings offer further support for a mediational model. Unfortunately, however, because so few studies have included well-validated measures of both general personality traits and coping strategies, it currently is impossible to specify the nature of these direct and indirect paths with any precision. We hope that the evidence we have presented will stimulate a new generation of research that clarifies the nature of the links among stress, coping, outcome, and the basic traits of personality.

Acknowledgment: We would like to thank Jeff Haig for his help in collecting the data reported in this chapter and C. R. Snyder for his helpful comments on an earlier version of this chapter.

References

1. Suls, J., & Fletcher, B. (1985). The relative efficacy of avoidant and nonavoidant coping strategies: A meta-analysis. *Health Psychology, 4,* 249–288.
2. Lazarus, R., & Folkman, S. (1984: *Stress, appraisal, and coping.* New York: Springer.
3. Costa, P. T., Jr., Somerfield, M. R., & McCrae, R. R. (1996). Personality and coping: A reconceptualization. In M. Zeidner & N. M. Endler (Eds.), *Handbook of coping* (pp. 44–61). New York: Wiley.
4. Suls, J., David, J. P., & Harvey, J. H. (1996). Personality and coping: Three generations of research. *Journal of Personality, 64,* 711–735.
5. Watson, D., & Hubbard, B. (1996). Adaptational style and dispositional structure: Coping in the context of the five-factor model. *Journal of Personality, 64,* 737–774.
6. Ayers, T. S., Sandler, I. N., West, S. G., & Roosa, M. W. (1996). A dispositional and situational assessment of children's coping: Testing alternative models of coping. *Journal of Personality, 64,* 923–958.
7. Carver, C. S., Scheier, M. F., & Weintraub, J. K. (1989). Assessing coping strategies: A theoretically based approach. *Journal of Personality and Social Psychology, 56,* 267–283.
8. Folkman, S., & Lazarus, R. S. (1980). An analysis of coping in a middle-aged community sample. *Journal of Health and Social Behavior, 21,* 219–239.
9. David, J. P. (1997). *Cross-situational consistency and temporal stability of coping behavior and the role of personality.* Unpublished doctoral dissertation, University of Iowa, Iowa City.
10. Diener, E., & Larsen, R. J. (1984). Temporal stability and cross-situational consistency of affective, behavioral, and cognitive responses. *Journal of Personality and Social Psychology, 47,* 871–883.
11. Epstein, S. (1979). The stability of behavior: I. On predicting most of the people much of the time. *Journal of Personality and Social Psychology, 37,* 1097–1126.
12. Watson, D., & Clark, L. A. (1992b). On traits and temperament: General and specific factors of emotional experience and their relation to the five-factor model. *Journal of Personality, 60,* 441–476.
13. Watson, D., Clark, L. A., & Harkness, A. R. (1994). Structures of personality and their relevance to psychopathology. *Journal of Abnormal Psychology, 103,* 18–31.
14. Costa, P. T., Jr., & McCrae, R. R. (1992). *Revised NEO Personality Inventory (NEO-PI-R) and NEO Five-Factor Inventory (NEO-FFI) professional manual.* Odessa, FL: Psychological Assessment Resources.
15. Eysenck, H. J., & Eysenck, S. B. G. (1968). *Manual for the Eysenck Personality Inventory.* San Diego, CA: Educational and Industrial Testing Service.
16. Eysenck, H. J., & Eysenck, S. B. G. (1975). *Manual of the Eysenck Personality Questionnaire.* San Diego, CA: Educational and Industrial Testing Service.

17. Tellegen, A. (1985). Structures of mood and personality and their relevance to assessing anxiety, with an emphasis on self-report. In A. H. Tuma & J. D. Maser (Eds.), *Anxiety and the anxiety disorders* (pp. 681–706). Hillsdale, NJ: Erlbaum.
18. Gough, H. G. (1987). *California Psychological Inventory* [Administrator's guide]. Palo Alto, CA: Consulting Psychologists Press.
19. Watson, D., & Clark, L. A. (1993). Behavioral disinhibition versus constraint: A dispositional perspective. In D. M. Wegner & J. W. Pennebaker (Eds.), *Handbook of mental control* (pp. 506–527). New York: Prentice-Hall.
20. Allport, G. W., & Odbert, H. S. (1936). Trait-names: A psycholexical study. *Psychological Monographs, 47*(1, Whole No. 211).
21. Digman, J. M. (1990). Personality structure: Emergence of the five-factor model. *Annual Review of Psychology, 41,* 417–440.
22. Goldberg, L. R. (1993). The structure of phenotypic personality traits. *American Psychologist, 48,* 26–34.
23. Cattell, R. B. (1945). The principal trait clusters for describing personality. *Psychological Bulletin, 42,* 129–161.
24. Cattell, R. B. (1946). *The description and measurement of personality.* Yonkers-on-Hudson, NY: World Book.
25. Digman, J. M., & Inouye, J. (1986). Further specification of five robust factors of personality. *Journal of Personality and Social Psychology, 50,* 116–123.
26. Norman, W. T., & Goldberg, L. R. (1966). Raters, ratees, and randomness in personality structure. *Journal of Personality and Social Psychology, 4,* 681–691.
27. McCrae, R. R., & Costa, P. T., Jr. (1985). Updating Norman's "adequate taxonomy": Intelligence and personality dimensions in natural language and in questionnaires. *Journal of Personality and Social Psychology, 49,* 710–721.
28. Mayer, J. D., & Gaschke, Y. N. (1988). The experience and meta-experience of mood. *Journal of Personality and Social Psychology, 55,* 102–111.
29. Watson, D. (1988). The vicissitudes of mood measurement: Effects of varying descriptors, time frames, and response formats on measures of Positive and Negative Affect. *Journal of Personality and Social Psychology, 55,* 128–141.
30. Diener, E., Smith, H., & Fujita, F. (1995). The personality structure of affect. *Journal of Personality and Social Psychology, 69,* 130–141.
31. Watson, D., & Tellegen, A. (1985). Toward a consensual structure of mood. *Psychological Bulletin, 98,* 219–235.
32. Watson, D., & Clark, L.A. (1994). *Manual for the Positive and Negative Affect Schedule-Expanded Form.* Unpublished manuscript, University of Iowa, Iowa City.
33. Mineka, S., Watson, D., & Clark, L. A. (1998). Comorbidity of anxiety and unipolar mood disorders. *Annual Review of Psychology, 49,* 377–412.
34. Clark, L. A., & Watson, D. (1991). Tripartite model of anxiety and depression: Psychometric evidence and taxonomic implications. *Journal of Abnormal Psychology, 100,* 316–336.

35. Clark, L. A., Watson, D., & Mineka, S. (1994). Temperament, personality, and the mood and anxiety disorders. *Journal of Abnormal Psychology, 103*, 103–116.
36. Watson, D., & Clark, L. A. (1995). Depression and the melancholic temperament. *European Journal of Personality, 9*, 351–366.
37. McCrae, R. R., & Costa, P. T., Jr. (1986). Personality, coping, and coping effectiveness in an adult sample. *Journal of Personality, 54*, 385–405.
38. Bolger, N. (1990). Coping as a personality process: A prospective study. *Journal of Personality and Social Psychology, 59*, 525–537.
39. Bolger, N., & Zuckerman, A. (1995). A framework for studying personality in the stress process. *Journal of Personality and Social Psychology, 69*, 890–902.
40. Breslau, N. Davis, G. C., & Andreski, P. (1995). Risk factors for PTSD-related traumatic events: A prospective analysis. *American Journal of Psychiatry, 152*, 529–535.
41. Headey, B., & Wearing, A. (1989). Personality, life events, and subjective well-being: Toward a dynamic equilibrium model. *Journal of Personality and Social Psychology, 57*, 731–739.
42. Ormel, J., & Wohlfarth, T. (1991). How neuroticism, long-term difficulties, and life situation change influence psychological distress: A longitudinal model. *Journal of Personality and Social Psychology, 60*, 744–755.
43. Suls, J., Green, P., & Hillis, S. (1998). Emotional reactivity to everyday problems, affective inertia, and neuroticism. *Personality and Social Psychology Bulletin, 24*, 127–136.
44. Costa, P. T., Jr., & McCrae, R. R. (1990). Personality: Another "hidden factor" in stress research. *Psychological Inquiry, 1*, 22–24.
45. Watson, D., & Clark, L. A. (1984). Negative affectivity: The disposition to experience aversive emotional states. *Psychological Bulletin, 96*,465–490.
46. Watson, D., & Pennebaker, J. W. (1989). Health complaints, stress, and distress: Exploring the central role of negative affectivity. *Psychological Review, 96*, 234–254.
47. Marco, C., & Suls, J. (1993). Daily stress and the trajectory of mood: Spillover, response assimilation, and chronic negative affectivity. *Journal of Personality and Social Psychology, 64*, 1053–1063.
48. Endler, N. S., & Parker, J. D. A. (1990). Multidimensional assessment of coping: A critical evaluation. *Journal of Personality and Social Psychology, 58*, 844–854.
49. Hooker, K., Frazier, L. D., & Monahan, D. J. (1994). Personality and coping among caregivers of spouses with dementia. *The Gerontologist, 34*, 386–392.
50. Amirkhan, J. H., Risinger, R. T., & Swickert, R. J. (1995). Extraversion: A "hidden" personality factor in coping? *Journal of Personality, 63*, 189–212.
51. Vickers, R. R., Jr., Kolar, D. W., & Hervig, L. K. (1989). *Personality correlates of coping with military basic training* (Report No. 89–3). San Diego, CA: Naval Health Research Center.

52. Watson, D., & Clark, L. A. (1991). *The Mood and Anxiety Symptom Questionnaire*. Unpublished manuscript, University of Iowa, Iowa City.

53. Baron, R. M., & Kenny, D. A. (1986). The moderator-mediator variable distinction in social psychological research: Conceptual, strategic, and statistical considerations. *Journal of Personality and Social Psychology*, *51*, 1173–1182.

54. Sher, K. J., & Trull, T. J. (1994). Personality and disinhibitory psychopathology: Alcoholism and antisocial personality disorder. *Journal of Abnormal Psychology*, *103*, 92–102.

55. Trull, T. J., & Sher, K. J. (1994). Relationship between the five-factor model of personality and Axis I disorders in a nonclinical sample. *Journal of Abnormal Psychology*, *103*, 350–360.

56. Kirmayer, L. J., Robbins, J. M., & Paris, J. (1994). Somatoform disorders: Personality and the social matrix of somatic distress. *Journal of Abnormal Psychology*, *103*, 125–136.

57. Vitousek, K., & Manke, F. (1994). Personality variables and disorders in anorexia nervosa and bulimia nervosa. *Journal of Abnormal Psychology*, *103*, 137–147.

58. Widiger, T. A., & Costa, P. T., Jr. (1994). Personality and the personality disorders. *Journal of Abnormal Psychology*, *103*, 78–91.

59. Widiger, T. A., & Trull, T. J. (1992). Personality and psychopathology: An application of the five-factor model. *Journal of Personality*, *60*, 363–393.

60. Berenbaum, H., & Fujita, F. (1994). Schizophrenia and personality: Exploring the boundaries and connections between vulnerability and outcome. *Journal of Abnormal Psychology*, *103*, 148–158.

61. Watson, D., & Walker, L. M. (1996). The long-term temporal stability and predictive validity of trait measures of affect. *Journal of Personality and Social Psychology*, *70*, 567–577.

62. Jardine, R., Martin, N. G., & Henderson, A. S. (1984). Genetic covariation between neuroticism and the symptoms of anxiety and depression. *Genetic Epidemiology*, *1*, 89–107.

63. Kendler, K. S., Heath, A. C., Martin, N. G., & Eaves, L. J. (1987). Symptoms of anxiety and symptoms of depression: Same genes, different environments? *Archives of General Psychiatry*, *44*, 451–457.

64. Kendler, K. S. (1996). Major depression and generalised anxiety disorder: Same genes, (partly) different environments—Revisited. *British Journal of Psychiatry*, *168 (Suppl. 30)*, 68–75.

65. Roy, M-A, Neale, M. C., Pedersen, N. L., Mathé, A. A., & Kendler, K. S. (1995). A twin study of generalized anxiety disorder and major depression. *Psychological Medicine*, *25*, 1037–1049.

66. Kendler, K. S., Neale, M. C., Kessler, R. C., Heath, A. C., & Eaves, L. J. (1993). A longitudinal twin study of personality and major depression in women. *Archives of General Psychiatry*, *50*, 853–862.

67. Kendler, K. S., Neale, M. C., Kessler, R. C., Heath, A. C., & Eaves, L. J. (1992). Major depression and generalized anxiety disorder: Same genes, (partly) different environments? *Archives of General Psychiatry*, *49*, 716–722.

68. Kendler, K. S., Walters, E. E., Neale, M. C., Kessler, R. C., Heath, A. C., & Eaves, L. J. (1995). The structure of the genetic and environmental risk factors for six major psychiatric disorders in women: Phobia, generalized anxiety disorder, panic disorder, bulimia, major depression, and alcoholism. *Archives of General Psychiatry, 52,* 374–383.

69. Watson, D., Clark, L. A., & Carey, G. (1988). Positive and negative affectivity and their relation to anxiety and depressive disorders. *Journal of Abnormal Psychology, 97,* 346–353.

70. Depue, R. A., & Iacono, W. G. (1989). Neurobehavioral aspects of affective disorders. *Annual Review of Psychology, 40,* 457–492.

71. Depue, R. A., Krauss, S., & Spoont, M. R. (1987). A two-dimensional threshold model of seasonal bipolar affective disorder. In D. Magnusson & A. Ohman (Eds.), *Psychopathology: An interactional perspective* (pp. 95–123). San Diego: Academic Press.

72. Depue, R. A., Luciana, M., Arbisi, P., Collins, P., & Leon, A. (1994). Dopamine and the structure of personality: Relation of agonist-induced dopamine activity to positive emotionality. *Journal of Personality and Social Psychology, 67,* 485–498.

73. Fowles, D. C. (1987). Application of a behavioral theory of motivation to the concepts of anxiety and impulsivity. *Journal of Research in Personality, 21,* 417–435.

74. Le Moal, M., & Simon, M. (1991). Mesocorticolimbic dopaminergic network: Functional and regulatory roles. *Physiological Reviews, 71,*155–234.

75. Fibiger, H. C., & Phillips, A. G. (1986). Reward, motivation, cognition: Psychobiology of mesotelencephalic dopamine systems. In F. E. Bloom (Ed.), *Handbook of physiology I: The nervous system* (Vol. 4, pp. 647–675). Bethesda, MD: American Physiological Society.

76. Willner, P. (1985). *Depression: A psychobiological synthesis.* New York: Wiley.

77. Wise, R. A., & Rompre, P.-P. (1989). Brain dopamine and reward. *Annual Review of Psychology, 40,* 191–225.

78. Meehl, P. E. (1975). Hedonic capacity: Some conjectures. *Bulletin of the Menninger Clinic, 39,* 295–307.

7

Coping Intelligently

Emotional Intelligence and the Coping Process

Peter Salovey
Brian T. Bedell
Jerusha B. Detweiler
John D. Mayer

Although it can be said that people cope with *life events*, coping is primarily a response to the *emotions*, particularly negative emotions, elicited by these events. This is because the meaningfulness of external events is, to a large extent, a function of their ability to arouse emotion. Of course, not all responses to emotional arousal are equally successful. At one extreme, there are people who consistently have difficulty coping with negative outcomes. These individuals never seem to get over the bad events in their lives. In contrast, there are those who even after the most saddening experience readily bounce back and move forward. These individuals seem almost happy to learn from life's setbacks, and they carry with them a heartening wisdom that inspires others to cope more effectively. What distinguishes the resilient person from the person who seldom copes effectively? The answer, we believe, has to do with emotional competencies—individuals differ in how well they perceive, express, understand, and manage emotional phenomena. These emotional competencies are components of a broader construct we have termed *emotional intelligence*. In this chapter, we will argue, specifically, that emotional intelligence influences responses to emotional arousal and, as a result, plays a significant role in the coping process.

Emotional intelligence involves the ability to monitor one's own and others' feelings and emotions, to regulate them, and to use emotion-based information to guide thinking and action. The competencies involved in emotional intelligence include (a) appraising and expressing emotions in the self and others, (b) assimilating emotion and thought, (c) understanding and analyzing emotions, and (d) regulating emotions to promote emotional and intellectual growth. In this chapter, we will apply the concept of emotional intelligence to the coping process. First, we will review a framework for understanding emotional intelligence and its component competencies. Then, we will describe how emotional intelligence can help us to understand coping strategies such as rumination, the elicitation of social support, and the disclosure of feelings.

The Origins of Emotional Intelligence

Most of us can think of individuals who seem to have considerable analytic intelligence—the skills measured by most intelligence tests—who nonetheless have great difficulty succeeding in their personal relationships or at work. It is clear that more is needed to succeed in life than possessing what psychologists have traditionally called "intelligence" (i.e., reasoning and analytical abilities in verbal and performance domains). Various nonintellectual characteristics may contribute to performance, including achievement motivation, self-efficacy, and other traits. Even in the realm of intelligence, however, there are other skills not tapped by traditional verbal and performance measures that clearly have something to do with emotions such as empathy, understanding the impact of one's behavior on other people's emotions, and the ability to regulate feelings. Some individuals may be high in emotional intelligence, others uniformly low, but a third, equally interesting, group shows great abilities on some aspects of emotional intelligence but profound deficits in others.

American psychology—like psychology in much of the rest of the world—has had a long tradition of considering thinking and feeling as polar opposites. On the one hand, there is *passion*, but on the other hand, *reason*. And traditionally, passion has not been thought of as something that assists reason. One traditional view of emotions in Western thought characterizes them as chaotic, haphazard, irrational, and immature. This view is reflected in the writings of classic scholars of 2000 years ago as well as the authors of American textbooks in psychology in the present century. For example, writing in the first century, B.C., Publilius Syrus exclaimed, "Rule your feelings, lest your feelings rule you." Similar sentiments can be found in many psychology textbooks of the twentieth century as well. For instance, P.T. Young (1, 2) described emotions as causing "a complete loss of cerebral control" and containing "no trace of conscious purpose" (pp. 457–458). Moreover, according to Young, emotions represent an "acute disturbance of the individual as a whole" (2, p. 263). Similar ideas can be found in a popular text by L. F. Schaffer and his colleagues (3), who noted that emotions are "a disorganized response, largely visceral, resulting from the lack of an effective adjustment" (p. 505).

Our view is that emotion and intelligence are not mutually contradictory. Rather, the emotional intelligence approach argues that emotions are adaptive and functional, and that they serve to organize cognitive activities and subsequent behavior—the passions *can* serve reason. This idea was captured by two early experimental psychologists, Robert Leeper and O. H.

Mowrer. In an influential and often-quoted paper, Leeper (4) noted that emotions "arouse, sustain, and direct activity" (p. 17). Mowrer (5) went one step further in claiming that "the emotions are of quite extraordinary importance in the total economy of living organisms and do not deserve being put into opposition with 'intelligence.' The emotions are, it seems, themselves a higher order of intelligence" (p. 308).

What is the source for the idea that emotions are a higher order of intelligence? We would argue that this perspective originated with Sir Charles Darwin, who in 1872, authored his classic book, *The Expression of Emotions in Man and Animal.* Darwin (6) argued that emotions are intelligent for two reasons: (a) they energize behavior that is required in certain situations (e.g., it is easier, if you are an animal in the wild, to run away when you feel fear than when you feel joy), and (b) they involve a signaling and communication system that has survival value for the other members of a species (e.g., the bared teeth of an angry face signal to others that an attack is imminent). Humans, of course, make use of this signaling system as well. For example, an infant will approach an unusual toy if he or she looks at mother and mother smiles, but will back away from the toy if mother looks fearful. If mother wears no particular facial expression (known as the "still face"), the infant may act quite distressed. For both animals and humans, this process is called *social referencing,* and it is an example of the intelligent use of emotional expressions.

Of course, more recent writers also have captured this idea that our emotions can be intelligent. A prominent example is Howard Gardner, who has identified the *intrapersonal intelligences* as one of seven areas of competence in his *multiple intelligences* perspective. In his book, *Frames of Mind*, Gardner (7) includes in the definition of intrapersonal intelligences "access to one's own feeling life—one's range of affects or emotions: the capacity instantly to effect discriminations among these feelings . . . label them . . . enmesh them in symbolic codes . . . and draw upon them as a mean of understanding and guiding one's behavior" (p. 239). Clearly, although the phrase *emotional intelligence* had not been used before 1990, the idea of an emotional intelligence has some history in psychological thought.

The Emotional Intelligence Framework

In 1990, two of the authors of this chapter (8) published a paper titled, simply, "Emotional Intelligence," in which we first described a framework for understanding the competencies involved in this domain. This framework emphasized competencies relevant to appraising and expressing emotions, regulating emotions, and using emotions in thought, in problem-solving, and to motivate behavior. We defined emotional intelligence at that time as "the ability to monitor one's own and others' feelings and emotions, to discriminate among them, and to use this information to guide one's thinking and actions" (p. 189).

In more recent work (9), we have refined this definition somewhat and have arrived at a model of emotional intelligence that includes four essential components:

1. Perception, appraisal, and expression of emotion.
2. Emotional facilitation of thinking.
3. Understanding and analyzing emotions; using emotional knowledge.
4. Adaptive regulation of emotion.

Appraisal and expression include both verbal and nonverbal behavior. First, we need to understand what we are feeling, and we need to be able to communicate our feelings using words and nonverbal expressions. Moreover, we need to understand the feelings of other people—both in their words and in their expressions. And, we need to be able to feel the emotions of other people, that is, to empathize with them. Second, we must recognize that emotions prioritize thinking, shape memory, create different problem-solving perspectives, and facilitate creativity. Third, to make use of our emotions, we must have a rich emotional vocabulary, and we must be able to understand emotional nuances, blends of feelings, and transitions from one emotion to another. Finally, we need to learn to regulate our emotions so that they are most appropriate to the task or situation at hand, and we need to learn to regulate the emotions of other people, to cheer them up when they are down, to engage them when we want them to listen to us. Although these skills are generally desirable, emotional intelligence should not be equated with character or morality. Emotional skills can also be used toward nefarious ends: sociopaths, for example, can be especially skilled at regulating the emotions of other people (10, 11).

What do we mean when we say that one can use emotions adaptively to help in problem solving and reasoning? A number of investigators (e.g., 12, 13) have argued that emotions create different mental sets that are more or less adaptive for solving certain kinds of problems. That is, different emotions create different information-processing styles. Happy moods facilitate a mental set that is useful for creative tasks in which one must think intuitively or expansively in order to make novel associations. Sad moods generate a mental set in which problems are solved more slowly with particular attention to detail using more focused and deliberate strategies. Palfai and Salovey argued that these two different information-processing styles (i.e., intuitive and expansive versus focused and deliberate) should be effective for two different kinds of problem-solving tasks—inductive problems like analogical reasoning and deductive logical tasks, respectively.

In order to test this idea, Palfai and Salovey (12) induced happy and sad moods in groups of college students by asking them to watch emotionally evocative films. They then asked them to solve analogical or deductive reasoning problems. The happy students were faster in solving the inductive (analogical) problems, and the sad students were faster in solving the deductive problems. These results indicate that certain kinds of moods make it easier to solve certain kinds of problems. The truly emotionally intelligent person may be aware of this phenomenon and may be able to adjust his or her mood accordingly. For instance, one of the authors of this chapter has difficulty writing scientific papers when he is "too" happy, and he often calms himself before starting a writing project by listening to sad music.

Attempts to Measure Emotional Intelligence

Although a great deal has been learned about the measurement of emotional intelligence over the past few years, there is still much work to be done. A valid measure of core emotional intelligence likely requires multidimensional instruments that rely on tasks and exercises rather than on self-report. Mayer, Caruso, and Salovey (14; see also 15) have developed a Multidimensional Emotional Intelligence Scale (MEIS) that relies on pencil-and-paper or computer-based emotion-related tasks rather than self-assessments. Some of the tasks included on the MEIS involve identifying the consensual feelings suggested by colors, abstract artistic designs, and pieces of music. In a study we did some years ago, the ability to identify the emotions suggested by colors and artistic designs correlated with traditional ratings of empathy (16). We have been refining our measurement techniques, examining such issues as reporting styles of emotions, alternative methods of assessing correct responses, and new tasks to measure emotional intelligence (17). The MEIS represents the culmination of this work.

Even before pursuing ability measures of emotional intelligence, we had been developing self-report measures of certain aspects of emotionally intelligent processes. The first three levels of emotional intelligence (perception, facilitation of thinking, and understanding) are generally best measured with ability tasks. The final level, which involves management and regulation, can benefit from the associated use of self-report measures for several reasons (see also 18). First, psychologists have come late to studying self-management of emotion, and it is important to understand such issues as the kinds of self-management people engage in, the relation between self-management and emotion, and the potential benefits and drawbacks of self-management. To accomplish this, we began examining the meta-, or reflective, experience of mood (19). Presently, there are two scales that we employ that represent meta-experience: one is a trait scale (20), and the other is a state scale (21). The remainder of this chapter examines some of the findings and implications emerging from this program research.

A Hierarchy of Emotional Coping

The importance of meta-mood skills and processes perhaps becomes most apparent under conditions of stress and coping, when individuals are forced to respond to emotions elicited by external events. To facilitate the application of emotional intelligence to the coping process, we have designed a hierarchy of emotional competencies that includes those components of emotional intelligence most relevant to coping. The Emotional Coping Hierarchy, depicted in Figure 7.1, describes three levels of emotional intelligence. On the first level are the basic emotional skills of perception, appraisal, and expression. On the second level are the two more sophisticated subcomponents of emotional knowledge: understanding and analysis. The third level of the hierarchy is reserved for emotional regulation. We believe that the *entire* hierarchy of emotional coping skills must be sufficiently developed and employed for successful coping to take place. A weakness lower in the hierarchy will interfere with more sophisticated skills and as a result will stall the coping process.

In one study, we have investigated the hypothesis that adapting successfully to a stressful experience depends, in part, on the capacity to attend to, discriminate among, and regulate feelings. Goldman, Kraemer, and Salovey (22) conducted a prospective study examining whether beliefs about one's moods, in particular, the belief that one can repair negative moods, are related to physical health complaints. The reasoning behind this study was that individuals who cannot repair or regulate their feelings may look to others for help in doing so. As a result, they may be more likely to seek the attention of a physician when they are feeling stressed because they do not know how to regulate these feelings themselves. Such individuals may simply be using the health care system as a mood regulation strategy. Of course, it is also possible that these individuals are actually more likely to become physically ill when under stress.

Goldman et al. (22) assessed 134 student volunteers at three different times during the semester: at the start of the year, during midterm examinations, and during final examinations. At these times, we administered the Trait Meta-Mood Scale (TMMS) as well as measures of stress, physical

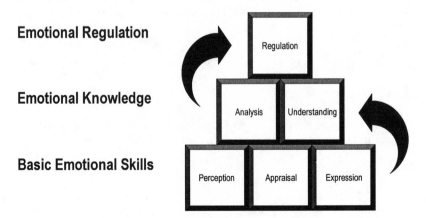

Figure 7.1. The Emotional Coping Hierarchy.

symptoms, and health center visits. When we divided the sample into three groups of people (those with a high degree of skill in repairing negative moods, those with average skills in this area, and those with low skills), interesting trends in health center visits emerged, depending on the level of stress people experienced. When stress was low, the three groups differed very little. But, as stress increased, those individuals who said that they cannot easily regulate their feelings were more likely to visit the health center, and those individuals who were good at repairing negative moods actually visited the health center less often.

Emotional Intelligence and the Coping Process

To date, few empirical studies have been carried out specifically focused on the impact of emotional intelligence on coping. Although we believe that emotional intelligence plays an important role in coping processes, little direct empirical evidence exists to support our claim. However, to facilitate our argument that the components of emotional intelligence are related to coping skills, we will discuss the links between emotional intelligence and three processes currently believed to be linked with coping skills: rumination, social support, and the disclosure of traumas.

Ruminative Coping

The experience of stressors is an unavoidable part of life. However, individuals differ substantially in how they respond to these stressors. One of the most natural responses to a stressful event is to spend time thinking about it. Some people give very little thought to such events, others give too much. Those people who are inclined to think excessively about the stressful event are said to be engaged in ruminative coping. Rumination is defined as "passively and repetitively focusing on one's symptoms of distress and the circumstances surrounding those symptoms" (23). Characteristics of ruminative coping include focusing on the symptoms of depressed mood, worrying that one will never feel better, and being unable to understand why one is feeling depressed. Caught up in ruminative thoughts, the individual often isolates herself from others. The current conceptualization of rumination is derived from Nolen-Hoeksema's (24) response styles theory of depression. The response styles theory suggests that people establish patterns of responding to depressed mood, and that these styles determine the success with which they will cope with depressive symptoms. Rumination, as a style of coping, tends to intensify and lengthen periods of depressed mood and, in turn, leads to greater difficulties in coping.

A number of laboratory and field studies have explored the association between ruminative coping and depression. These studies have supported the prediction that rumination maintains depressed moods, whereas distraction (i.e., focusing on external stimuli) can lead to a decrease in negative affect. In one study, for example, participants who engaged in a ruminative task showed maintenance of an induced negative mood, whereas participants who were led through an engaging distraction task were able to ameliorate their depressed mood (25). In the field, Nolen-Hoeksema and Morrow (26) explored the effect of ruminative coping following the 1990 Loma Prieta earthquake in California. They found that people who had a more ruminative response style before the earthquake exhibited higher levels of depression 10 days after the event. More recently, Nolen-Hoeksema, McBride, and Larson (23) found that newly bereaved men who had demonstrated greater tendencies toward ruminative coping before their loss experienced longer and more severe periods of depression after their partner's death. These are but a few of the studies that lend support to the hypothesis that rumination is a maladaptive coping strategy. In other words, individuals inclined to ruminate are apt to experience more intense and longer-lasting periods of depression when faced with stressors and, as a result, they do not cope effectively.

Given what we know about the relationship between rumination and coping, where does emotional intelligence fit in? The most basic component of emotional intelligence is the ability to appraise and express emotions accurately. This component involves the ability to recognize emotions within oneself and to identify accurately what one is feeling. This also encompasses the ability to express and articulate one's feelings and to define what these feelings mean (9). People tend to vary with respect to how much attention they give to emotions and, in turn, the clarity with which they perceive their moods. Ruminative responses to depressed mood have been described as "a type of self-focused attention, an emotion-focused attention" (27, p. 332). Using vocabulary from the emotional intelligence literature, we would argue that individuals who ruminate are those who exhibit tendencies to focus *excessively* on the perception and appraisal of their mood states. This excessive amount of attention may be motivated, in part, by an inability to make sense of one's emotional experience and the need for some kind of meaning-making activity (cf. 28, 29). Although a moderate amount of attention to one's mood may be both adaptive and advantageous, high levels of attention may, in fact, be counterproductive in the act of coping.

We believe that successful processing of intrusive thoughts may depend on skills related to the activation, experience, and modification of feelings. Salovey et al. (20) examined the relation of individual differences in beliefs about attention to, clarity, and regulation of feelings (as measured by the Trait Meta-Mood Scale) to sustained negative affect and the intensity, insistency, controllability, and negativity of ruminative thoughts that followed a distressing stimulus. In this study, we asked 78 student volunteers to come to the laboratory and told them that they would be participating in two studies, one involving watching television and a second one on the stream of consciousness. First, a film clip was presented. The video clip was a 12-minute segment of a documentary on drinking and driving. The film contained graphic footage of serious automobile accidents and the emergency room/hospital sequences that followed. Victims also described the nature of their traumas.

At this point, the experimenter described the supposed purpose of the "second experiment" and the rationale of the thought sampling procedure. The instructions asked subjects to (a) focus on whatever thoughts, feelings, and images they were experiencing at the time of a prearranged signal, (b) jot down a few select words to describe the thought on a page in a thought sampling record, and (c) answer the questions that appeared on the bottom of each page with regard to the recorded thought. Four items were included at the bottom of each page that asked subjects to rate the positiveness, intensity, insistency, and controllability of their recorded thoughts.

Watching the drunk driving film had a powerful impact on mood. Our participants reported relatively high levels of positive mood before the film, but mood reports just after the film dropped substantially. In addition, recovery of positive mood by the end of the experiment (after the thought sampling task) was best predicted by the Clarity subscale of the Trait Meta-Mood Scale (TMMS). Those individuals who reported that they were usually very clear about their feelings were more likely to rebound from the induced negative mood.

To analyze the ruminative nature of the thought samples, participants were divided into three groups based on their scores on the Clarity subscale of the TMMS. Those individuals whose scores fell into the upper quartile were considered to possess high emotional clarity. Those who scored in the lower quartile were considered to possess low clarity. Scores for the remaining subjects were classified in the average range. Individuals who experienced their moods clearly showed a reduction in their negative thoughts over time. The average and low Clarity individuals, in contrast, continued to ruminate. Thus, it appears that individuals who reported being very clear about their feelings experienced a significant decline in ruminative thought over time when compared to individuals who reported being unclear about their moods. These results support our hypothesis that clarity in discriminating feelings is important in mood repair following a negative and/or stressful event.

Swinkels and Giuliano (30) conducted a similar series of studies on the monitoring and labeling of mood states. These researchers describe mood monitoring as the tendency to focus attention on one's mood and to scrutinize one's mood state, analogous to the Attention subscale of the TMMS. They define mood labeling as the ability to identify and give a name to the mood that is being experienced, a construct very much like the Clarity subscale of the TMMS. They suggest that mood monitoring allows a person to track the progress of his or her moods. However, they note that mood monitoring may not always be productive. Although general awareness of one's moods is adaptive, when the process of mood monitoring becomes more extreme or vigilant, it may be harmful to the individual's emotional well-being. Mood labeling is different from mood monitoring in that being able to label a mood suggests that the individual has reached some degree of understanding of the mood itself. In a sense, the act of mood labeling allows the individual to identify the mood and use what is known about the mood to help carry out future thoughts and behaviors.

In their investigation of mood monitoring and labeling, Swinkels and Giuliano (30) found support for their hypothesis that mood monitoring (i.e., attention to negative emotions) leads to greater rumination than does mood labeling. They found that higher scores on a measure of mood monitoring were significantly related to a greater amount of ruminative thinking displayed in free responses to questions such as, "List some of the specific strategies that you use to cheer yourself up" (30). Scores on a measure of mood labeling, however, were not predictive of rumination. These findings converge with those of our study (20), in which depression was shown to be correlated with high attention to emotions but low clarity in discriminating feelings. Recall that Salovey et al. (20) found that clarity predicted the recovery of a positive mood following a stressful event induced in the laboratory. Furthermore, individuals who reported that they were able to experience feelings more clearly tended to show a decrease in ruminative thought over time. Gaining emotional clarity appears to aid the individual in breaking out of a ruminative cycle.

Together, these studies suggest that excessive attention to negative moods leads to rumination, but that clarity in labeling one's feelings short-circuits ruminative processes. This ruminative process, if it is not kept in check, may maintain negative moods and hinder the coping process. Thus, it is not attention, per se, that is maladaptive. Instead, it is the inability to find clarity and understanding that leads to poor coping. Gaining clarity and labeling one's emotions are critical first steps in enabling a person to repair a negative mood state (30).

Successfully monitoring and appraising one's mood does not, however, forge a direct path to a healthy resolution of the coping process. When an individual comes to recognize that his or her experience of negative emotionality has reached the point of diminishing returns, he or she must begin regulating the experience. As Nolen-Hoeksema and colleagues have demonstrated, brooding over failures and drowning in sorrows leads only to greater depression. A healthier strategy would be to control more carefully how one thinks about a negative life event and to choose to act or think in ways that would help one feel better. This strategy comprises the component of emotional intelligence referred to as regulation, or the ability to engage reflectively or detach from an emotion depending upon its informativeness or utility (9). Adaptive regulation of emotion should play a central role in the process of coping more generally and the experience of rumination more specifically. Emotionally intelligent individuals should be more adept at directing their thoughts away from uninformative negative emotions.

Nolen-Hoeksema and Morrow have argued that one of the most effective approaches for disengaging from a ruminative coping cycle is distraction

(25, 31). People who are trapped in a ruminative coping process are likely to think about and focus on their negative moods without doing anything to relieve their symptoms (23). Negative moods that are maintained by ruminations appear to interfere with the individual's ability to engage in successful problem solving (32). Individuals who are skilled at regulating emotions, however, should be better able to move to repair their emotional state. Lyubomirsky and Nolen-Hoeksema (32) demonstrated that when people use pleasant activities to relieve their moods, they show better problem-solving skills and fewer negative thoughts. The ability to manage emotions in oneself by moderating negative emotions and enhancing pleasant ones is considered one of the most advanced skills within the reflective regulation of emotion (9).

Engaging in distraction is different, however, from avoiding negative affect all together. A careful balance between the experience of the emotion and the use of distraction must be reached in order to achieve successful coping. An additional component of reflective regulation is the ability to understand emotions without exaggerating or minimizing their importance (9). An emotionally intelligent individual must be able to determine when it is appropriate to engage in distraction behaviors and what types of distraction behaviors have functional value. An emotionally intelligent strategy would be to take advantage of opportunities for *healthy* distraction, such as seeking out others for social support. Nolen-Hoeksema suggests that the more socially isolated a person is, the more opportunities there will be to ruminate. Indeed, the availability of high quality social support, among other things, may influence the individual's tendency to ruminate (24). The role of emotional intelligence in the development and use of social support is discussed in the next section.

Social Support

As we have begun to see in the discussion of rumination, social support appears to play a critical role in successful and healthy coping. To be sure, the literature on social support and coping is vast, and the resounding conclusion is that social support has a direct and immediate impact on one's ability to cope with stressors (see 33 for a review). We would like to argue that emotionally intelligent individuals are more likely to gain access to rich social support networks and that they are more likely to rely on these networks during times of stress.

Researchers have described two ways that social support benefits individuals: directly and as a buffer against the effects of stressful life events (34, 35). The direct effects hypothesis suggests that social support enhances mental and physical health regardless of the amount of stress present in a person's life. The buffering hypothesis, on the other hand, suggests that social support intervenes between the stressful event and the stress experience; social support helps the individual avoid stress-elicited health problems. Research indicates that both hypotheses are valid—social support has

positive direct and buffering effects on psychological adjustment to stressful events, recovery from illnesses, and even mortality risk (36, 37, 38, 39).

The health-enhancing consequences of social support were illustrated
by Spiegel et al. (40), who followed women diagnosed with breast cancer
for one year and found that patients who were randomly assigned to a
cancer support group reported significantly more energy, less tension, less
confusion, less fatigue, and fewer ineffective or maladaptive coping strategies. These findings have been replicated by other investigators (e.g., 41,
42). Similarly, a review of 26 longitudinal studies found that being married
(a powerful source of social support) is negatively related to mortality and
to the recurrence of symptoms in myocardial infarction and coronary artery
disease patients (43). Social support also is important for those who are not
themselves sick, but who care for the sick or elderly. Better caregiver well-
being has been associated with greater social support and activity (44, 45).
And finally, social support has a direct effect on the immune system. Researchers have found that the cellular immune response system is sup-
pressed in lonely individuals (46, 47), and at least one study has provided
direct evidence that the feelings of belonging and security brought about
by social support facilitate the recovery of sick individuals by mobilizing
their immune systems (48). These findings convincingly demonstrate that
social support critically influences the effectiveness with which individuals cope.

We would argue that emotional intelligence predicts whether individuals will have developed a strong social network, and whether they will
seek out social support during times of great stress. Along these lines, social
support researchers have speculated that individuals differ in their utilization of social support. That is, some people may be better able to develop
and utilize social support networks (49). Consider, for example, the development of social support networks among children. Parenting has a strong
effect on a child's social engagement. Kahen and colleagues (50) have found
that when fathers are emotionally volatile, their children's play tends to be
disengaged. But when fathers are warm and emotionally responsive, their
children exhibit more self-disclosure during play. Similarly, children who
openly express positive feelings toward their peers more often have emotionally communicative mothers (50). As a result of parenting, then, it is
likely that a child develops a style of social interaction that either facilitates
or undermines the development of a strong social support network. The
consequences of having or lacking social support can be substantial. In one
study, how children were perceived socially by their peers in the third
grade was a better predictor of mental health problems over the next 11
years than grade-point averages, IQ scores, teachers ratings, absenteeism,
and nurses' ratings of physical health (51). Furthermore, children who report the most loneliness tend to be those who are viewed as less prosocial
and more aggressive by both teachers and peers, and young children who
are rejected by their peers are significantly more lonely than other children
(52).

We believe that children's development of social support illustrates the role of emotional intelligence in this area. Specifically, children learn from role models how to process and regulate emotional information and experiences. The emotional intelligence that emerges from this learning process influences how a child interacts with her peers, which determines how successful she will be at developing a supportive group of friends (9). Gottman and his colleagues have made a similar point in their research on meta-emotion (53). They find that parents' awareness of their own sadness and tendencies to coach their children about their anger have a considerable impact on children's emotion regulation abilities. At age five, children whose parents possess these meta-emotional abilities show less negative play styles and physiological distress. At age eight, these same children show fewer behavioral problems, higher academic achievement in mathematics and reading, and better physical health. Thus, when emotionally intelligent behavior is modeled, children are better equipped to form essential social ties. As we have discussed, these social ties have positive direct effects and will provide a buffer against stress and negative life events.

Of course, emotional intelligence influences adults' social skills and relationships as well. For example, we have argued elsewhere (54) that people who help others may be more likely to receive social support later when they need it. Ironically, this suggests that altruism can be used as a means of emotional self-regulation—individuals who help others may incur the short-term costs of helping in order to build their long-term social resources. Those who are skilled at such a strategy are more likely to work well within a social network and to acquire and maintain close relationships. As a result, they are more likely to benefit from the positive effects of social support, especially when they are attempting to cope with a negative event. Clearly, many people have good social support networks. It seems possible, however, that emotionally intelligent individuals will be more likely to build, maintain, and rely on social networks because of their skills. Emotional intelligence not only enables individuals to build solid social ties, but it also enables them to recognize the emotional benefits of utilizing their social networks in times of stress. Thus, emotionally intelligent individuals should be more likely to seek out their family (if not too toxic) and form and maintain friendships as a means of coping because they understand how important emotional sharing and support is in the coping process.

To summarize, emotional intelligence equips individuals with many of the skills that are needed to build solid and supportive social networks. Understanding that social support provides an emotional buffer against stressful events, these individuals will be more likely to utilize their social resources throughout the coping process. As a result, emotionally intelligent individuals are more likely to experience negative life events against a backdrop of social resources.

Emotional Disclosure

The importance of disclosing emotional experiences as part of the coping process was foreshadowed in our discussions of rumination and social support. Reaching out for social support characterizes effective coping. Internalizing emotions through ruminative thinking does not. Pennebaker (see chapter 4 in this volume) has studied the effects of emotional disclosure extensively and finds that the simple act of disclosing emotional experiences in writing, even anonymously, improves individuals' subsequent physical and mental health (see 61 for a review). For instance, students assigned to write about a traumatic emotional experience subsequently made fewer health center visits and received higher grades than students assigned to write about a trivial topic (e.g., 55, 56). The benefits of emotional disclosure also include broadly enhanced immunological functioning (e.g., 57), and many studies have observed decreases in self-reported physical symptoms, distress, and depression (e.g., 58; cf. 57, 59). These impressive findings have proved robust across dozens of studies conducted by several investigators and among such disparate populations as college students, maximum security prisoners, and recently unemployed professionals (see 60 for a meta-analysis).

How exactly does writing or talking about negative life events facilitate coping? The answer to this question is not entirely clear. However, Pennebaker (61) offers two possible models of disclosure's underlying mechanism. The *inhibition model of psychosomatics* is drawn from both psychodynamic and psychophysiological theorizing and research. This model suggests that inhibition is a form of stressful, physiological work that burdens and hence impairs both physical and mental health. Emotional disclosure lifts the burden of inhibition and thus improves health. The *cognitive changes model*, on the other hand, emphasizes the benefits of cognitive housekeeping. The individual's thoughts and feelings about a traumatic experience become progressively more organized through repeated disclosures. This cognitive housekeeping is essential because traumatic life events dramatically alter our experiences of the world—they may leave us victimized, on our own, terminally ill, or otherwise vulnerable. The individual must struggle to restructure his or her view of the world in order to assimilate such changes. The disclosure of traumas facilitates this process. Through the structure of language, disturbing experiences become more coherent and are given a meaningful place in the individual's world. The mind thus adapts and moves on less cluttered.

Although the inhibition model is theoretically consistent with the beneficial effects of disclosure, evidence linking emotional disclosure to decreases in inhibition (and, in turn, to improved health) is lacking. In contrast, the cognitive changes model is consistent with related research and is quickly gaining direct empirical support of its own. Consider, for instance, Wegner's work on ironic processes (e.g., 62), which has shown that attempts to inhibit a thought actually increase the availability of that thought. This ironic result presumably occurs because the repressed thought is maintained in order to determine how successful the act of repression has been. Wegner's research suggests that repression of a traumatic experience would only serve to maintain thoughts of the experience. This conclusion is consistent with the cognitive changes model—even if a person tries to repress a traumatic experience, the experience will continue to challenge the thoughts and feelings until it is resolved adequately. Added support for the cognitive changes model comes from Pennebaker and his colleagues (63, 64), who have provided convincing evidence that specific cognitive changes mediate the benefits of emotional disclosure. Written disclosures characterized by increased insight and causal thinking are most apt to lead to improved physical health. Similarly, health improves most when individuals use the appropriate balance of emotion words in disclosing traumas (i.e., a moderate amount of negative emotion words accompanied by a greater amount of positive emotion words). These contingencies make it clear that a person must confront, make sense of, and integrate a trauma in order to cope effectively.

Emotional intelligence is closely related to aspects of personality involving openness to experience and the repression of thoughts and feelings. It is not surprising, then, that we can apply the emotional intelligence framework to emotional disclosure. Individuals must be able to recognize that they are experiencing emotions that require a response. Those who are unable to perceive and appraise their own emotional states accurately may fail to recognize the origin of their troubles. If so, the coping process will stall, precluding effective emotional disclosure. In our own work, individuals open to emotional experience (even when negative) report lower levels of depression than those who claim to "fight the feeling" or that "everything is okay" (65).

Beyond this basic level, and more particular to emotional disclosure, are how emotional knowledge and the ability to regulate emotion can facilitate disclosure. We believe that the linguistic features characterizing effective emotional disclosure (i.e., insight, causal thinking, and a balance of emotion) reflect a person's ability to understand, analyze, and actively regulate their emotions. Insight and causal thinking are associated with the understanding and analysis of the emotions surrounding traumatic experiences. People who are able to recognize their emotional responses to a trauma as natural, who can see the trauma and their emotions in the broader context of their lives, and who can make positive attributions about the trauma and their emotions must have a strong sense of what emotions are and how emotions arise from life experiences and, more important, from one's construal of these experiences. Compared to those who continue to be overwhelmed by their negative life experiences, these emotionally intelligent individuals are more likely to cope effectively. They are more likely to engage in the disclosure process through personal writing (e.g., diaries, journals) and through sharing their thoughts and feelings with friends and family simply because they have the emotional knowledge to do so effectively. Moreover, emotional knowledge should motivate emotional disclosure to begin with, especially when it is understood that writing or sharing is an efficient means of organizing and, thus, regulating one's emotions.

Pennebaker's findings complement the research on rumination by demonstrating that the outward, linguistic expression of traumatic experiences facilitates the coping process. Similarly, Pennebaker has observed that individuals naturally turn to others in order to discuss and make sense of negative life events (66), a point that acknowledges that disclosure is more often social than anonymous. Thus, emotional disclosure is closely tied to social support as well as rumination. Recognizing that these three aspects of coping are interrelated helps define the coping process. For example, a person's social support network, if it is strong, should prevent rumination by inviting the disclosure of negative emotional experiences. We believe that the framework of emotional intelligence further illuminates the interrelationship of these aspects of coping and, in doing so, further defines the coping process. Specifically, the perspective of emotional intelligence is that individuals have skills that enable them to avoid rumination, build and utilize social support, and effectively disclose traumas. In the final section of this chapter, we discuss how the framework of emotional intelligence can be used as a guide to intervene in the coping process, and we further illustrate the common emotional competencies that we believe underlie these aspects of coping.

The Application of Emotional Intelligence

Readers may ask at this point whether the framework of emotional intelligence can be used to intervene to enhance the coping process. Clinicians may wonder if it serves as a useful guide to assessing and treating their clients' reactions to negative life events. Individuals who are having difficulty coping may wonder if they are handling their emotions "intelligently." These are questions worth asking. Indeed, we are optimistic about both clinical and personal applications of emotional intelligence. Yet, we feel uneasy about recent claims touting emotional intelligence as the comprehensive solution to a variety of psychosocial problems, from ineffective managerial styles to inner-city turmoil (e.g., 67). Emotional intelligence is certainly no cure-all. Nonetheless, the framework of emotional intelligence appears to be a promising means of addressing some of life's problems. We envision it as a tool that can help us understand ourselves better, those around us, and the challenges we face. With this caveat in mind, we advocate the judicious application of this tool to instances of problematic coping.

At the very least, individuals and clinicians may benefit simply because the framework of emotional intelligence calls greater attention to the importance of *emotional competencies*. Sufficient attention is already paid to emotion, but the attention is largely unfocused and dismissive. Emotions often are viewed as renegade mental states that must be reigned in by reason, otherwise, our emotions will "run away with us." When we separate emotion and reason in this way, setting them at opposition, we fail to appreciate their subtle interrelationship. Emotions are not renegade mental states. Rather, they serve as a compelling and rational source of information about one's surroundings and inner states, and they play an important role as motivators (4). The significance of emotion, both informationally and motivationally, clarifies the relationship between emotion and reason. It is much more of an alliance than a conflict. The framework of emotional intelligence acknowledges this by refocusing the attention paid to emotion on the emotional competencies involved in negotiating the emotion-reason alliance. Some clinical perspectives are already quite compatible with this view (e.g., 68), attitudes that are less dismissive with respect to emotional competence are creeping into other schools of therapy as well.

Although calling greater attention to emotional competencies is a good first step, we originally proposed the framework of emotional intelligence in order to enumerate and describe *specific* emotional competencies. Indeed, we believe the framework's greatest strength is that it establishes a hierarchy of emotional competencies (69). The Emotional Coping Hierarchy should serve as a guide to pinpointing where the process of coping breaks down (i.e., at the level of basic emotional competencies, emotional knowledge, or emotional regulation). Of course, a great deal of empirical work still needs to be carried out, but it is not difficult to imagine how we would apply this framework. For example, imagine that you are acquainted with the following person.

Carol is a writer. She has made a career out of her writing and has little trouble publishing in national magazines and newspapers. She is admired in the profession and has been described as creative, insightful, inspired, and thought-provoking. Carol does most of her writing at home and finds her greatest inspiration in the winter-time, writing in front of the fireplace. Her closest companion and friend is Percy, her dog, who Carol has had since her writing career began over seven years ago.

Late one evening, after eight grueling hours of work, Carol decides to run to the grocery store and treat herself to a midnight snack. She returns one hour later to find her home surrounded by firetrucks and engulfed in flames. Already, the damage is irreparable. Her home has been completely destroyed. Among her lost possessions is a collection of writings, including the only copy of what would have been her first full-length novel. Far worse, Carol learns that the fire and emergency crew arrived too late to save Percy. Her previously fulfilling life has been forever altered. Over the next few weeks, Carol sinks into a deep depression. She is immobilized, constantly revisiting the fire. She feels useless, cut-off from friends and family, and utterly alone. After nearly a year, Carol's depression has not lifted. She remains withdrawn and has not returned to writing. Gradually, friends' attempts to comfort Carol grow less frequent. Many give up, weary of having their efforts rejected and unable to understand why Carol remains despondent. Carol knows she cannot go on living this way, and yet she cannot bring herself to move on.

If you knew Carol, what would you do? Where and at what point did Carol's coping skills break down? These are not simple questions to answer, but you might begin by considering Carol's ability to assess and identify the emotions she has been experiencing. Thinking back to her work as a writer, you remember people describing her as "in touch with the human experience." Although her skilled insight into other people's lives may not generalize to insight into her own life, you might assume that Carol's basic abilities to perceive and express emotion are superb. Moreover, the quality and depth of Carol's writing exhibits an amazing ability to understand the way emotions work. You remember, for example, Carol skillfully describing the plight of a widowed young mother on welfare who simultaneously felt intense love and torturous anger toward her dead husband. If Carol is able to label, express, and understand emotions so well, then perhaps her difficulties lie elsewhere. Perhaps Carol's problem is that she is unable to *apply* her emotional knowledge and insight when she is the one who needs help. What, if anything, has Carol done to regulate her emotions? Has she written about her emotions? If not, Carol's failure to cope effectively may stem primarily from her inability to move beyond rumination and on to regulation of her emotional experience.

Although the link between emotional intelligence and coping does not provide a clear strategy for changing Carol's behavior, it does provide a rationale for deciding where to intervene. After evaluating Carol's situation, you may decide that she needs to be motivated, in small steps, to resume her writing. Perhaps more immediately, she needs to be distracted. Or maybe she needs help in opening up to her friends and family. The benefit of taking the perspective of emotional intelligence is further illustrated by contrasting Carol with a second woman, Suzanne, who does not share Carol's writerly insights into emotions. After experiencing a traumatic car wreck, Suzanne immediately distracts herself by jumping back into a busy social life. Nevertheless, she has as much difficulty coping as Carol. It seems that Suzanne refrains from talking to others about the event, not because of an inability to apply emotional skills, but because of an inability to label, express, and understand her emotional experiences. Before attempting to regulate her emotions, Suzanne may need to learn the vocabulary for expressing her emotions. We employ these examples in order to help illustrate how the construct of emotional intelligence is subdivided into specific competencies. When an individual has difficulty coping, the problem may be attributable to one or more of these competencies. Although a solution to the individual's problem does not follow directly from this perspective, it is clear that a successful intervention must address the level at which emotional skills are weak or lacking.

This discussion raises a very important issue. Emotional intelligence is sometimes described as a trait. That is, you either have it or you don't. We wish to convey the idea that all people can learn and use emotionally intelligent strategies. The use of such strategies may be easier and more natural for some people than for others, but it is our belief that we all can work to increase our emotional competencies. The challenge is in being able to recognize where, for a given individual, emotional skills are deficient. This makes it possible, for instance, to determine where the coping process breaks down and enables us to intervene at that point.

Teaching Emotional Literacy in the Classroom

Rather than waiting until a person experiences difficulty coping with a stressful experience and then applying the emotional intelligence framework, it makes sense to consider how emotionally intelligent skills might be fostered prior to times of stress. Along these lines, we can examine how emotionally intelligent skills might be taught to children. All over the United States, school systems are currently implementing curricula in which children in elementary school, junior high school, and high school are learning about their feelings quite explicitly. These emotional intelligence curricula appear under different names and with a variety of stated goals. For example, in the New York City Public School System, the program is organized around the theme of learning to resolve conflicts creatively. In the New Haven, Connecticut, public schools, a similar program is called the social development curriculum. It emphasizes social problem solving as well as lessons on physical health (alcohol, drugs, AIDS, etc.). The Nueva School, a private school in California, emphasizes emotions for their own sake in a larger program called *Self Science*. These programs are described by Goleman (67) and Salovey and Sluyter (70).

The teachers in the New Haven and the California programs instruct their students quite directly about feelings. In New Haven, for example, elementary school students learn a "feeling" vocabulary. At the Nueva School in California, art projects are incorporated as a way of expressing different feelings. Although we endorse the principles underlying these kinds of programs, we are a bit concerned about them. Some school curricula involving emotions teach about feelings divorced from any other aspects of the children's lives. Yet, out in the world, emotions occur in a context. We would like to see feelings discussed in the context of other school activities. For example, children should learn about how to handle frustration in the context of a math class. They should learn about complex emotions like envy when they receive their report-card grades. And they should study the emotions of characters in the stories they read. We would like to see emotions integrated with the rest of the curriculum. For example, athletes need to learn how to harness emotions like anger, joy, and fear so that they facilitate performance rather than debilitate it. Skills in regulating emotion in oneself and others are often important in athletics. These competencies can be developed in vivo, that is, as part of instruction in a sport, dance, or other physical activity. As teachers, school administrators, parents, counselors, and other related professionals, we have opportunities to teach children and adults about their emotions all the time.

Although these kinds of programs are popular at the moment, many have not been evaluated adequately. We don't really know if they work. Optimistic claims are made about the benefits of classes on emotional literacy— that they will reduce drug use, school drop-out, violence in the schools— and we share this optimism. Nonetheless, we will only be able to speak with confidence about the value of these programs after they have been subjected to rigorous, controlled evaluation.

Conclusion

In this chapter we have argued that coping, as a response to emotion, is influenced by a person's emotional intelligence. Individuals who are emotionally intelligent accurately perceive and appraise their emotional states, know how and when to express their feelings, and can effectively regulate their mood states. These competencies facilitate successful coping through a number of distinct processes—they forestall rumination, prompt emotional insight and disclosure, and often lead to increased use of social support. And, of course, emotional intelligence may influence the coping process in ways beyond these. Although we have discussed substantial evidence that is consistent with this view, more research is needed that directly examines the relationship between emotional intelligence and the coping process. For example, demonstrating that interventions designed to improve emotional competencies do, in fact, foster effective coping would provide particularly compelling evidence in support of our position. In many ways, however, the significance of emotional intelligence is self-evident—problematic coping is often attributable (and quite clearly so) to a breakdown in emotional coping skills. The strength of the emotional intelligence framework lies in its ability to describe a hierarchy of specific emotional competencies that lead to effective coping. These skills are required to respond successfully to emotion. They enable the individual to cope intelligently.

References

1. Young, P. T. (1936). *Motivation of behavior.* New York: John Wiley & Sons.
2. Young, P. T. (1943). *Emotion in man and animal: Its nature and relation to attitude and motive.* New York: John Wiley & Sons.
3. Schaffer, L. F., Gilmer, B., & Schoen, M. (1940). *Psychology.* New York: Harper & Brothers.
4. Leeper, R. W. (1948). A motivational theory of emotions to replace "emotions as disorganized response." *Psychological Review, 55,* 5–21.
5. Mowrer, O. H. (1960). *Learning theory and behavior.* New York: Wiley.

6. Darwin, C. (1965/1872). *The expression of the emotions in man and animals.* Chicago: University of Chicago Press.
7. Gardner, H. (1983). *Frames of mind.* New York: Basic Books.
8. Salovey, P., & Mayer, J. D. (1990). Emotional intelligence. *Imagination, Cognition, and Personality, 9,* 185–211.
9. Mayer, J. D., & Salovey, P. (1997). What is emotional intelligence? In P. Salovey & D. J. Sluyter (Eds.), *Emotional development and emotional intelligence* (pp. 3–31). New York: Basic Books.
10. Salovey, P., Hsee, C., & Mayer, J. D. (1993). Emotional intelligence and the self-regulation of affect. In D. M. Wegner & J. W. Pennebaker (Eds.), *Handbook of mental control* (pp. 258–277). Englewood Cliffs, NJ: Prentice-Hall.
11. Salovey, P., & Mayer, J. D. (1994). Some final thoughts about personality and intelligence. In R. J. Sternberg & P. Ruzgis (Eds.), *Personality and intelligence* (pp. 303–318). Cambridge, England: Cambridge University Press.
12. Palfai, T. P., & Salovey, P. (1993). The influence of depressed and elated mood on deductive and inductive reasoning. *Imagination, Cognition, and Personality, 13,* 57–71.
13. Schwarz, N. (1990). Feelings as information: Informational and motivational functions of affective states. In E. T. Higgins & E. M. Sorrentino (Eds.), *Handbook of Motivation and Cognition* (Vol. 2, pp. 527–561). New York: Guilford Press.
14. Mayer, J. D., Caruso, D., & Salovey, P. (1997). *Emotional intelligence meets traditional standards for an intelligence.* Manuscript under review.
15. Mayer, J. D., Salovey, P., & Caruso, D. (1997). *Emotional IQ test* [CD-ROM version]. Needham, MA: Virtual Knowledge.
16. Mayer, J. D., DiPaolo, M., & Salovey, P. (1990). Perceiving the affective content in ambiguous visual stimuli: A component of emotional intelligence. *Journal of Personality Assessment, 54,* 772–781.
17. Mayer, J. D., & Geher, G. (1996). Emotional intelligence and the identification of emotion. *Intelligence, 22,* 89–113.
18. Bar-On, R. (1997). *EQi: Bar-On Emotional Quotient Inventory.* Toronto: Multi-Health Systems, Inc.
19. Mayer, J. D., & Gaschke, Y. N. (1988). The experience and meta-experience of mood. *Journal of Personality and Social Psychology, 55,* 102–111.
20. Salovey, P., Mayer, J. D., Goldman, S., Turvey, C., & Palfai, T. (1995). Emotional attention, clarity, and repair: Exploring emotional intelligence using the Trait Meta-Mood Scale. In J. Pennebaker (Ed.), *Emotion, disclosure, and health* (pp. 125–154). Washington, DC: American Psychological Association.
21. Mayer, J. D., & Stevens, A. (1994). An emerging understanding of the reflective (meta-) experience of mood. *Journal of Research in Personality, 60,* 100–111.
22. Goldman, S. L., Kraemer, D. T., & Salovey, P. (1996). Beliefs about mood moderate the relationship of stress to illness and symptom reporting. *Journal of Psychosomatic Research, 41,* 115–128.
23. Nolen-Hoeksema, S., McBride, A., & Larson, J. (1997). Rumination and

psychological distress among bereaved partners. *Journal of Personality and Social Psychology, 72*, 855–862.

24. Nolen-Hoeksema, S. (1991). Responses to depression and their effects on the duration of depressive episodes. *Journal of Abnormal Psychology, 100*, 569–582.

25. Morrow, J., & Nolen-Hoeksema, S. (1990). Effects of responses to depression on the remediation of depressive affect. *Journal of Personality and Social Psychology, 58*, 519–527.

26. Nolen-Hoeksema, S., & Morrow, J. (1991). A prospective study of depression and posttraumatic stress symptoms after a natural disaster: The 1989 Loma Prieta earthquake. *Journal of Personality and Social Psychology, 61*, 115–121.

27. Butler, L. D., & Nolen-Hoeksema, S. (1994). Gender differences in responses to depressed mood in a college sample. *Sex Roles, 30*, 331–346.

28. Baumeister, R. F. (1991). *Meanings of life*. New York: Guilford.

29. Frankl, V. E. (1955). *The doctor and the soul*. New York: Knopf.

30. Swinkels, A., & Giuliano, T. A. (1995). The measurement and conceptualization of mood awareness: Monitoring and labeling one's mood states. *Personality and Social Psychology Bulletin, 21*, 934–949.

31. Nolen-Hoeksema, S., & Morrow, J. (1993). Effects of rumination and distraction on naturally occurring depressed mood. *Cognition and Emotion, 7*, 561–570.

32. Lyubomirsky, S., & Nolen-Hoeksema, S. (1995). Effects of self-focused rumination on negative thinking and interpersonal problem solving. *Journal of Personality and Social Psychology, 69*, 176–190.

33. Stroebe, W., & Stroebe, M. (1996). The social psychology of social support. In E. T. Higgins & A. W. Kruglanski (Eds.), *Social psychology: Handbook of basic principles* (pp. 597–621). New York: Guilford Press.

34. Cohen, S., & Wills, T. A. (1985). Stress, social support and buffering. *Psychological Bulletin, 98*, 310–357.

35. Cohen, S., & Syme, S. L. (Eds.) (1985). *Social support and health*. Orlando, FL: Academic.

36. Holahan, C. J., Moos, R. H., Holahan, C. K., & Brennan, P. L. (1997). Social context, coping strategies, and depressive symptoms: An expanded model with cardiac patients. *Journal of Personality and Social Psychology, 72*, 918–928.

37. House, J. S., Landis, K. R., & Umberson, D. (1988). Social relationships and health. *Science, 241*, 540–545.

38. Sarason, I. G., Sarason, B. R., & Pierce, G. R. (1994). Social support: Global and relationship-based levels of analysis. *Journal of Social and Personal Relationships, 11*, 295–312.

39. Taylor, S. E. (1990). Health psychology: The science and the field. *American Psychologist, 45*, 40–50.

40. Spiegel, D., Bloom, J., & Yalom, I. (1981). Group support for patients with metastatic cancer. *Archives of General Psychiatry, 38*, 527–533.

41. Ferlic, M., Goldman, A., & Kennedy, B. J. (1979). Group counseling in adult patients with advanced cancer. *Cancer, 43*, 760–766.

42. Maisiak, R., Cain, M., Yarbo, C., & Josof, L. (1981). Evaluation of

TOUCH: An oncology self-help group. *Oncology Nursing Forum, 8*, 10–25.

43. Reifman, A. (1995). Social relationships, recovery from illness, and survival: A literature review. *Annals of Behavioral Medicine, 17*, 124–131.

44. Haley, W. E., Levine, E. G., Brown, S. L., & Bartolucci, A. A. (1987). Stress, appraisal, coping, and social support as predictors of adaptational outcome among dementia caregivers. *Psychology and Aging, 2*, 323–330.

45. Haley, W. E., Roth, D. L., Coleton, M. I., & Ford, G. R. (1996). Appraisal, coping, and social support as mediators of well-being in Black and White family caregivers of patients with Alzheimer's disease. *Journal of Consulting and Clinical Psychology, 64*, 121–129.

46. Glaser, R. (1985). Stress-related impairments in cellular immunity. *Psychiatry Research, 16*, 233–239.

47. Kiecolt-Glaser, J. K., Garner, W., Speicher, C. E., Penn, G. M., Holliday, J., & Glaser, R. (1984). Psychosocial modifiers of immunocompetence in medical students. *Psychosomatic Medicine, 46*, 7–14.

48. Jemmott, J. B., III, & Locke, S. E. (1984). Psychosocial factors, immunologic mediation, and human susceptibility to infectious diseases: How much do we know? *Psychological Bulletin, 95*, 78–108.

49. Dunkel-Schetter, C., Folkman, S., & Lazarus, R. S. (1987). Correlates of social support receipt. *Journal of Personality and Social Psychology, 53*, 71–80.

50. Kahen, V., Katz, L. F., & Gottman, J. M. (1994). Linkages between parent-child interaction and conversations of friends. Special Issue: From family to peer group: Relations between relationships systems. *Social Development, 3*, 238–254.

51. Cowen, E. L., et al. (1973). Long term follow-up of early detected vulnerable children. *Journal of Consulting and Clinical Psychology, 41*, 438–446.

52. Cassidy, J., & Asher, S. R. (1992). Loneliness and peer relations in young children. *Child Development, 63*, 350–365.

53. Hooven, C., Gottman, J. M., & Katz, L. F. (1995). Parental meta-emotion structure predicts family and child outcomes. *Cognition and Emotion, 9*, 229–264.

54. Salovey, P., Mayer, J. D., & Rosenhan, D. L. (1991). Mood and helping: Mood as a motivator of helping and helping as a regulator of mood. *Review of Personality and Social Psychology, 12*, 215–237.

55. Cameron, L. D., & Nicholls, G. (1998). Expression of stressful experiences through writing: Effects of a self-regulation manipulation for pessimists and optimists. *Health Psychology, 17*, 84–92.

56. Pennebaker, J. W., Colder, M., & Sharp, L. K. (1990). Accelerating the coping process. *Journal of Personality and Social Psychology, 58*, 528–537.

57. Pennebaker, J. W., Kiecolt-Glaser, J. K., & Glaser, R. (1988). Disclosure of traumas and immune function: Health implications for psychotherapy. *Journal of Consulting and Clinical Psychology, 56*, 239–245.

58. Greenberg, M. A., & Stone, A. A. (1992). Emotional disclosure about traumas and its relation to health: Effects of previous disclosure and

trauma severity. *Journal of Personality and Social Psychology, 63,* 75–84.
59. Petrie, K. J., Booth, R. J., Pennebaker, J. W., Davison, K. P., & Thomas, M.G. (1995). Disclosure of trauma and immune response to a hepatitis B vaccination program. *Journal of Consulting and Clinical Psychology, 63,* 787–792.
60. Smyth, J. M. (1998). Written emotional expression: Effect sizes, outcome types, and moderating variables. *Journal of Consulting and Clinical Psychology, 66,* 174–184.
61. Pennebaker, J. W. (1997). Writing about emotional experiences as a therapeutic process. *Psychological Science, 8,* 162–166.
62. Wegner, D. M., Erber, R., & Zanakos, S. (1993). Ironic processes in the mental control of mood and mood-related thought. *Journal of Personality and Social Psychology, 65,* 1093–1104.
63. Pennebaker, J. W., Mayne, T. J., & Francis, M. E. (1997). Linguistic predictors of adaptive bereavement. *Journal of Personality and Social Psychology, 72,* 863–871.
64. Pennebaker, J. W., & Francis, M. E. (1996). Cognitive, emotional, and language processes in disclosure. *Cognition and Emotion, 10,* 601–626.
65. Mayer, J. D., Salovey, P., Gomberg-Kaufman, S. & Blainey, K. (1991). A broader conception of mood experience. *Journal of Personality and Social Psychology, 60,* 100–111.
66. Pennebaker, J. W., & Harber, K. D. (1993). A social stage model of collective coping: The Loma Prieta earthquake and the Persian Gulf War. *Journal of Social Issues, 49,* 125–145.
67. Goleman, D. (1995). *Emotional intelligence.* New York: Bantam.
68. Safran, J. D., & Greenberg, L. S. (1991). *Emotion, psychotherapy, and change.* New York: Guilford.
69. Mayer, J. D., & Salovey, P. (1995). Emotional intelligence and the construction and regulation of feelings. *Applied and Preventive Psychology, 4,* 197–208.
70. Salovey, P., & Sluyter, D. (Eds.) (1997). *Emotional development and emotional intelligence: Implications for educators.* New York: Basic Books.

8

Learned Optimism in Children

Andrew J. Shatté
Karen Reivich
Jane E. Gillham
Martin E. P. Seligman

We live in an "age of melancholy" (1). Our children succumb to depression at progressively younger ages and at progressively higher rates. Scientific inquiry over the last two decades has identified several cognitive and behavioral deficits implicated in the etiology of childhood depression and, of these, pessimistic explanatory style is perhaps the most researched. Within the last decade a handful of researchers have begun work on empirical validation of protocols designed to redress faulty thinking in depressed children.

This chapter examines a depression prevention program for children developed at the University of Pennsylvania. In this chapter we focus on two related cognitive-behavioral risk factors for depression in children; learned helplessness and pessimistic explanatory style. First, we briefly profile childhood depression. Second, we outline the nature of learned helplessness and pessimism in children. Third, we offer two conceptualizations of learned optimism. Narrowly defined, learned optimism is the skill of reattributing one's pessimistic explanations to more optimistic causes. More broadly formulated, it is a set of skills that promotes cognitive flexibility and resiliency in children. Within this framework we describe our program, the Penn Optimism Program, which aims to "inoculate" children against depression with the skills of learned optimism.

Childhood Depression

The lifetime prevalence of major depression in the United States has increased dramatically in the last two generations (2). This is in part due to decreases in the mean age of onset observed over the same time period (3).

Current estimates indicate that almost 10% of children experience clinical depression before the age of 14, and up to 20% of adolescents have a major depressive episode before the end of their high school years (4, 5).

In spite of sound epidemiological evidence indicating increased risk for children, the development and validation of effective treatments for child and adolescent depression have lagged behind the adult research. Two historical factors have contributed to this. Only recently have clinicians and researchers acknowledged that children can be clinically depressed (6), and that child depression is phenomenologically similar to the adult disorder (7). Furthermore, prior to the 1970s, the existing psychotherapeutic interventions for adult depression were predominately psychoanalytic in orientation. These therapies were considered inappropriate for children and young adolescents, who, it was argued, were yet to complete their psychosexual development.

The advent of cognitive therapy for depression paved the way for new treatments of childhood depression (8, 9). Three lines of research converged to indicate that cognitive techniques were germane to the treatment of depression in children. First, cognitive therapies are demonstrably effective in treating adult depression (10). Second, as proposed by cognitive theorists, the efficacy of the therapy is mediated by change in the patient's maladaptive thoughts (11). Third, depressive children tend to make the same cognitive distortions associated with the adult disorder, and these maladaptive styles of thinking have been causally implicated in the development of depression in children and adolescents (12–15). Specifically, children whose thinking style is pessimistic are significantly more likely to fail and become depressed than their optimistic peers.

Helplessness and Pessimism

A hallmark feature of depression is the individual's perceived lack of control over her world and her future; a sense of helplessness that leads to hopelessness (16). A seminal animal model of uncontrollability was developed in the 1960s by Martin Seligman and his colleagues (17, 18). As graduate students in an animal learning laboratory, they conducted a series of trials in which dogs in two experimental conditions were administered noninjurious electric shocks. Dogs in the first condition were able to turn off the shock with a simple lever push. The animals in the second condition were unable to escape the shocks. They were experimentally "yoked" with those in the first condition to ensure equivalent amounts of electric shock across condition, but they had no lever and no control.

Some twenty-four hours later, all of the dogs were put through a second learning paradigm. They were placed in a shuttlebox—a small box divided in two by a low barrier. When the floor of one side of the box was electrified, the dogs in the lever condition learned, within two or three trials, to escape across the barrier. The dogs who had no control in the first experiment never attempted escape. They overgeneralized learning from a situation in which they clearly did not have control, to one in which they truly did. They had learned to be helpless.

The "learned helplessness" model was readily extended to human behavior. When people are subjected to uncontrollable noise, for example, fully two-thirds fail to switch off highly preventable noise in a subsequent phase of the experiment (19). However, not everyone becomes helpless in the wake of an uncontrollable, aversive event. Revision of the theory was required to account for the resilient third. The reformulated model integrated helplessness with the cognitive variable of explanatory style (20). By so doing, learned helplessness was modified from a theory of stimulus-operant-response to one of stimulus-interpretation-response.

We are predisposed to analyze and interpret the events that befall us in life (21). We attribute them to cause, and we imbue them with meaning for ourselves and our future. This seems particularly true of negative events, perhaps because the threats they pose are more salient to survival than the boon provided by positive events. And it is as true of preadolescent children as it is of adults. When a child argues with a school friend, to what does she attribute the disagreement? Does she put it down to the recent divorce of her friend's parents, or does she instead believe "my friend's a jerk"? Does she think "all friendships have their ups and downs," or does she say to herself "I'm just no good with people?"

If we analyze these very different explanations, we see they vary across three dimensions. First, some will believe that the argument is all their fault ("I'm so irritable"; internal), while others attribute it to the friend or to circumstances ("she's a jerk" or "she's upset over her parents' divorce"; external). Second, some will attribute the argument to an enduring cause ("I don't have what it takes to be a good friend"; stable), while others will see the cause as short-lived ("all friendships go through ups and downs"; unstable). Third, some believe that the cause of the argument undermines almost everything they do ("I'm just not good with people"; global), while others will confine the operation of that cause to a relatively narrow domain ("I don't deal well with people as upset as she"; specific). Pessimists tend to explain negative events in terms of internal, stable, and global causes, and attribute positive events to external, unstable, and specific causes. Conversely, optimists tend to explain negative events as due to external, unstable, and specific causes, while ascribing positive outcomes to internal, stable, and global attributes.

In the reformulation, emphasis shifted from uncontrollable aversive events to the *perceived* uncontrollability of aversive events. Perception of control is mapped onto the three dimensions of explanatory style. One's own behavior is generally more amenable to control than that of another. Given that we want adversity to end and will exert whatever control we have to end it, those negative events perceived as uncontrollable will also be seen as stable over time. So, internal and unstable attributions typically denote high levels of controllability. For example, imagine your child explains the argument with her friend in the following way: "we argued because I was cranky, and I was cranky because I stayed up too late watching TV last night." It should be relatively easy for the child to change her TV viewing so that crankiness rarely interferes in her social world again. External-stable explanations indicate low controllability, because to gain control over them one must effect another's disposition or an environmental constant (e.g., stop the friend from being a jerk, or cause her parents to reconcile). Attributions to internal-stable or external-unstable causes usually represent a middle level of control (e.g., "I'm not good with sad people," "she's in a bad mood"). Global attributions indicate loss of control— that the cause of the problem cannot be contained. In essence, the more pessimistic the attribution, the less the degree of perceived control.

Optimism and pessimism are best conceptualized as poles on a continuum. We tend to reflexively explain negative events at a habitual level of pessimism, which can be measured with a quick and easy pencil and paper test (22). Furthermore, in the absence of active intervention, our degree of pessimism remains constant across the lifespan (23). For these reasons our degree of optimism-pessimism is referred to as an "explanatory *style*." The adult literature demonstrates that pessimists are at elevated risk for compromised performance in sports (24), reduced productivity in the workplace (25), academic failure (26), depressed mood (27), and even death from coronary heart disease (28).

Pessimism in children is measured using the Children's Attributional Style Questionnaire (CASQ), developed for ages 8 to 14 (29). The CASQ consists of 48 forced-choice items, in which the child is presented with a hypothetical positive or negative event and asked to choose between two possible causes. On each item, two of the dimensions are held constant across the two explanations and the third is varied. For example, respondents are presented with "a good friend tells you that he hates you" and must choose between "my friend was in a bad mood that day" and "I wasn't nice to my friend that day." These attributions are both relatively unstable and specific, but the former is external and the latter internal. Sixteen items are designed to tap each of the three dimensions. Internal, stable, and global scores for each of the positive and negative hypothetical events can be combined into composite positive and composite negative scores (CP and CN). A summary optimism score (CPCN) is derived by subtracting CN from CP. Internal consistency and test-retest reliability is best with these three composites (30).

Examination of explanatory style in children began in earnest as recently as the mid 1980s. Research since indicates that children's causal attributions, especially those for negative events, stabilize into a style by about age nine (31) and that, as with adults, pessimism leads to an array of age-relevant problems. Pessimism causes depressive symptoms in children (30). The pessimistic child tends to underachieve academically (32, 33) and has fewer and less satisfying peer relationships (34).

Can the maladaptive consequences of pessimism be averted? Is explanatory style changeable? Cognitive therapy does produce positive change in explanatory style. This appears not to be true of drug therapies, even when the degree of depressive symptom relief is comparable. Furthermore, change in explanatory style is an important mediator of both treatment and relapse prevention effects (35). That is, those depressed patients who become more optimistic over the course of cognitive therapy not only benefit more from the therapy, but are also more robust against subsequent bouts of depression.

The Penn Optimism Program (POP) attempts to equip at-risk children with these same skills.

Challenging Pessimism

The Penn Optimism Program (POP)

The Penn Optimism Program (POP) is a 12-week (24-hour), school-based intervention which is delivered in groups of 10 to 12 children. In our initial iterations of POP, participants were not diagnosably depressed, but were at risk for depression due to high levels of family conflict, low levels of family cohesion, or the early onset of mild levels of depressive symptomatology. In POP we have attempted to distill the essential skills of cognitive therapy, calibrate them to a child's developmental age, and present them in a preventive mode. The result is a manualized, activities-based curriculum which reads much more like a school course than a therapy.

Reference to an "optimism program" may invoke notions of a protocol designed purely to make pessimists more optimistic; a "reattribution training," as it is often labeled. Reattribution is an important skill to which substantial content is devoted in POP. But relegating optimism to change in causal explanations is optimism narrowly defined (36). The causal attributions we make are rich in context and meaning. They reflect our past successes and failures. They are snapshots of our current cognitive biases. And they entail predictions about our futures. When a child concludes that she failed a history test because she "didn't study enough," she is implicitly adding that in the future she can avoid academic failure by studying more. Conversely, when she attributes to a pessimistic cause like "I'm just plain stupid," she endows her academic future with hopelessness.

In addition, causal explanations frame the problems in our lives and therefore also determine the goals we set and the solutions we generate. Some children in interpersonal settings seem particularly prone to biased attributions and consequently to poor social problem solving. Accurate predictions and effective problem solving are skills which we include as learned optimism, broadly defined.

Causal Reattribution: Flexibility and Accuracy

In POP, the skill of reattribution is set within the framework of Albert Ellis's ABC model (37, 38). Ellis argued that we intuitively believe that activating events lead to emotional and behavioral consequences (A→C, e.g., fail a history test and so give up and become depressed), but that this intuition is wrong because it omits a crucial mediating variable. According to Ellis, activating events invoke certain beliefs in us, and it is these beliefs that make sense of how we feel and what we do (i.e., A→B→C). Beck and colleagues focus on automatic thoughts; those beliefs that occur reflexively in the wake of negative events (9, 39, 40). Attributions represent an important subset of automatic thoughts.

The first three sessions of POP teach the skill of causal reattribution. But more fundamentally these sessions try to convey to the participant the notions of cognitive flexibility and accuracy.

Sessions 1 and 2 are devoted to developing flexibility. Adults and even children get themselves into explanatory ruts. Their explanations for negative events form rapidly and reflexively and exist on the periphery of awareness. Therefore, we must first teach the children to slow down their thinking in order to identify their automatic attributions. Second, we guide them to an understanding of the emotional and behavioral impact of these thoughts, as predicted by the ABC model. We describe this to our students as the link between thoughts and feelings and present it in the form of three-panel cartoons like that in Figure 8.1.

POP participants learn how to recognize pessimistic and optimistic thoughts and to analyze them according to the three dimensions of explan-

Figure 8.1. Illustration of the ABC model using a three-panel cartoon.

atory style. With the aid of role-plays and stories, they learn about the mechanism of self-fulfilling prophecy, by which pessimistic thoughts lead to depression and failure while optimistic thoughts do not. When Greg, a pessimist, is turned down at the school dance, for example, he thinks: "I got rejected because I'm ugly and nobody likes me." The emotional consequence of this thought is that Greg feels sad. The behavioral consequence is that he clings to the wall for the rest of the evening. By taking himself off the dance floor, he ensures that he does not get to dance. This only serves to corroborate his initial belief, rendering it even less likely that he dances at the next event. Linking back to helplessness and explanatory style, Greg's attribution of the event to highly internal, stable, and global causes leads him to quit and to fail to exert control over elements of the situation which are in fact changeable.

Most important, however, we encourage the students to generate alternative causal attributions; explanations outside of their typically narrow band of optimism-pessimism. We ask them to be as creative as possible, without vetting their responses, and we help them trace the very different consequences they would experience were they to endorse the alternative attribution. Imagine if Greg were to respond with a more external, unstable, or specific response, such as "she must not feel like dancing," or even "that girl probably doesn't like me." What are the alternative emotional and behavioral consequences for him? He will probably experience some sadness, but significantly less than the thought "I'm ugly" will generate in a 12-year-old child. His more optimistic thoughts make it rational for him to persist, and his persistence will, in all likelihood, lead him to a dance partner (see Figure 8.2). This newfound cognitive flexibility continues as a central theme in POP, applied not only to causal attributions, but also to predictions about the future and the search for goal-compatible problem-solving strategies.

While Sessions 1 and 2 promote the expansion of the children's attributional repertoire, Session 3 is devoted to funneling down to accuracy. The lay notion of optimism is one of resolutely refusing to see bad events as bad. This is encapsulated in facile phrases like "turning grey skies into blue," "looking at the world through rose-colored glasses," or "seeing the glass as half-full." Even some clinicians and researchers have communicated to us their belief that reattribution is the process of shaping optimistic explanations, regardless of the evidence. This, however, has never been our understanding of that skill. Rather for us, reattribution is the practice of supplanting pessimism with optimism only "to the extent that reality permits" (36).

In POP, the skills of generating alternatives (cognitive flexibility) and evaluating the evidence for and against each is paralleled with the work of a detective. Endorsing one's initial attribution without considering other possible causes is analogous to arresting the first suspect. Glibly reattributing to a more optimistic cause is equally irrational.

Problems in life almost never have a single cause. Rather, they are a consequence of a multiplicity of contributing factors. So, in analyzing the

Figure 8.2. Demonstrating reattribution with the three-panel cartoon.

cause of a problem, a good detective first lists several candidates. In response to asking herself why she failed the history exam, she not only arrives at the explanation "I'm just plain stupid," but also lists "I didn't put in enough hours of study," "I didn't study the right material in the right way," "the teacher has it in for me," and "I'm just not good at history" to name a few.

POP participants are taught how to review their lives and solicit information from others to help in evaluating the accuracy of each causal self-statement. Older children are assisted in determining the relative contribution of each cause that has implications for problem solving. Devoting more time to study for the next exam is only beneficial if the child also studies the right material in the right way. Similarly, coaxing her parents to meet with the principal about the teacher's animosity will not help if the exam failure is due to inadequate study. You cannot solve a problem until you know what the problem is.

Some children are habitually more optimistic than the evidence warrants. This typically manifests itself on the internal-external dimension. In the wake of an exam failure, they may automatically assume it's because "the teacher hates me." We encourage these children to generate and evaluate more internal attributions in order to take responsibility for what they are truly culpable. Their overly optimistic response may preserve their self-esteem and mood, but it is not reality-based and so does not lend itself to effective solutions. Our task with children who habitually externalize blame is to guide them to greater dexterity in generating more pessimistic attributions. However, the children in our programs more often show a depressogenic attributional style. When these children become more accurate in their causal explanations, they are moving toward the optimistic end of the continuum.

Determining a problem-solving strategy is also a logical funneling process. Focal causes are delineated from the candidate list on the basis of the evidence implicating them in the problem. Once isolated, their changeability can be examined. Highly stable factors are less amenable to change (e.g., "I'm just not all that smart"). Although such a cause may play a large role, it is maladaptive to allocate limited problem-solving resources to its resolution. If unstable factors (e.g., study habits) contribute at all, then some scope for improvement is afforded the student. Study habits can be monitored and alterations made and tested against subsequent exams. If the child truly adheres to the new study regimen but still no change is evident, then different causes should be examined and new solutions sought and tested. Eventually the weight of the evidence may indeed indicate that the student truly is just not cut out to be a historian. In spite of all her efforts to improve in the course, the student may have reached asymptote on grade or academic interest. Perhaps then a cost-benefit analysis may point toward reallocating her study time and energy to different subjects. If asymptote is reached across her academic life, then she should be encouraged to explore nonacademic talents and interests, while studying enough to maintain the best grades she can. Her depressogenic or anxiety-invoking beliefs about her future (e.g., "I'll never amount to anything") can be subjected to the same scrutiny, as described in the next section.

It is in this way that learned optimism plays out in problem solving. The optimistic child is not Pollyanna. When problems arise, she seeks out those causes which are most implicated and most changeable. The pessimist becomes helpless because he automatically settles on a unitary stable and global cause and so can find no leverage for change. The optimist remains resilient because her cognitive skills lead her to find and exert control whenever and wherever possible, but always "to the degree that reality permits" (36).

Applying the Skills to Predictions

Depression and anxiety are highly comorbid in both adults and children (41). The same cognitive errors and distortions which produce depression when applied to past events may lead to anxiety when operating on possible futures. Indeed, as we saw earlier, causal attributions are imbued with predictions about the future.

Some of the children in our program are experiencing high levels of parental conflict at home. The pessimists among them report that when their parents argue, or even fight, they have a stream of thoughts like the following:

What did I do wrong this time? I know they're fighting because of me. What's wrong with me? I'm always messing up. They get angry with me and they fight with each other. They're always arguing and they always will. They'll probably get divorced like Mike's parents. My mom will be so unhappy. She'll never get over it. My dad will move away and I'll never see him again. I'll never be happy again.

Her causal attribution is highly pessimistic. She not only blames herself ("I did something wrong"), she also assigns the cause to what seems like a highly stable, dispositional aspect of herself (something is "wrong with me"). When we make predictions about the future, it is rational to take current circumstances into account. Because she attributes the fighting to stable causes, she necessarily projects into a bleak future. "My parents will get divorced because they don't care about me, and they don't care about me because there is something wrong with me." If one assumes the cause of the fighting is permanent, one must also assume that the fighting will continue.

Her attribution to cause is probably inaccurate. Parents often fight *about* the child, but they rarely fight *because* of the child. However, disputing this single attribution may not be sufficient to significantly reduce her hopelessness. Her negative view of the future is probably supported by an entire network of pessimistic beliefs which feed into her predictions. "My mother will never be happy again because I just don't have what it takes to help her." "My father will leave forever because he doesn't care about me, and he doesn't care about me because I just can't connect with anyone." "I'll never be happy again because bad things make me sad, and I have no control over my mood nor the events in my life." These are causal attributions for projected future events.

If we scrutinize her self-statements about the future, we notice that whenever there is ambiguity, her pessimism leads her to predict the worst. She has offered up an implicit causal chain:

parents' fighting → divorce → absent father

She perceives a 1:1 correspondence between each step in the chain; fighting will lead to divorce, and divorce means that she will rarely or never see her father again. This process is called "catastrophizing" (see chapter 12 in this volume). While her predicted outcome is possible, it is unlikely. First, most married couples argue but most do not divorce. Second, within those 45% of marriages that do end in divorce, in most cases the children do have access to both parents.

The process of disputing such catastrophic beliefs is called "decatastrophizing." In this skill, the children are asked to again use their cognitive flexibility, this time in generating several possible futures as alternatives to the pessimism-driven outlook they automatically conceived. Flexibility can be maximized by providing a structure within which the child generates alternatives. We first ask the child to generate and list the worst possible outcomes for the current situation. For the pessimists, these are the very thoughts over which they habitually ruminate. Next, we prompt for some best possible outcomes, with the caveat that they must be about as improbable as the worst list (e.g., "I'll never be happy again" can be counterpoised with "they will never argue again"). Finally, the child generates most likely outcomes. By extracting the worst-case scenarios the child feels validated. Without generating best-case outcomes children may fail to see the low probability of their worst fears. Worst and best lists serve to calibrate their evaluation using evidence.

The worst, best, and most likely lists can be used to inform problem-solving strategy. Most time and energy should be devoted to the outcomes in the most likely list. Strategies can be implemented now to minimize the chances that bad outcomes occur and maximize any positive outcomes. However, one or two of the worst-case scenarios may be so maladaptive that some time should be devoted to averting those consequences.

The child who makes pessimistic attributions for past events also projects her pessimism into the future. Like a bad detective, she assumes her most catastrophic thoughts will inevitably be realized, and this perception leads to helplessness in the present. The optimistic child recognizes that predicted futures are testable hypotheses that can be evaluated by evidence. How much do other parents argue? Of her friends whose parents have divorced, how many have access to both parents and how many are *never* happy again? They use this information to reshape their predictions, identify the most likely, and act to exert control where they can.

Applying the Skills to the Social World

We have outlined and demonstrated the use of learned optimism skills with causal attributions and with catastrophic predictions. There are indications that for some children, negative social interactions evoke a particular style of attributional bias, to which the skills of learned optimism can be successfully applied. In this section we examine attributions in the social domain.

Research within the last decade has identified five information-processing steps required for competent social interaction (42). For a child to respond appropriately to the behavior of a peer, she must first attend to and encode the verbal and nonverbal cues displayed by the peer. Second, she must use those cues to accurately interpret the peer's motivation for behaving as he did. Third, she must generate an array of possible responses, evaluate the consequences of enacting each, and then, fourth, select the most appropriate. Fifth, she must successfully enact the selected behavioral response.

Peer-rejected and aggressive children commonly show deficits at one or more of these stages (43). For example, visualize the melee that can be the middle school playground. Imagine a child who finds himself face down on the ground without knowing how he got there. Was he pushed or accidentally bumped, and by whom? Some children in negative interpersonal situations such as these tend to assume that the other's intentions were malevolent, and they selectively attend to cues that support that assumption. This hostile attributional bias often leads them to select and enact aggressive responses. From the perspective of their peer who truly meant no malice, this aggressive response seems unprovoked, and so they tend to respond in kind. The true level of hostility is embellished through the distorted lens of the child's hostile attributional bias—and so the cycle of aggression continues.

POP attempts to build skills at all five stages of the social-cognitive process. Children are taught basic behavioral skills to delay their initial impulse to act. Instead, they learn to identify and distance themselves from their automatic hostile attribution. Like a good detective, they draw up a list of suspects (generate alternatives), and look for clues (evaluate evidence) to determine the relative contribution of the candidate causes they have generated. They learn how to view the situation from another's perspective, the better to determine the true motivation of the playground instigator. The children use decision-making skills acquired in an earlier session to choose the most appropriate course of action, and learn strategies to help enact that option (e.g., assertiveness).

Depressed children are more likely to make hostile attributions than their nondepressed peers (44). When faced with an aversive social situation, the pessimist will invoke a self-fulfilling prophecy—an interactive aggression spiral that brings upon himself the very behavior against which he is so vigilant. The optimistic child has learned to see the world more accurately and so is primed to choose a more prosocial course of action.

Empirical Evaluation of POP

POP is predicated on the skills of learned optimism outlined above. These are complemented with lessons on assertiveness, negotiation, relaxation techniques, anger, and sadness control, dealing with procrastination, social skills, and decision making. The 12–session protocol is fully scripted and manualized (45).

The first empirical trial of POP was conducted with fifth- and sixth-grade children in two middle schools in the suburbs of Philadelphia (46, 47) (design and methodology is fully described in Jaycox, Reivich, Gillham, & Seligman, 1994). The children selected for the program were at risk for depression based on their self-report of depressive symptomatology and their perception of parental conflict in the home. Both prevention and control condition children completed the Children's Depression Inventory

(CDI) (48) and the CASQ at six measurement points; pre, post, and every six months for two years.

POP children experienced significantly fewer depressive symptoms than their control peers at every measurement point from post-test through the two-year follow-up. The clinical significance of these data was also indicated, with 38% of children in the control group suffering moderate to severe levels of depressive symptomatology by the two-year follow-up, compared with 12% in the prevention condition (see Figure 8.3; in this comparison, moderate to severe depressive symptoms is defined as a score greater than 18 on the CDI).

A central aim of POP is to guide children toward more accurate causal attributions for the negative events in their lives. Children at risk for depression tend to exhibit depressogenic thinking styles, such as pessimism. They habitually respond with pessimistic attributions without determining their accuracy. Therefore, for these children, thinking more accurately is equated with thinking more optimistically. Results from this first trial did indeed demonstrate that children in POP developed significantly more optimistic explanatory styles compared with their control peers over the follow-up period (see Figure 8.4). Furthermore, mediational analyses indicated that this positive change in explanatory style led to depressive symptom relief in the prevention group children.

This study demonstrated the two premises essential to our program of research. First, children can become more optimistic when equipped with a set of cognitive skills. Second, this change in explanatory style has prophylactic effects against depression.

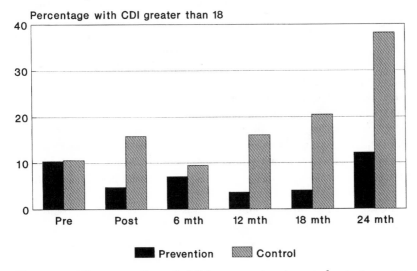

Figure 8.3. The proportion of children experiencing moderate to severe levels of depressive symptoms.

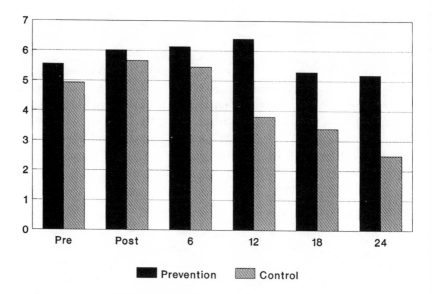

Higher scores represent greater optimism

Figure 8.4. Explanatory style by condition and time (numbers represent months).

Conclusions and Future Directions

In this chapter we have described the childhood depression risk factors of learned helplessness and explanatory style. We have outlined a learned optimism program designed to redress them. Narrowly defined, learned optimism is the process of reattribution; modifying one's causal explanations to fit reality. Typically, this entails adopting a more optimistic explanation for negative events. More comprehensively formulated, learned optimism is a set of cognitive-behavioral skills that children can use to ameliorate the effects of pessimism and catastrophic thinking and to improve social problem solving. At its core, the program equips children with greater flexibility and resiliency.

Our research platform continues to be one of dissemination and empirical validation. To this end, in the last two years we have trained middle-school teachers as program providers. In addition, we have implemented research methodologies designed to answer some important questions about the mechanisms of change in POP. We believe that systematic examination of dissemination and process issues will enable us to more effectively "inoculate" children against the epidemic of depression.

References

1. Klerman, G. (1979, April). The age of melancholy. *Psychology Today,* 37–88.

2. Robins, L.N., Helzer, J.E., Weissman, M.M., Orvaschel, H., Gruenberg, E., Burke, J.D., & Reiger, D.A. (1984). Lifetime prevalence of specific psychiatric disorders in three sites. *Archives of General Psychiatry, 41,* 949–958.

3. Reich, T., Van Eerdewegh, P., Rice, J.P., & Mullaney, J. (1987). The familial transmission of primary major depressive disorder. *Journal of Psychiatric Research, 21(4),* 613–624.

4. Lewinsohn, P.M., Hops, H., Roberts, R., & Seeley, J. (1993). Adolescent psychopathology: I. Prevalence and incidence of depression and other DSM-III-R disorders in high school students. *Journal of Abnormal Psychology, 102,* 110–120.

5. Garrison, C.Z., Schluchter, M.D., Schoenbach, V.J., & Kaplan, B.K. (1989). Epidemiology of depressive symptoms in young adolescents. *Journal of the American Academy of Child and Adolescent Psychiatry, 28(3),* 343–351.

6. Cytryn, L., McKnew, D.H., & Bunney, W.E. (1980). Diagnosis of depression in children: A reassessment. *American Journal of Psychiatry, 137,* 22–25.

7. Kovacs, M. & Beck, A.T. (1977). An empirical-clinical approach toward a definition of childhood depression. In J.G. Schulterbrandt & A. Raskin (Eds.), *Depression in childhood: Diagnosis, treatment and conceptual models.* New York: Raven Press.

8. Beck, A.T. (1967). *Depression: Causes and treatment.* Philadelphia: University of Pennsylvania Press.

9. Beck, A.T. (1976). *Cognitive therapy and the emotional disorders.* New York: International Universities Press.

10. Beck, A.T., Hollon, S.D., Young, J.E., Bedrosian, R.C., & Budenz, D. (1985). Treatment of depression with cognitive therapy and amitriptyline. *Archives of General Psychiatry, 42,* 142–148.

11. DeRubeis, R.J., Evans, M.D., Hollon, S.D., Garvey, M.J., Grove, W.M., & Tuason, V.B. (1990). How does cognitive therapy work? Cognitive change and symptom change in cognitive therapy and pharmacotherapy for depression. *Journal of Consulting and Clinical Psychology, 58(6),* 862–869.

12. Kashani, J.H., Husain, A., Shekim, W.O., Hodges, K.K., Cytryn, L., & McKnew, D.H. (1981). Current perspectives on childhood depression: An overview. *American Journal of Psychiatry, 138(2),* 143–153.

13. Butler, L., Miezitis, R.F., Friedman, R., & Cole, E. (1980). The effect of two school-based intervention programs on depressive symptoms in preadolescents. *American Educational Research Journal, 17(1),* 111–119.

14. Hammen, C. (1988). Self-cognitions, stressful events, and the prediction of depression in children of depressed mothers. *Journal of Abnormal Child Psychology, 16(3),* 347–360.

15. Kaslow, N.J., Rehm, L.P., & Siegel, A.W. (1984). Social-cognitive and cognitive correlates of depression in children. *Journal of Abnormal Child Psychology, 12(4),* 605–620.

16. Abramson, L.Y., Metalsky, G.I., & Alloy, L.B. (1989). Hopelessness depression: A theory-based subtype of depression. *Psychological Review, 96,* 358–372.

17. Overmier, J.B., & Seligman, M.E.P. (1967). Effects of inescapable shock upon subsequent escape and avoidance learning. *Journal of Comparative and Physiological Psychology, 63*, 23–33.
18. Seligman, M.E.P., & Maier, S.F. (1967). Failure to escape traumatic shock. *Journal of Experimental Psychology, 74*, 1–9.
19. Hiroto, D.S., & Seligman, M.E.P. (1975). Generality of learned helplessness in man. *Journal of Personality and Social Psychology, 31*, 311–327.
20. Abramson, L.Y., Seligman, M.E.P., & Teasdale, J.D. (1978). Learned helplessness in humans: Critique and reformulation. *Journal of Abnormal Psychology, 87*, 49–74.
21. Heider, F. (1958). *The psychology of interpersonal relations.* New York: John Wiley & Sons.
22. Peterson, C., & Seligman, M.E.P. (1984). Causal explanations as a risk factor for depression: Theory and evidence. *Psychological Review, 91*, 347–374.
23. Burns, M.O., & Seligman, M.E.P. (1989). Explanatory style across the lifespan: Evidence for stability over 52 years. *Journal of Personality and Social Psychology, 56*, 471–477.
24. Seligman, M.E.P., Nolen-Hoeksema, S., Thornton, K.M., & Thornton, N. (1990). Explanatory style as a mechanism of disappointing athletic performance. *Psychological Science, 1*, 143–146.
25. Schulman, P., & Seligman, M.E.P. (1986). Explanatory style predicts productivity among life insurance sales agents. *Journal of Personality and Social Psychology, 50*, 832–838.
26. Peterson, C., & Barrett, L. (1987). Explanatory style and academic performance among university freshmen. *Journal of Personality and Social Psychology, 53*, 603–607.
27. Metalsky, G.I., Abramson, L.Y., Seligman, M.E.P., Semmel, A., & Peterson, C. (1982). Attributional styles and life events in the classroom: Vulnerability and invulnerability to depressive mood reactions. *Journal of Personality and Social Psychology, 43*, 612–617.
28. Buchanan, G.M. (1995). Explanatory style and coronary heart disease. In G.M. Buchanan & M.E.P. Seligman (Eds.), *Explanatory style.* Hillsdale, NJ: Erlbaum.
29. Kaslow, N.J., Tannenbaum, R.L., & Seligman, M.E.P. (1978). *The KASTAN: A children's attributional style questionnaire.* Unpublished manuscript. University of Pennsylvania.
30. Seligman, M.E.P., Peterson, C., Kaslow, N.J., Tannenbaum, R.L., Alloy, L.B., & Abramson, L.Y. (1984). Attributional style and depressive symptoms in children. *Journal of Abnormal Psychology, 93*, 235–238.
31. Nolen-Hoeksema, S., Girgus, J.S., & Seligman, M.E.P. (1986). Learned helplessness in children: A longitudinal study of depression, achievement, and explanatory style. *Journal of Personality and Social Psychology, 51*, 435–442.
32. Johnson, C.C., Myers, L., Webber, L.S., & Hunter, S.M. (1997). Learned helplessness with excess weight and other cardiovascular risk factors in children. *American Journal of Health Behavior, 21(1)*, 51–59.
33. Paul, G., Girgus, J.S., Nolen-Hoeksema, S., & Seligman, M.E.P. (1989, April). Precursors of deficits in children's academic achievement. Pa-

per presented at the meetings of the Eastern Psychological Association, Philadelphia.

34. Toner, M.A., & Munro, D. (1996). Peer-social attributions and self-efficacy of peer-rejected preadolescents. *Merrill-Palmer Quarterly, 42(3)*, 339–357.

35. Hollon, S.D., DeRubeis, R.J., Evans, M.D., Wiemer, M.J., Garvey, M.J., Grove, W.M., & Tuason, V.B. (1992). Cognitive therapy and pharmacotherapy for depression: Singly and in combination. *Archives of General Psychiatry, 49*, 774–781.

36. Seligman, M.E.P. (1981). A learned helplessness point of view. In L.P Rehm (Ed.). *Behavior therapy for depression: Present status and future directions.* New York: Academic Press.

37. Ellis, A. (1962). *Reason and emotion in psychotherapy.* New York: Lyle Stuart.

38. Ellis, A., & Grieger, R. (1977). *Handbook of rational-emotive therapy.* New York: Springer.

39. Rush, A.J., Beck, A.T., Kovacs, M., & Hollon, S. (1977). Comparative efficacy of cognitive therapy and pharmacotherapy in the treatment of depressed outpatients. *Cognitive Therapy and Research, 1*, 17–18.

40. Beck, A.T., Rush, A.J., Shaw, B.F., & Emery, G. (1979). *Cognitive Therapy of Depression.* New York: Guilford Press.

41. Nilzon, K.R., & Palmerus, K. (1997). Anxiety in depressed school children. *School Psychology International, 18(2)*, 165–177.

42. Dodge, K. (1986). A social information processing model of social competence in children. In M. Perlmutter (Ed.), *Cognitive perspectives on children's social and behavioral development.* Hillsdale, NJ: Erlbaum.

43. Dodge, K.A., & Frame, C.L. (1982). Social cognitive biases and deficits in aggressive boys. *Child Development, 53*, 620–635.

44. Quiggle, N.L., Garber, J., Panak, W.F., & Dodge, K.A. (1992). Social information processing in aggressive and depressed children. *Child Development, 63*, 1305–1320.

45. Gillham, J.E., Jaycox, L.H., Reivich, K., Seligman, M.E.P., & Silver, T. (1990). *Penn Optimism Program: Depression Prevention for School Children—Leader's Manual.* Unpublished manuscript. University of Pennsylvania.

46. Jaycox, L.H., Reivich, K.J., Gillham, J.E., & Seligman, M.E.P. (1994). Prevention of depressive symptoms in school children. *Behaviour Research and Therapy, 32(8)*, 801–816.

47. Gillham, J.E., Reivich, K.J., Jaycox, L.J., & Seligman, M.E.P. (1995). Prevention of depressive symptoms in schoolchildren: Two-year follow-up. *Psychological Science, 6(6)*, 343–351.

48. Kovacs, M. (1985). The Children's Depression Inventory (CDI). *Psychopharmacology Bulletin, 21*, 995–1124.

9

Optimism

Charles S. Carver
Michael F. Scheier

Optimists are people who expect good things to happen to them; pessimists are people who expect bad things to come their way. These concepts have a distinguished history in folk wisdom. It's long been believed that this fundamental difference among people is important in many, if not all, facets of life. Although folk wisdom sometimes turns out to be less than accurate, this particular piece of folk wisdom is receiving a considerable degree of support in contemporary research. As we describe later on, optimists and pessimists differ in several ways that have a big impact on their lives. They differ in how they approach problems and challenges in life, and they differ in the manner—and the success— with which they cope with adversity.

The colloquial definitions of optimism and pessimism that are found in dictionaries turn on people's expectations for the future—positive and negative, respectively. Scientific approaches to these constructs also turn on expectations for the future. In so doing, these approaches connect the concepts of optimism and pessimism to a long tradition of expectancy-value models of motivation. The result of this connection is that the optimism construct, though originating in folk wisdom, is also firmly grounded in decades of theory and research on human motives and how they are expressed in behavior.

Expectancy-Value Models of Motivation

Let's begin by briefly exploring the elements of the expectancy-value approach to motivation, to better understand the dynamics that underlie optimism and pessimism and how they influence human experience (1). The expectancy-value viewpoint begins with the assumption that behavior is organized around the pursuit of goals. Goal concepts are given a variety of labels by different theorists, and there are several differences among them (for discussion of several such differences, see chapters 10 and 11 in this volume). At present, however, what we want to emphasize is what they have in common.

Goals are values that people take either as desirable or as undersirable (the latter are what you might think of as "anti-goals"). People try to fit their behaviors (and indeed their very selves) to values they see as desirable, and they try to keep away from values they see as undesirable. The more important the goals are to the person, the greater is the element of *value* that underlies the motivation. Without having a goal that they value, people have no reason to act.

The second conceptual element in the expectancy-value viewpoint is *expectancy*—a sense of confidence or doubt about the attainability of the goal value. If the person lacks confidence, again there will be no action. That's why a lack of confidence is sometimes referred to with the phrase "crippling doubt." Doubt can impair effort both before the action begins and while it's ongoing. Only if people have sufficient confidence will they surge into action and remain engaged in effort. When people have confidence about an eventual outcome, their efforts will continue even in the face of enormous adversity.

Variations in Breadth

The fact that goals vary in specificity—from the very general, to those that pertain to a particular domain of life, to the very concrete and specific— suggests that people have a comparable range of variations in expectancies (1, 2). To put it more concretely, you can be confident or doubtful about having a fulfilling life, about performing well in most socially evaluative circumstances, about winning a particular tennis match, about finding healthy food for dinner, or about tying your shoes.

Which of these sorts of expectancies matter? Probably all of them do. Expectancy-based theories generally suggest either explicitly or implicity that behavior is predicted best when the level of specificity of the expectancy matches that of the behavior. Sometimes it's argued that prediction is best when taking into account a combination of several levels of specificity. However, many outcomes in life have multiple causes. Further, people often face situations they've never experienced before, and situations that unfold and change over time. It has been suggested that in circumstances such as these, generalized expectations are particularly useful in predicting behavior and emotions (3).

The same principles that apply to focused confidence also apply to the generalized sense of optimism and pessimism. When we talk about optimism and pessimism, the sense of confidence that's at issue is simply more diffuse and broader in scope. Thus, when confronting a challenge of any type, optimists should tend to take a posture of confidence and persistence (even if progress is difficult or slow). Pessimists should be more doubtful and hesitant. This divergence should also be displayed—and perhaps even amplified—under conditions of serious adversity. Optimists are likely to assume the adversity can be handled successfully, in one fashion or another, whereas pessimists are likely to anticipate disaster (see also chapter 12 in this volume). These differences in how people approach stressful circumstances prove to have important implications for the manner in which people cope (4).

Variations in Conception and Assessment

Expectancies are pivotal in contemporary theories of optimism, but there are at least a couple of ways to think about expectancies and how to measure them, leading to two distinct literatures. One approach measures expectancies directly, asking people to indicate the extent to which they believe that their future outcomes will be good or bad. This is the approach we've taken in our work (4). Our own approach thus adds little further conceptual complexity to what we've said so far. Expectancies that are generalized—expectancies that pertain more or less to the person's entire life space—are what we mean when we use the terms optimism and pessimism.

In 1985 we developed a measure called the Life Orientation Test, or LOT (3), to assess differences between people in optimism and pessimism. Currently, we use a briefer form of the LOT, called the Life Orientation Test-Revised, or LOT-R (5). Table 9.1 contains the six items of the LOT-R. Available evidence (5) suggests that the LOT-R possesses good internal consistency (Cronbach's alpha for the scale tends to be in the high .70s to low .80s) and relatively stable test-retest reliability (usually falling in the lower to mid .70s). Because of the extensive item overlap between the original scale and the revised scale, correlations between the two scales are very high, often exceeding .90 (5).

We should perhaps also note explicitly that both the LOT and the LOT-R provide continuous distributions of scores. Although we refer throughout the chapter to optimists and pessimists as though they were distinct categories, this is a matter of descriptive convenience. People actually range from the very optimistic to the very pessimistic, with most falling somewhere in the middle.

The other approach to assessing optimism makes the assumption that people's expectancies for the future derive from their understanding of the causes of events in the past (6–7). If attributions or explanations for past failures in some domain focus on causes that are stable, the person's expectancy for the future in that domain will be for bad outcomes, because the cause is seen as relatively permanent and thus likely to remain in force. If attributions for past failures focus on cases that are unstable, then the outlook for the future may be brighter, because the cause may no longer be

Table 9.1 Items Making Up the Life Orientation Test-Revised (LOT-R)

1. In uncertain times, I usually expect the best.
2. It's easy for me to relax. (Filler)
3. If something can go wrong for me, it will.[a]
4. I'm always optimistic about my future.
5. I enjoy my friends a lot. (Filler)
6. It's important for me to keep busy. (Filler)
7. I hardly ever expect things to go my way.[a]
8. I don't get upset too easily. (Filler)
9. I rarely count on good things happening to me.[a]
10. Overall, I expect more good things to happen to me than bad.

Note: Respondents indicate the extent of their agreement with each item using a 5-point Likert scale, ranging from "strongly disagree" to "strongly agree." After reverse coding the negatively worded items (those identified with the supercript "a"), the six relevant items are summed to produce an overall score (filler items are not included in the scoring). From M. F. Scheier, C. S. Carver, & M. W. Bridges (1994), Distinguishing optimism from neuroticism (and trait anxiety, self-mastery, and self-esteem): A reevaluation of the Life Orientation Test. *Journal of Personality and Social Psychology, 67,* 1063–1078. Reprinted with permission of the American Psychological Association and the authors.

in force. If explanations for past failures are global (apply to many aspects of life), the person's expectancy for the future across many domains will be for bad outcomes, because the causal forces are at work everywhere. If the explanations are specific, however, the outlook in other areas of life may be brighter because the causes don't apply there.

Attributions can be to a particular area of action (e.g., playing tennis), or to a moderately broad domain (e.g., performance in evaluative situations), but they are usually treated at an even broader level. That is, it's often assumed that people have "explanatory styles," which bear on the person's whole life space (see chapters 8 and 12 in this volume). The theory that's identified with the term "explanatory style" holds that optimism and pessimism are defined by adaptive versus problematic patterns of explanation (6–7).

Although these two approaches to conceptualizing and measuring optimism have important differences, we focus here on their commonality. They share the theme that expectations for the future are an important determinant of people's actions and subjective experiences. Optimism is the expectation that you will have good outcomes in life, even if you're presently facing adversity. Pessimism is the expectation of bad outcomes—the sense that the adversity won't be overcome.

These two approaches to optimism and pessimism have led to their own research literatures, each of which sheds light on the nature and function of optimism and pessimism (see also Snyder's discussion of hope, another closely related member of the theoretical family in chapter 10 of this volume). In what follows, we focus mostly on optimism as operationalized by Scheier and Carver (3–5)—that is, in terms of self-reported generalized expectancies.

Possible Origins of Optimism and Pessimism

Regardless of whether you think of optimism in terms of analyses of causal processes or in terms of confidence and doubt per se, there are several ways to think about how optimism comes to exist as a quality of personality. For example, many aspects of personality are genetically influenced. Is optimism one of them? The answer seems to be yes. The results of twin studies suggest that optimism, whether assessed in terms of generalized expectancies or in terms of explanatory style, is subject to genetic influence (8, 9).

As is always true in considering heritability, there remains a question about whether optimism is *itself* heritable, or whether it displays heritability because it's closely related to some other aspect of biologically based temperament. Optimism relates both to neuroticism and to extraversion, and both of these qualities are known to be genetically influenced (Watson, David, and Suls discuss these qualities of temperament in chapter 6 of this volume). Although it appears that optimism and pessimism are distinguishable from these temperaments (5), it may be that the observed heritability of optimism is a product of these associations.

Another potential influence on having an optimistic versus pessimistic outlook on life is early childhood experience. Many theories maintain that early childhood is an important time in the formation of personality. For example, Erikson's well-known theory of personality development (10) holds that infants who experience the social world as predictable develop a sense of "basic trust," whereas those who experience the world as unpredictable develop a sense of "basic mistrust." These qualities aren't all that different from the general sense of optimism and pessimism.

Similarly, discussions of attachment hold that some infants are securely attached in their relationships, others are not (11–12). This model has also been extended to discussions of the attachments that adults have to important relationships in their lives (13). As it happens, insecurity of adult attachment is related to pessimism. This finding suggests the possibility that optimism may derive in part from the early childhood experience of secure attachment to a caregiver (see also 6, 14).

Whether optimism and pessimism turn out to derive from genetic influences or from early experiences in life, they are qualities of personality that are basic to the person. They influence how people orient to all the events of their lives, how they define the nature of the realities they experience (cf. the discussion in chapter 2 this volume). The qualities of optimism and pessimism influence people's subjective experiences when confronting problems in life, and they also influence the actions people engage in to try to deal with these problems. Thus, when we ask the question, "Do optimists and pessimists differ in how they react to adversity?'' the answer has at least two parts. One part concerns differences in feelings of well-being versus distress. The other part concerns differences in how people act to deal with the adversity. These two themes are explored in the next two sections.

Optimism and Subjective Well-Being Under Adversity

When people confront adversity or difficulty in their lives, they experience a variety of emotions, ranging from excitement and eagerness, to anger, anxiety, and depression. The balance among these feelings appears to relate to people's degree of optimism or pessimism. Optimists are people who expect to have positive outcomes, even when things are difficult. This confidence should yield a mix of feelings that is relatively positive. Pessimists expect negative outcomes. This doubt should yield a greater tendency toward negative feelings—anxiety, guilt, anger, sadness, or despair (1, 4).

Over the past decade or so, many studies have examined relationships between optimism and distress in groups of people facing difficulty or adversity. The range of stressors involved in this research is very broad. Studies have examined the experiences of students entering college (15), employees of businesses (16), and survivors of missile attacks (17). Studies have measured the responses of people caring for cancer patients (18) and people caring for Alzheimer's patients (19, 20). Research has examined experiences of people dealing with medical procedures such as childbirth (21), abortion (22), coronary artery bypass surgery (23–24), attempts at in vitro fertilization (25), and bone marrow transplantation (26). Yet other studies have looked at how people deal with a diagnosis of cancer (27–28) and the progression of AIDS (29). Thus, many of the studies focus on people who are undergoing truly serious life crises, rather than just dealing with the ordinary problems of daily life.

Some of the studies of this group are more limited than others. In many cases the researchers examined responses to a difficult event, but did so at only one time point. What's known from these studies is that pessimists experienced more distress after the event in question. What is not known is whether the pessimists may have had more distress even before the event. It's far more useful to examine people repeatedly and see how their distress shifts over time and circumstances. Of course, it's sometimes impossible to recruit participants before the event you're interested in (e.g., it's hard to know when an earthquake will occur, so it's hard to recruit people two weeks before the earthquake). But even in cases where participants weren't recruited before the event, it's useful to examine the process of adaptation to the event across an extended period. Some of the studies that make up this literature on stress and subjective well-being did assess participants at multiple time points, and we will focus on these studies here.

One early study of the effect of optimism on emotional well-being (21) examined the development of depressed feelings after childbirth. Women in this study completed the LOT and a depression scale in the last third of their pregnancy. They then completed the depression measure again three weeks after their babies were born. Optimism related to lower depression symptoms at the initial assessment. More important, optimism predicted lower levels of depressive symptoms post-partum, even when controlling for the initial levels. Thus, optimism seemed to confer a resistance to the development of depressive symptoms after having a baby.

A similar point is made by a more recent study (30), which also examined the effects of optimism on psychological adjustment during pregnancy. Women completed the LOT during their first prenatal clinic visit. During the last trimester of their pregnancy, the women's anxiety was assessed, as well as the extent to which they were maintaining positive states of mind. Optimism was a significant predictor of each. The predictive association of optimism with anxiety was negative, whereas the association with positive states of mind was positive.

Other research investigated the reactions of men who were undergoing and recovering from coronary artery bypass surgery (24). Patients completed questionnaires the day before surgery, six to eight days after surgery, and six months postsurgery. Prior to surgery, optimists reported lower levels of hostility and depression than did pessimists. A week after surgery, optimists reported feeling more relief and happiness, greater satisfaction with their medical care, and greater satisfaction with the emotional support they had received from friends. Six months after surgery, optimists reported higher quality of life than pessimists. In a follow-up of the same patients five years after surgery, optimists continued to experience greater subjective well-being and general quality of life compared to pessimists. All these differences remained significant when medical factors were statistically controlled.

Another study on optimism and quality of life after coronary artery bypass surgery (23) assessed participants one month prior to surgery and eight months after surgery. Analysis revealed that optimism was negatively related to presurgical distress. Further, controlling for presurgical life satisfaction, optimism was positively related to postsurgical life satisfaction. Further analysis revealed that the general sense of optimism appeared to operate on feelings of life satisfaction through a more focused sense of confidence about the surgery. That is, the general sense of optimism about life seems to have been funneled into a specific kind of optimism regarding the surgery and from there to satisfaction with life.

Optimism has also been studied in the context of other kinds of health crises. One study examined the effect of optimism on psychological adaptation to treatment for early-stage breast cancer (27). Diagnosis and treatment for breast cancer is a traumatic experience, and cancer is a life-threatenting disease. However, prognosis for early-stage cancer is relatively good. This experience thus provides sufficient ambiguity about what will happen in the future to permit individual differences in optimism to be readily expressed. Patients in this study were interviewed six times: at the time of diagnosis, the day before surgery, 7 to 10 days after surgery, and 3, 6, and 12 months later. Optimism was assessed (using the LOT) at the time of diagnosis and was used to predict distress levels at the subsequent time points.

Optimism inversely predicted distress over time, above and beyond the effect of relevant medical variables and beyond the effects of earlier distress. That is, the prediction of distress at 3, 6, and 12 months after surgery was significant, even when the immediately prior level of distress was controlled. Thus, optimism predicted not only lower initial distress, but also resilience to distress during the year following surgery.

Another medical situation that's been studied with respect to optimism effects is infertility—a problem that causes a good deal of unhappiness to a good many people (31). A procedure called in vitro fertilization is one way to circumvent fertility problems, but it doesn't always work. Researchers focused in this study on people whose attempts were unsuccessful (25). Approximately eight weeks before the attempt, the researchers measured optimism, specific expectancies for fertilization success, coping strategies, distress levels, and the impact of the infertility on participants' lives. Two weeks after notification of a negative pregnancy test, distress was assessed by phone. Neither demographics, obstetric history, marital adjustment, nor the rated effect of infertility on subjects' lives predicted this time-2 distress—but optimism did. Controlling for time-1 distress, pessimism was in fact the strongest predictor of time-2 distress.

Yet another recent study examined the influence of optimism on adjustment to abortion (22). One hour prior to an abortion, women completed measures of optimism, self-esteem, self-mastery, self-efficacy, and depression. Depression and psychological adjustment were assessed 30 minutes after the abortion and again three weeks later. Optimists had less preabortion depression, better postabortion adjustment, and better three-week adjustment than did pessimists. The authors of the study concluded that optimism relates to psychological adjustment both directly and also indirectly through a sense of personal efficacy.

Not only does optimism have a positive effect on the psychological well-being of people dealing with medical conditions, but it also influences the psychological well-being of people who are acting as caregivers to patients. One project supporting this conclusion studied a group of cancer patients and their caregivers, and found that caregivers' optimism related to a number of caregiver well-being variables (18). Optimism was related to lower symptoms of depression, less impact of caregiving on physical health, and less impact on caregivers' daily schedules. Caregiver optimism thus predicted caregiver reactions to the burdens of caring for a family member with cancer and did so independent of patient variables. Similar results have been found in research on caregiver spouses of Alzheimer's patients (19–20), with optimism relating to lower levels of depression and higher levels of psychological well-being.

Although much of the evidence for the relationship between optimism and psychological well-being comes from samples such as people facing health threats and people caring for seriously ill relatives, other studies have looked at samples of people undergoing events that are difficult but far less extreme. For example, the start of a person's college years is a difficult and stressful time, and researchers have examined students making their adjustment to their first semester of college (15). Optimism, self-esteem, and a number of other variables were assessed when the students first arrived on campus. Measures of psychological and physical well-being were obtained at the end of the semester. Higher levels of optimism upon entering college predicted lower levels of psychological distress at the end of the semester. The relationship was independent of effects due to self-esteem, locus of control, desire for control, and baseline mood.

Optimism, Pessimism, and Coping

As the evidence reviewed in the previous section makes clear, optimists experience less distress than pessimists when dealing with difficulties in their lives. Is this just because optimists are more cheerful than pessimists? Apparently not, because the differences often remain, even when statistical controls are incorporated for previous levels of distress. There must be other explanations. Do optimists do anything in particular to cope that helps them adapt better than pessimists? Many researchers are now investigating this possibility as a potential mechanism through which optimism confers psychological benefits. In this section we consider the strategies that optimists and pessimists tend to use and the broader meaning of these strategies.

In many respects, this discussion turns out to be a more detailed depiction of the broad behavioral tendencies we discussed earlier in the chapter, when we were describing expectancy-value models of motivation. That is, people who are confident about the future exert continuing effort, even when dealing with serious adversity. People who are doubtful about the future are more likely to try to push the adversity away as though they can somehow escape its existence by wishful thinking, more likely to do things that provide temporary distractions but don't help solve the problem, and sometimes even give up trying. Both the effort and the removel of effort can be expressed in a variety of ways, and those expressions—coping reactions and coping strategies—are the focus of this section.

Differences in coping methods used by optimists and pessimists have been found in a number of studies. One early project (32) asked undergraduates to recall the most stressful event that had happened to them during the previous month and complete a checklist of coping responses with respect to that event. Optimism related positively to problem-focused coping, especially when the stressful situation was perceived to be controllable. Optimism also related to the use of positive reframing and (when the situation was perceived to be uncontrollable) with the tendency to accept the reality of the situation. In contrast, optimism related negatively to the use of denial and the attempt to distance oneself from the problem.

These findings provided the first indication that optimists not only use problem-centered coping, but also use a variety of emotion-focused coping techniques, including striving to accept the reality of difficult situations and putting the situations in the best possible light. These findings hint that optimists may enjoy a coping advantage over pessimists, even in situations that cannot be changed.

Other research has studied differences in dispositional coping styles among optimists and pessimists (33–34). As with situational coping, optimists reported a dispositional tendency to rely on active, problem-focused coping, and they reported being more planful when confronting stressful events. Pessimism was associated with the tendency to disengage from the goals with which the stressor is interfering. While optimists reported a tendency to accept the reality of stressful events, they also reported trying to see the best in bad situations and to learn something from them. (They seem to try to find benefits in adversity, a process that Tennen and Affleck discuss in greater detail in chapter 13 in this volume.) In contrast, pessimists reported tendencies toward overt denial and substance abuse, strategies that lessen their awareness of the problem. Thus, in general terms optimists appear to be active copers and pessimists appear to be avoidant copers.

Other projects have studied the relationship between optimism and coping strategies in more specific contexts. For example, consider the work environment. Research has found that optimists used more problem-focused coping than pessimists (self-control and directed problem solving [35]). Pessimists used more emotion-focused coping (including both the use of social support and avoidance of being with people, and self-indulgent escapism such as sleeping, eating, and drinking). Another study, focusing on executive women (36), found that optimists appraised and evaluated daily hassles differently than did pessimists. Optimistic women expected gain or growth from stressful events and reported coping indicative of acceptance, expressiveness, and tension reduction. They also reported using their social support in stressful circumstances rather than withdrawing, distancing, or engaging in self-blame.

Several studies described earlier in this chapter also provide evidence of relationships between optimism and coping and between coping and emotional well-being. One study of coronary artery bypass surgery (24) assessed the use of attentional-cognitive strategies as ways of dealing with the experience. Before surgery, optimists were more likely than pessimists to report that they were making plans for their future and setting goals for their recovery. Optimists, as compared to pessimists, also tended to report being less focused on the negative aspects of their experience—their distress emotions and physical symptoms. As Stanton and Franz discuss in chapter 5 of this volume, focusing on emotions can have varying consequences, depending on the nature of the focusing. In this case, however, the focusing was simply an enhanced awareness of the distress, which we suspect was not very adaptive. Indeed, the fact that pessimists focused on negative aspects of their experience raises the possibility that they are vulnerable to catastrophizing, a reaction discussed by Peterson and Moon in chapter 12 of this volume.

Once the surgery was past, optimists were more likely than pessimists to report seeking out and requesting information about what the physician would be requiring of them in the months ahead. Optimists were also less likely to report trying to suppress thoughts about their physical symptoms. Results from path analyses suggested that the positive impact of optimism on quality of life six months post-surgery occurred through the indirect effect of differences in coping.

The study of adaptation to failed in vitro fertilization that was described earlier (25) also examined coping. Although the researchers did not find a relationship between optimism and instrumental coping, they did find that pessimism related to escape as a coping strategy. Escape, in turn, related to greater distress after the fertilization failure. In addition, optimists were more likely than pessimists to report feeling that they benefited somehow from the failed fertilization experience (e.g., by becoming closer to their spouse).

The study of AIDS patients described earlier (29) also provides information regarding coping. In general, optimism was associated with active coping strategies. Optimism predicted positive attitudes and tendencies to plan for recovery, seek information, and reframe bad situations so as to see their most positive aspects. Optimists made less use of fatalism, self-blame, and escapism, and they didn't focus on the negative aspects of the situation or try to suppress thoughts about their symptoms. Optimists also appeared to accept situations that they could not change, rather than trying to escape those situations.

Several studies have examined the relationship between optimism and coping among cancer patients. One study followed women who were scheduled for breast biopsy (37). Optimism, coping, and mood were assessed the day before biopsy and (among women who received a cancer diagnosis) again 24 hours before surgery and three weeks after surgery. Women with a benign diagnosis completed a second assessment that corresponded to either the second or the third assessment of the cancer group. Pessimistic women in this study used more cognitive avoidance in coping with the upcoming diagnostic procedure than did optimists. This avoidance contributed significantly to distress prior to biopsy. Indeed, cognitive avoidance proved to be a mediator of the association of pessimism with prebiopsy distress. Cognitive avoidance prebiopsy also predicted postbiopsy distress among women with positive diagnoses.

Another study of cancer patients, mentioned earlier in the chapter, examined the ways women cope with treatment for early-stage breast cancer during the first full year after treatment (27). Optimism, coping (with the diagnosis of cancer), and mood were assessed the day before surgery. Coping and mood were also assessed 10 days postsurgery, and at three follow-up points during the next year. Both before and after surgery, optimism was associated with a pattern of reported coping tactics that revolved around accepting the reality of the situation, placing as positive a light on the situation as possible, trying to relieve the situation with humor, and (at pre-surgery only) taking active steps to do whatever there was to be done. Pessimism was associated with denial and behavioral disengagement (giving up) at each measurement point.

The coping tactics that related to optimism and pessimism also related strongly to the distress that subjects reported. Positive reframing, acceptance, and the use of humor were all related inversely to self-reports of distress, both before surgery and after. Denial and behavioral disengagment were positively related to distress at all measurement points. At the six-month point a new association emerged, such that distress was positively related to another kind of avoidance coping: self-distraction. Not unexpectedly, given the pattern of the correlations, further analyses revealed that the effect of optimism on distress was largely indirect through coping, particularly at postsurgery.

Other studies have also looked for a mediational role of coping in the relationship between optimism and psychological well-being. In the college adaptation study described earlier (15), optimistic students were more likely than pessimistic students to engage in active coping and less likely to engage in avoidance coping. Avoidance coping was associated with poorer adjustment, and active coping was (separately) associated with better adjustment. The paths from optimism to well-being through coping were significant. Thus, as in the health studies, the beneficial effects of optimism in this context seemed to be operating at least in part through the differences in coping.

Similarly, in the study described earlier concerning adjustment to pregnancy (30), optimistic women were more likely than pessimistic women to engage in constructive thinking (i.e., the tendency to think about and solve daily problems in an effective way). Further, as with optimism, constructive thinking also correlated negatively with later anxiety and positively with later positive states of mind. Subsequent analyses revealed that the association between optimism and each of these markers of psychological adjustment was mediated through the tendency of optimists to engage in constructive thinking.

In sum, these studies indicate that optimists differ from pessimists both in their stable coping tendencies and in the kinds of coping responses that they spontaneously generate when confronting stressful situations. Optimists also differ from pessimists in the manner in which they cope with serious disease and with concerns about specific health threats. In general (see Table 9.2), findings from this research suggest that optimists tend to use more problem-focused coping strategies than do pessimists. When problem-focused coping is not a possibility, optimists turn to adaptive emotion-focused coping strategies such as acceptance, use of humor, and positive reframing. Pessimists tend to cope through overt denial and by mentally and behaviorally disengaging from the goals with which the stressor is interfering.

It is particularly noteworthy that optimists turn toward acceptance in uncontrollable situations, whereas pessimists turn more to the use of active attempts at denial. Although both tactics seem to reflect emotion-focused coping, there are important qualitative differences between them that may, in turn, be associated with different qualities of outcomes. More concretely, denial (the refusal to accept the reality of the situation) means attempting to adhere to a worldview that is no longer valid. In contrast, acceptance implies a restructuring of one's experience so as to come to grips with the reality of the situation that one confronts. Acceptance thus may involve a deeper set of processes, in which the person actively works through the experience, attempting to integrate it into an evolving worldview.

The active attempt to come to terms with the existence of problems may confer special benefits to acceptance as a coping response. We should be very clear here, however, about the sort of acceptance we are talking about. The kind of acceptance we have in mind is a willingness to admit that a problem exists or that an event has happened—even an event that may irrevocably alter the fabric of the person's life. We are *not* talking about a stoic resignation, a fatalistic acceptance of the negative consequences to which the problem or event might lead, no matter how likely those consequences might be. The latter kind of acceptance does not confer a benefit at all.

Consider, for example, someone diagnosed with an illness such as a terminal cancer or AIDS. The ultimate outcome in both cases may be death. Yet, the person can accept the fact that he or she is terminally ill without

Table 9.2 Coping Tendencies of Optimists and Pessimists

Optimists	Pessimists
Information seeking	Suppression of thoughts
Active coping and planning	Giving up
Positive reframing	Self-distraction
Seeking benefit	Cognitive avoidance
Use of humor	Focus on distress
Acceptance	Overt denial

simultaneously succumbing to the feeling that he or she is "as good as dead." The latter sort of acceptance, or resignation, may well promote a kind of functional death, in which the person prematurely disengages from the opportunities of life. Consistent with this idea, there are findings suggesting that people who react to illness diagnoses with stoic resignation, or passive acceptance of their own impending death, actually die sooner than those who exhibit less of these qualities (38–41).

In contrast to resignation to the ultimate consequence of the diagnosis, limited acceptance of the diagnosis per se may have very different consequences. It may cause people to reprioritize their lives, to realistically revise and cut back on long-term goals, and to use what time they have left in constructive and optimal ways. Stated somewhat differently, by accepting the fact that life may be compromised (but not over), people may be impelled to develop a more adaptive set of parameters within which to live the life they have left. It is in this spirit that we have speculated that acceptance serves the purpose of keeping the person goal-engaged and indeed "life-engaged"(1).

Promotion of Well-Being

In describing the manner in which optimists and pessimists cope with adversity, several other studies are worth noting. These studies don't deal with coping per se, but they make points that are closely related to the points we've made regarding coping. Some of these are studies of proactive processes, processes that promote good health and well-being. The reasoning behind the studies is that people who are optimistic about their personal future may take active steps to ensure the positive quality of that future. This behavior would be much the same as engaging in problem-focused coping activities, except there's no particular stressor threatening the person. The "problem" in this case is simply the problem of ensuring good health and well-being, no matter what circumstances might arise in the future.

One study looking at the possibility of individual differences in health promotion followed a group of heart patients who were participating in a cardiac rehabilitation program (42). Optimism among participants was related to greater success in lowering levels of saturated fat, body fat, and global coronary risk. Optimism was also related to increases in level of exercise across the rehabilitation period. Another study investigated the lifestyles of coronary artery bypass patients five years after their surgery. This study found that optimists were more likely than pessimists to be taking vitamins, to be eating low-fat foods, and to be enrolled in a cardiac rehabilitation program (4).

Heart disease isn't the only aspect of health-related behavior that's been related to optimism. Another obvious health risk related to people's behavior is HIV infection. By avoiding certain sexual practices (e.g., sex with unknown partners), people reduce their risk of infection. One study of HIV-negative gay men revealed that optimists reported having fewer anonymous sexual partners than did pessimists (29). This finding suggests that optimists were making efforts to reduce their risk, thereby safeguarding their health.

Other studies have examined the health-related habits reported by groups of people with no particular salient health concerns. At least two such projects found associations in which optimists reported more health-promoting behaviors than pessimists (43–44). Taken together, the various studies that we've described in the preceding paragraphs suggest that optimism is associated with behaviors aimed at promoting health and reducing health risk.

Consistent with this pattern is research showing conclusively that optimists aren't simply people who stick their heads in the sand and ignore threats to their well-being. Rather, they display a pattern of attending selectively to risks—risks that both are applicable to them and also are related to serious health problems (45). If the potential health problem is minor, or if it's unlikely to bear on them personally, optimists don't show this elevated vigilance. Only when the threat matters does it emerge. This fits the idea that optimists scan their surroundings for threats to their well-being, but save their behavioral responses for threats that are truly meaningful.

Pessimism and Health-Defeating Behaviors

Another set of studies to consider in this context represent the reverse of the proactive effort at establishing and maintaining well-being. We characterized optimists throughout this discussion as being persistent in the attempts to reach desired goals. This includes persistence in coping with the onset of serious adversity, and it includes active efforts to promote well-being even apart from adversity. The theory from which we've operated also suggests that people who are pessimistic are less likely to display such persistence. There is, in fact, considerable evidence that pessimists engage in behaviors that have adverse consequences for well-being, that the tendency to give up can have serious—even deadly—consequences.

One behavior that may stem from the giving-up tendency is various forms of substance abuse. Substance abuse in general, and excessive alcohol consumption in particular, are often seen as taking place in the service of an escape from problems. If so, it follows that pessimists should be more vulnerable than would otherwise comparable optimists to engaging in this pattern of maladaptive behavior. At least three studies have produced findings that fit this picture.

One was a study of women with a family history of alcoholism. Pessimists in this group were more likely than optimists to report having drinking problems (46). Another study of drinking examined people who had been treated for alcohol abuse and were now entering an aftercare program. This study found that pessimists were more likely to drop out of the aftercare program and to return to drinking than optimists (47). The final study (30) examined substance use among a group of pregnant women. Optimists were less likely to engage in substance abuse during the course of their pregnancies than were pessimists. These studies converge in showing that pessimists display one form of disengagement—substance abuse—more than optimists.

People can give up in many ways. Substance abuse such as alcohol consumption dulls awareness of failures and problems. People can turn their backs on their problems by distracting themselves with other activities. Even sleeping sometimes serves the purpose of escaping from situations that we don't want to face. Sometimes, though, giving up is far more complete than this. Sometimes people give up not just on specific goals, but on all the goals that make up their lives. In such an extreme case, suicide may be the result. Some people are more vulnerable to this event than others. It's commonly assumed that depression is the best indicator of suicide risk. But research has found that pessimism (as measured by the Hopelessness scale) is a stronger predictor of this act—the ultimate disengagement from life (48).

In sum, there is evidence that the general sense of pessimism is one source of influence that can lead people into self-defeating patterns of living. The result can be less persistence, more use of avoidance coping in dealing with problems, health-damaging behavior, and potentially even an impulse to escape from life altogether. It is arguable that when there's no confidence about the future, there's simply nothing to sustain life (1).

Is Optimism Always Better than Pessimism?

The picture we've painted throughout this chapter is one in which optimists are virtually always better off than pessimists. The evidence we've reviewed indicates that they are less distressed when times are tough, they cope in ways that foster better outcomes for themselves, and they're better at taking the steps necessary to ensure their futures continue to be bright. Although there are certainly times and situations in which optimists are only minimally better off than pessimists, and probably cases where they have no advantage at all, there's remarkably little evidence that optimists are ever *worse* off than pessimists.

Several people have suggested the possibility that such situations may exist, that optimism may be potentially damaging (49, 50). And, indeed, there is logic behind this hypothesis. For example, too much optimism might potentially lead people to ignore a threat until it's too late, or might lead people to overestimate their ability to deal with an adverse situation, resulting in poorer outcomes.

Most of the data reviewed in the preceding sections indicate that this is generally not the case. On the other hand, there are a couple of studies which suggest the possibility that optimists may not always take action to enhance their future well-being. Goodman, Chesney, and Tipton (51) studied the extent to which a group of adolescent girls at risk for HIV infection sought out information about HIV testing and agreed to have a test performed. Those higher in optimism were less likely to expose themselves to the information about HIV testing and were less likely to follow through with an actual test than were those lower in optimism (see also [52]).

These findings contradict the evidence reviewed earlier. Why the findings diverge in this way is not clear. Goodman et al. noted that the average level of optimism among these adolescent girls was substantially lower than the levels typically seen in other samples; this difference may somehow have played a role in the results. Alternatively, perhaps the results do not really contradict previous findings at all. Perhaps it seems so only because of the absence of other data that would render the findings more understandable. For example, no information was gathered in this study about the knowledge the girls had concerning the serostatus of their sexual partners. Perhaps optimists had gone to greater lengths than pessimists to verify that their partners were HIV-negative. If so, they would have had less need to seek out HIV-relevant information or have their HIV status tested. Obviously, more work is needed for these questions to be resolved.

The idea that optimists may fail to take steps to protect themselves against threats is one potential way in which optimism can work against a person. Another possibility worth considering is that the worldview of an optimist might be more vulnerable than that of a pessimist to the shattering impact of a traumatic event. Such an event is more consistent with the pessimist's worldview than with the optimist's. Given the diagnosis of metastatic cancer, the experience of a violent rape, or having one's home destroyed by fire or flood, will the optimist react worse than the pessimist? Will optimists be less able to rebuild the shattered assumptions of their lives? (See the Janoff-Bulman chapter of this volume for a broader discussion of related issues.) All of these possibilities are legitimate to raise. Any of them might occur. However, we're aware of no evidence that any of them systematically *does* occur.

Perhaps the lack of support for the idea that optimists respond worse to a shattering event reflects a more general lack of information about how qualities of personality relate to responses to trauma, or to experiences such as terminal illness. In reality, there isn't a great deal of information on these questions. However, at present, we don't expect optimists to respond adversely. Rather, we expect them to reset their sights on their changed realities and to continue to make the best of the situations they are facing. Pessimists may find that their worldviews are confirmed by trauma or disaster, but we doubt that pessimists will take much satisfaction in this confirmation. Rather, their experience will be the continuing anticipation of yet further adversity.

Can Pessimists Become Optimists?

Given the wide variety of ways in which the life of the optimist is better than the life of the pessimist, there's good reason to want to be in the former category instead of the latter. There's a problem, though, for those of us who aren't optimists at present. Earlier in the chapter we discussed the possible origins of optimism and pessimism in inheritance and in early childhood experience. Both of these pathways to the creation of an optimistic or pessimistic outlook on life suggest that the quality in question is relatively pervasive and relatively permanent. Genetically determined qualities are by definition part of your fundamantal make-up and can be expected to exert a virtually unending influence on your behavior. Similarly, aspects of your worldview that are acquired early in life are the foundation from which you proceed to experience the *rest* of the events in your life. The more firmly shaped is that foundation, the more enduring is its influence.

If the quality of pessimism is that deeply embedded in a person's life, can it be changed? The answer seems to be a cautious yes (chapter 8 in this volume describes one approach to doing so among children; see also 14). It seems clear that change in an optimistic direction is possible. However, there remain questions about how large a change can be reasonably expected and how permanent the change will be. There also remain questions about whether an induced optimistic view on life will act in the same way— have the same beneficial effects—as a naturally occurring optimistic view.

There are many ways to try to turn a pessimist into an optimist. The most straightforward approach may be the group of techniques known collectively as "cognitive-behavioral therapies." Indeed, trying to turn either generalized or focused pessimists into optimists seems an apt characterization of the main point of these therapies. Their earliest applications were to problems such as depression and anxiety (53). The logic behind the therapies was that people with these problems make a variety of unduly negative mental distortions (e.g., "I can't do anything right"). The unrealistically negative cognitions cause negative affect (dysphoria, anxiety) and set the person up to behave maladaptively (by not trying). In cases such as this, the cognitive distortions closely resemble what we would imagine to be the interior monologue of the pessimist.

If inappropriately negative cognitions and self-statements define the nature of the problem, the goal of the cognitive therapies is to change the cognitions, to make them more positive, and to thereby diminish distress and allow more adaptive behaviors to emerge. Many techniques have been devised for producing these changes. In general, this approach to therapy begins by having people pay closer attention to their experience, to identify both points where distress arises and the cognitions associated with (or immediately preceding) these points. The idea is to give the person a better awareness of what are now automatic thoughts. In many cases, the cognitions in question turn out to be pessimistic beliefs. Once the beliefs have been isolated, they can be challenged and changed. (This attempt to deal with pessimistic beliefs by shifting them has an interesting resemblance to positive reframing, which was described earlier in the chapter as a useful coping strategy.)

Another method often used is personal efficacy training. The focus of such procedures is on increasing specific kinds of competence or control (e.g., by assertiveness training or social skill training). However, the specific techniques often address thoughts and behaviors that relate to a more general sense of pessimism. For example, problem-solving training, teaching people to select and define obtainable subgoals, and decision-making training all improve the ways in which a person handles a wide range of everyday situations.

Although the development of positive expectations is an important goal of these therapies, it is also important to recognize that it can be counterproductive to try to immediately substitute an unquestioning optimism for an existing doubt. Sometimes the reason for pessimism is that people have unrealistically high aspirations for themselves. They demand perfection in themselves, hardly ever find it, and as a result develop doubts about their adequacy. This tendency must be countered by establishing more realistic goals and identifying which situations must be accepted rather than changed. The person must learn to relinquish unattainable goals and set alternative goals to replace those that cannot be attained.

Concluding Comment

It is commonly held that positive thinking is good and negative thinking is bad. The advice given to the student taking an exam, the athlete competing at the Olympics, and the patient facing a life-altering diagnosis is to "think positive." Are there really benefits to such positive thinking? The answer is an emphatic yes. A growing literature supports the idea that expectations for the future have an important impact on how people respond in times of adversity or difficulty. The expectations influence the manner in which people confront these difficulties, and they influence the success—both emotional and behavioral—with which people deal with the difficulties. We have yet to see clear evidence of a case in which holding positive expectations for one's future is deterimental. There are many questions that are yet unanswered: for example, about the precise mechanism by which optimism influences subjective well-being, and about potential pathways by which optimism may influence physical well-being. But we are optimistic about the future of work in this area, optimistic that research will continue to unravel the paths by which positive thinking benefits people.

Acknowledgment: Preparation of this chapter was facilitated by support from the National Cancer Institute (CA64710 and CA64711).

References

1. Carver, C. S., & Scheier, M. F. (1998). *On the self-regulation of behavior.* New York: Cambridge University Press.
2. Armor, D. A., & Taylor, S. E. (1998). Situated optimism: Specific outcome expectancies and self-regulation. In M. Zanna (Ed.), *Advances in experimental social psychology* (Vol. 30, pp. 309–379). San Diego: Academic Press.
3. Scheier, M. F., & Carver, C. S. (1985). Optimism, coping and health: Assessment and implications of generalized outcome expectancies. *Health Psychology, 4*, 219–247.
4. Scheier, M. F., & Carver, C. S. (1992). Effects of optimism on psychological and physical well-being: Theoretical overview and empirical update. *Cognitive Therapy and Research, 16*, 201–228.
5. Scheier, M. F., Carver, C. S., & Bridges, M. W. (1994). Distinguishing optimism from neuroticism (and trait anxiety, self-mastery, and self-esteem): A reevaluation of the Life Orientation Test. *Journal of Personality and Social Psychology, 67*, 1063–1078.
6. Peterson, C., & Seligman, M. E. P. (1984). Causal explanations as a risk factor for depression: Theory and evidence. *Psychological Review, 91*, 347–374.
7. Seligman, M. E. P. (1991). *Learned optimism.* New York: Knopf.
8. Plomin, R., Scheier, M. F., Bergeman, C. S., Pedersen, N. L., Nesselroade, J. R., & McClearn, G. E. (1992). Optimism, pessimism, and mental health: A twin/adoption analysis. *Personality and Individual Differences, 13*, 921–930.
9. Schulman, P., Keith, D., & Seligman, M. E. P. (1991). Is optimism heritable? A study of twins. *Behavior Research and Therapy, 31*, 569–574.
10. Erikson, E. H. (1968). *Identity: Youth and crisis.* New York: Norton.
11. Bowlby, J. (1988). *A secure base: Parent-child attachment and healthy human development.* New York: Basic Books.
12. Ainsworth, M. D. S., Blehar, M. C., Waters, E., & Wall, T. (1978). *Patterns of attachment.* Hillsdale, NJ: Erlbaum.
13. Hazan, C., & Shaver, P. R. (1994). Attachment as an organizational framework for research on close relationships. *Psychological Inquiry, 5*, 1–22.
14. Snyder, C. R., McDermott, D., Cook, W., & Rapoff, M. A. (1997). *Hope for the journey: Helping children through the good times and the bad.* Boulder, CO: Westview Press.
15. Aspinwall, L. G., & Taylor, S. E. (1992). Modeling cognitive adaptation: A longitudinal investigation of the impact of individual differences and coping on college adjustment and performance. *Journal of Personality and Social Psychology, 61*, 755–765.
16. Long, B. C. (1993). Coping strategies of male managers: A prospective analysis of predictors of psychosomatic symptoms and job satisfaction. *Journal of Vocational Behavior, 42*, 184–199.
17. Zeidner, M., & Hammer, A. L. (1992). Coping with missile attack: Resources, strategies, and outcomes. *Journal of Personality, 60*, 709–746.
18. Given, C. W., Stommel, M., Given, B., Osuch, J., Kurtz, M. E., & Kurtz,

J. C. (1993). The influence of cancer patients' symptoms and functional states on patients' depression and family caregivers' reaction and depression. *Health Psychology, 12*, 277–285.

19. Hooker, K., Monahan, D., Shifren, K., & Hutchinson, C. (1992). Mental and physical health of spouse caregivers: The role of personality. *Psychology and Aging, 7*, 367–375.

20. Shifren, K., & Hooker, K. (1995). Stability and change in optimism: A study among spouse caregivers. *Experimental Aging Research, 21*, 59–76.

21. Carver, C. S., & Gaines, J. G. (1987). Optimism, pessimism, and postpartum depression. *Cognitive Therapy and Research, 11*, 449–462.

22. Cozzarelli, C. (1993). Personality and self-efficacy as predictors of coping with abortion. *Journal of Personality and Social Psychology, 65*, 1224–1236.

23. Fitzgerald, T. E., Tennen, H., Affleck, G., & Pransky, G. S. (1993). The relative importance of dispositional optimism and control appraisals in quality of life after cornonary artery bypass surgery. *Journal of Behavioral Medicine, 16*, 25–43.

24. Scheier, M. F., Matthews, K. A., Owens, J. F., Magovern, G. J., Lefebvre, R. C., Abbott, R. A., & Carver, C. S. (1989). Dispositional optimism and recovery from coronary artery bypass surgery: The beneficial effects on physical and psychological well-being. *Journal of Personality and Social Psychology, 57*, 1024–1040.

25. Litt, M. D., Tennen, H., Affleck, G., & Klock, S. (1992). Coping and cognitive factors in adaptation to in vitro fertilization failure. *Journal of Behavioral Medicine, 15*, 171–187.

26. Curbow, B. Somerfield, M. R., Baker, F. Wingard, J. R., & Legro, M. W. (1993). Personal changes, dispositional optimism, and psychological adjustment to bone marrow transplantation. *Journal of Behavioral Medicine, 16*, 423–443.

27. Carver, C. S., Pozo, C., Harris, S. D., Noriega, V., Scheier, M. F., Robinson, D. S., Ketcham, A. S., Moffat, F. L., & Clark, K. C. (1993). How coping mediates the effect of optimism on distress: A study of women with early stage breast cancer. *Journal of Personality and Social Psychology, 65*, 375–390.

28. Friedman, L. C., Nelson, D. V., Baer, P. E., Lane, M., Smith, F. E., & Dworkin, R. J. (1992). The relationship of dispositional optimism, daily life stress, and domestic environment to coping methods used by cancer patients. *Journal of Behavioral Medicine, 15*, 127–141.

29. Taylor, S. E., Kemeny, M. E., Aspinwall, L. G., Schneider, S. G., Rodriguez, R., & Herbert, M. (1992). Optimism, coping, psychological distress, and high-risk sexual behavior among men at risk for Acquired Immunodeficiency Syndrome (AIDS). *Journal of Personality and Social Psychology, 63*, 460–473.

30. Park, C. L., Moore, P. J., Turner, R. A., & Adler, N. E. (1997). The roles of constructive thinking and optimism in psychological and behavioral adjustment during pregnancy. *Journal of Personality and Social Psychology, 73*, 584–592.

31. Stanton, A. L., & Dunkel-Schetter, C. (Eds.). (1991). *Infertility: Perspectives from stress and coping research.* New York: Plenum.

32. Scheier, M. F., Weintraub, J. K., & Carver, C. S. (1986). Coping with stress: Divergent strategies of optimists and pessimists. *Journal of Personality and Social Psychology, 51,* 1257–1264.

33. Carver, C. S., Scheier, M. F., & Weintraub, J. K. (1989). Assessing coping strategies: A theoretically based approach. *Journal of Personality and Social Psychology, 56,* 267–283.

34. Fontaine, K. R., Manstead, A. S. R., & Wagner, H. (1993). Optimism, perceived control over stress, and coping. *European Journal of Personality, 7,* 267–281.

35. Strutton, D., & Lumpkin, J. (1992). Relationship between optimism and coping strategies in the work environment. *Psychology Reports, 71,* 1179–1186.

36. Fry, P. S. (1995). Perfectionism, humor, and optimism as moderators of health outcomes and determinants of coping styles of women executives. *Genetics, Social, and General Psychology Monographs, 121,* 211–245.

37. Stanton, A. L., & Snider, P. R. (1993). Coping with breast cancer diagnosis: A prospective study. *Health Psychology, 12,* 16–23.

38. Reed, G. M., Kemeny, M. E., Taylor, S. E., et al. (1994). "Realistic acceptance" as a predictor of decreased survival time in gay men with AIDS. *Health Psychology, 13,* 299–307.

39. Greer, S., Morris, T., & Pettingale, K. W. (1979). Psychological response to breast cancer: Effect on outcome. *Lancet, 2,* 785–787.

40. Pettingale, K. W., Morris, T., & Greer, S. (1985). Mental attitudes to cancer: An additional prognostic factor. *Lancet, 1,* 750.

41. Greer, S., Morris, T., Pettingale, K. W., et al. (1990). Psychological response to breast cancer and 15-year outcome. *Lancet, 1,* 49–50.

42. Shepperd, J. A., Maroto, J. J., & Pbert, L. A. (1996). Dispositional optimism as a predictor of health changes among cardiac patients. *Journal of Research in Personality, 30,* 517–534.

43. Robbins, A. S., Spence, J. T., & Clark, H. (1991). Psychological determinants of health and performance: The tangled web of desirable and undesirable characteristics. *Journal of Personality and Social Psychology, 61,* 755–765.

44. Steptoe, A., Wardle, J., Vinck, J., Tuomisto, M., Holte, A., & Wichstrm, L. (1994). Personality and attitudinal correlates of healthy lifestyles in young adults. *Psychology and Health, 9,* 331–343.

45. Aspinwall, L. G., & Brunhart, S. N. (1996). Distinguishing optimism from denial: Optimistic beliefs predict attention to health threats. *Personality and Social Psychology Bulletin, 22,* 993–1003.

46. Ohannessian, C. M., Hesselbrock, V. M., Tennen, H., & Affleck, G. (1993). Hassles and uplifts and generalized outcome expectancies as moderators on the relation between a family history of alcoholism and drinking behaviors. *Journal of Studies on Alcohol, 55,* 754–763.

47. Strack, S., Carver, C. S., & Blaney, P. H. (1987). Predicting successful completion of an aftercare program following treatment for alcoholism: The role of dispositional optimism. *Journal of Personality and Social Psychology, 53,* 579–584.

48. Beck, A. T., Steer, R. A., Kovacs, M., & Garrison, B. (1985). Hopelessness and eventual suicide: A 10-year prospective study of patients hos-

pitalized with suicidal ideation. *American Journal of Psychiatry, 142,* 559–563.

49. Tennen, H., & Affleck, G. (1987). The costs and benefits of optimistic explanations and dispositional optimism. *Journal of Personality, 55,* 377–393.

50. Schwarzer, R. (1994). Optimism, vulnerability, and self-beliefs as health-related cognitions: A systematic overview. *Psychology and Health, 9,* 161–180.

51. Goodman, E., Chesney, M. A., & Tipton, A. C. (1995). Relationship of optimism, knowledge, attitudes, and beliefs to use of HIV antibody test by at-risk female adolescents. *Psychosomatic Medicine, 57,* 541–546.

52. Perkins, D. O., Lesserman, J., Murphy, C., et al. (1993). Psychosocial predictors of high-risk sexual behavior among HIV-negative gay men. *AIDS Education and Prevention, 5,* 141–152.

53. Beck, A. T. (1967). *Depression: Clinical, experimental, and theoretical aspects.* New York: Harper & Row.

10

Hoping

C. R. Snyder
Jen Cheavens
Scott T. Michael

Hope in Historical Perspective

Let us begin by revisiting the myth of Pandora, which is the most famous historical touchstone involving hope. To vent his emotions toward the mortal Prometheus for stealing fire from the gods, Zeus sent the maiden Pandora to earth with a "treasure chest" filled mostly with evil creatures. Instructing Pandora to keep the box closed, Zeus knew that she would not be able to do so (this appears to be one of the first examples of reverse psychology). Indeed, Pandora opened the lid, and Zeus gained his revenge. As the story goes, however, Pandora realized her mistake as the evils spewed from the chest, and she scurried to replace the lid. By the time that the box was covered again, however, hope supposedly was the only force remaining inside.

This myth has been interpreted so as to place hope as a consolation for the other troubles of life (1). The subsequent historical views of hope have had two-sides—a blessing and a curse. Sophocles and Nietzsche, for example, railed at "evil" hope as being a motive that only prolonged human torment. Saint Paul and Martin Luther, on the other hand, elevated hope to the same high level as love, suggesting that it is synonymous with everything that is good and truthful. Tillich (2) attempted a reconciliation of the good and bad perspectives of hope, writing that "hope is easy for the foolish, but hard for the wise. Everybody can lose himself into foolish hope, but genuine hope is something rare and great" (p. 17). Indeed, twentieth-century writers generally share the view that "genuine" hope is good and "foolish" hope is bad; the difficulty with this seeming solution, however, is that these writers offered no insights in distinguishing these two types of hope. To compound the confusion regarding "genuine" and "foolish" hope further, it has been argued that the seemingly "foolish" hope at times may produce positive therapeutic outcomes (3).

Because they do not distinguish between mental and bodily states, the proponents of holistic medicine readily accept hope-related cures as being "genuine." The more traditional medical community, however, with its underlying Cartesian dualism assumptions, views these nonphysical cures as being fake. Equating hope with a placebo, large segments of the medical profession hold that such cures are ingenuine and therefore illegitimate. Nevertheless, a small yet vocal group of physicians (e.g., 3, 4, 5, 6, 7, 8, 9 10, 11) have suggested that hope not only is legitimate, but that it is also inherent in all medical and nonmedical approaches to healing (see 12).

From the late 1950s to the 1960s, several psychiatrists (e.g., 5, 8, 13, 14, 15) and psychologists (e.g., 16, 17, 18, 19, 20) provided more systematic approaches to the study of hope. These authors not only assumed that hope was worthy of investigation, but they also generally agreed that it tapped the *positive expectation for goal attainment*. The wider scientific community remained skeptical, however, and generally was not influenced by this newer perspective. In this latter regard, the noted psychotherapy researcher Jerome Frank (5) speculated that such lack of interest in this "new" hope reflected inaccurate historical stereotypes, as well as concerns about how it would impact on the more established and traditional models of treatment.

In the mid-1970s, there was a renewed interest in hope and positive emotions, largely due to the burgeoning psychological research and writings related to stress, coping, and illness (see chapter 1). Many coping researchers suggested that negative thoughts and emotions are part of the etiology of illness, that they interfere with social support, suppress coping efforts in general, and even may undermine medical recovery (see 21, 22, for reviews). Several writers (6, 11, 23, 24) reasoned that if negative thoughts and emotions could block recovery, then positive processes, such as hope, might promote it. Bolstering this latter view, subsequent researchers have shown that enhanced self-evaluations and perceptions of control or mastery are related positively to psychological and physical well-being (see 25, 26, 27, 28, 29, for reviews).

Increasingly in the 1980s and 1990s, investigators have developed specific theoretical viewpoints about the coping benefits that flow from positive cognitive and emotional motivational states. Many of these researchers present their work in this volume. As but one small strand in this strengthening line of work, we will explore the topic of hope in this chapter. In order, we will discuss the definition of a new model of hope, along with instruments to measure it in adults and children. Likewise, we will describe the adaptive sequelae of elevated levels of hope for a variety of coping arenas, along with the presently sparse literature on increasing hope. We also will explore how hope can be applied to special populations. Finally, we will close with speculations about future directions for research and applications of this hope concept.

Defining New Hope

Dictionary definitions typically describe hope as the perception "that something desired may happen." Building upon this definition by emphasizing the importance of goals, previous scholars have described hope as a unidimensional construct involving an overall perception that goals can be met (e.g., 5, 8, 13, 14, 15, 16, 17, 18, 20, 30, 31, 32). These earlier writers also suggest that expectancies for goal-attainment can be used to explain a variety of behaviors, including those involving mental and physical health. Although assuming goal-directedness and its adaptiveness, these writers did not emphasize the cognitive processes that are tied to goal-directed thinking. The present model of hope draws upon goal concepts (see 33, 34) and expands on the previous views in order to more fully elucidate the cognitive process of hope.

Definition

According to this new theory, hope is a thinking process in which people have a sense of agency and pathways for goals (26, 35, 36, 37, 38, 39, 40). Together, goals, pathways, and agency form the motivational concept of hope. This definition clearly is *cognitive* in nature and, as such, stands in contrast to other more emotion-based models of hope (41, 42). In more specific terms, we have defined hope as "a reciprocally derived sense of successful (a) agency (goal-directed determination) and (b) pathways (planning of ways to meet goals)" (37). Although the agency and pathways of hope are additive, reciprocal, and positively related, they are not synonymous. To sustain movement toward life goals, both the sense of agency and pathways must be operative. Thus, although agency and pathways are necessary to define hope, neither alone is sufficient. Also, hope does not entail just one iteration of thinking, in which a person first assesses agentic and then the available pathways thoughts, thereafter initiating goal-directed behaviors; nor is it the case that one pathways thought unleashes the agency thinking that leads to goal-directed behavior. Instead, at all stages of goal-directed behavior, the iterations of agency/pathways and pathways/agency thought continue and build on one another.

Goal Thoughts

The desired target of hopeful thought is the goal. Goal objects are constantly in our thoughts so that we can respond effectively to our environment. Goals are preeminent in hopeful thought, with high-hope persons clearly conceptualizing their goals, and low-hope people being more uncertain about their goals (26). Such goals can be short-term (e.g., finishing this sentence), or more long-term with several other subgoals (e.g., completing the editing of this coping book).

Pathway Thoughts

Two additional and pivotal thoughts accompany goal thinking. First, pathway thoughts tap perceptions of being able to produce one or more workable routes to goals. In most instances, there is one centrally conceived route that is the focus for the mental journey to a particular goal. It is common, however, to anticipate a goal by conjuring more than one effective route.

Agency Thoughts

Second, agentic thought reflects the perceived ability to begin, as well as to continue, movement along a selected pathway to a goal. Agentic thought provides the motivational force to pursue goals via the imagined pathways. As such, agency is the source of mental energy in the present hope model.

Barriers

According to hope theory, the unimpeded pursuit of goals should produce positive emotions, whereas goal barriers may yield negative feelings. Thus, within our model, *goal pursuit thoughts drive emotional experiences.* In this regard, research in our laboratory (correlational and causal designs) shows that goal blockages lead to negative emotional responses (40). Similarly, research in other laboratories reveals that difficulties in the pursuit of important goals undermine well-being (43, 44, 45, 46, 47, 48), as compared to the opposite temporal sequence in which lowered well-being hampers subsequent goal pursuits (49, 50).

Given that the foundation of hope theory rests on goal thought, anything that interferes with either pathway or agency thinking should affect subsequent coping (see 36, 51). In the context of hope theory, successful coping rests on thinking so as to achieve one's desired goals.

Although barriers can and do promote negative emotional reactions, high- as compared to low-hope people do not experience the same degree of negativeness when impeded. This more adaptive, positive emotional response probably occurs because higher hope people can generate additional, alternative paths when blocked via the original route (26, 35). Equally important, when confronted with blockages, higher hope people sense that they can use their alternate routes and have the motivation to put these plans into action.

Therefore, hopeful thought not only operates to facilitate success during unimpeded goal pursuits, but it is also especially helpful when encountering barriers. Accordingly, higher hope helps people to deal more successfully with the stressful events in their lives.

Measuring Hope

Once a new psychological theory is clearly defined, an important next step is the development and validation of instruments that reflect the basic tenets of the theory. In the case of hope theory, we have produced individual differences measures that can be used with children and adults. This work is described briefly in this section.

The Children's Hope Scale

The basic components of hope should be established by age three, with the ensuing preschool, middle, and adolescent years serving to solidify such hopeful thought (for reviews, see chapter 3 of 26, chapter 1 of 39). Unless there is a profoundly negative series of events, a child's hope should be stable across the developmental period. Although hope is in place by the time of toddlerhood, a minimum level of language skills is necessary to respond to self-report instruments. Therefore, we developed and validated the Children's Hope Scale (CHS) for children in the second grade and beyond.

As shown in Appendix A, the CHS is a six-item self-report index. It is appropriate for children ages 8 through 16 (38). There are three items each for the agency and pathways components. The CHS has been given to many samples of children in various locations across the United States. The two-component factor structure is stable, allowing for the separate study of children's agency or pathways; nevertheless, because the hope concept rests on the combination of the two components, we would suggest aggregating these in order to garner the more meaningful index of hope. The CHS evidences acceptable internal (alphas in high .70s and .80s) and test-retest (.70s) reliabilities, thereby meeting the psychometric standards for self-report instruments (52). The CHS also has displayed convergent and discriminant validity in terms of yielding predicted relationships with other self-report scales for children.

The Adult Trait Hope Scale

Additionally, we have developed and validated a trait hope measure for persons age 15 and older (37). This 12-item Hope Scale, shown in Appendix B, includes four agency and four pathway items, as well as four distracter items. With coefficient alphas in the high .70 to .80 range, and consistently high test-retest coefficients (.70s to .80s), the Hope Scale surpasses the psychometric standards related to reliability. A variety of factor analytic studies support the existence of the agency and pathway factors; moreover, a confirmatory analysis suggests that the two subscales contribute to the overarching hope construct (53). Lastly, this Hope Scale exhibits convergent and discriminant validity in that it yields predicted relationships to other related self-report indices.

The Adult State Hope Scale

We also have developed the Adult State Hope Scale in order to tap ongoing goal-directed thoughts at any given moment in time (40). Shown in Appendix C, the State Hope Scale is made up of three agency and three pathways items. These state items were reworded from the dispositional Hope Scale so as to reflect the present tense. The State Hope Scale has high internal reliability (coefficient alphas in the .90s); likewise, the State Hope Scale has modest test-retest coefficients (.50s to .90s), as would be expected of an instrument that is sensitive to fluctuations in goal-directed thought over time. The State Hope Scale manifests acceptable construct validity in that four studies have shown it to be responsive to variations in goal-directed thought at particular points in time; moreover, the scale has demonstrated concurrent and discriminant validity in terms of its relations to other state self-report indices.

Individual Differences in Hope and Markers of Successful Coping

The previous definition suggests that high hope should be related to enhanced problem-solving strategies (pathways), as well as the motivation to undertake those pathways (agency). On these points, the initial evidence suggests that both adults (37) and children (38) with high-hope experience benefits related to psychological adjustment, achievement, problem solving, and health-related problems. We will treat each issue in turn.

Hope and Psychological Adjustment

Hope is related to psychological adjustment in several ways. One way in which psychological adjustment is affected by hope is through the belief in one's self. Snyder, Hoza, et al. (38) found that high-hope is related to perceived competency in several life areas in children. In this study, hope was positively correlated with perceptions of scholastic competence ($rs = .35$ to .59), social acceptance ($rs = .23$ to .43), athletic ability ($rs = .26$ to .35), and physical appearance ($rs = .00$ to .46). Therefore, hopeful thinking in children is related to the belief that one has the necessary competence to accomplish a specified goal.

In addition to perceived competence, psychological adjustment is related to hope. For example, research has shown that level of hope, as measured by the State Hope Scale, is positively related to state measures of positive affect ($rs = .55$ to .65) and negatively related to state measures of negative affect ($rs = -.47$ to $-.50$) (40). Beyond these correlational findings, manipulations aimed at increasing hope show parallel increases in positive affect (40). Therefore, hope increases with more positive feeling states and decreases with more negative feeling states. Additionally, higher hope is related to more positive thinking states. In this regard, Snyder, Sympson, and colleagues (40) asked participants to report and rate their major thoughts for each day over 28 days. The results showed that high hope was related to significantly more positive thoughts and significantly fewer negative thoughts. Further, the State Hope Scale correlated positively with the ratings of positive thoughts and negatively with the ratings of negative thoughts. Taken together, this evidence suggests that higher hope individuals both feel more positively and think more positively on a day-to-day basis. This finding is supported by evidence that indicates high- as compared to low-hope college students report feeling more confident, inspired, energized, eager, and challenged by their goals (37). Thus, it appears that the high-hope individual feels invigorated and thinks positively in terms of meeting goals, while the low-hope individual feels overwhelmed and thinks negatively in terms of meeting goals.

Another component of psychological adjustment is the presence of positive feelings toward oneself. Evidence indicates that high-hope individuals feel good about themselves on a fairly regular basis. For example, hopeful thinking in children is associated with an increased feeling of self-worth (rs = .23 to .55) (38). The increased feeling of self-worth is also found in adults with high hope (rs = .35 to .75) (54, 40). The relationship between hope and self-worth generalizes to diverse arenas involving performance, social relations, and appearance (40). In adults, hope has a significant positive correlation with self-esteem (55). Further, higher hope is associated with lower levels of depression (38). This latter relationship may be due, in part, to the different attributional styles of individuals with high and low hope. The depressive attributional style is one in which a person makes more internal, stable, and global explanations for bad events, and external, stable, and global explanations for good events (56). Thus, persons with depression-related feelings are unable to distance themselves from negative events, whereas they simultaneously do associate themselves with positive events. In this regard, high-hope children tend to have internal, stable and global attributions for positive events, and external, stable, and global attributions for negative events (38). This indicates that high-hope children are able to associate themselves with positive events in their environments and distance themselves from negative events in their environments. This is an adaptive coping process through which children may increase their perceptions of competency and reduce their feelings of depression. Other research indicates that hope has a significant inverse relationship ($r = -.42$) (55) with Beck Depression Inventory scores (57).

A final adaptive coping process related to hope and psychological adjustment is the ability to view oneself and present oneself in a positive light. Research has shown that hope scores have slight positive correlations with scores on social desirability measures in both children (rs = .21 to .27) (38) and adults ($r = .30$) (37). For adults, there is also a small, positive correlation between hope and positive self-presentation ($r = .28$) (37). Thus, it appears that higher hope children and adults have a slight tendency to make positive distortions when viewing themselves. Other authors have posited a relationship between positive distortions and adaptive coping (28, 29, 58). Individuals with "positive self-illusions," as they are termed by the authors, often use active coping strategies to deal with adverse events (58). Positive self-illusions may be a form of active coping, wherein an individual responds to stressful events with an inflated sense of personal control and overly optimistic expectations about the future as a means of dealing with such events.

An example of this positive illusion phenomenon can be found within a sample of women with breast cancer. The authors found that the presence of positive self-distortions and the perception of control over the disease predicted better adjustment to breast cancer (59). Thus, it may be argued that some positive distortion is reflective of adaptive coping with adversity, and it may well be that hopeful persons manifest such illusions (25). Related to this latter point, Taylor and Armor (58) suggest that people who employ positive self-illusions tend to make more favorable appraisals of their abilities to deal with stressful situations, which implies a link between positive self-illusions and hope. Hopeful individuals make plans and execute them in response to adverse situations, and they have confidence in the ability of their problem-solving skills to implement these plans and achieve the adjoining goal(s). This information, taken with the findings that high-hope children and adults tend to be less depressed, have higher self-worth, and perceive themselves as competent, elucidates the adaptive features of high hope in terms of psychological adjustment.

Hope and Achievement

In addition to the advantages related to psychological adjustment, high-hope individuals tend to have increased performances in the achievement arenas. Although hope is not significantly related to intelligence (38) as measured by standardized tests for children, it is related to achievement (38), as measured by the Iowa Basic Test of Skill (60). The Iowa Basic Test of Skill is a commonly used measure of achievement for kindergarten through twelfth-grade students. In addition to the first-order correlation between hope and achievement, it should be noted that hope scores augmented the predicted achievement scores on the Iowa Basic Test of Skill after the variance due to self-worth had been removed.

This increased achievement propensity in the cognitive realm does not stop in childhood. Recent research suggests that high-hope college students also have increased success in the academic realm (61). In this study, a sample of college freshmen (100 men and 100 women) was given the dispositional Hope Scale and then the academic progress was tracked over the next six years. The results indicated that both grade point average and graduation status were predicted by level of hope. Hope was significantly and positively correlated with grade point average. When the sample was divided into high- and low-hope categories, high-hope individuals had significantly higher grade point averages than did the low-hope individuals (Ms = 2.85 vs. 2.43, respectively). Graduation status also was differentially predicted by the dispositional measure of hope. The results indicated that more high- as compared to low-hope students graduated, while more low- as compared to high-hope students were dismissed from the university in poor standing. The aforementioned relationships between hope and both grade point average and graduation status remained even after removing the variance due to ACT scores. This suggests that high hope is related to collegiate achievement beyond the students' previous knowledge base. The relationship between hope and grade point average also has been demonstrated with two samples of collegiate athletes (54). These studies found that level of hope was positively and significantly related to semester grade point average, and that the magnitude of this relationship remained when the variance due to cumulative grade point average was removed.

Another achievement realm in which hope may confer advantages is athletics. A study by Curry et al. (54) looked at hope as it relates to collegiate athletic performance. The study found that the combination of dispositional and state hope (as measured by the indices described earlier in this chapter) accounted for 56% of the variance related to performance at track meets for female, collegiate athletes. Additionally, measures of self-esteem, confidence, and mood did not significantly augment the prediction of performance. Results also showed that hope provided additional predictive information about performance beyond natural ability. That is to say, while coaches' ratings of natural ability significantly predicted track performances, this prediction was significantly enhanced by dispositional Hope Scale scores taken at the beginning of the track season. Thus, athletic achievement is accentuated by the combination of increased motivation and increased perceptions of the ability to generate routes to goals (i.e., agency and pathways goal thinking or hope).

Hope and Problem Solving

Research also has supported the theoretical premise that hope is positively related to problem solving. In studies designed to validate the dispositional Hope Scale, a number of findings emerged that support the view that hope is an important factor in coping and problem solving (see 37, for a review). Holleran and Snyder (62) studied the relationship between hope, negative affectivity, optimism, and problem-focused coping. They found that hope is a significant, unique predictor of problem-focused coping when controlling for negative affectivity and optimism, and that neither negative affectivity nor optimism added any significant unique predictive value above that of hope. In another study directly related to hope and coping (63), hope predicted both active coping (i.e., taking steps to overcome effects of stressors in a direct and effortful manner) and planning (i.e., producing strategies to cope with stressors) when controlling for both positive and negative affectivity. Thus, the effects of hope on coping and problem solving cannot be explained by the mediating effects of affectivity.

Furthermore, high-hope students have reported that they focus on success rather than failure while pursuing goals, and that they rely on adaptive coping strategies in pursuing goals, even in the face of significant obstacles (37). Other studies from our research program have demonstrated positive relations between hope and increased perceived problem-solving ability (55), number of active life goals (64), preference for difficult goals (65), and perceptions of past success and the probability of future goal-attainment (66). Consequently, problem solving is related to enhanced number of goals (goal-directed thinking), the perception of finding ways to reach goals (pathways thinking), and the perception of succeeding in reaching one's goals (agency thinking).

Hope and Health-Related Concerns

We have reasoned elsewhere (36, 51, 67) that hope should confer advantages as people attempt to cope with illness-related problems. On this point, there are three reported studies relating hope to health, all of which suggest that there are benefits accruing for those with higher hope. First, in the recovery process following spinal cord injury, higher hope was related to better coping and less depression (68). Second, in a study of nurses working in a high-pressure hospital unit, those with higher hope were less likely to report burnout (69). Third, higher hope adolescent burn survivors engaged in fewer behaviors that would undermine recovery (70). These burn survivors also had a greater number of successful interactions with others and a higher level of global self-worth.

Other studies also suggest a relationship between higher hope and better health-related outcomes. On a cold pressor task, which measures pain tolerance, high-hope individuals experienced less pain and tolerated pain almost twice as long as did the low-hope individuals (71). This suggests that high-hope individuals may be able to better tolerate pain by employing coping mechanisms that somehow reduce the perceived level of the pain. When asked to elucidate the nature of their coping strategies to handle the pain of the cold pressor task, the higher hope persons listed more strategies and reported a higher likelihood of using the strategies listed.

In another study, high-hope college women evidenced more knowledge about cancer and more hope-specific coping responses to an imaginal task of coping with cancer than did low-hope college women; moreover, this effect remained when controlling for academic achievement, experience with cancer (in family or friends), and negative affectivity (72). What is also noteworthy about this imaginal task is that the higher hope women displayed superior coping throughout the stages of dealing with cancer (i.e., from prevention, to detection, to treatment, and adjustment thereafter). We propose that these findings relate to coping with health-related concerns because knowledge about and readiness to cope with serious disease or related health problems is intimately connected with actual coping and/or prevention. Higher levels of hope thus are likely to aid in adjustment to illnesses and other health-related concerns.

In a study of 36 males and 126 females who had been receiving treatment for arthritis for at least six months, Laird (73) focused upon predictors of the patients' coping. Although the results revealed that active prayer and adherence to religion related to positive outcomes, when Hope Scale scores were entered into the predictive equation, the power of these other variables disappeared. That is to say, hope provided significant and unique predictive variance for these arthritis patients in terms of their specific functioning in lower extremities, upper extremities, and affect, as well as overall functioning on the Arthritis Impact Measurement Scales (74).

Hope also appears to be related to the ability to find benefits when facing the adversity of illness. Affleck and Tennen (75; see also chapter 13 in this volume) discuss findings from an ongoing research project that they are conducting concerning the psychological adjustment of individuals living with fibromyalgia, a chronic disease which involves a great deal of pain. Participants with higher levels of dispositional hope reported finding more benefits from their experience with the disease than those with lower levels of hope, even when controlling for optimism and pessimism. The authors suggest that hope plays a unique role in the formation of positive appraisals of adverse situations. Affleck and Tennen also discuss the role of benefit-reminding as an active coping strategy and its adaptive functions in dealing with illness and other adversity. In the same study discussed above, when the pathways component of hope was partialed out, the correlation between benefit-finding and benefit-reminding was no longer significant, indicating that the ability to plan routes to goals, based on beliefs in the benefits that arise from adversity, plays a crucial role in the use of benefit-reminding as a coping strategy.

While hope appears to play a promising role in adjustment to illness or injury, surely there must be a level of symptom severity whereafter hope abates. On this point, one study looked at the correlation between levels of hope and disease severity in a sample of African-American children with sickle cell disease (76). In this study, hope scores were negatively correlated with disease severity ($r = -.44$). What this study suggests is that there may be limits to hopeful thinking when the level of the illness becomes truly severe. Indeed, this latter point is a tenet of hope theory in that hope is posited to diminish when enduring and profound goal impediments are encountered.

All of the previous studies are based on the various individual differences measures of hope that we have developed and validated for adults and children. The benefits for higher hope children and adults have related to coping and performances in a variety of arenas, including academics, sports, problem-solving ability, and health. It also should be emphasized that, in comparison to optimism, negative affectivity, positive affectivity, locus of control, mood, depression, athletic aptitude, cognitive-intellectual aptitude, and helplessness, the hope scales have provided unique and augmenting variance in predicting outcome markers. Thus, hope appears to be a fairly robust predictor of various coping-related outcome markers, and this predictive capability is not diminished in any major degree by other individual differences indices that would reflect counterexplanations.

Interventions for Hope and Markers of Successful Coping

To date, there are only two reported intervention studies that have employed the tenets of hope theory. First, Klausner et al. (77) developed a specific hope theory-based intervention in order to more systematically explore the therapeutic implications of hope theory. Research participants were older adults (M age $= 67$) who met the criteria for major depressive disorder and who were already outpatients. They were randomly assigned to either a hope/goal-focused or a reminiscence intervention. Approximately 80% of the group was white, and 20% was Hispanic, with an equal mix of women and men. There were 13 participants per each intervention group. For the hope/goal-focused intervention group, explicit suggestions taken from *The Psychology of Hope* (26) were utilized over 10 sessions in order to help the group participants to set goals, and to think about themselves and their goals so as to produce pathways and the related agency motivation. The goals were doable ones such as to plant a rose bush, or to get to the shopping center, and there were weekly homework assignments and discussions about how this new manner of thinking was working. These hope/goal-focused intervention sessions were quite structured and ended with individualized behavioral practice assignments. The control comparison group of reminiscences was based on Butler's (78) life review model, and sessions involved the recall of memories at the various stages in the participants' lives. This approach was selected as a comparison because previous research indicates that it works to reduce depression in older persons (see 79).

Persons were evaluated at the beginning and end of the interventions. Assessments included both self-report and observations. Results showed that both groups significantly reduced depression after the interventions. For the hope/goal-focused intervention group only, however, hopelessness and anxiety significantly lessened, and the State Hope Scale scores increased reliably; moreover, social interaction with family members increased for the hope/goal-focused intervention, but not for the reminiscence group. Turning to between-group differences, the hope/goal-focused intervention decreased 15 points on the Hamilton Depression Rating Scale (80), moving the mean of this group from major depression to no depression at all. In comparison, the reminiscence group dropped only 4.6 points on the Hamilton, leaving them still in the major depression category. It also is informative to note that the hope/goal-focused intervention group became quite proactive, whereas the reminiscence group was very passive. For example, the hope/goal-focused intervention group members brought refreshments and snacks, whereas the reminiscence group's lack of enthusiasm is captured in one member's "out of the blue" announcement that "Well, I'm not baking anything!" At the end of the hope/goal-focused intervention group, however, the members actually presented small gifts to each leader and thanked them for what had been accomplished.

A second study (81) has been performed to test a pretreatment hope package. This study was conducted at a community mental health center. Clients ($N = 120$) were randomly assigned to a five-week orientation group or a five-week waiting list prior to 12 weeks of individual therapy. The orientation group consisted of five weekly 1.5 hour meetings. Group size was limited to approximately 16 participants per group. The orientation meetings were designed to prepare clients for individual therapy, and they emphasized the hope theory notions of establishing goals to address problem issue(s), and developing skills to cope (both agentic and pathways content). Clients assigned to the waitlist were required to wait five weeks from completion of intake to the beginning of individual therapy. Independent variables included pretreatment assignment (yes, no) and level of hope (high, low) as measured by the Hope Scale at intake. Dependent measures of wellbeing (four items developed expressly for this study, with an alpha of .79), level of functioning (82), and the State Hope Scale were administered at intake and four times during individual therapy. The final sample ($N = 98$) was largely female, white, unmarried, with a high school education.

At baseline, higher hope was associated with greater well being, superior functioning, fewer symptoms, and superior coping and capacity to regulate emotional distress (81). In regard to the effectiveness of the orientation group, in comparison to high-hope people, those low in hope reported greater responsiveness to a pretherapy orientation group on the dependent measures of well-being, level of functioning, and state hope. This study is promising on three fronts. First, the pretreatment individual differences in hope significantly predicted well-being, level of functioning, symptoms, and reported coping. Second, it indicates that a pretreatment package for hope can be delivered effectively in the context of a community mental health center. Third, the hope pretreatment tended to have beneficial effects precisely for the group of incoming clients—those low in hope—who are most in need of help.

Hope and the ISMs: Sexism, Racism, and Ageism

One general premise of hope theory is that persons who are consistently blocked in their goal pursuits over time should be lower in hope than persons who do not experience such impediments (26). In this regard, there are at least three sources of prejudice—sex, race, and age—that can enforce differential access to goals. For example, the traditional societal blockages of sexism would suggest that men have been allowed access to more goals than women. Likewise, with racism, members of minority racial groups in America have not had as free access to desirable goals as have Caucasians. Finally, with ageism, the older as compared to younger persons are not allowed to pursue the same desirable goals. Therefore, with sexism, racism, and ageism, the predictions would be that the favored, as compared to the unfavored, persons should have freer access to goals and, by inference, higher hope. We address the data on each of these points next.

The Results of Sexism: Female and Male Differences in Hope?

The active, goal-directed thinking that characterizes hope would suggest an obvious gender difference: Males, with their supposed agentic approach to things, should have higher hope than women. Indeed, the gender stereotype literature traditionally has described men in terms of instrumental characteristics, and women as being aligned toward expressive and communal matters (83, 84). In our research with both children (38) and adults (37), however, we have *never* found any gender differences. What can explain this apparent anomaly? On this issue, recent research reveals that *both* sexes are predominantly oriented to task or instrumental activities (85, 86). In the interactions of men and women in groups, therefore, we may expect that when it comes to goal-directed thinking, *more similarities than differences between the genders should emerge.*

The Results of Racism: Ethnic Differences in Hope?

Two samples of children have been used to test for racial differences in level of hope (38). Racial differences did not emerge in either of the samples. Additionally, in a study of college students, the African American, Caucasian, Hispanic, and Native American students reported higher Hope Scale scores than did the Asian American students (87). Certainly, further studies are necessary to ascertain whether there are any consistent racial differences in hope. As we wrote in the beginning of this section on the ISMs, those minority group members who have met extensive goal-blockages in their lives should have their dispositional hope undermined. There is one study that applies, albeit indirectly, to this argument. We examined the level of hope in a sample of minority adolescents who were exposed to violence. The teenagers (80% African American, 9% biracial, 6% Caucasian, and 5% Hispanic) who had witnessed violence, but who had less personal experience with violence to their loved ones, reported the highest levels of hope (88). When the violence had personally impacted on these minority adolescents, however, their hope was lower. By implication, therefore, if members of minority groups are more likely to be in environments of violence, then the predicted lower levels of hope may appear. In this latter regard, of course, the issue of greater importance may be socioeconomic status rather than race. That is to say, perhaps it is the violence and other possible impediments that are more commonly associated with the lower end of the socioeconomic spectrum that deplete hope. Clearly, more research is needed on this topic.

The Results of Ageism: Age Differences in Hope?

The research at this point has not suggested any differences between young and old individuals with high hope. Thus, children (38), adolescents (88), and adults (37) seem to manifest reasonably high levels of hope in several life areas. We make this inference based on the average responses that people make to our self-report indices. For the Children's Hope Scale, for example, the average response is "A lot of the time" (i.e., a 4 on a 6–point continuum) when asked to indicate the applicability of the hope items (38). For the dispositional and State Hope Scales, the average response is "Somewhat true" (i.e., a 6 on an 8–point continuum) in regard to the applicability of the hope item content (37, 40). As previously stated, the theory of hope suggests that the propensity for high hope is developed in childhood and that high hope children should retain this prophylactic level of hope into adulthood, barring a series of intensely, negative goal blockage events (26). Whether ageism itself results in sufficient goal-blockage to yield lower hope in older adults is unknown at this time. Therefore, it will be important to test the age difference hope question with longitudinal data.

Future Directions of Hope Research and Applications

As discussed throughout this chapter, there are a number of correlational findings that suggest a role for hope in the coping process, but there have only been a few studies of the direct relation of hope to coping, and even fewer concerning the application of hope theory as an intervention to increase psychological adjustment to stressful events and adverse situations. Given the lack of research findings in these areas, we are left to speculate about the causal role of hope in coping. In this section, we briefly will discuss future research directions for studying the effectiveness of hope as an intervention, the helper transfer of hope to clientele, and applications of hope theory and measurement to applied coping issues.

Hope as an Intervention

Elsewhere, we have made the case that hope is the common positive factor across differing therapeutic interventions (12). As the next step in our program of research, we are planning to study the effectiveness of writing about hope components as a means to increase both physical and psychological health. In their seminal study, Pennebaker and Beall (89) found that writing about traumatic events increased both psychological adjustment and general physical health. These findings have been supported by a growing body of research (90, 91, 92, 93). We plan to study if writing about hope components will lead to similar increases in physical and psychological health. Further, if writing about hope leads to physical and psychological benefits, we are interested in the conditions that produce this benefit. One condition will examine the act of writing about hope alone. Thus, participants will be asked to describe their past goal accomplishments and their present goal plans. A second condition will look at the act of writing about hope in response to distressing events. Consequently, participants will be asked to recount traumatic events and the effects these events have had on levels of hope through changes related to goal thinking, pathway generation, and level of motivation. Thus, how hope is affected by trauma initially will be examined through narratives of participants. The latter case bears similarities to the theory of benefit-finding discussed earlier (see 75, and chapter 13 in this volume). This research may lead to the designing of a hope-based writing intervention that can be used alone or as an adjunct to psychotherapy. Another possibility is to study the use of hope-reminding (reminding oneself about past goal accomplishments as a means to deal with stressful events) as an active coping strategy. Hope-reminding bears obvious similarities to benefit-reminding (75).

We also have an ongoing intervention project aimed at using children's stories in order to build hope (for an overview of this narrative approach to teaching children to be more hopeful, read the Snyder, McDermott, et al. volume [39] entitled *Hope for the Journey: Helping Children through the Good Times and the Bad*). The premise of this latter work is that one of the most effective ways to reach and influence children is to work within their personal narratives. Consequently, building messages about defining goals and finding ways to reach those goals into children's stories may benefit children who do not innately possess these skills. These stories also may prime children to view obstacles in their environments as challenges to be overcome as opposed to insurmountable roadblocks. Our unfolding program of applied research in teaching children to have more hopeful stories is similar to the seminal work conducted by Seligman and his colleagues (see the Seligman, Reivich, Jaycox, and Gillham volume (94) entitled *The Optimistic Child*, as well as chapter 8 in this volume by Shatté, Reivich, Gillham, and Seligman).

Lastly, we are implementing hope interventions for adults. In these interventions, we are formulating a hope training module, which builds on three prerequisite skills related to the ability to conceptualize and define goals, to generate routes to those goals (both primary routes and secondary routes), and to sustain motivation on any given route to a goal (26). The presentation of the training could take several different forms. For example, we have considered group formats with trained facilitators, book or manual formats with less contact from a facilitator, and lesson plans delivered through audio tapes which would remove the role of the facilitator. Obviously, hope training also could be done in a one-on-one format.

Hope as a Helper Characteristic

We also have suggested in other writings (12, 26) that the helper's hope may be contagious in the sense of influencing other people. There presently is only one study that bears on this issue, however, and it is limited in that it is correlational in design and contains a questionable index of patient hope. More specifically, in this study (95), the hope of staff members in a head injury unit correlated positively with their ratings of hope in patients. Such findings, of course, may be entirely perceptual on the part of the helpers and, as such, it would be informative in future research to ascertain whether helpers' hope correlates with other valid markers of hope in their patients. More important, causal designs elucidating the possible transfer of helper to patient hope are warranted.

Hope to Cope

Hope may play an integral role in the use of other coping strategies. First, there may be a moderating effect of hope, such that high-hope individuals may have greater success in implementing other coping strategies. In this regard, whatever the specifics of such strategies may be, high- as compared to low-hope people have greater confidence in their ability to implement plans and in the probability of those plans succeeding (37). Accordingly, it follows that increased motivations to use particular strategies, combined with well-thought-out plans of how to do so, would lead to better success in the use of various coping strategies.

Second, high-hope individuals, particularly those with elevated pathways thinking, should be more willing to try differing coping strategies. The strategies, themselves, represent possible pathways to the goal of better adjustment or decreased distress. High-hope people also have alternate pathways to reach their goals if the selected pathway is blocked (26). Thus, a high-hope individual who is experiencing distress in her personal life may generate several pathways to alleviate this distress. She may seek guidance from a therapist, pray, partake in physical activity, and read books that address her issues. In other words, she finds several routes to the goal of feeling better. A low-hope individual, on the other hand, may conceive of only one coping strategy and, if that strategy is blocked, she will be without a feasible alternative. In short, the high- as compared to low-hope person has a more flexible approach to dealing with impediments to goals.

Third, hope may play a role in the effectiveness of medical treatments for illnesses and injuries. Because of their higher motivation (agentic thought), high- rather than low-hope individuals should be more likely to comply with treatment regimens.

We believe that the coping process is intimately linked to the hoping process. As we have illustrated, a high level of hope enables people to strive toward their goals, overcome obstacles, feel good about themselves, and to ward off negative emotions. These advantages are all instrumental to the process of adaptive coping. Coping often entails the experiencing of an obstacle, followed by subsequent attempts to move past that obstacle. Hope provides a framework that allows us to understand why some individuals surpass the obstacles in their lives with relative ease, whereas others remain stymied by such obstacles. Further, the present model of hope allows us to comprehend how people emerge from encounters with obstacles and are better off. As a case in point, breast cancer survivors state that their lives have been improved by their experiences with this disease (59). Using the hope framework, we can see how cancer survivors may have adopted new life goals and have found alternative pathways to reach those goals, as well as renewed mental energy to use those pathways. Hoping, like coping, often involves reworked life priorities and activities.

As we come to better understand the process of hope, we expect that we will better understand the process of coping. The present study of hope theory is still in its infancy. The findings to date allow us to speculate about the ways in which hope is related to coping. Future studies that rigorously test hope interventions will further this knowledge. As we learn more about how to increase hope, especially for those persons low in hope, we also will better understand how to help people to cope with the inevitable obstacles that they will encounter.

References

1. Smith, M. B. (1983). Hope and despair: Keys to the socio-psycho-dynamics of youth. *American Journal of Orthopyschiatry, 53*(3), 388–399.
2. Tillich, P. (1965). The right to hope. *The University of Chicago Magazine, 58*, 16–22.
3. Frank, J. D. (1973). *Persuasion and healing* (Rev. ed.). Baltimore: Johns Hopkins University Press.
4. Ader, R. (1981). *Psychoneuroimmunology.* New York: Academic Press.
5. Frank, J. D. (1968). The role of hope in psychotherapy. *International Journal of Psychiatry, 5*, 383–395.
6. Frank, J. D. (1975). The faith that heals. *The Johns Hopkins Medical Journal, 137*, 127–131.
7. Locke, S., & Colligan, D. (1986). *The healer within: The new medicine of mind and body.* New York: Mentor Books.
8. Menninger, K. (1959). The academic lecture on hope. *The American Journal of Psychiatry, 116*, 481–491.

9. Pelletier, K. R. (1979). *Holistic medicine: From stress to optimum health.* New York: Delacorte Press, Seymour Lawrence.
10. Siegel, B. S. (1986). *Love, medicine, and miracles.* New York: Harper & Row.
11. Simonton, O. C., Matthews-Simonton, S., & Creighton, J. L. (1978). *Getting well again.* New York: Bantam Books.
12. Snyder, C. R., Michael, S., & Cheavens, J. (in press). Hope as a psychotherapeutic foundation of nonspecific factors, placebos, and expectancies. In M. A. Huble, B. Duncan, & S. Miller (Eds.), *Heart and soul of change.* Washington, DC: American Psychological Association.
13. Frankl, V. E. (1992). *Man's search for meaning: An introduction to logotherapy* (4th edition). Boston: Beacon.
14. Melges, R., & Bowlby, J. (1969). Types of hopelessness in psychopathological processes. *Archives of General Psychiatry, 20,* 690–699.
15. Schachtel, E. (1959). *Metamorphosis.* New York: Basic Books.
16. Cantril, H. (1964). The human design. *Journal of Individual Psychology, 20,* 129–136.
17. Farber, M. L. (1968). *Theory of suicide.* New York: Funk and Wagnall's.
18. Mowrer, O. H. (1960). *The psychology of hope.* San Francisco: Jossey-Bass.
19. Schmale, A. H., & Iker, H. P. (1966). The affect of hopelessness and the development of cancer. *Psychosomatic Medicine, 28,* 714–721.
20. Stotland, E. (1969). *The psychology of hope.* San Francisco: Jossey-Bass.
21. Cohen, F. (1979). Personality, stress, and the development of physical illness. In G. C. Stone, F. Cohen, & N. Adler (Eds.), *Health psychology: A handbook* (pp. 77–111). San Francisco: Jossey-Bass.
22. Cohen, F. & Lazarus, R. S. (1979). Coping with the stress of illness. In G. C. Stone, F. Cohen, & N. Adler (Eds.), *Health Psychology: A handbook* (pp. 217–254). San Francisco: Jossey-Bass.
23. Cousins, N. (1976). Anatomy of an illness (as perceived by the patient). *New England Journal of Medicine, 295,* 1458–1463.
24. Mason, R. C., Clark, G., Reeves, R. B., & Wagner, B. (1969). Acceptance and healing. *Journal of Religion and Health, 8,* 123–142.
25. Snyder, C. R. (1989). Reality negotiation: From excuses to hope and beyond. *Journal of Social and Clinical Psychology, 8,* 130–157.
26. Snyder, C. R. (1994b). *The psychology of hope: You can get there from here.* New York: Free Press.
27. Taylor, S. E. (1989). *Positive illusions: Creative self-deception and the healthy mind.* New York: Basic Books.
28. Taylor, S. E., & Brown, J. D. (1988). Illusion and well-being: A social psychological perspective on mental health. *Psychological Bulletin, 103,* 193–210.
29. Taylor, S. E., & Brown, J. D. (1994). Positive illusions and well-being: Separating fact from fiction. *Psychological Bulletin, 116,* 21–26.
30. Erickson, R. C., Post, R., & Paige, A. (1975). Hope as a psychiatric variable. *Journal of Clinical Psychology, 31,* 324–329.
31. Gottschalk, L. A. (1974). A hope scale applicable to verbal samples. *Archives of General Psychiatry, 30,* 779–785.

32. Lewin, K. (1938). The conceptual representation and measurement of psychological states. *Contributions to Psychological Theory, 1,* 1–36.

33. Lee, T. W., Locke, E. A., & Latham, G. P. (1989). Goal setting theory and job performance. In L. A. Pervin (Ed.), *Goal concepts in personality and social psychology* (pp. 291–326). Hillsdale, NJ.: Lawrence Erlbaum Associates.

34. Pervin, L. A. (1989). Goal concepts in personality and social psychology: A historical introduction. In L. A. Pervin (Ed.), *Goal concepts in personality and social psychology* (pp. 1–17). Hillsdale, NJ: Erlbaum.

35. Snyder, C. R. (1994a). Hope and optimism. In V. S. Ramachandran (Ed.), *Encyclopedia of human behavior* (pp. 535–542). Orlando, FL: Academic Press.

36. Snyder, C. R. (1998). A case for hope in pain, loss, and suffering. In J. H. Harvey, J. Omarzu, & E. Miller (Eds.), *Perspectives on loss: A sourcebook.* pp. 63–79. Washington DC: Taylor & Francis.

37. Snyder, C. R., Harris, C., Anderson, J. R., Holleran, S. A., Irving, L. M., Sigmon, Yoshinobu, L., Gibb, J., Langelle, C., & Harney, P. (1991). The will and the ways: Development and validation of an individual-differences measure of hope. *Journal of Personality and Social Psychology, 60,* 570–585.

38. Snyder, C. R., Hoza, B, Pelham, W. E., Rapoff, M., Ware, L., Danovsky, M., Highberger, L., Rubinstein, H., & Stahl, K. J. (1997). The development and validation of the Children's Hope Scale. *Journal of Pediatric Psychology, 22,* 399–421.

39. Snyder, C. R., McDermott, D., Cook, J. W., & Rapoff, M. (1997). *Hope for the journey: Helping children through the good times and the bad.* Boulder, CO: Westview.

40. Snyder, C. R., Sympson, S. C., Ybasco, F. C., Borders, T. F., Babyak, M. A., & Higgins, R. L. (1996). Development and validation of the State Hope Scale. *Journal of Personality and Social Psychology, 70,* 321–335.

41. Averill, J. R, Catlin, G., & Chon, K. K. (1990). *Rules of hope.* New York: Springer-Verlag.

42. Farran, C. J., Herth, A. K., & Popovich, J. M. (1995). *Hope and hopelessness: Critical clinical constructs.* Thousand Oaks, CA: Sage.

43. Diener, E. (1984). Subjective well-being. *Psychological Bulletin, 95,* 542–575.

44. Emmons, R. A. (1986). Personal strivings: An approach to personality and subjective well-being. *Journal of Personality and Social Psychology, 51,* 1058–1068.

45. Little, B. R. (1983). Personal projects: A rationale and method for investigation. *Environment and Behavior, 15,* 273–309.

46. Omodei, M. M., & Wearing A. J. (1990). Need satisfaction and involvement in personal projects: Toward an integrative model of subjective well-being. *Journal of Personality and Social Psychology, 59,* 762–769.

47. Palys, T. S., & Little, B. R. (1983). Perceived life satisfaction and organization of personal projects systems. *Journal of Personality and Social Psychology, 44,* 1221–1230.

48. Ruehlman, L. S., & Wolchik, S. A. (1988). Personal goals and interpersonal support and hindrance as factors in psychological distress and well-being. *Journal of Personality and Social Psychology, 55,* 293–301.

49. Brunstein, J. C. (1993). Personal goals and subjective well-being: A longitudinal study. *Journal of Personality and Social Psychology, 65,* 1061–1070.

50. Little, B. R. (1989). Personal projects analysis: Trivial pursuits, magnificent obsessions, and the search for coherence. In D. M. Buss and N. Cantor (Eds.), *Personality psychology: Recent trends and emerging directions* (pp. 230–245). New York: Springer.

51. Snyder, C. R. (1996). To hope, to lose, and to hope again. *Journal of Personal and Interpersonal Loss, 1,* 1–16.

52. Nunnally, J. C. (1978). *Psychometric theory* (2nd edition). San Francisco: Jossey-Bass.

53. Babyak, M. A., Snyder, C. R., & Yoshinobu, L. (1993). Psychometric properties of the Hope Scale: A confirmatory factor analysis. *Journal of Research in Personality, 27,* 154–169.

54. Curry, L. A., Snyder, C. R., Cook, D. L., Ruby, B. C., & Rehm, M. (1997). The role of hope in academic and sport achievement. *Journal of Personality and Social Psychology, 73,* 1257–1267.

55. Gibb, J. (1990). *The Hope Scale revisited: Further validation of a measure of individual differences in the hope motive.* Unpublished manuscript. University of Illinois-Champaign, and University of Kansas-Lawrence.

56. Kaslow, N. J., Tanenbaum, R. L., & Seligman, M. E. P. (1978). *The KASTAN-R: A children's attributional style questionnaire (KASTAN-R-CASQ).* Unpublished manuscript, University of Pennsylvania.

57. Beck, A. T., Ward, C. H., Mendelsohn, M., Mock, J., & Erbaugh, J. (1961). An inventory for measuring depression. *Archives of General Psychiatry, 4,* 53–63.

58. Taylor, S. E., & Armor, D. A. (1996). Positive illusions and coping with adversity. *Journal of Personality, 64,* 873–898.

59. Taylor, S. E., Lichtman, R. R., & Wood, J. V. (1984). Attributions, beliefs about control, and adjustment to breast cancer. *Journal of Personality and Social Psychology, 46,* 489–502.

60. Hieronymous, A. N., & Hoover, H. D. (1985). *Iowa Test of Basic Skills.* Chicago: Riverside.

61. Snyder, C. R., Wiklund, C., & Cheavens, J. (1998). *Hope and success in college: Making the grades, graduating, or dropping-out?* Unpublished manuscript, University of Kansas, Lawrence, Kansas.

62. Holleran, S., & Snyder, C. R. (1990). *Discriminant and convergent validation of the Hope Scale.* Unpublished manuscript. University of Kansas, Lawrence, Kansas.

63. Sigmon, S. T., & Snyder, C. R. (1990). *The independent contributions of positive and negative affect and hope in predicting psychological health.* Unpublished manuscript. University of Kansas, Lawrence, Kansas.

64. Langelle, C. (1989). *An assessment of hope in a community sample.* Master's thesis. University of Kansas, Lawrence, Kansas.

65. Harris, C. B. (1988). *Hope: Construct definition and the development of an individual differences scale.* Doctoral dissertation. University of Kansas, Lawrence, Kansas.

66. Anderson, J. R. (1988). *The role of hope in appraisal, goal-setting, ex-*

pectancy, and coping. Doctoral dissertation. University of Kansas, Lawrence, Kansas.

67. Snyder, C. R., Irving, L. M., & Anderson, J. R. (1991). Hope and health. In C. R. Snyder & D. R. Forsyth (Eds.) *Handbook of social and clinical psychology: The health perspective* (pp. 285–305). Elmsford, NY: Pergamon.

68. Elliott, T. R., Witty, T. E., Herrick, S., & Hoffman, J. T. (1991). Negotiating reality after physical loss: Hope, depression, and disability. *Journal of Personality and Social Psychology, 61,* 608–613.

69. Sherwin, E. D., Elliott, T. R., Rybarczyk, B. D., Frank, R. G., Hanson, S., & Hoffman, J. (1992). Negotiating the reality of care giving: Hope, burnout, and nursing. *Journal of Social and Clinical Psychology, 11,* 129–139.

70. Barnum, D. D., Snyder, C. R., Rapoff, M. A., Mani, M. M., & Thompson, R. (1998). Hope and social support in the psychological adjustment of pediatric burn survivors and matched controls. *Children's Health Care, 27* (1), 15–30.

71. Snyder, C. R., & Brown, J. (1998). *Hope as related to perceived severity and tolerance of physical pain.* Unpublished manuscript. University of Kansas, Lawrence, Kansas.

72. Irving, L. M., Snyder, C. R., & Crowson, J. J. (1998). Hope and coping with cancer by college women. *Journal of Personality, 66* (2), 195–214.

73. Laird, S. P. (1991). *A preliminary investigation into the role of prayer as a coping technique for adult patients with arthritis.* Doctoral dissertation. University of Kansas, Lawrence, Kansas.

74. Meenan, R. F., Gertman, P. M., & Mason, J. H. (1980). Measuring health status in arthritis: The Arthritis Impact Measurement Scales. *Arthritis and Rheumatism, 23,* 146–152.

75. Affleck, G., & Tennen, H. (1996). Construing benefits from adversity: Adaptational significance and dispositional underpinnings. *Journal of Personality, 64,* 899–922.

76. Kliewer, W., & Lewis, H. (1995). Family influences on coping processes in children with sickle cell disease. *Journal of Pediatric Psychology, 20,* 511–525.

77. Klausner, E. J., Clarkin, J. F., Spielman, L., Pupo, C., Abrams, R., & Alexopoulas, G. (1997). *Goal-focused group psychotherapy for late-life depression.* Unpublished manuscript, Department of Psychiatry, The New York Hospital-Cornell Medical Center, White Plains, NY.

78. Butler, R. (1974). Successful aging and the role of life review. *Journal of the American Geriatric Society, 22,* 529–535.

79. Arean, P. A., Perri, M. G., Nezu, A. M., Schein, R., Christopher, F., & Joseph, T. (1993). Comparative effectiveness of social problem-solving therapy and reminiscence therapy as treatments for depression in older adults. *Journal of Consulting and Clinical Psychology, 61,* 1003–1010.

80. Hamilton, M. (1960). A rating scale for depression. *Journal of Neurology, Neurosurgery, and Psychiatry, 23,* 56–62.

81. Irving, L., Snyder, C. R., Gravel, L., Hanke, J., Hilberg, P., & Nelson, N. (1997, April). *Hope and effectiveness of a pre-therapy orientation group for community mental health center clients.* Paper presented at the Western Psychological Association Convention, Seattle.

82. Howard, K. I., Lueger, R. J., Maling, M. S., & Martinovich, Z. (1993). A phase model of psychotherapy outcome: Causal mediation of change. *Journal of Consulting and Clinical Psychology, 61*, 678–685.

83. Block, J. H. (1973). Conceptions of sex-roles: Some cross-cultural and longitudinal perspectives. *American Psychologist, 28*, 512–526.

84. Rosenkrantz, P., Vogel, S., Bee., H., Broverman, I., & Broverman, D. M. (1968). Sex-role stereotypes and self-concepts in college students. *Journal of Consulting and Clinical Psychology, 32*, 287–295.

85. Anderson, L. R., & Blanchard, P. N. (1982). Achievement attributions and self-instructions under competitive and individualistic goal structures. *Journal of Educational Psychology, 76*, 478–487.

86. Eagly, A. H., Karau, S. J., & Makhijani, M. G. (1995). Gender and the effectiveness of leaders: A meta-analysis. *Psychological Bulletin, 117*, 125–145.

87. Munoz-Dunbar, R. (1993). *Hope: A cross-cultural assessment of American college students.* Master's thesis. University of Kansas, Lawrence, Kansas.

88. Hinton-Nelson, M. D., Roberts, M. C., & Snyder, C. R. (1996). Exposure to violence and early adolescent's perceptions of hope and vulnerability to victimization. *American Journal of Orthopsychiatry, 66*, 346–353.

89. Pennebaker, J. W., & Beall, S. K. (1986). Confronting a traumatic event: Toward an understanding of inhibition and disease. *Journal of Abnormal Psychology, 95*, 274–281.

90. Greenberg, M. A., & Stone, A. A. (1992). Emotional disclosure about traumas and its relation to health: Effects of previous disclosure and trauma severity. *Journal of Personality and Social Psychology, 63*, 75–84.

91. Hughes, C. F., Uhlmann, C., & Pennebaker, J. W. (1994). The body's response to processing emotional trauma: Linking verbal text with autonomic activity. *Journal of Personality, 62*, 565–585.

92. Pennebaker, J. W., Colder, M., & Sharp, L. K. (1990). Accelerating the coping process. *Journal of Personality and Social Psychology, 58*, 528–537.

93. Pennebaker, J. W., Kiecolt-Glaser, J. K., & Glaser, R. (1988). Disclosure of traumas and immune function: Health implications for psychotherapy. *Journal of Consulting and Clinical Psychology, 56*, 239–245.

94. Seligman, M. E. P., Reivich, K., Jaycox, L., & Gillham, J. (1995). *The optimistic child.* Boston: Houghton Mifflin.

95. Couch, J. A. (1989). *The Hope Scale and head injury rehabilitation: Staff ratings as a function of client characteristics.* Doctoral dissertation. University of Kansas, Lawrence, Kansas.

Appendix A: The Children's Hope Scale

Directions: The six sentences below describe how children think about themselves and how they do things in general. Read each sentence carefully. For each sentence, please think about how you are in most situations. Place a check inside the circle that describes YOU the best. For example, place a check (✓) in the circle (◯) above "None of the time," if this describes you. Or, if you are this way "All of the time," check this circle. Please answer every question by putting a check in one of the circles. There are no right or wrong answers.

1. I think I am doing pretty well.

◯	◯	◯	◯	◯	◯
None of the time	A little of the time	Some of the time	A lot of the time	Most of the time	All of the time

2. I can think of many ways to get the things in life that are most important to me.

◯	◯	◯	◯	◯	◯
None of the time	A little of the time	Some of the time	A lot of the time	Most of the time	All of the time

3. I am doing just as well as other kids my age.

◯	◯	◯	◯	◯	◯
None of the time	A little of the time	Some of the time	A lot of the time	Most of the time	All of the time

4. When I have a problem, I can come up with lots of ways to solve it.

◯	◯	◯	◯	◯	◯
None of the time	A little of the time	Some of the time	A lot of the time	Most of the time	All of the time

5. I think the things I have done in the past will help me in the future.

◯	◯	◯	◯	◯	◯
None of the time	A little of the time	Some of the time	A lot of the time	Most of the time	All of the time

6. Even when others want to quit, I know that I can find ways to solve the problem.

○	○	○	○	○	○
None of the time	A little of the time	Some of the time	A lot of the time	Most of the time	All of the time

Notes: When administered to children, this scale is not labeled "The Children's Hope Scale," but is called "Questions About Your Goals." To calculate the total Children's Hope Scale score, add the responses to all six items, with "None of the time" = 1; "A little of the time" = 2; "Some of the time" = 3; "A lot of the time" = 4; "Most of the time" = 5; and, "All of the time" = 6. The three odd-numbered items tap agency, and the three even-numbered items tap pathways. From C. R. Snyder, B. Hoza, et al. The development and validation of the Children's Hope Scale, *Journal of Pediatric Psychology* © (1997), Vol. 22(3), p. 421. Reprinted with the permission of the Journal and the senior author.

Appendix B: The Adult Trait Hope Scale

Directions: Read each item carefully. Using the scale shown below, please select the number that best describes YOU and put that number in the blank provided.

> 1 = Definitely False
> 2 = Mostly False
> 3 = Somewhat False
> 4 = Slightly False
> 5 = Slightly True
> 6 = Somewhat True
> 7 = Mostly True
> 8 = Definitely True

_____ 1. I can think of many ways to get out of a jam.
_____ 2. I energetically pursue my goals.
_____ 3. I feel tired most of the time.
_____ 4. There are lots of ways around any problem.
_____ 5. I am easily downed in an argument.
_____ 6. I can think of many ways to get the things in life that are important to me.
_____ 7. I worry about my health.
_____ 8. Even when others get discouraged, I know I can find a way to solve the problem.
_____ 9. My past experiences have prepared me well for my future.
_____ 10. I've been pretty successful in life.
_____ 11. I usually find myself worrying about something.
_____ 12. I meet the goals that I set for myself.

Notes: When administering the scale, it is called "The Future Scale." The Agency subscale score is derived by summing items # 2, 9, 10 and 12; the Pathway subscale score is derived by adding items # 1, 4, 6, and 8. The total Hope Scale score is derived by summing the four Agency and the four Pathway items. From C. R. Snyder, C. Harris, et al., The will and the ways: Development and validation of an individual differences measure of hope, *Journal of Personality and Social Psychology,* © (1991), Vol. 60, p. 585. Reprinted with the permission of the American Psychological Association and the senior author.

Appendix C: The Adult State Hope Scale

Directions: Read each item carefully. Using the scale shown below, please select the number that best describes *how you think about yourself right now* and put that number in the blank before each sentence. Please take a few moments to focus on yourself and what is going on in *your life at this moment.* Once you have this "here and now" set, go ahead and answer each item according to the following scale:

1 = Definitely False
2 = Mostly False
3 = Somewhat False
4 = Slightly False
5 = Slightly True
6 = Somewhat True
7 = Mostly True
8 = Definitely True

_____ 1. If I should find myself in a jam, I could think of many ways to get out of it.

_____ 2. At the present time, I am energetically pursuing my goals.

_____ 3. There are lots of ways around any problem that I am facing now.

_____ 4. Right now, I see myself as being pretty successful.

_____ 5. I can think of many ways to reach my current goals.

_____ 6. At this time, I am meeting the goals that I have set for myself.

Notes: The Agency subscale score is derived by summing the three even-numbered items; the Pathways subscale score is derived by adding the three odd-numbered items. The total State Hope Scale score is derived by summing the three Agency and the three Pathways items. Scores can range from a low of 6 to a high of 48. When administering the State Hope Scale, it is labled as the "Goals Scale For the Present." From C. R. Snyder, S. C. Sympson, et al. Development and validation of the State Hope Scale. *Journal of Personality and Social Psychology,* © (1996), Vol. 70, p. 335. Reprinted with the permission of the American Psychological Association and the senior author.

11

Mastery-Oriented Thinking

Carol S. Dweck
Lisa A. Sorich

In our society, it is often assumed that success is simply a matter of basic ability: Those who have high ability will typically display high achievement while those who have lower ability will typically fall short. Our work, however, shows that many bright students show striking underachievement, and that many who may have seemed less bright end up achieving a great deal more than one would have predicted.

What is it then that determines achievement? Is it self-esteem? Is it those who have high opinions of their ability who become successful, and those who have poorer opinions of themselves who fall behind? Our work shows that, on the whole, students' estimates of their ability (their self-esteem vis-à-vis their intelligence) do not tell us who will succeed. As we will see, students differ greatly in whether they are able to *sustain* their confidence in their ability in the face of setbacks—and this is crucial—but just having a high opinion of your intellect is far less important than one might think.

Then is it students' motivation that is most important—their desire to do well, to succeed, to achieve? Although this is undoubtedly an influence, as we will see many students who care very deeply about succeeding are still underachieving.

Our research has shown that a crucial factor in achievement is students' ability to cope with challenges and setbacks. The students who love challenges, who are willing to take risks, and who thrive when they hit obstacles are the ones who achieve up to, or beyond, their apparent potential. These students may not start out being highly skilled, but they become skilled over time. The students who are afraid of challenges, who avoid risks, and who wilt when they fail (or run from failure situations) are the ones who lose ground over time.

This chapter is about these two different coping styles and the psychology that lies behind them. We will show how students who display the less adaptive, "helpless" coping pattern think differently about their intelligence (they think it is a fixed trait), focus on different goals in achievement situations (they are more concerned with showing they have a lot of intelligence than they are with learning), and interpret their failures in different ways (they think failure signifies a lack of intelligence). These students see challenge as a threat; it holds the danger of revealing weaknesses and showing them to lack intelligence. Indeed, we will see that in some ways it is these students' overconcern with doing well and proving they are smart that stands in the way of their success.

In contrast, the students who display the more adaptive, "mastery-oriented" pattern think of their intelligence as something they can cultivate over time (not something that is just fixed), focus on the goal of learning (not just looking smart), and interpret their failures as meaning they need more effort or a new strategy (not as signifying a deficiency in their endowment). These students see challenge as a welcome opportunity, as a chance to stretch their skills and become smarter.

We also will look at how these patterns emerge in early childhood, and at the kinds of feedback that adults give to foster the helpless and mastery-oriented coping styles. One might think that praising children's abilities after a job well done is what would foster adaptive coping. This, after all, would be expected to raise children's intellectual self-esteem and allow them to confront challenges with confidence. However, we present research to show that praising children's abilities or intelligence, even when it is well-deserved, does not promote mastery-oriented coping. In fact, it promotes the opposite. As we will see, by focusing students on measuring their intelligence, such praise can create a helpless response to setbacks.

In summary, in this chapter we will first describe helpless and mastery-oriented thinking, and how they influence students' motivation and learning. Then we will delve into the psychology behind the two patterns; and finally, we will present new research on the kinds of experiences that create helpless and mastery-oriented thinking—exploring the sometimes surprising implications for motivational practices.

Helpless and Mastery-Oriented Coping Styles

Two decades ago, building on research in learned helplessness (1, 2), Diener and Dweck (3, 4) spelled out two very different patterns of reaction to failure. In one, the *helpless pattern*, students quickly blame their ability, give up, and show a sharp deterioration in performance. In the other, the *mastery-oriented pattern*, students remain focused and effective. Instead of doubting their competence, they take action to surmount the problem. Our studies have shown us that helpless and mastery-oriented thinking is not a matter of ability, but a matter of "mind-set." Let us now look more closely at these different mind-sets.

In the studies by Diener and Dweck, late grade-school students worked on a series of concept-formation problems. They succeeded on the first problems, with training given as needed, but failed on the later ones. We were most interested in how students' thoughts, feelings, and problem-solving strategies changed as they went from success to failure, and, to examine this, a number of steps were taken.*

First, we used a task that allowed us to pinpoint the level of students' problem-solving strategies on each trial. In this way, we could tell whether their strategies improved, stayed the same, or declined as they hit the failure trials.

Second, we asked students to talk aloud, and specifically to verbalize their thoughts and feelings about the task, as they went about trying to solve the problems. We gave them license to hold forth on any topic whatsoever, and they did.

Third, after the failure trials (and, in some studies, after the success trials as well) we asked students a number of questions about their perceptions of their performance and their predictions about their future performance.

Before these experimental sessions students had been categorized into two groups: Those who were likely to display a helpless response to the failure and those who were likely to display a mastery-oriented one. This was done on the basis of an attribution questionnaire that had predicted persistence versus nonpersistence following failure in past research (5). (Those who tended to attribute their failures to a lack of effort were predicted to display the more mastery-oriented response.) But here we were interested in the entire pattern of thoughts, feelings, and behaviors—not just attributions—that might unfold as the students encountered failure.

When we looked at the ways in which the two groups confronted failure, striking differences were evident. Soon after the onset of the failure problems, many children in the helpless group spontaneously began to denigrate their intellectual competence. They concluded from the failure that their memory was deficient or that they lacked intelligence.

The students in the mastery-oriented group drew no such conclusion. They didn't seem to analyze the reasons for their failure at all, and, in fact, didn't seem to think they *were* failing. They recognized that the task had gotten harder and that they would have to strive to find ways to solve these new, more difficult problems. This is precisely what they set about doing. For example, they gave themselves instructions on ways to improve their performance—by concentrating harder or by reviewing the feedback they

---

*It is important to note that in every study involving failure, we take extensive precautions to ensure that everyone leaves the experiment feeling quite proud of their performance. We do this by giving students mastery experiences and mastery training at the end of the session on the failure problems.

had been given on that problem—and they monitored themselves to make sure they were implementing these strategies properly. In short, these students, rather than seeing failure as a sign that their intelligence was inadequate, saw their difficulty as a cue to go into high gear.

Many of the students in the helpless group had recognized that the problems were now harder, but they still thought they were intellectually deficient for not being able to solve them right away. Unlike the mastery-oriented students, they did not give themselves the time and leeway to learn how to master the new challenge. In line with blaming their abilities, the helpless students lost confidence in their chances for future success. In contrast, the mastery-oriented students retained a high degree of confidence that they would eventually succeed on these new problems if they continued to work at them. Some of them practically begged for additional chances to solve the failure problems, even after the problem was declared over.

What were the emotions that the two groups of students expressed during the success and then the failure problems? As you might expect, everyone expressed a fair degree of positive emotions while they were succeeding, but this positive affect dissipated rapidly as the helpless group encountered difficulty. Instead, they began to express a range of negative emotions from sadness to boredom. In striking contrast, the mastery-oriented group continued to enjoy the problems, and some even expressed increased positive affect in the face of difficulty. They said such things as "I love a challenge," "Mistakes are our friends," or "You know, I was hoping this would be informative." In other words, they relished the challenge they were confronting.

What happened to the performance of the two groups? Over half of the students in the helpless group suffered a clear decline in the level of their problem-solving strategies. Many of them slipped into strategies that were typical of preschoolers and that would not have worked to solve even the original easier problems. Most of the members of the mastery-oriented group, in contrast, maintained or improved the level of problem-solving strategy they were using. Indeed, a full quarter of them taught themselves how to use new and more sophisticated strategies than they had ever used before. Some even solved the problems that were supposed to be considerably beyond them.

Thus, while the helpless group became discouraged and condemned their intelligence, the mastery-oriented group pulled up their sleeves and applied themselves assiduously to the task at hand. Further, because the new problems were quite difficult, the helpless group unjustly denigrated their ability and were excessively pessimistic about their future performance. Thus, the helpless response included distorted thinking. In contrast, the mastery-oriented group recognized that the problems had become more difficult. Free from preoccupation with negative self-judgments, they remained focused on the task and were realistically optimistic in predicting their future performance.

Next, we showed that these two mind-sets could affect the quality of children's learning as they attempted to master new material in their classroom. In a study by Licht and Dweck (6), fifth-graders were given a new unit to learn in their classrooms: Psychology: Why People Do the Things They Do. They received programmed instruction booklets that taught them the principles of operant learning. What they learned, essentially, was that when they performed an action and a good thing happened, they were likely to perform that action again in the future. When they did something and a bad thing happened, they were less likely to do that thing again. If a big bad thing and a little good thing happened, they were still not likely to perform the action again, and so on.

After students read the first instructional booklet, they were given a seven-question mastery test. They were considered to have mastered the material if they got all seven questions correct, because the questions were all based directly on the material they had just studied. If students did not attain mastery on the first try, they were given a review booklet and another mastery test. In all, they had four opportunities to demonstrate their mastery.

We wanted to look at the effects of initial confusion on children's mastery of the material. We reasoned that in many school subjects, but particularly in math, students are often confronted at the beginning of a new unit with periods of confusion. New concepts and new conceptual frameworks are introduced, and the student may have no idea how these new concepts are related to anything he or she has learned before. The resulting period of confusion, we thought, might have a negative impact on helpless students. As with the failure problems in our previous studies, initial difficulty with new material would be likely to cause the helpless students to call their ability into question, and perhaps impede their learning of subsequent material. The same period of confusion, however, should not hinder the mastery-oriented students in the least.

To test this idea, we gave students two different versions of the initial instruction booklet. In both versions, we inserted a few paragraphs on "imitation" near the beginning of each booklet. In half the cases, these paragraphs were written in a clear, straightforward way, but in the other half of the cases, they were written in a tortuous, confusing fashion. These passages were completely irrelevant to the real material that the students were supposed to learn, and so the confusing passage did not rob them of any information they needed to master the psychological principles they were being taught later on in the booklet. Nonetheless, would the confusing paragraphs cause deficits in learning for the helpless children?

As in our previous studies, students were classified into helpless and mastery-oriented groups on the basis of their responses to an attribution questionnaire, with those who attributed their failures more to effort being assigned to the mastery-oriented group. Thus, there were four experimental groups: mastery-oriented and helpless children, who received either the initial booklet without the confusing passage or the initial booklet with the confusing passage.

What we found was that when students received the booklet with no confusion, the helpless and mastery-oriented groups showed the same degree of learning. More than two-thirds of the children in both groups demonstrated their mastery of the material within the experimental session. This showed that the two groups had equal ability at the task. However, when students received the booklet that contained the confusing paragraphs, a strong difference emerged. As in the no confusion condition, over 70% of the mastery-oriented students mastered the material. In contrast, only about one-third of the helpless group was able to learn the material when it was preceded by the confusing paragraphs. Thus, the helpless group was thrown off by the confusion, despite the fact that they had four chances to go over the subject matter and repeat the test. This study showed that helpless and mastery-oriented thinking affects children not only on laboratory tasks, but also in realistic classroom learning situations.

Although we had shown the striking contrasts between the helpless and mastery-oriented patterns, many questions remained. Primary among them was: If the two groups of students have essentially equal ability, why does one group respond to challenging achievement situations with negative emotions, diminished confidence, and impairment of performance, whereas the other group responds with enthusiasm and effective effort? We soon began to suspect that these two different mind-sets grew out of the different ways that students viewed achievement situations and the different goals they had for themselves in those situations.

Students' Achievement Goals

Elliott and Dweck (7) set out to test the idea that it was the goals that students set for themselves that gave rise to the helpless and mastery-oriented patterns. We identified two classes of goals that students could pursue in achievement situations: performance goals and learning goals. With a performance goal, the student's aim is to gain favorable judgments of his or her competence (or avoid unfavorable judgments of it)—that is, to look smart. In contrast, a learning goal is one in which the student's aim is to increase his or her competence—that is, to get smarter.

It is important to understand that both kinds of goals are natural, necessary, and pretty much universal. Everyone wants their ability to be esteemed by others and everyone wants to learn new things. The difference among students lies in how much they value each goal, and whether they are willing to sacrifice one goal for the other. In the study by Elliott and Dweck, we showed that when students are overly focused on performance goals—when they are overconcerned with how their ability is being judged—they are vulnerable to a helpless response to failure. This is especially true when they have low confidence in their ability.

In contrast, when students are focused on learning goals, they show a mastery-oriented response to failure, even when they have low confidence in their ability. This is because their goal is not to prove their ability but to improve it. You don't necessarily need to feel you already have the ability in order to pursue improvement in a mastery-oriented way.

Over and over we've seen that performance goals, by focusing students on measuring their ability by their performance, can make them vulnerable to a helpless pattern in the face of failure. Learning goals, by instead focusing students on the effort and strategies they need for learning, foster a mastery-oriented stance toward difficulty (8, 9, 10, 11).

However, a question that remained was why some students are so concerned about measuring their intellectual ability, while others invest themselves in increasing their ability.

Students' Theories of Intelligence

We noted that students with a performance goal seemed to be treating their ability as if it were a static quality, something that they could assess, but not alter—while those with a learning goal acted as though they thought of their ability as something that could be developed. Perhaps, we reasoned, the two groups of students actually had fundamentally different ideas about the nature of their intellectual ability.

Bandura and Dweck (12) set out to test the idea that it was the beliefs students had about their intelligence that generated the performance versus learning goal orientations, and the subsequent helpless versus mastery responses. They identified two theories that students could hold about their intelligence. One, called an "entity theory," was the idea that intelligence is a fixed entity, a deep-seated personal quality that could not be changed. The other, called an "incremental theory" was the idea that intelligence is an attribute that can be developed through one's intellectual efforts.

We hypothesized that students who held the entity theory, believing that intelligence is fixed, would be concerned with demonstrating that they had a goodly amount of it. They would thus pursue performance goals, seeking opportunities that would display their intelligence to good advantage and avoiding situations that contained the risk of revealing intellectual inadequacies. In contrast, we predicted that students who held the incremental theory would be more concerned with getting smarter. They would not want to waste their time showing off their intellect, when they could be developing it.

In a series of studies, we have shown that the different theories of intelligence do indeed set up the different goals (10, 13). Whether we measure students' existing theories of intelligence or induce students, through experimental manipulations, to adopt one view over the other, we find that holding an entity theory fosters performance goals, whereas holding an incremental theory fosters learning goals. Indeed, we find that holding an entity theory fosters both performance goals and a helpless response to failure, whereas holding an incremental theory fosters learning goals and a mastery-oriented response to failure.

We also have found that students with different theories of intelligence have different attitudes toward effort. Those with an entity theory, who worry about assessing their intelligence, believe that effort is a measure of your intellectual ability. If you have to work hard at something, they believe, it means you must not have high ability in that area. Conversely, if you have high ability, you shouldn't have to work hard. So, for them, by applying effort you risk showing that you lack ability.

Those students with an incremental theory of intelligence, who are oriented toward learning, do not see effort as a way of measuring their intellect. They see it as a tool for learning. For them, high effort is what turns on people's ability, allows them to use it to the fullest, and ultimately increases their ability. Far from undermining intellectual ability, then, effort is what supports and creates it.

Two recent studies of students making the transition to junior high school illustrates this relation between students' theories of intelligence, their goals, their beliefs about effort, and their helpless versus mastery-oriented responses to failure. These studies also demonstrate the important impact these mind-sets can have on students' actual school achievement.

Theories of Intelligence and School Achievement

We have looked at the impact of these mind-sets on achievement across the junior high school transition for a very important reason. This is the time that many students, especially academically successful ones, meet their first real challenge. This is often when the school work suddenly becomes harder and the grading becomes more stringent. In the previous years, in grade school, students are typically in a more protective and personalized learning environment, where compliance and a degreee of diligence alone often guarantee success in the classroom. In junior high school they must confront new challenges in a more independent way, and academic failure may loom as a real possibility for the first time (14). This is the time, then, that we would expect the helpless and mastery-oriented patterns to have a real impact on achievement. In two separate studies we have found just this—that students' theories of intelligence predict helpless and mastery-oriented responses to the new achievement challenge, strongly predicting students' level of achievement as they make the transition to junior high school.

In the first study, MacGyvers (Henderson) and Dweck (15) measured students' theories of intelligence at the beginning of seventh grade, the first year of junior high school. We could thus classify them as entity or incremental theorists. For each student, we also had their sixth-grade grades and achievement test scores, and, at the end of their first semester of seventh grade, we recorded the grades they earned that semester.

Our first question was: How did the students do compared to how one would expect them to do on the basis of their sixth-grade achievement? Was their current achievement best predicted by their previous achievement, or by their theories of intelligence? What we found was that the students' theories of intelligence were the best predictor of their seventh-grade grades. Students who believed intelligence to be fixed showed a clear decline in class standing on the whole, relative to what would have been predicted from their previous achievement level. Thus, entity theorists who had been low achievers in the sixth grade tended to remain low in achievement, while many of those who had been among the high achievers the previous year had fallen into the ranks of the lower achievers.

In contrast, the students with an incremental theory of their intelligence showed gains in their class standing on the whole. Those who had been high achievers tended to remain high, and many of those who had been lower achievers in sixth grade blossomed into being higher achievers—that is, their class standing had risen appreciably.

Our results also showed that the entity theorists displayed the other key aspects of the helpless pattern, whereas the incremental theorists showed a clear mastery-oriented pattern. Specifically, the two groups differed not only in their performance in the face of challenge (as we have just noted), but also in their attributions for setbacks and in the affect with which they confronted the challenge of junior high school. The students with an entity theory of their intelligence were significantly more likely than their incremental counterparts to say that a poor grade in junior high school meant that they had low intellectual ability. The incremental theorists were significantly more likely to say that a poor grade reflected on their effort or their study strategy. The entity theorists were also more likely to report anxiety and apprehension about their junior high schoolwork—even before they had received their lower report card grades.

Our next study (16) fleshed out these findings and provided more insight into the ways in which helpless and mastery-oriented children confront achievement challenges. Here, once again, we studied students who were beginning their first year in junior high. In contrast to the students in the last study, who were mostly Caucasian and lived in semirural Midwest towns, the students in this study were largely minority students who lived in a major northeastern city. Once again, we had the achievement test scores that the students had earned the previous year (in sixth grade) and again we measured students' theories about their intelligence as they embarked on junior high school. We also assessed their learning and performance goals, their confidence in their ability, their beliefs about effort, and their reactions to hypothetical failures. We then waited to see what grades they earned at the end of the semester.

When we classified students into entity and incremental theorists, we saw that they had virtually identical achievement test scores (in both English and math) the previous year. They also had identical degrees of confidence in their ability as they confronted the seventh grade. Yet once again, confidence was not enough, for when we examined the grades they earned during their first two years of junior high, we saw large differences. Incremental theorists earned significantly higher grades than entity theorists in both English and math.

Entity and incremental theorists also differed in a number of other ways. As expected, they preferred different achievement goals. Most students endorsed both performing well and learning as general goals. However, when the two goals were placed in conflict, as they often may be in the real world, incremental theorists were far more interested in learning than in simply performing well. They wanted to meet challenges and acquire new skills rather than have easy work that would make them look smart. Entity theorists, on the other hand, tended to prefer performance goals over learning. They were willing to sacrifice learning in order to look smart, and unwilling to sacrifice short-term performance in order to learn.

When we looked at students' attitudes toward effort, we saw, first, that entity theorists had a strong desire to minimize the effort they put into their schoolwork. In fact, the goal of minimizing effort was as important to them as learning or performing well. Thus, the entity theorists were burdened with conflicting interests: the goals of doing well had to compete with an equally strong aversion to the very effort required to attain them.

The two groups also differed in their beliefs about the meaning and utility of effort. Incremental theorists more strongly believed that expending effort was an effective way of using your ability, while entity theory theorists believed that expending effort was a sign that you did not have ability. Finally, incremental theorists more strongly believed that effort was a key ingredient in success.

These differences in beliefs about effort are likely causes of the subsequent disparity in academic attainment over the transition to junior high school. If entity theorists believe that effort is not effective in bringing about success, that effort means you're not smart, and that it is highly desirable to minimize the effort you put into academic tasks, this cannot help but put them at a disadvantage. Incremental theorists, in contrast, essentially sing the praises of effort—as a way of turning on ability and bringing about success.

Indeed, on our hypothetical failure scenarios (where students were asked to imagine that they had received a poor test grade despite a moderate degree of studying), incremental theorists said they would respond by studying harder the next time. Entity theorists said, more often than incremental theorists, that they would consider cheating the next time!

In sum, in two studies that examined real-world coping with important challenges, the mastery-oriented approach shown by the incremental students yielded significantly better results—emotionally and intellectually—

than the more helpless responses shown by the entity theorists. From these findings we see how the different theories of intelligence, and the helpless versus mastery-oriented coping styles they create, have a clear role to play in academic settings.

How Early Do These Patterns Begin?

We used to think that young children (below the age of 8 or 9) were immune to a helpless response. They were thought by researchers to be entirely mastery-oriented. Why? Because it was found that young children do not really know very much about intelligence or think of it as a fixed trait. Therefore, they should not engage in the intelligence-blaming of entity theorists when they hit failure, and thus, they should not show a helpless response. It also was believed that young children are very effort-oriented, and that to the extent that they think about intelligence, they view it as being synonymous with effort. This should make them more mastery-oriented. It also made sense to us that young children, as they approached the most challenging tasks of their lives, should be mastery-oriented. One needs to be extremely persistent to learn how to walk and talk and learn about the world. Unfortunately, we were wrong. Although many, many young children are indeed mastery-oriented, a sizable proportion are not.

We have now performed extensive research with young children, as young as preschool age, and we have found clear evidence of a helpless response. At least one-third of young children show signs of helpless responding when they experience failure or receive criticism—including self-blame, negative affect, lowered persistence, and a lack of constructive strategies (17, 18, 19, 20, 21, 22, 23).

Why did we find evidence of a helpless response pattern in young children when others had not? First, we gave our young participants tasks and measures that were meaningful to them and failures they could understand. For example, we gave them vivid jig-saw puzzles that they sometimes could not finish.

Second, we began to realize that children did not need to know anything at all about intelligence to show a helpless response. Maybe questions about intelligence are paramount to older children, but young children are not really in the thick of academic schoolwork and worrying about how smart they are. They do have concerns, however, and for these young children, socialization issues are paramount. They are in the midst of being taught what is right and wrong, what is good and bad. Thus, it should be issues of whether they are good or bad children that preoccupy them, and it should be in this area that they show their vulnerability to a helpless response. And this is precisely what we found.

In a study with kindergartners (20), for example, the helpless children, after their failure, said they felt as though they were not good and not nice children. The mastery-oriented children rarely reported such feelings. In this study, and another as well (18), children were asked to role-play (with dolls) their parents' and their teacher's reactions to their mistakes. Compared to the mastery-oriented children, the helpless children role-played a great deal more criticism, and even punishment, from these socialization agents. This again showed that the helpless children felt as though they were bad when they failed.

What did the mastery-oriented children think and feel when they failed? Interestingly, they were also preoccupied with issues of goodness and badness, but they simply assumed that they were still good children despite their errors. For instance, in their role-playing of adult responses to their work, many mastery-oriented children had the adult reassure the child (the doll that represented them) that they were still good, but that they needed to work harder, practice more, and correct the mistakes that they had made. In other words, in contrast to the helpless children, many of whom simply had the adults proclaim the child's badness, these children had the adult provide reassurances of goodness along with constructive strategies for remedying the failure.

We saw that with the older children, helpless and mastery-oriented children had different beliefs about the nature of intelligence—whether it was a fixed trait that could be judged from their performance or whether it was a malleable quality that could be increased through effort. Do young children hold analogous beliefs about badness? Heyman, et al. (20) found that they do. Helpless young children are far more likely than their mastery-oriented peers to believe that badness is a stable trait—and that it can readily be judged from children's behavior, even their academic behavior.

This means that the model of helpless versus mastery-oriented beliefs and behavior that we formulated for older children also applies to younger ones. Young helpless children believe that the trait in question is a fixed quality that can be judged from their performance; they blame that quality when they fail and fall into a helpless response. Young mastery-oriented children believe that the qualities in question are malleable ones that can be improved through their effort; they focus on that effort when they fail, and display a constructive and determined mastery-oriented response to setbacks.

A critical remaining question, however, is this: What socialization practices lead children to adopt a helpless or a mastery-oriented pattern? Are there things that parents or teachers do that create one mode or the other? We took a hint from the role-playing that the young children did—the fact that the young helpless children role-played judgmental reactions from parents and that the young mastery-oriented children role-played more effort and strategy suggestions—and we set out to see whether these different kinds of reactions can actually create helpless and mastery-oriented responses in children.

A researcher might observe parents with their children, see what kinds of feedback practices the parents use, and see whether these practices are linked to the coping styles of their children. But this wouldn't tell you which came first, the feedback practices of the parents, or the coping styles of the children. What we chose to do was to create an experimental situation in which children were given different kinds of feedback by an adult. We then checked to see whether this feedback fostered a helpless or mastery-oriented response to setbacks in the children.

We had shown in a number of previous studies that, counter to what one might think, we could actually generate helpless and mastery-oriented reactions in children by creating the right circumstances. In other words, even though children might come into our experiment with one coping style, if we set up the right "psychology" in the situation (e.g., the right theory, goal, or attribution), we could foster the other coping style. For example, we found that when we highlighted one or another type of goal, we influenced not only the childrens' choice of task, but their responses to difficulty. When we emphasized a performance goal (by telling children that their performance on a task would be "evaluated by experts"), children chose a task that would "show what they could do." When we highlighted a learning goal (by telling children they could develop skills that would help them in their schoolwork), children chose a difficult task that would entail errors, but from which they were told they could learn. Subsequently, when the children experienced failure, many of the children with the induced performance goal showed the typical helpless response of negative emotions, denigration of their ability, and deteriorating strategies. In contrast, the children who had been given a learning goal retained a mastery-oriented coping style (7).

Thus, powerful factors in the situation can actually change someone's coping style at least for the moment. Our goal here was to see whether different kinds of feedback from adults would function in this way and set up a psychological situation that would promote either the helpless or mastery-oriented coping style.

We were interested in the effects of both criticism and praise, because we believed that how parents and teachers respond to children's successes could be as important as how they respond to children's errors or failures. Our results were clear and striking (24). Let us take the results of the criticism first. What we found was that judgmental criticism—criticism that reflected on the child's traits or on the child as a whole—fostered a strong helpless reaction in response to later setbacks: negative emotions, self-blame and feelings of badness, and a lack of constructive reactions. The overwhelming percentage of children that displayed these maladaptive responses to judgmental criticism undoubtedly included many who would ordinarily have displayed a mastery-oriented reaction. In contrast, criticism indicating that more effort or a new strategy was called for set up a very mastery-oriented reaction when children later encountered obstacles, even for children who presumably would ordinarily have reacted in a helpless fashion. (Feedback that simply criticized the behavior and not the child was in between. It did not lead to as much self-condemnation as the judgmental feedback, but it did not create as strong a mastery-oriented pattern as the effort/strategy feedback.)

This study showed that feedback from adults could readily shape children's coping styles. It also showed that judgmental criticism could teach children to judge themselves and their deepest underlying qualities from their performance, so that when their performance was poor they concluded that they were deficient and unworthy. This inference then interfered with the quality of their coping. Thus, these coping styles are not simply innate dispositions. Rather, they are the product of beliefs and expectations that can be fostered by others' reactions.

It is perhaps unsurprising that negative judgmental criticism, with its implicit threat of rejection, should make children more likely to feel apprehensive about failure and exhibit a helpless response. But might praise that reflected on the child or on his/her qualities also have a negative effect on coping? This would be highly counterintuitive because in our society we tend to believe, for example, that telling children that they are smart when they perform well is a real confidence booster and can only enhance motivation and coping. Thus, educators have been advised to praise children's abilities and performance to increase their self-esteem and, consequently, their academic confidence and performance.

On the other hand, it is possible that praising either the child as a whole or his/her qualities following good performance or behavior might carry the same message as the judgmental criticism: That your basic qualities can be judged from your performance—so that when the child later performs poorly, s/he turns the previous positive judgment into a negative one. If this is true, then judgmental praise, as desirable and ego-boosting as it may seem, carries a hidden message that can lead to a helpless response to later setbacks.

To test these ideas about praise, we set up a series of studies with both young (kindergarten) and older (fifth grade) children (24). In every case, we found that praise for the child as a whole or praise for the child's traits (e.g., his or her intelligence) after a job well done created a significantly greater helpless response to subsequent difficulty than did praise that was directed toward the child's effort/strategy or toward the behavior or performance itself. Effort/strategy praise consistently created the most mastery-oriented coping styles. It is not that children were not very happy to receive the praise that reflected on their traits or on them as a whole. They were very pleased to be so judged. It is simply that this praise backfired when the children later hit obstacles: If the good performance meant they were smart and worthy, then the bad performance, they surmised, meant they were not smart and not worthy.

To convey the flavor of these studies, let us look at the experiments with fifth graders. Here, following success on an intellectual problem-solving task, children received one of three forms of praise. The children in the intelligence-praise group were told: "Wow, you got (10) right. That's a really good score! You must be really smart at this." The children in the effort praise group were told: "Wow, you got (10) right. That's a really good score! You must have tried really hard." And the children in the control group were told simply: "Wow, you got (10) right. That's a really good score!" Unlike the children in the intelligence praise or the effort praise groups, the children in the control group were not given any particular interpretation of their good score.

What impact did the different forms of praise have? As suggested above, the intelligence praise made children feel good in the short run (though actually no better than the other forms of praise), but when they then encountered a more difficult set of problems, on which they did more poorly, the children in the intelligence praise group fell apart. They were the ones who now thought they were not smart—that is, they interpreted the failure to mean that they lacked intelligence. The children in the effort praise group simply took the failure to mean they needed to try harder. Thus, by telling children they are smart when they succeed, the intelligence praise led them to believe they were not smart when they didn't.

The children in the intelligence praise group also showed other problems. After the failure, they reported less enjoyment of the task than any of the other groups and the least desire to take the problems home to practice. This means that the initial intelligence praise made the students turn off to the material when they weren't doing well at it—just the time when they needed to practice more, not less.

Moreover, when students were given another opportunity to work on the kind of problem on which they had done well initially, the children who had gotten the intelligence praise now did the worst of any group, even though they were equal to the other groups at the start. Once they felt they weren't smart at the task, they no longer performed well. In fact, they did worse than they had done on the first trial, even though they now had more practice on the task. The children who received effort praise did the best of all the groups on this last trial; they also showed significant improvement from the first trial to the last. This means that the intelligence praise not only made children feel bad about themselves when the problems got hard, but also actually led to impaired performance. This was not because they no longer cared about performing well, as our next finding showed.

Perhaps our most striking and disheartening finding was that intelligence praise made performing well so important that children lied about their scores. On this measure, we asked children to write a description of the task for a child in another school, and on the sheet we asked them to write down the score they had achieved on the task. When we looked at the scores children had reported to this unknown peer, we saw that about 40% of the children in the intelligence praise group lied about the score they had earned, and of course, they lied in the direction of enhancing their scores. Very few of the children in the other groups falsified their scores. This means that performing well meant so much about their intelligence to these children that they were led to lie about how well they had done, even to a child they would never meet. It also means, as noted above, that the performance deficit shown by this group was not due to a lessened emphasis placed by these children on performing well. The performance deficit occurred *despite* their strong desire to do well—just as we've seen with the helpless children all along.

It appears, then, that intelligence praise sets children up for a helpless response when they later encounter difficulty, whereas effort praise sets children up for a mastery-oriented response. Yet we found differences between the groups even before they encountered difficulty. Specifically, after the initial praise, children were asked what kinds of tasks they would like to work on in the future. They were given a choice between "performance goal tasks" that would allow them to look smart but not learn anything new, and "learning goal tasks" that would allow them to learn something new and important, but contained the risk of errors or confusion and thus might not allow them to look smart.

We found in study after study that the students who received intelligence praise just wanted to keep on looking smart—the clear majority of them chose the performance goal task, even though it meant that they sacrificed the opportunity for new learning. This was true even under the most favorable performance conditions, when they had met with nothing but success. In contrast, the effort praise children overwhelmingly chose the learning goal task. Instead of worrying about how smart they were, they were free to pursue development. Thus, some aspects of the helpless versus mastery-oriented patterns, such as challenge avoidance versus challenge seeking, may emerge even without the catalyst of actual failure, when the situation promotes one or the other motivational system.

What was also interesting was that the effects of the different forms of praise were just as strong for children who were, in fact, very good at the task and for children who were less proficient. This means that intelligence praise can be harmful even when it's "true."

These studies have taught us a powerful lesson about the causes of the helpless and mastery-oriented coping styles. It is not just harsh or negative treatment that can impair children's coping. Even extremely positive and well-meant feedback can be detrimental. Anything that causes children to focus on their traits and to worry about measuring them by their performance can create vulnerability, even though adults may think they are boosting children's self-esteem with trait compliments.

Implications and Future Directions

These findings suggest we should be careful of labeling children "gifted" or "bright," lest we promote an entity theory of intelligence, and an overemphasis on looking smart. The inevitable challenges associated with higher level achievement guarantee that even very bright children will experience periods of difficulty and initial confusion. A strong personal investment in maintaining the status of a "gifted" student could make a child especially sensitive to any sort of failure, and thus vulnerable to a helpless response. Our findings suggest that robust self-confidence does not come from preoccupation with assessments of one's intellectual ability. Rather, it comes from feeling that one can continually develop one's ability by applying effort.

Is it enough simply to praise effort? Might it not become routine and tiresome? There are many ways to praise effort and strategy when complimenting a child's good performance. For example, the adult can show great enthusiasm for the product itself, and find various aspects of it to ask about and compliment. He or she can ask about how the child came up with various ideas and made choices and compliment them. Recognition can focus on the process by which the task was accomplished, rather than on the child's attributes. Such praise, more subtle and convincing than simply saying "You must have worked so hard," nevertheless implicitly conveys the value of effort and strategy by focusing attention on the child's active role in accomplishment. It can easily be argued that this kind of interest in a child's work is far more appreciative than simply looking at the work and complimenting a trait. Moreover, as we have seen, this kind of reaction not only rewards children for the work they have done, but teaches them a value system and a coping style that will serve them well in the future (25).

In our current research, we are exploring further how the different theories about intelligence may be transmitted to children by parents, teachers, and peers. We are also examining in more detail precisely *how* students' theories of intelligence influence their academic outcomes, seeking to pinpoint the critical combination of beliefs and behaviors that give incremental theorists their advantage.

Another line of research involves looking at the impact of the individual's self-theories on coping with social setbacks, such as rejection. We have seen that beliefs about one's intellectual attributes can have a powerful influence on successful coping in the academic realm, setting up the contrasting mastery-oriented and helpless patterns. Similarly, some people cope better than others with social difficulty: Where some people respond poorly to social setbacks, feeling rejected and blaming their own attributes, others are more resilient, maintaining self-confidence and finding constructive ways to respond to challenges in their relationships with others. Thus, we are showing how beliefs about one's own personality can generate helpless versus mastery-oriented responses in social settings (26, 27).

Finally, we are finding that people who believe in fixed traits differ from those who believe in malleable qualities not only in their self-judgments, but also differ in how they judge others. A series of recent studies shows that entity theorists consistently stereotype others more than do incremental theorists. They believe more strongly in existing stereotypes and they form new ones more readily. Thus, people's theories have important implications both for their personal achievement and for how they conduct their social lives (28, 29).

Conclusion

What can we now say about helpless and mastery-oriented thinking? We can conclude that helpless thinking revolves around measuring the self and worrying how the self will appear and be judged if one makes errors or performs poorly. This mind-set leads to a host of maladaptive thoughts, feelings, and behaviors: fear of challenge and avoidance of effort, as well as denigration of ability, plunging expectations of success, and impaired performance in the face of difficulty. It is not difficult to see how this pattern can stand in the way of success. If students are afraid to apply effort or are unable to apply it effectively when it is most needed, this cannot help but hinder their achievement.

Mastery-oriented thinking, in contrast, revolves around the task at hand and focuses on effort and strategies. Mastery-oriented students think about how to accomplish something, not about whether they're smart or not. For them, effort is the way to put their skills into motion, to surmount challenges, to accomplish their goals, and to increase their abilities. Mastery-oriented students are certainly aware when they don't know something or don't know how to do something, but they don't take this to mean that they are incompetent. They take it to mean they have effort to put in and learning to do.

We have begun to learn how these different patterns of achievement motivation can affect children's actual performance in the academic realm. In particular, when confronting a challenging transition, the advantages of focusing on developing rather than demonstrating one's ability become clear. Children who held an incremental theory of their intelligence were more successful in negotiating this transition. Children who held an entity theory performed less well, despite their emphasis on performance. The helpless pattern, fueled by fear of inadequacy, is triggered by challenge and difficulty. However, only in a challenging learning environment is high achievement likely to flower.

Resilience in the face of challenge and setbacks is a highly valued attribute—one sometimes treated as some mysterious gift of nature. The coping styles we have described are, at bottom, resilient and nonresilient ways of responding to challenge. Far from being unfathomable, they are clearly set up by different sets of beliefs and different resulting motivational systems. When we give children, implicitly or explicitly, the message that their ability is fixed and can be measured from their performance, we very likely undermine their mastery-oriented inclinations and promote helplessness— even when the message is couched in praise. In contrast, if we emphasize development and focus on those aspects of achievement over which the child has control, such as effort and strategy, we enhance the development of resilient, mastery-oriented coping.

References

1. Seligman, M. (1974). Depression and learned helplessness. In R.J. Friedman & M.M. Katz (Eds.), *The psychology of depression: Contemporary theory and research.* Washington, D.C.: Winston Wiley.
2. Miller, W., & Seligman, M. (1975). Depression and learned helplessness in man. *Journal of Abnormal Psychology, 84,* 228–238.
3. Diener, C., & Dweck, C. (1978). An analysis of learned helplessness: Continuous changes in performance, strategy, and achievement cognitions following failure. *Journal of Personality and Social Psychology, 36,* 451–461.
4. Diener, C., & Dweck, C. (1980). An analysis of learned helplessness: II. The processing of success. *Journal of Personality and Social Psychology,* 39, 940–952.
5. Dweck, C., & Reppucci, N. (1973). Learned helplessness and reinforcement responsibility in children. *Journal of Personality and Social Psychology, 25,* 109–116.
6. Licht, B., & Dweck, C. (1984). Sex differences in achievement orientations: Consequences for academic choices and attainments. In M. Marland (Ed.), *Sex differentiation and schooling.* London: Heinemann.
7. Elliott, E., & Dweck, C. (1988). Goals: An approach to motivation and achievement. *Journal of Personality and Social Psychology, 54,* 5–12.
8. Ames, C., & Archer, J. (1988). Achievement goals in the classroom: Students' learning strategies and motivation processes. *Journal of Education Psychology, 80,* 260–267.
9. Farrell, E., & Dweck, C. (1985). *The role of motivational processes in transforming learning.* Doctoral dissertation, Harvard University.
10. Dweck, C., & Leggett, E. (1988). A social-cognitive approach to motivation and personality. *Psychological Review, 95,* 256–273.
11. Pintrich, P., Roeser, R., & DeGroot, E. (1994). Classroom and individual differences in early adolescents' motivation and self-regulated learning. *Journal of Early Adolescence, 14,* 139–161.
12. Bandura, M., & Dweck, C. (1985). *Self-conceptions and motivation: Conceptions of intelligence, choice of achievement goals, and patterns of cognition, affect and behavior.* Unpublished manuscript, Harvard University.
13. Zhao, W., Dweck, C., & Mueller, C. (1998). Implicit theories and vulnerability to depression-like responses. Manuscript submitted for publication.
14. Eccles, J., Midgley, C., Wigfield, A., Buchanan, C., Reuman, D., Flanagan, C., & Mac Iver, D. (1993). The impact of stage-environment fit on young adolescents' experiences in schools and in families. *American Psychologist, 48,* 90–101.
15. Henderson, V., & Dweck, C. (1990). Achievement and motivation in adolescence: A new model and data. In S. Feldman & G. Elliot (Eds.), *At the threshold: The developing adolescent.* Cambridge, MA: Harvard University Press.

16. Sorich, L., & Dweck, C. (1997). *Psychological mediators of student achievement in the transition to junior high school.* Unpublished manuscript, Columbia University.
17. Cain, K., & Dweck, C. (1995). The development of children's achievement, motivation patterns and conceptions of intelligence. *Merrill-Palmer Quarterly, 41*, 25–52.
18. Hebert, C., & Dweck, C. (1985). *Mediators of persistence in preschoolers: Implications for development.* Unpublished manuscript, Harvard University.
19. Heyman, G., & Dweck, C. (1998). Children's thinking about traits: Implications for judgements of the self and others. *Child Development, 64*, 391–403.
20. Heyman, G., Dweck, C., & Cain, K. (1992). Young children's vulnerability to self-blame and helplessness. *Child Development, 63*, 401–415.
21. Smiley, P., & Dweck, C. (1994). Individual differences in achievement goals among young children. *Child Development, 65*, 1723–1743.
22. Dweck, C. (1991). Self-theories and goals: Their role in motivation, personality, and development. In R. Dienstbier (Ed.), *Nebraska Symposium on Motivation, Vol. 38; Perspectives on Motivation* (pp. 199–255). Lincoln: University of Nebraska Press.
23. Dweck, C. (in press). The develoment of early self-conceptions: Their relevance for motivational processes. In J. Heckhausen & C.S. Dweck (Eds.), *Motivation and self-regulation across the life span.* Cambridge: Cambridge University Press.
24. Mueller, C., & Dweck, C. (1998) Praise for intelligence can undermine children's motivation and performance. *Journal of Personality and Social Psychology, 75*, 33–52.
25. Snyder, C.R. (1994). *The psychology of hope.* New York: Free Press.
26. Erdley, C., Cain, K., Loomis, C., Dumas-Hines, F., & Dweck, C. (1997). The relations among children's social goals, implicit personality theories, and response to social failure. *Developmental Psychology, 33*, 263–272.
27. Dweck, C., Goetz, T., & Strauss, N. (1980). Sex differences in learned helplessness: (IV) An experimental and naturalistic study of failure generalization and its mediators. *Journal of Personality and Social Psychology, 38*, 441–452.
28. Levy, S., Stroessner, S., & Dweck, C. (1998) Stereotype formation and endorsement: The role of implicit theories. *Journal of Personality and Social Psychology, 74*, 1421–1436
29. Levy, S., & Dweck, C. (1998). The impact of children's static vs. dynamic conceptions of people on stereotype formation. Manuscript submitted for publication.

12

Coping with Catastrophes and Catastrophizing

Christopher Peterson
Christina H. Moon

The word *catastrophe* first entered everyday language as a description of the last event of a tragedy, where the protagonist falls victim to his or her destiny, an occurrence intended by the playwright to stir pity or terror among onlookers. Catastrophes of course exist outside the dramatic realm. Origin myths like the Garden of Eden notwithstanding, we can assume that catastrophes, with or without such a label, have existed throughout the history of humankind. War, famine, and pestilence made the lives of our distant ancestors short, brutish, and cruel; our lives today differ—on average—by being longer. Psychologists have been drawn to the study of catastrophes, and a considerable literature exists that describes the causes and consequences of terrible life events. One of our purposes here is to review what is known about catastrophes and how to avoid them or at least how to minimize their deleterious effects.

The word *catastrophize* is derived from catastrophe but has a different connotation, referring not to objective events but rather to a person's tendency to think that bad events are worse than they really are. This tendency can set into motion a self-fulfilling prophecy. So, bad events may follow in the wake of catastrophizing, although these should be located not within our destinies but simply within ourselves. Psychologists also have been drawn to the study of catastrophizing, and again, a considerable literature exists that describes the causes and consequences of this cognitive style. Our second purpose is to review what is known about catastrophizing, again with a focus on how to avoid or to minimize this way of thinking.

But our overarching purpose here is to argue that we must jointly consider catastrophes and catastrophizing in order to help people thrive in the real world. Once we take a look at what the research reveals, any stark contrast between objective events imposed from outside the person (catastrophes) and subjective appraisals of these events arising from inside the person (catastrophizing) cannot be maintained. Catastrophes are not always or even typically random events; catastrophizing does not always or even typically involve delusional thinking. Catastrophes and catastrophizing mutually influence one another, and useful advice about how to "cope" cannot target just the world or just the person.

Our argument does not involve blaming those who experience catastrophes or those who catastrophize (1). People do not choose their risk factors, and life is not a Greek tragedy. The power of a psychological perspective is that it shifts our focus from moral certainties to statistical generalizations, thereby providing targets for intervention. Nonetheless, there is a tension. The popular psychology of catastrophes uses the language of victimology. The person who experiences a catastrophe is regarded as a bystander, and catastrophes are regarded as lightning bolts that strike anyone. These assumptions are not always true. Catastrophes are predictable, at least in part from catastrophizing tendencies. Without blaming individuals in a moral sense, we still need to encourage them to change how they think and behave, thereby making catastrophes less likely.

Catastrophes

What qualifies an event as a catastrophe? These are disasters that would be recognized as such by virtually all onlookers. An automobile accident in which one's spinal cord was severed would be a catastrophe, as would a violent rape or a cancer diagnosis during the prime of life. Losing one's savings to a swindler would probably qualify, and so too might seeing one's child make a terrible choice for a spouse.

One rubric under which psychologists study catastrophes is that of *trauma*. In defining trauma for the purpose of a diagnosis of post-traumatic stress disorder (PTSD), DSM-III-R pointed to events falling outside the realm of common experience (2). However, the authors of DSM-IV recognized that catastrophes may, unfortunately, be rather common, and instead offered a more substantive definition: "An event or events that involved actual or threatened death or serious injury, or a threat to . . . physical integrity . . . (3 p. 428). Examples cited include military combat, violent assault, kidnapping, torture, natural disasters, and severe automobile accidents.

We can quarrel with the DSM-IV definition, which is biased toward somatic as opposed to psychological threat. Certainly, events with "only" a psychological impact can be construed as traumatic, and here it is instructive to consider the broader range of *major life events* studied by epidemiologists. In Holmes and Rahe's (4) well-known measure of life events requiring social readjustment, we find listed not only physical injuries but also psychological ones, like a moving violation, mortgage, or loss of a job.

A distinction sometimes made within the trauma literature is between *intentional trauma* and *nonintentional trauma* (5). Rape or assault involves someone deliberately perpetrating a trauma on someone else. Car crashes, except in action movies, are not intentional in this sense.

There are probably no firm distinctions between traumas as defined by DSM-IV, major life events like those listed on the social readjustment scale, and more mundane *hassles* (6) once we take into account how people construe these events. Any bad occurrence—one arousing negative affects such as fear, anxiety, guilt, or shame—can be a catastrophe for people if they think about it in terms that produce these feelings. We will return to this point when we talk about the mutual influence between objective catastrophes and subjective catastrophizing, but let us for the time being focus only on the most severe catastrophes.

Prevalence of Severe Trauma

However we chose to define catastrophes, they are common. Table 12.1 compiles estimates of the prevalence of various traumas in the United States as determined by four recent surveys. Although the estimates of specific trauma categories vary somewhat, due to variations in the samples and in how questions were posed to respondents (7), nonintentional trauma appears much more common than intentional trauma.

The same conclusion follows when we look at trauma that results in death. In the United States, the majority of deaths due to injury result from unintentional trauma, chiefly motor vehicle crashes, but also falls, drowning, fires and burns, poisoning, choking, and exposure (5). Psychologists have been more likely to study intentional trauma than unintentional trauma, but the sheer numbers of people affected does not justify this disproportionate interest. In the contemporary United States, unintentional trauma is among the leading causes of death, particularly for children and young adults, and it is the number one cause of lost years of productivity.

Risk Factors for Severe Trauma

Traumatic injuries are often described as *accidents*, but if this term conveys a sense of randomness, it is misleading. Some good generalizations can be made about the factors that put people at risk for so-called accidents (8, 9, 10). Young males from the lower class constitute the majority of the trauma population in the contemporary United States. Lifestyle appears to be the operative mechanism. If one does the sorts of things that put oneself in situations where accidents might happen, then eventually they will happen. Reckless driving, the use of alcohol, access to firearms, preference for dangerous hobbies: These are the ingredients for catastrophe.

There are also psychological risk factors for catastrophes. Although researchers seem reluctant to describe accident-proneness per se as a trait,

Table 12.1 Some Recent Prevalence Estimates of Lifetime Exposure to Trauma in the United States

Sample	Adolescents	Adults	Adults	Adults
Researchers	(Giaconia et al.)	(Norris et al.)	(Kessler et al.)	(Breslau et al.)
Date	1995	1992	1995	1991
n	384	1,000	8,098	1,007
Any trauma	43%	69%	56%	39%
Combat	—	9	3	—
Rape	2	4	5	16
Robbery/physical assault	7	15	9	10
Seeing someone hurt or killed	13	30	25	7
Natural disaster	1	13	16	1
Threat/narrow escape	4	15	13	3
Injury/accidents	10	34	20	6
News of someone else's death or injury/accident	13	30	—	—

From Giaconia, R. M., Reinherz, H. Z., Silverman, A. B., Pakiz, B., Frost, A. K., & Cohen, E. (1995). Traumas and post-traumatic stress disorder in a community population of older adolescents. *Journal of American Academy of Child and Adolescent Psychiatry, 34,* 1369–1380.

Norris, F. H. (1992). Epidemiology of trauma: Frequency and impact of different potentially traumatic events on different demographic groups. *Journal of Consulting and Clinical Psychology, 60,* 409–418.

Kessler R. C., Sonnega A., Bromet, E., Hughes, M., & Nelson C. B. (1995). Posttraumatic stress disorder in the National Comorbidity Survey. *Archives of General Psychiatry, 52,* 1048–1060.

Breslau, N., Davis, G. D., Andreski, P., & Peterson, E. (1991). Traumatic events and posttraumatic stress disorder in an urban population of young adults. *Archives of General Psychiatry, 48,* 216–222.

there are traits that predict whether someone has accidents (11, 12). So, extraversion, sensation-seeking, risk-taking, hostility, and neuroticism are linked with catastrophes. Again, lifestyle seems to be the mechanism that leads from traits to actual traumas. Personality characteristics draw us into the fast lane or keep us safe on the sidewalk; these habitual settings determine what ensues, including accidents (13).

There are more transient psychological risk factors for catastrophes, including depression, stress, and fatigue (14, 15). Studies further suggest that stress can affect one's propensity toward accidents by compromising peripheral vision (16). Social support buffers against the accident-facilitating aspects of stress (17).

Ways of thinking about events also can put someone at risk for catastrophes. Most generally, appraisal of events sets into operation (or not) behavior that can make accidents more likely versus less likely. Not recognizing the danger of a situation is an obvious example, and is why household poisons need to kept away from children and pets who lack the cognitive wherewithal to understand that they are potentially lethal. Fatalism has been linked to accidents, probably because these beliefs rationalize passivity which then makes mishaps more likely. So, researchers have looked at people who do not evacuate their homes in the wake of warnings about hurricanes, tornadoes, volcanic eruptions, and the like (e.g., 18, 19, 20). Those who stay behind are not blithe optimists, as we might think. Rather, they believe that catastrophes are inevitable, so why bother to get out of their way?

Consequences of Severe Trauma

Mortality is a possible consequence of severe trauma, but even among those who survive in a physical sense, there may be a psychological cost. The most frequently studied psychological consequence of catastrophes is PTSD, and one recent survey estimated that the lifetime prevalence among contemporary Americans is almost 8% (21). PTSD frequently cooccurs with other psychological disorders, and outcomes like depression, anxiety, and substance abuse may follow in the wake of severe trauma (22). Indeed, comorbidity is high among the psychological problems following catastrophes, probably because one problem predisposes others. For example, trauma patients who later developed PTSD reported higher levels of peritraumatic dissociation, more severe depression, anxiety, and intrusive symptoms one week following their injury (23).

Researchers have looked at who is more likely to show psychological consequences in the wake of a traumatic event. Among the risk factors are prior histories of traumatic events and/or psychological difficulties (24). In a study of acute reactions by survivors of a train collision, Hagstrom (25) found that the elderly passengers had more difficulty in coping with their trauma than did the younger passengers, and that women tended to be more engrossed with the accident and displayed more avoidant behavior than did men.

The type of trauma matters as well. For example, sexual assault is particularly likely to produce PTSD. In general, the more severe the stressor, of any type, and the greater the degree of exposure to it, the more likely it is to result in PTSD and other difficulties. In contrast, education and social support limit severe psychological consequences (26, 27, 23).

Among the consequences of trauma are changes in how people think about themselves and the world. Janoff-Bulman (28), for example, showed how a variety of traumas take a toll on one's sense that the world is a just place, that others can be trusted, and that one is efficacious. Beliefs of this sort may put someone at further risk for bad events and bad reactions to these events. Among individuals with PTSD, those with a more pessimistic way of explaining the causes of bad events have a more severe version of the disorder (29, 30, 31, 32). Along these lines, Greenberg (33) studied the role of cognitive processing in the wake of a catastrophe and noted that trauma survivors evidenced different forms of rumination, the most dysfunctional of which involved a seemingly endless cycle that eventually intensified psychological distress. Bryant and Harvey (34) studied motor vehicle accident survivors and found that intrusive PTSD symptoms like nightmares and flashbacks were more common among individuals with an avoidant coping style. So, catastrophes reside in a vicious circle along with catastrophizing.

Catastrophizing

Like catastrophes, catastrophizing has been studied under various rubrics. Common to all approaches to catastrophizing is the notion that people make more of bad events than the facts warrant. Mole hills become mountains; mountains become the Himalayas. Catastrophizers overstate the severity of a bad event and understate their ability to cope with what it presents. Given events take on greater significance than they merit. As already emphasized, what makes catastrophizing more than just an eccentricity involving exaggeration is that it can set into operation a self-fulfilling prophecy. Consider an individual who interprets every ache and pain as a sign of a serious physical disease. Taken to an extreme over time, this tendency becomes Briquet's syndrome (aka somatization disorder), one of the most intractable of the somatoform disorders. The person's life revolves around imagined illnesses, and she may elect unnecessary operations, which can create actual physical damage (35).

Theoretical Approaches to Catastrophizing

The most general approach to catastrophizing is implicit in the perspective on coping introduced by Lazarus and Folkman (36). According to these theorists, coping starts with how people appraise a challenging situation and what they might do about it. In *primary appraisal*, the person asks "What is at stake?" And in *secondary appraisal*, the person asks, "What can I do about it?" If the answers are, respectively, "lots" and "little," then the person may well have catastrophized the situation and will be unlikely to be able to cope successfully with it. Other theorists have focused on more specific aspects of catastrophizing; let us mention some of these perspectives (see also chapters 2, 4, 5, 8, 9, 10, 11, 13, and 14 in the present volume).

Cognitive Bases of Emotional Disorders.   Beck's (37) theories of anxiety and depression propose a catastrophizing style as the cognitive basis for these emotional disorders. Catastrophizing takes two forms. First, the individual entertains a *schema* about himself and the world that creates and maintains an emotional disorder. In the case of anxiety, he feels fragile and overly vulnerable to what the world may present. In the case of depression, he feels that he and the world are bad.

Second, the person prone to emotional disorders uses a variety of *logical errors* that maintain these extreme views. Many of these errors that Beck distinguishes involve catastrophizing: selectively focusing on evidence that confirms the negative, while ignoring the evidence that would point to a more benign view of things (38).

Ellis (39), in his rational-emotive theory, similarly took catastrophizing to task by labeling this tendency as one toward *irrational beliefs*. People who endorse ideas that exaggerate the importance of singular occurrences, who confuse wants and needs, and who look at things in dichotomous fashion are at risk for anxiety and disorder. The Dysfunctional Attitudes Scale is a common operationalization of irrational beliefs of the type Ellis emphasized (40). Here are some paraphrased examples:

- I am nothing if someone I love does not love me in return.
- Asking for help is a sign of weakness.
- Making a mistake should upset anyone.

The catastrophizing character of these irrational beliefs is obvious. A similar scale is the Irrational Beliefs Test, and again, many of its items involve blatant catastrophizing (41).

According to Beck and Ellis, catastrophizing is objectionable because it is illogical or irrational, but this is a difficult characterization to maintain if it means that we can describe people as inaccurate versus accurate thinkers. Taylor (42) argued that most people entertain *positive illusions*: widespread beliefs that they are talented, that things will work out well in the end, and that this is the best of all possible worlds. These beliefs are no more accurate than the doomsday thinking of the most confirmed catastrophizer, but they usually serve individuals better because they maintain good cheer and perseverance.

Explanatory Style.   Our own research has been concerned with *explanatory style*, defined as an individual's habitual tendency to explain bad events with causes that are stable ("it's going to last forever") versus unstable, global ("it's going to undermine everything") versus specific, and internal ("it's me") versus external (43). The notion of explanatory style emerged from the attributional reformulation of helplessness theory, where it was introduced to explain variations in response to actual bad events (44). When these events occur to individuals, they ask why, and their answers dictate how they respond. Stable and global explanations put people at risk for helplessness: passivity, low morale, and such outcomes as depression and illness. Internal explanation puts individuals at risk for the loss of self-esteem.

The constellation of internal, stable, and global causes for bad events has been characterized as a helpless, depressive, or pessimistic style—the opposite constellation of efficacious or optimistic. The three dimensions of explanatory style frequently covary and have similar correlates: depression, anxiety, poor achievement, and passive coping. At times, it makes sense to examine the three dimensions separately (45). For example, stability and globality are consistently associated with physical illness, whereas internality usually is not (46), perhaps because it conflates self-blame *and* an assertion of efficacy ("next time things will be different") (47, 48).

When we consider just stability and globality, we sometimes describe them as comprising a common dimension of hopelessness. Stability can be interpreted as fatalism (because the causes of bad events in the past will continue to exert a negative effect in the future), and globality can be construed as a style of catastrophizing (because the cause of any given bad event will bring about many other bad events).

The attribution reformulation of helplessness theory is a *diathesis-stress model*, proposing that the conjunction of objective bad events and a pessimistic explanatory style is necessary for negative outcomes to ensue. This position stems from the roots of the helplessness approach in the experimental psychology of animal learning, where bad events (i.e., noncontingent electric shocks) are controlled by the researcher and presented randomly to research subjects.

When applied to research with people, the attributional reformulation has usually focused only on the cognitive diathesis, which proves a consistent correlate of expected outcomes. Part of this emphasis results from the availability of simple ways of measuring explanatory style, namely, a self-report questionnaire dubbed the Attributional Style Questionnaire (ASQ; 49) and a content analysis procedure (CAVE [Content Analysis of Verbatim Explanations]; 50) that allows written or spoken material to be scored for explanatory style.

When researchers look as well at the occurrence of bad events, the evidence is checkered for the diathesis-stress prediction. Occasional studies find that bad events and explanatory style interact to predispose outcomes like depression, but support is much stronger for a main effect of explanatory style. Taking this evidence at face value, we need to ask why explanatory style predisposes negative outcomes, even in the absence of objectively imposed bad life events. Bad events—whether catastrophes, traumas, major life events, or mundane hassles—do not randomly occur to people; they are not imposed on people like uncontrollable shocks are imposed on laboratory animals, independently of whatever the individual brings to the situation or does once in it. Bad events are more likely to occur to some people than to others, and among the risk factors for the occurrence of bad events is a pessimistic explanatory style. The diathesis causes the stress, rendering the diathesis-stress conceptualization unwieldy.

Needed is an approach that studies events and cognitive styles—and especially their reciprocal influences—over time; this might shed more light on catastrophes and catastrophizing than the more typical research designs. A modest example of this sort of design is a study of explanatory style and illness by Dykema, Bergbower, and Peterson (51). These researchers studied 101 college students over a one-month period. At Time One, their research participants completed the ASQ and a baseline measure of recent physical illness (e.g., "how many days of class have you missed because of illness"). At Time Two, they again completed a measure of recent physical illness and reported on the occurrence of major life events since Time One, as well as the extent to which they felt hassled by everyday demands like having to take care of a pet or a plant.

These researchers explicitly tested the diathesis-stress hypothesis with a multiple regression formula, predicting to Time Two illness after holding constant Time One illness and entering explanatory style and life events (or hassles) into the equation, followed by the product of explanatory style and life events (or hassles). Contrary to the helplessness reformulation, neither life events nor hassles interacted with explanatory style to predict illness. Rather, a hopeless explanatory style (stable + global causal attributions for bad events) predicted increased perceptions of hassles which in turn predicted illness, even when the baseline measure of illness was held constant. Explanatory style can apparently have a direct effect on outcomes, in this case illness, because it leads individuals to see the world as a stressful place in which to live.

Catastrophizing Pain.   One more line of research deserves mention here, in which investigators explicitly label what they study as *catastrophizing.* Their focus is on how people react to pain. Chronic pain disorders invariably start with an actual illness or injury. These disorders are maintained, however, by certain ways of thinking that make the pain worse than it might be if other ways of thinking were entertained. Where is the reality of the pain? It resides both in the nerve endings and in the way a person thinks.

Sullivan, Bishop, and Pivot (52) developed the Pain Catastrophizing Scale (PCS), a self-report instrument whose items were suggested by open-ended inquiries in previous studies. They wrote items that captured frequently mentioned themes, and administered the resulting questionnaire to hundreds of individuals who were asked to focus on a past painful experience and indicate the degree to which they had entertained each of the thoughts listed. A factor analysis revealed three interpretable factors, identified by Sullivan et al. as rumination, magnification, and helplessness (see Table 12.2).

Composite scores on the PCS predicted how subjects responded in a laboratory experiment in which they were exposed to a painful task (a cold pressor procedure), and how actual patients responded to a painful medical procedure (an electrodiagnostic evaluation). In both studies, individuals identified as high catastrophizers reported more pain-related thoughts, more distress, and more pain than their low catastrophizing counterparts. Future researchers might consider rewording the items of the PCS and ask-

Table 12.2 Paraphrased Items from the Pain Catastrophizing Scale

Rumination items
  I cannot get the pain out of my mind.
  More than anything I want the pain to stop.
  I cannot think of anything except how much it hurts.

Magnification items
  I am afraid the pain will get worse.
  I think of other experiences involving pain.
  I wonder whether something more serious will happen.

Helplessness items
  I cannot go on.
  I cannot stand it any more.
  It overwhelms me.
  It is never going to get better.
  There is nothing I can do to stop the pain.

From Sullivan, M. J. L., Bishop, S. R., Pivot, J. (1995). The Pain Catastrophizing Scale: Development and Validation. *Psychological Assessment, 7,* 524–532.

ing people to respond vis-à-vis any stressful occurrence; such a measure might serve as a standard operationalization of catastrophizing.

An Integrative Investigation of the Dimensions of Catastrophizing

Consider our own efforts to take a broad look at what catastrophizing entails. As discussed, people have a variety of reactions to bad events that can be classified as catastrophizing. Each of these reactions has been the subject of theoretical and empirical work, but most psychologists have championed their own constructs as the most important dimension of catastrophizing. Is this reasonable?

Our review of the relevant literature led us to identify 13 important dimensions for appraising bad events. In each case, the endpoints of the dimension can be construed as a catastrophizing style versus a noncatastrophizing style. Four of these dimensions are properties of the events themselves (as perceived by the individual):

- undesirable versus desirable
- unpredictable versus predictable
- uncontrollable versus controllable
- recurrent versus nonrecurrent

Four dimensions are properties of the causal attributions made for the events:

- internal versus external
- stable versus unstable
- global versus specific
- uncontrollable versus controllable

Three other dimensions describe parameters of the perceived consequences of bad events:

- stable versus unstable
- global versus specific
- uncontrollable versus controllable

Finally, the remaining two dimensions pertain to how the individual copes with the events:

- success versus failure
- difficulty versus ease

These 13 dimensions may not be exhaustive, but they are representative of the main thrust of cognitive theorizing about what determines reactions to bad events.

We studied 140 college students over a four-week interval. At Time One, they responded to the Beck Depression Inventory (BDI), a frequently used measure of the extent of an individual's distress and dysphoria. At Time Two, they returned and again completed the BDI along with descriptions of the "four worst events" that had happened to them during the past month. After briefly characterizing each bad event, they rated the event, its cause, its consequence, and their coping on 7-point scales along the 13 dimensions just discussed.

We collapsed each of the ratings across the four events, which was justified because they were intercorrelated in each case. The immediate interpretation of this convergence is that people have characteristic styles of construing bad events, but we also must consider the possibility that there is a common reality responsible for the sorts of bad events that befall a given individual. Indeed, both possibilities are probably the case.

We factor analyzed these composite ratings. Two clean and clear factors emerged. Each of the dimensions unambiguously loaded on just one of these factors, with the exception of the undesirability of the event, which loaded on neither. This means that the other dimensions of appraisal are not just redundant with the severity of the event itself. The first factor can be identified as one of control, and it was comprised of the following ratings:

- unpredictable events
- uncontrollable events
- external causes
- uncontrollable causes
- uncontrollable consequences

The second factor can be identified as one of magnitude because it was made up of the following ratings:

- recurring events
- stable causes
- global causes
- stable consequences
- global consequences
- failed coping
- difficult coping

This magnitude factor seems to capture what most theorists mean by catastrophizing.

We formed scales reflecting these two factors and found that the catastrophizing scale was correlated with Time Two BDI scores, even when Time One BDI scores were statistically controlled. Interestingly, the control factor proved unrelated to BDI scores. We were able to replicate these findings fully in a similar study of 170 college students, this time finding as well that a measure of illness symptoms was predicted by catastrophizing but not by control.

These results have several implications for how we might think about catastrophizing. They show that theorists may have made a mistake slicing the appraisal pie. The critical factors are not whether catastrophizing involves the event, the cause, the consequences, or the coping, but instead whether these perceptions involve the locus and magnitude of the event and its aftermath. Control is accorded great importance by many theories, but at least when our research subjects made sense of its various instantiations, these proved less important than magnitude. We have elsewhere commented on psychology's preoccupation with personal control (54), but perhaps more emphasis is indicated on catastrophizing, whether or not there is self-blame involved.

Catastrophes and Catastrophizing

Our thesis here is that catastrophes and catastrophizing mutually influence one another and interact to predispose negative outcomes. Several recent studies by our research group support this assertion. These studies deal with explanatory style, understood to mean stability and globality of attributed causes for bad events, but the aforementioned comments about the larger meaning of catastrophizing probably apply. We suspect that similar results would obtain regardless of just how catastrophizing is operationalized.

Catastrophes Predispose Catastrophizing

One prediction from this perspective is that catastrophizing is reality-based. Although catastrophizing is not isomorphic with what has actually happened, people who have experienced catastrophes should nonetheless be more likely to catastrophize. Greening and Dollinger (55) surveyed 455 adolescents in 15 schools in the Midwest and classified them according to their degree of exposure to severe weather trauma (i.e., lightning strikes, tornadoes, floods). The greater the exposure to a given trauma, the higher one's expected risk of dying from that trauma. In this study, changes in risk perception were specific to a given trauma: Exposure to lightning increased the perceived likelihood of dying from lightning but not from a flood, and so on.

However, studies of explanatory style suggest that exposure to catastrophes can have even more general effects on catastrophizing (54). For example, Bunce, Larsen, and Peterson (56) studied a group of 58 undergraduates at the University of Michigan. These research participants completed a variety of personality measures, including the ASQ. They also reported if at any point in their lives they had experienced one of these traumatic events:

- death of a parent
- death of a sibling
- rape or incest
- a fire which destroyed their home
- permanent physical disability

If such an event had ever occurred, they reported when.

Of the 58 research participants, 28 had experienced one of these traumas, a lifetime prevalence similar to those from national surveys. When traumatized individuals were compared to their nontraumatized counterparts with respect to ASQ responses, they explained events in a more pessimistic fashion. Among individuals who had experienced a trauma, the earlier it had occurred, the more pessimistic their explanatory style ($r=.27$), although because of the small sample size, this correlation fell somewhat short of conventional significance. If this result is valid, it suggests that early trauma results in more catastrophizing than does later trauma, perhaps because the catastrophe-catastrophizing cascade has been in operation for a longer time.

Catastrophizing Predisposes Catastrophes

Another prediction is that catastrophizing makes catastrophes more likely. Here we have some data showing that explanatory style predicts the likelihood of catastrophes, and indeed, death from them (57). Our study investigated explanatory style and mortality among participants in the Terman Life-Cycle Study.

This investigation began in 1921–22, when most of the 1,528 participants were in public school. The average birth date for children in the sample was 1910, with a standard deviation of four years. Most of the children were preadolescents when first studied; those still living are now in their eighties. Data were collected prospectively, without any knowledge of eventual health or longevity. The original sample has been followed ever since, with attrition (except by death) of less than 10%. For most of those who have died (about 50% of males and 35% of females as of 1991), year of death and cause of death are known.

In 1936 and 1940, the participants completed open-ended questionnaires about difficult life events. Examples include:

> 1936: Have any disappointments, failures, bereavements, uncongenial relationships with others, etc., exerted a prolonged influence upon you? Describe.
> 1940: What do you regard as your most serious fault of personality or character?

Their responses included causal explanations, which we content analyzed for explanatory style with the CAVE technique. We determined the associations between dimensions of explanatory style on the one hand and time of death and cause of death on the other.

Among the 1,182 participants for whom explanatory style scores were available, mortality information was known for 1,179. Among this group, the numbers of deaths as of 1991 were 148 from cancer (85 men, 63 women), 159 from cardiovascular disease (109 men, 50 women), 57 from accidents or violence (40 men, 17 women), 87 from other (known) causes (50 men, 37 women), and 38 from unknown causes (24 men, 14 women).

To investigate the association between the dimensions of explanatory style and mortality (through 1991), Cox Proportional Hazards regression analyses were used and checked with logistic regression analyses. When all three attributional dimensions were examined simultaneously, only globality was significantly associated with mortality risk. Results from the logistic regressions (predicting to a dichotomous variable of survival to at least age 65 versus dying before age 65) similarly found that only the odds ratio for globality was significant.

Next we investigated whether globality was differentially related to specific causes of death by comparing Gompertz models. When comparing a model with both sex and globality as predictors but constraining the effects of globality to predict equally across all causes of death with an unconstrained model (in which globality was allowed to predict differentially to separate causes of death), we found that the unconstrained model fit better than that of the constrained model. This finding was also obtained when participants who did not survive until at least 1945 were eliminated.

A closer examination revealed that globality best predicted deaths by accident or violence and from unknown causes. The risk ratios associated with other causes were greater than one but not significantly above chance. As we have argued, globality taps a style of catastrophizing about bad events, expecting them to occur across diverse situations. Such a style can be hazardous, as the present results show, presumably because of its association with passive coping, social estrangement, and risky decision-making (54). Deaths by accident or violence may result from a fatalistic lifestyle, one more likely to be followed by males than by females. Perhaps deaths due to unknown causes may similarly reflect an incautious lifestyle.

Explanatory style, at least as measured here, showed no specific link to death by cancer or cardiovascular disease. Some of the interesting speculation concerning explanatory style and poor health has centered on physiological mechanisms, but behavioral and lifestyle mechanisms are probably more typical and more robust (46). We were unable to identify a single behavioral mediator, however, which may mean that there is no simple set of health mediators set into operation by globality.

We have recently conducted a second study, more modest in scope, that links explanatory style not to fatal "accidents" but to more mundane mishaps. This was a cross-sectional investigation, which means that the direction of causality is ambiguous. If we take the results at face value, though, they suggest that stability and globality of explanatory style are associated with the tendency to have accidents requiring medical attention. If enough of these accidents occur, then one is apt to be fatal, as the Terman study demonstrated.

At the University of Michigan, 440 introductory psychology students completed a variety of questionnaires the first day of class, including a question about "how many accidents have you experienced in the past 24 months that required medical attention," a standard phrasing from epidemiological surveys of traumatic accidents. They also completed an abbreviated version of the ASQ that asked them how they usually explained bad events: with stable (versus unstable) causes and with global (versus specific) causes. These ratings were entwined and so were combined into a single hopelessness score. Also available for the research participants was information pertinent to other variables previously linked to accident-proneness: gender, ethnicity, handedness, depression, anger, and impulsivity.

These variables were included in a multiple regression formula to predict the number of reported mishaps (see Table 12.3). These variables were entered in blocks, with the composite explanatory style score the final predictor examined. The zero-order correlations were modest but more or less replicated what is known about risk factors for so-called accidents. Explanatory style remained a significant predictor, even when all the other variables had been entered. Individuals who explained bad events in a hopeless fashion were more likely to have experienced recent accidents requiring medical attention.

The Interaction of Catastrophes and Catastrophizing

One more aspect of our argument about the relationship between catastrophes and catastrophizing is that both must be considered in making sense

Table 12.3 Predictors of Recent "Accidents"

Predictor	Zero-order r	Beta
Gender (male = 1; female = 0)	.13*	12*
Ethnicity (white = 1; nonwhite = 0)	.01	.02
Handedness (right = 1; nonright = 0)	−.11*	−.10*
Depression	.09*	.05
Anger	−.04	.00
Impulsivity	.08*	.06
Explanatory style	.12*	.11*

Note: Variables entered in a multiple regression equation in blocks are separated by spaces in the table, from top to bottom; $R^2 = .04$, $p < .007$; *$p < .05$.

of people's well-being. Let us describe a recently completed study by our research group that supports this premise (58). We started with the hypothesis that measures of explanatory style are psychologically relevant only to the degree that these measures are based on attributions for events to which individuals have devoted some thought. If individuals offer attributions off the tops of their heads, measures of explanatory style are not likely to be psychologically relevant and thus minimally if at all correlated with external criteria of well-being (59). Said another way, if events have actually occurred to an individual, his or her causal explanations concerning them are most pertinent to well-being.

We administered to 70 college students a version of the ASQ asking for causal attributions about these events:

- You have trouble sleeping.
- You have a serious injury.
- You can't find a job.
- You can't get the work done that others expect of you.
- You don't help a friend who has a problem.
- You have financial problems.
- A friend is very angry with you.
- You have a serious argument with someone in your family.

They were also asked to indicate how frequently they had actually experienced events like these. (In the typical version of the ASQ, this inquiry is not made: Respondents are merely asked to "imagine" various bad events occurring to them and to offer causal explanations for these occurrences, which may or may not be hypothetical.) We also asked our research participants to describe the low points of their lives during the last 10 years, which we scored for explanatory style with the CAVE technique. Similarly, we asked them to describe the worst thing that could happen to them in the next 10 years, which we again content analyzed for explanatory style. We also administered a measure of depressive symptoms.

We expected the ASQ explanatory style to correlate with depressive symptoms, but that this would occur chiefly or only when respondents had actually experienced events like those for which explanations were offered. We expected CAVE explanatory style to correlate with depressive symptoms, but that this would occur chiefly or only when the narratives were about past events as opposed to future ones. Results confirmed these hypotheses (see Table 12.4).

The eight events on the ASQ were rated as somewhat common by the research participants (the median of the mean ratings was 2.9 on a 7-point scale) but also showed variability (the median standard deviation was 1.47). To test the hypothesis that ASQ explanatory style would correlate positively with depressive symptoms to the degree that respondents had actually experienced the events, a multiple regression formula was computed to test the moderating effect of event frequency. Depressive symptoms were predicted by first entering a composite explanatory style score (internality + stability + globality) and the mean frequency of events in a single block along with gender, followed by an interaction term (the mean across events of [internal + stable + global ratings] x frequency). Only the interaction term was a significant predictor of depressive symptoms, showing explanatory style (catastrophizing) is related to well-being only when it is measured with respect to events that have actually happened.

Coping

Part of the reason catastrophes are catastrophic is that they are difficult events with which to cope. Nonetheless, we do have some advice about what people might do to reduce the negative consequences of catastrophes. This advice is—we hope—informed by some of the points already made in the chapter.

General Considerations

First, catastrophes are common, especially unintentional traumas. Nevertheless, the risk for at least some of these can be minimized by raising people's awareness of how frequently terrible things occur. Most people greatly underestimate the chances of most bad events occurring to them, a tendency so widespread that it has received its own name: *unrealistic optimism* (60). This topic has been studied by asking people to estimate their risk, relative to other people, of experiencing various negative life events such as illnesses or car crashes. The robust finding is that the average person sees himself or herself as below average in risk, a result which of course cannot be accurate. This optimistic bias in risk perception can be decried

Table 12.4 Explanatory Style and Depressive Symptoms

Measure	r with BDI
ASQ	
internality	.20*
stability + globality	.29**
CAVE: "low points" in the past	
internality	.05
stability + globality	.34**
CAVE: "worst thing" in the future	
internality	.10
stability + globality	−.02

$*p < .10; **p < .05.$
From Park, C., Moon, C. H., & Peterson, C. (1997). *Explanatory style and depressive symptoms: A multimethod investigation.* Unpublished manuscript, University of Michigan.

because it leads a person to neglect preventive measures, but it can be combated in part by providing people with the facts.

Many catastrophes can be prevented from occurring in the first place. If some of the well-known risk factors for catastrophes can be reduced, so too can the catastrophes themselves. Just in the past few decades, progress has been made on many fronts. In the United States, for example, overall alcohol consumption is down; smoking and most drug use are for the most part down; seat-belt usage is up; bungee jumping is now illegal and thus down, as it were. Speed limits were reduced, with a huge savings of lives, although now they have been raised again, and we can assume that mortality due to motor vehicle crashes will again rise. Stated so starkly, these societal changes seem the province of legislation or public heath, but psychologists have a legitimate role to play in the primary prevention of catastrophes (61). Public health campaigns often consist solely of information and moral exhortation; their messages reach some but not all of the population (62). More successful are campaigns that take into account the psychological makeup of the targeted individuals.

Bandura's (63) theory of self-efficacy makes a useful distinction between outcome expectations ("this behavior leads to this outcome") and efficacy expectations ("I can perform this behavior"). Both expectations are needed to encourage behavior change. Applied to catastrophes, the individual for example must believe that not drinking will lead to a longer and better life and further that he is capable of refraining from alcohol consumption. In the language of the present chapter, catastrophizing can undercut behavior change if people believe that bad events are inevitable and/or that they are not able to do what is necessary to prevent them.

Second, many catastrophes occur because an individual's lifestyle—occupational and recreational—puts him or her in situations where bad things are likely to occur. It may be useful in future research to distinguish aspects of lifestyle that involve acts of commission versus those that involve acts of omission. Driving too fast would be an example of the former and not buckling one's seatbelt would be an example of the latter. Perhaps catastrophizing, as a rationalization of passivity, is more of a risk factor for omissions than for commissions.

In any event, to the degree that lifestyle represents choice, people can be encouraged to choose differently. *Risk homeostasis theory* provides a useful perspective on why people voluntarily put themselves in risky situations (64). According to this theory, each individual accepts a given level of subjectively estimated risk in exchange for benefits he or she hopes to receive. A corollary is that people will modify their behavior to maintain an optimal risk level. Here we have an explanation for why drivers will go faster or follow more closely as the objective hazard of a section of road decreases. The reduction of risk-taking in one domain of life may be counteracted by an increase in another domain. We cannot simply eliminate all risks for individuals. Many public health intervention programs seem to take as their goal the complete elimination of all risk with regard to behavior and lifestyle, but this goal is not realistic. A better strategy would be to legitimize the taking of intellectual or psychological risks as opposed to those involving immediate and blatant threats to physical well-being.

Third, one of the influences on catastrophes is catastrophizing, and one of the influences on catastrophizing is catastrophes. Either one encourages the other, but so too should the converse of each work against the other. Catastrophizing is based in reality but not identical to it. Any intervention that helps an individual distinguish what he fears from what actually might happen would serve to break him out of this vicious circle.

It is glib to tell someone just "think differently" because this admonition begs the question of how one might do so. Belief systems have considerable inertia (65). In order to cope with a trauma, people must begin with the way in which they think about themselves and the world around them (66). This can be very difficult. Some survivors of catastrophes not only fail to rebuild their shattered assumptions, but they also may develop highly dysfunctional strategies of "coping," such as self-injury. Self-injury following trauma is not well understood, but it may represent attempts to reveal unmet wants or needs in symbolic fashion, to reorganize one's view of oneself, and/or to dissociate oneself from the entire coping process (67).

Theorists suggest that schemas tend to be organized according to a mixture of three different principles (68):

- consistency
- accuracy
- self-aggrandizement

Each of these principles can maintain catastrophizing. The role of consistency in maintaining a catastrophic view of things is obvious, and so too is the role of accuracy, once we acknowledge that the determinants of catastrophizing include actual catastrophes.

In most cases, self-aggrandizement works against catastrophizing, but at least occasionally a person may defensively exaggerate the negative significance of events. This is the essence of the psychoanalytic formula for paranoia (69). Believing oneself at the center of pervasive persecution may not make one happy, but it does make one feel important.

Any attempt to change a person's catastrophizing style must acknowledge the (partial) basis of catastrophizing in reality. There are circumstances in which catastrophizers are correct. In a well-known demonstration, Alloy and Abramson (70) showed that depressed college students were more likely in a laboratory experiment to recognize correctly that they could not control events that were happening to them. Nondepressed individuals apparently do not consider the possibility that they lack control, even in situations where this is objectively true. This phenomenon has been dubbed the "sadder but wiser" effect. There is debate about how general the actual effect might be—we think it would be premature to select world leaders on the basis of how depressed they might be—but the debate reminds us again that we cannot across-the-board describe catastrophizers as illogical or inaccurate.

Accurate or inaccurate, there are circumstances in which a catastrophizing perspective proves functional, at least in the short run. Norem and Cantor (71) described a cognitive style they dubbed *defensive pessimism*, in which people exaggerate the likelihood of failure as a means of curbing their anxiety at a task. Keeping one's expectations in check blunts the possibility of subsequent disappointment and may actually allow a person to do better than giving free rein to wants and wishes (cf. 72). In the long run, defensive pessimism has costs, not the least of which is social estrangement, as defensive pessimists turn off their friends by making frequent dire predictions that prove groundless.

Fourth, catastrophizing may be a more critical aspect of the appraisal of bad events than self-blame and thus demands more attention in interventions. Guilt and inappropriate responsibility are popular targets in psychotherapy, and heightened self-esteem and empowerment popular goals. But these guiding assumptions are incomplete if they ignore the insidious tendency to exaggerate the magnitude of bad events, regardless of how they are construed with respect to personal control.

Tennen and Affleck (73) reviewed the research literature on self-blame for traumatic events and how people adjust to them. Results are inconsistent, and these reviewers suggested that a focus on *other-blame* might be more productive because here the results are consistent in that blaming others for misfortunes is associated with poor functioning. This finding seems at odds with the attributional reformulation of helplessness theory because "other people" represent an external attribution. However, in the reviewed studies, the other people typically blamed were either people per se or individuals like spouses or children who play large roles in one's life. In either case, this type of explanation taps catastrophizing, and its link with negative outcomes is unsurprising.

Specific Strategies

The literature contains no shortage of specific strategies for preventing, containing, and treating the negative effects of catastrophes and catastrophizing. Most are drawn from the cognitive-behavioral arena (74, 75). In this concluding section, we briefly mention some representative approaches.

Prevention.   Research at the University of Pennsylvania showed that depression among children can be prevented in the first place by teaching cognitive and social problem-solving skills (76, 77). Changes in explanatory style, from pessimistic to optimistic, were among the important mechanisms of this intervention (see chapter 8 of the present volume). Along these lines, Fresco, Craighead, Sampson, and Koons (78) showed that young adults can be encouraged through a self-administered program to think in less catastrophizing ways. We predict that follow-ups of these samples, if possible, would show not only decreased incidence of depression but also a lower rate of traumatic events. Indirect evidence for this prediction already exists. Among athletic teams that introduce stress management programs involving similar interventions, "accidental" injuries show a notable decrease (79).

Containment.   Immediately following a catastrophe, interventions are possible that contain its effects so that trauma does not translate itself into full-blown PTSD. Debriefing—recounting the details of a trauma in a factual way—can decrease emotional reactivity among injured individuals (80). Debriefing is probably most effective when combined with support groups and meetings with family members. Along these lines, Foa, Hearst-Ikeda, and Perry (81) developed a brief cognitive-behavioral program for rape survivors. Its components included an interview about the rape, information about reactions to rape, discussion about guilt and blame, and training in specific coping strategies. This program limited the development of PTSD.

Treatment.   What about people who have already experienced a catastrophic event and have a catastrophizing style of thinking? Beck's (37) cognitive therapy and Ellis's (39) rational-emotive therapy specifically target catastrophizing beliefs and accordingly should be helpful for individuals trapped in the catastrophe-catastrophizing cascade (cf. 82). Ellis (83) specifically addressed traumatic events in the context of rational-emotive therapy, recommending that the therapist needs to understand the role the traumatic event occupies in the individual's larger belief system. Because those who have experienced traumatic events, especially intentional trauma, are not only catastrophizers but also socially estranged, any therapeutic intervention needs to occur in an explicitly supportive context (84).

Trauma engenders many attempts at coping; avoidance and wishful thinking were among the most commonly reported strategies among a group of trauma survivors attending a stress clinic (85). None of these common strategies seemed to mitigate distress. In contrast, the less frequently used strategies of positive reappraisal and distancing did seem effective, suggesting that these might be explicitly encouraged in interventions that follow trauma.

Indeed, we know that people can be taught to cope better in the wake of a catastrophic event. There is a large literature on coping with respect to chronic pain. Useful strategies include (86, 87, 88):

- decatastrophizing
- diverting attention elsewhere
- ignoring or suppressing pain
- increasing activity level
- reinterpreting pain
- relaxing and deep breathing

Some of these techniques are specific to pain, but others are generally applicable, such as decatastrophizing and reinterpreting. An important qualification of any advice concerning coping emerges from research into the effectiveness of these strategies. Studies with pain patients suggest that the various cognitive-behavioral interventions used to encourage coping with pain do *not* work for patients who catastrophize (e.g., 89, 90, 91). If catastrophizing does not change, then nothing else will help. The importance of catastrophizing tendencies is underscored, and the therapist must take them into account and make changing them a priority.

References

1. Ryan, W. (1978). *Blaming the victim* (Rev. ed.). New York: Random House.
2. American Psychiatric Association. (1987). *Diagnostic and statistical manual of mental disorders* (3rd ed., Rev.). Washington, DC: author.
3. American Psychiatric Association. (1994). *Diagnostic and statistical manual of mental disorders* (4th ed.). Washington, DC: author.
4. Holmes, T. H., & Rahe, R. H. (1967). The social readjustment rating scale. *Journal of Psychosomatic Research, 11,* 213–218.
5. Baker, S. P., O'Neill, B., Ginsburg, M. J., & Li, G. (1992). *The injury fact book* (2nd ed.). New York: Oxford University Press.
6. Kanner, A. D., Coyne, J. C., Schaefer, C., & Lazarus, R. S. (1981). Comparison of two modes of stress measurement: Daily hassles and uplifts versus major life events. *Journal of Behavioral Medicine, 4,* 1–39.
7. Robertson, L. S. (1992). *Injury epidemiology.* New York: Oxford University Press.

8. Breslau, N., Davis, G. C., & Andreski, P. (1995). Risk factors for PTSD-related traumatic events: A prospective analysis. *American Journal of Psychiatry, 152,* 529–535.

9. McKenna, F. P. (1982). The human factor in driving accidents: An overview of approaches and problems. *Ergonomics, 25,* 867–877.

10. Norris, F. H. (1992). Epidemiology of trauma: Frequency and impact of different potentially traumatic events on different demographic groups. *Journal of Consulting and Clinical Psychology, 60,* 409–418.

11. Dahlback, O. (1991). Accident-proneness and risk-taking. *Personality and Individual Differences, 12,* 79–85.

12. McKenna, F. P. (1983). Accident-proneness: A conceptual analysis. *Accident Analysis and Prevention, 15,* 65–71.

13. Buss, D. M. (1987). Selection, evocation, and manipulation. *Journal of Personality and Social Psychology, 53,* 1214–1221.

14. Harvey, M. R. (1996). An ecological view of psychological trauma and trauma recovery. *Journal of Traumatic Stress, 9,* 3–23.

15. Stuart, J. C., & Brown, B. M. (1981). The relationship of stress and coping ability to incidence of disease and accidents. *Journal of Psychosomatic Research, 25,* 255–260.

16. Williams, J. M., & Andersen, M. B. (1997). Psychosocial influences on central and peripheral vision and reaction time during demanding tasks. *Behavioral Medicine, 22,* 160–167.

17. Petrie, T. A. (1992). Psychosocial antecedents of athletic injury: The effects of life stress and social support on female collegiate gymnasts. *Behavioral Medicine, 18,* 127–138.

18. Bauman, D. B., & Sims, H. H. (1974). Human response to the hurricane. In G. F. White (Ed.), *Natural hazards: Local, national, and global* (pp. 25–30). New York: Oxford University Press.

19. Slovic, P., Kunreuther, H., & White, G. F. (1974). Decision processes, rationality, and adjustment to natural hazards. In G. F. White (Ed.), *Natural hazards, Local, national, and global* (pp. 187–205). New York: Oxford University Press.

20. Withey, S. B. (1962). Reaction to uncertain threat. In G. W. Baker & D. F. Chapman (Eds.), *Man and society in disaster* (pp. 93–123). New York: Basic Books.

21. Kessler, R. C., Sonnega, A., Bromet, E., Hughes, M., & Nelson, C. B. (1995). Posttraumatic stress disorder in the National Comorbidity Survey. *Archives of General Psychiatry, 52,* 1048–1060.

22. Green, B. L. (1994). Psychosocial research in traumatic stress: An update. *Journal of Traumatic Stress, 7,* 341–362.

23. Shalev, A. Y., Peri, T., Canetti, L., & Schreiber, S. (1996). Predictors of PTSD in injured trauma survivors: A prospective study. *American Journal of Psychiatry, 153,* 219–225.

24. Peterson, C. (1996). *The psychology of abnormality.* Fort Worth: Harcourt Brace.

25. Hagstrom, R. (1995). The acute psychological impact on survivors following a train accident. *Journal of Traumatic Stress, 8,* 391–402.

26. Hoffart, A. & Martinsen, E. W. (1993). Coping strategies in major depressed, agoraphobic, and comorbid in-patients: A longitudinal study. *British Journal of Medical Psychology, 66,* 143–155.

27. Joseph, S., Dalgleish, T., Thrasher, S., & Yule, W. (1995). Crisis support and emotional reactions following trauma. *Crisis Intervention and Time-Limited Treatment, 1,* 203–208.
28. Janoff-Bulman, R. (1992). *Shattered assumptions: Toward a new psychology of trauma.* New York: Free Press.
29. Joseph, S., Yule, W., & Williams, R. (1993). Post-traumatic stress: Attributional aspects. *Journal of Traumatic Stress, 6,* 501–513.
30. McCormick, R. A., Taber, J. I., & Kruedelbach, N. (1989). The relationship between attributional style and post-traumatic stress disorder in addicted patients. *Journal of Traumatic Stress, 2,* 477–487.
31. Mikulincer, M., & Solomon, Z. (1988). Attributional style and combat-related posttraumatic stress disorder. *Journal of Abnormal Psychology, 97,* 308–313.
32. Wolfe, V. V., Gentile, C., & Wolfe, D. A. (1989). The impact of sexual abuse on children: A PTSD formulation. *Behavior Therapy, 20,* 215–228.
33. Greenberg, M. A. (1995). Cognitive processing of traumas: The role of intrusive thoughts and reappraisals. *Journal of Applied Social Psychology, 25,* 1262–1296.
34. Bryant, R. A. & Harvey, A. G. (1995). Avoidant coping style and post-traumatic stress following motor vehicle accidents. *Behaviour Research & Therapy, 33,* 631–635.
35. Barsky, A. J. (1988). *Worried sick: Our troubled quest for wellness.* Boston: Little, Brown.
36. Lazarus, R. S., & Folkman, S. (1984). *Stress, appraisal, and coping.* New York: Springer.
37. Beck, A. T. (1976). *Cognitive therapy and the emotional disorders.* New York: International University Press.
38. Cook, M. L., & Peterson, C. (1986). Depressive irrationality. *Cognitive Therapy and Research, 10,* 293–298.
39. Ellis, A. (1962). *Reason and emotion in psychotherapy.* New York: Stuart.
40. Weissman, A. N. (1979). *The Dysfunctional Attitudes Scale: A validational study.* Doctoral dissertation, University of Pennsylvania.
41. Jones, R. G. (1969). A factored measure of Ellis' irrational belief systems, with personality and maladjustment correlates. *Dissertation Abstracts International, 29,* 11–13.
42. Taylor, S. E. (1989). *Positive illusions.* New York: Basic Books.
43. Peterson, C., & Seligman, M. E. P. (1984). Causal explanations as a risk factor for depression: Theory and evidence. *Psychological Review, 91,* 347–374.
44. Abramson, L. Y., Seligman, M E. P., & Teasdale, J. D. (1978). Learned helplessness in humans: Critique and reformulation. *Journal of Abnormal Psychology, 87,* 49–74.
45. Carver, C. S. (1989). How should multi-faceted personality constructs be tested? Issues illustrated by self-monitoring, attributional style, and hardiness. *Journal of Personality and Social Psychology, 56,* 577–585.
46. Peterson, C., & Bossio, L. M. (1991). *Health and optimism.* New York: Free Press.
47. Brewin, C. (1982). Self-blame in accidental injury. In C. Antaki & C.

Brewin (Eds.), *Attributions and psychological change: Applications of attributional theories to clinical and educational practice* (pp. 119–134). London: Academic Press.

48. Bulman, R. J., & Wortman, C. B. (1979). Attributions of blame and coping in the "real world": Severe accident victims react to their lot. *Journal of Personality and Social Psychology, 35,* 351–363.

49. Peterson, C., Semmel, A., von Baeyer, C., Abramson, L. Y., Metalsky, G. I., & Seligman, M. E. P. (1982). The Attributional Style Questionnaire. *Cognitive Therapy and Research, 6,* 287–299.

50. Peterson, C., Schulman, P., Castellon, C., & Seligman, M. E. P. (1992). CAVE: Content analysis of verbatim explanations. In C. P. Smith (Ed.), *Motivation and personality: Handbook of thematic content analysis* (pp. 383–392). New York: Cambridge University Press.

51. Dykema, K., Bergbower, K., & Peterson, C. (1995). Pessimistic explanatory style, stress, and illness. *Journal of Social and Clinical Psychology, 14,* 357–371.

52. Sullivan, M. J. L., Bishop, S. R., & Pivot, J. (1995). The Pain Catastrophizing Scale: Development and validation. *Psychological Assessment, 7,* 524–532.

54. Peterson, C., Maier, S. F., & Seligman, M. E. P. (1993). *Learned helplessness: A theory for the age of personal control.* New York: Oxford University Press.

55. Greening, L., & Dollinger, S. J. (1992). Illusions (and shattered illusions) of invulnerability: Adolescents in natural disaster. *Journal of Traumatic Stress, 5,* 63–75.

56. Bunce, S. C., Larsen, R. J., & Peterson, C. (1995). Life after trauma: Personality and daily life experiences of traumatized people. *Journal of Personality, 63,* 165–168.

57. Peterson, C., Seligman, M. E. P., Yurko, K. H., Martin, L. R., & Friedman, H. S. (1998). Catastrophizing and untimely death. *Psychological Science 9,* 127–130.

58. Park, C., Moon, C. H., & Peterson, C. (1997). *Explanatory style and depressive symptoms: A multimethod investigation.* Unpublished manuscript, University of Michigan.

59. Taylor, S. E., & Fiske, S. T. (1978). Salience, attention, and attribution: Top of the head phenomena. In L. Berkowitz (Ed.), *Advances in experimental social psychology* (Vol. 10, pp. 249–288). New York: Academic Press.

60. Weinstein, N. D. (1989). Optimistic biases about personal risks. *Science, 246,* 1232–1233.

61. Winett, R. A., King, A. C., & Altman, D. G. (1989). *Health psychology and public health: An integrative approach.* Elmsford, NY: Pergamon.

62. Peterson, C., & Stunkard, A. J. (1989). Personal control and health promotion. *Social Science and Medicine, 28,* 819–828.

63. Bandura, A. (1986). *Social foundations of thought and action.* Englewood Cliffs, NJ: Prentice-Hall.

64. Wilde, G. J. (1994). *Target risk.* On line: http//pavlov.psyc.queensu.ca/target

65. Quine, W. V., & Ullian, J. S. (1978). *The web of belief* (2nd ed.). New York: Random House.

66. Janoff-Bulman, R. & Frieze, I. H. (1983). A theoretical perspective or understanding reactions to victimization. *Journal of Social Issues, 39,* 1–17.
67. Connors, R. (1996). Self-injury in trauma survivors: I. Functions and meanings. *American Journal of Orthopsychiatry, 66,* 197–206.
68. Peterson, C. (1997). *Psychology: A biopsychosocial approach* (2nd ed.). New York: Longman.
69. Freud, S. (1911). Psycho-analytic notes on an autobiographical account of a case of paranoia (dementia paranoides). *Standard edition* (Vol. XII). London: Hogarth.
70. Alloy, L. B., & Abramson, L. Y. (1979). Judgment of contingency in depressed and nondepressed students: Sadder but wiser? *Journal of Experimental Psychology: General, 108,* 441–485.
71. Norem, J. K., & Cantor, N. (1986). Defensive pessimism: "Harnessing" anxiety as motivation. *Journal of Personality and Social Psychology, 51,* 1208–1217.
72. Rothbaum, F., Weisz, J. R., & Snyder, S. S. (1982). Changing the world and changing the self: A two-process model of perceived control. *Journal of Personality and Social Psychology, 42,* 5–37.
73. Tennen, H., & Affleck, G. (1990). Blaming others for threatening events. *Psychological Bulletin, 108,* 209–232.
74. Kuch, K., Cox, B. J., & Evans, R. J. (1996). Posttraumatic stress disorder and motor vehicle accidents: A multidisciplinary overview. *Canadian Journal of Psychiatry, 41,* 429–434.
75. Scott, M. J. (1997). Post-traumatic stress disorder: A cognitive-contextual approach. *Counselling Psychology Quarterly, 10,* 125–137.
76. Gillham, J., Reivich, K. J., Jaycox, L. H., & Seligman, M. E. P. (1995). Prevention of depressive symptoms in schoolchildren: Two-year follow-up. *Psychological Science, 6,* 343–351.
77. Jaycox, L. H., Reivich, K. J., Gillham, J., & Seligman, M. E. P. (1994). Prevention of depressive symptoms in schoolchildren. *Behaviour Research and Therapy, 32,* 801–816.
78. Fresco, D. M., Craighead, L. W., Sampson, W. S., & Koons, A. N. (1997). *Self-administered optimism training: Teaching pessimists to be more optimistic.* Unpublished manuscript, University of North Carolina.
79. Davis, J. O. (1991). Sports injuries and stress management: An opportunity for research. *The Sport Psychologist, 5,* 175–182.
80. FitzGerald, M. L., Braudaway, C. A., Leeks, D. & Padgett, M. B. (1993). Debriefing: A therapeutic intervention. *Military Medicine, 158,* 542–545.
81. Foa, E. B., Hearst-Ikeda, D., & Perry, K. J. (1995). Evaluation of a brief cognitive-behavioral program for the prevention of chronic PTSD in recent assault victims. *Journal of Consulting and Clinical Psychology, 63,* 948–955.
82. Seligman, M. E. P., Castellon, C., Cacciola, J., Schulman, P., Luborsky, L., Ollove, M., & Downing, R. (1988). Explanatory style change during cognitive therapy for unipolar depression. *Journal of Abnormal Psychology, 97,* 13–18.
83. Ellis, A. (1994). Post-traumatic stress disorder (PTSD): A rational emo-

tive behavioral therapy. *Journal of Rational-Emotive and Cognitive Behavior Therapy, 12,* 3–25.

84. Herman, J. (1992). *Trauma and recovery.* New York: Basic Books.
85. Charlton, P. F. C., & Thompson, J. A. (1996). Ways of coping with psychological distress after trauma. *British Journal of Clinical Psychology, 35,* 517–530.
86. Muse, M. (1986). Stress-related, posttraumatic chronic pain syndrome: Behavioral treatment approach. *Pain, 25,* 389–394.
87. Rosenstiel, A. K., & Keefe, F. J. (1983). The use of coping strategies in chronic low back pain patients: Relationship to patient characteristics and current adjustment. *Pain, 17,* 33–44.
88. Vallis, T. M. (1984). A complete component analysis of stress inoculation for pain tolerance. *Cognitive Therapy and Research, 8,* 313–329.
89. Geisser, M. E., Robinson, M. E., Keefe, F. J., & Weiner, M. L. (1994). Catastrophizing, depression and the sensory, affective and evaluative aspects of chronic pain. *Pain, 59,* 79–83.
90. Heyneman, N. E., Fremouw, W. J., Gano, D., Kirkland, F., & Heiden, L. (1990). Individual differences and the effectiveness of different coping strategies for pain. *Cognitive Therapy and Research, 14,* 63–77.
91. Spanos, N. P., Radtke-Bodorik, L., Ferguson, J. D., & Jones, B. (1979). The effects of hypnotic susceptibility, suggestions for analgesia, and the utilization of cognitive strategies on the reduction of pain. *Journal of Abnormal Psychology, 88,* 282–292.

13

Finding Benefits in Adversity

Howard Tennen
Glenn Affleck

The discovery of benefits among individuals experiencing adversity is well documented (1) and plays a prominent role in theories of cognitive adaptation to threatening circumstances (2, 3), and in an emerging literature on post-traumatic growth (4) and psychological thriving (5). Yet the conceptual status of benefit-finding is equivocal and its potential relationship to personality remains speculative. In this chapter we summarize the prevalence of benefit-finding, primarily among people facing medical problems, and describe the emotional and health advantages associated with finding benefits in adversity. We then turn to evidence and informed speculation relating benefit-finding to the personality characteristics that are discussed at length in other chapters of this volume. These include optimism (see chapters 8 and 9), extraversion, neuroticism (see chapter 6 in this volume), and hope (see chapter 10 in this volume). We offer five alternative conceptualizations of benefit-finding and present previously unpublished findings that distinguish benefit-related cognitions as adaptive beliefs—*benefit-finding*—from active efforts to recall benefits as coping strategies during difficult times—*benefit-reminding*. Finally, we propose a direction for future research and consider the implications of this area of inquiry for clinical practice.

The Prevalence of Benefit-Finding in Major Medical Problems

Many studies of the psychological aspects of major medical problems have included queries about any gains, benefits or advantages that participants might have found after weeks or years of contending with these problems.

In each of these studies a *majority* of informants cited benefits or gains from their adversity. This evidence comes from studies of heart attack survivors (6); women with breast cancer (7); survivors of spinal cord injuries (8); individuals who have lost their sense of taste and smell (9); women with impaired fertility (10); patients with chronic rheumatic diseases (11); stroke victims and their caregivers (12); parents of infants hospitalized in newborn intensive care units (13); and mothers of children with insulin-dependent diabetes (14). Aldwin (15), Calhoun and Tedeschi (16), and Park and Folkman (17) describe still other studies of benefit-finding in the face of adversity.

We find it remarkable that most people are able to describe benefits or gains across this range of threatening medical situations. Equally remarkable is that those who had more time to consider possible benefits were *no* more likely to report benefits than those who were only recently confronted with the threatening circumstance. Thus, if finding benefits reflects a temporally unfolding process, it is one that unfolds rather quickly. And there is no support in these studies that benefit-finding is a transient cognitive adaptation that gives way to other adaptive preferences. If it were transient, we would have found less benefit-finding among individuals who had more chronic medical conditions. Finally, these findings emerge across assessment methods. Although the evidence of benefit-finding derives in large part from answers to direct interview questions about what, if any, positive consequences ensued from the persons' experiences, in several studies participants answered multi-item questionnaires in which they endorsed benefits that could have accrued from their medical conditions (9, 18).

Several categories of perceived benefits cut across these problems and echo what has been found in studies of other types of threatening events (3, 4). For example, one common theme is the strengthening of relationships with family and friends. Another is the perception of positive personality change, including greater patience, tolerance, empathy, and courage. Yet another commonly reported benefit is a valued change in life's priorities and personal goals. Other benefits appear relatively specific to health-related adversity. As a case in point, many men believe that their heart attacks taught them the importance of health behavior practices for living a long life (6). And mothers often reported that their infants' hospitalizations in intensive care units opened their eyes to the dedication and caring attitudes of health care professionals (13). Later in this chapter, we attempt to tie the kinds of benefits people experience to aspects of personality.

The Benefits of Benefit-Finding

Most of the evidence linking benefit-finding to positive adaptation and well-being comes from cross-sectional studies. Benefit-finding relates to less negative affect in cancer patients (19); less depression and greater meaningfulness in life in stroke victims (12); less psychological distress in infertile women (10) and victims of taste and smell loss (9); superior psychological adjustment in women with breast cancer (7); and less mood disturbance and intrusive thoughts in mothers of acutely ill newborns (13). Because it is difficult to disentangle temporal precedence in these cross-sectional studies, their findings also can mean that those who are better adjusted to these problems find it easier to construe positive aspects of their experience. Or, perhaps positive adjustment and the ability to find benefits are both influenced by differences in the severity of the problem.

We are aware of only two longitudinal studies of the predictive significance of benefit-finding. Prior to their child's discharge from a newborn intensive care unit, Affleck, Tennen, and Rowe (13) asked mothers whether they had found any benefits from their child's hazardous delivery and prolonged hospitalization. Seventy-five percent of these mothers cited at least one benefit, including improved relationships with family and friends, the importance of keeping life's problems in perspective, increased empathy, positive changes in their personality, and the conviction that their child was now even more precious to them. Mothers who had cited no benefits from their child's newborn intensive care, however, reported more mood disturbance and psychological distress six and 18 months later, even when their mood at the time they were asked to describe any benefits was partialed from these relations. The ability of benefit-finding to predict later emotional well-being also was independent of an objective severity index of the child's medical problems, echoing what Thompson (12) found in a study of stroke survivors and what Tennen, Affleck, and Mendola (9) documented among individuals with taste and smell loss. Thus, it appears that benefit-finding *predicts* emotional well-being and is not confounded by objective measures of the severity of the problem.

These mothers' ability to find benefits not only predicted their own well-being, but also their child's actual developmental test scores 18 months later. This relation remained significant, even when we controlled for mothers' predischarge mood, age, education, parity, and the severity of infants' perinatal medical problems. This discovery is critical because it extends the positive outcomes of benefit-finding beyond the realm of self-report.

Another demonstration of the predictability of objective outcomes from earlier benefit-finding comes from a cohort of heart attack survivors who participated in an unusually long prospective study (6). After seven weeks of recovery from their initial heart attack, 58% of these men cited benefits, including anticipated changes in lifestyle, increased enjoyment, valued lessons about the importance of health behavior, and positive changes in their values and life philosophies. Eight years later, those men who had construed benefits were in significantly better cardiac health and also were less likely to have suffered a subsequent attack. These predictive relations remained significant, even after controlling for age, socioeconomic status, and severity of initial attack. It may be tempting to argue that benefit-finding predicted morbidity "simply" because those who referred to anticipated lifestyle and health behavior changes actually made such changes, which in turn produced superior cardiac health. But as anyone who has worked in a cardiac rehabilitation program (or, for that matter, anyone who has tried to stop smoking or maintain a weight loss diet) will attest, the road from appreciating the benefits of health behavior to cardiac health eight years later is filled with motivational, interpersonal, social, and medical obstacles. The possible mechanisms through which benefit-finding predicted subsequent cardiac health in this study and predicted infant development in the Affleck et al. (13) study deserve subsequent attention and replication.

In summary, research on the adaptational correlates of benefit-finding among individuals facing serious medical problems has documented its unique ability to predict emotional well-being. This, along with initial evidence that benefit-finding also may confer long-term health benefits, is a good reason to investigate *why* this positive appraisal of threatening events is related to positive adaptational outcomes. Our starting point is how benefit-finding relates to personality.

Personality and Benefit-Finding: The Usual Suspects Generate Little Light

Personality's relation to perceived benefits and gains has been considered in the literature on "thriving" (5) and "crisis-induced personal transformation" (4), in recent formulations of "stress-related growth" (19), and it has been implied in many studies of cognitive adaptation to threatening events. The strategy of investigators examining personality in relation to perceived benefits or gains reminds us of the classic scene from *Casablanca* in which Captain Louis Renault initiates a police investigation by demanding that the "usual suspects" be "rounded up" (20). Psychological investigators similarly have rounded up the usual moderational and mediational suspects without a fully developed theory of benefit-finding. As a result of this strategy, the proposed personality correlates of benefit-finding are identical to proposed correlates in totally unrelated areas of investigation (21); moreover, these are personal characteristics already suspected of being dimensions of one another (22). Although there may be some benefits to sticking to the usual suspects, we have argued previously that this approach runs the distinct risk of uncovering only what one already suspected (20). We now review the usually suspected candidates for finding benefits in adversity.

Personality has great appeal as a way of explaining psychological adaptation during a crisis and in its aftermath. Although the proportion of individuals reporting benefits or gains suggests that such perceptions are common, many survivors of adversity do not experience positive consequences from their plight, and these individuals could well differ from their benefit-finding counterparts in general or specific personality characteristics.

Over the years, authors have linked adversity-related benefit-finding to an *internal locus of control* (23); a *belief in a just world* (24); *dispositional optimism* (18, 19); and, *extraversion* and *openness to experience* (25). Because the empirical literature is limited, we follow the review strategy we employed in our previous discussions of this literature (1, 20) as we focus on those personality dimensions that have received the greatest theoretical attention. Specifically, we consider how dispositional optimism/pessimism, cognitive and self-complexity, and dispositional hope, each of which emphasizes the pursuit of personal goals in the face of obstacles, relate to benefit-finding. We then address the potential role played by the "Big Five" personality constellation (26).

Dispositional Optimism

Moos and Schaefer (27), O'Leary and Ickovics (5), Tennen et al. (9), and Tedeschi and Calhoun (4) have hypothesized that dispositional optimism, or the generalized expectancy for positive outcomes (28), may anticipate the perception of benefits or gains following threatening events. Optimists show superior adaptation to medical stressors, including coronary artery bypass surgery (29), childbirth (30), failed in-vitro fertilization (31), and HIV-positive status (32); moreover, on conceptual grounds, optimistic as compared to pessimistic individuals might be more inclined to extract a sense of benefit from adversity because of their positive interpretation of ongoing events.

Several studies using the Life Orientation Test (LOT) of dispositional optimism and pessimism (28) already have shown that perceptions closely related to benefit-finding are aligned with optimistic expectations. For example, Fontaine, Manstead, and Wagner (33) found that dispositional optimism was associated with "positive reinterpretation" as a strategy of coping with life stressors. Curbow, Somerfield, Baker, Wingard, and Legro (34) reported that among individuals undergoing bone marrow transplantation, greater optimism was associated with reports of positive life changes and personal growth. And Carver, Pozo, Harris, Noriega, Scheier, Robinson, et al. (35) found that optimists were more likely to use "positive reframing" as a coping strategy before and after breast cancer surgery. In a study that measured situation-specific optimism, Affleck, Tennen, and Rowe (13) showed that mothers who maintained more optimistic expectancies for their premature infant's development were more likely to find benefits in the neonatal intensive care crisis.

Tennen, Affleck, Urrows, Higgins, and Mendola (18) examined how dispositional optimism and benefit-finding relate to one another and operate in the day-to-day symptoms, mood, and functioning of individuals with rheumatoid arthritis, a chronic, painful, and disabling illness. After completing the LOT and a measure of perceived benefits from their chronic pain drawn from the *Inventory of Perceived Control Beliefs* (IPCB; 36), research participants reported for 75 consecutive days about their pain intensity, mood, and pain-related activity limitations (e.g., missing work and cutting back on planned social activities). As predicted, those scoring higher on the LOT were significantly more likely to endorse benefits from their illness.

Perceiving benefits from living with chronic pain also correlated with diary keepers' positive daily mood. In this regard, we wondered whether the relation between perceived benefits and daily mood might be explained by the tendency of dispositional optimists both to construe these benefits from their suffering and to experience more positive mood states. As expected, controlling for dispositional optimism attenuated the relation between benefit-finding and mood. But enthusiasm for the idea that optimism "explains" the association between perceiving benefits and well-being is dampened when we consider recent refinements in the measurement of optimism. First, it appears that the LOT measures two relatively orthogonal constructs: optimism *and* pessimism (22). Accordingly, our analysis relating optimism, perceived benefits, and mood may be flawed because it failed to distinguish between optimism and pessimism.

A second refinement of the LOT recommended by Scheier, Carver, and Bridges (37) is even more critical to the specificity of the relation between optimism and perceived benefits in adversity. Two of the four items originally claimed to measure optimism appear instead to measure the ability to extract positive value from negative circumstances: "I always look on the bright side of things" and "I'm a believer in the idea that 'every cloud has a silver lining.' " Thus, any apparent relation between optimism and benefit-finding may simply be due to overlapping measures of the capacity to extract something positive from an otherwise grim experience, one dispositional (as measured by these two items on the LOT) and the other more specific to the threatening circumstance (as assessed by questions regarding perceived benefits).

When we reanalyzed the data reported by Tennen et al. (18) to separate optimism from pessimism and the expectancy from the benefit-finding components of optimism, we found that although benefit-finding remained significantly correlated with the original four-item optimism scale, even when pessimism was partialed from the association, the two-item optimism scale without its dispositional benefit-finding items did not correlate significantly with the benefits participants derived from their illness, nor did it confound the association between benefit-finding and well-being. These findings suggest that the shared variation between optimism as measured by the original LOT and benefit-finding may be attributable to predictor-criterion item overlap. Both published findings and our reanalysis of previously published data render equivocal the role of dispositional optimism in benefit-finding, at least among those facing major medical problems. The recent and welcome refinements in the LOT offer investigators an opportunity to revisit the findings linking optimism and pessimism to benefit-finding among individuals facing adversity.

Although the relation between optimism and benefit-finding remains uncertain because of the aforementioned concerns, investigators and theorists have not been reticent to propose mechanisms mediating their association. These purported mediators converge on the idea that optimists experience benefits in the face of threat because they try harder: optimists are active, problem-oriented copers (4) who, because of their active efforts, have an edge in dealing with acute challenges (27). Several theorists have suggested that the efforts optimists exert to reframe negative experiences in a positive light similarly propels them toward actual positive transformations (4, 5). That the experience of benefits is related to effortful strategies is an untested assumption to which we will return later in this chapter.

Cognitive and Self-Complexity

Cognitive complexity shares with dispositional optimism/pessimism the ability to achieve personal goals despite barriers. Harvey (38) theorized that the more complex one's conceptual system, the greater should be one's ability to achieve "adequate means of fate control . . . and a greater mastery over what would otherwise be a capricious, unpredictable, and overwhelming environment" (38, p. 249). In the face of adversity, cognitively complex individuals should be better able to pursue alternative goals and find more flexible ways of achieving them, allowing them to see threat as an opportunity to change their life goals, values, or priorities in desirable ways.

Linville's (39) elaboration of the concept of *self*-complexity refines this argument. Linville documented that individuals who display high self-complexity—reflecting a greater number of discrete roles or identities used to organize self-schemas—adapt better to adversity, presumably because they are less likely to suffer global effects on self-representation. Bringing additional specificity to this hypothesis, Morgan and Janoff-Bulman (40) suggested that the complexity of *positively* valenced self-representations should best predict adaptation to events that threaten personal identities and roles. They indeed found that psychological adjustment to lifetime traumas (e.g., death of a parent, physical abuse, sexual assault) was superior among those who continued to hold many more independent positive self-representations (e.g., "hard-working," "focused," "imaginative," "motivated") than among trauma survivors with fewer independent positive self-representations (cf. 41). Although we believe that self-complexity may hold considerable promise as a personality moderator of the capacity to find benefits in adversity, the promise of cognitive complexity in relation to benefit-finding will only be realized through fully prospective inquiries.

Dispositional Hope

Dispositional hope is yet another personality construct that rests on the perceived accessibility of desired goals. Hope differs from optimism/pessimism in that it encompasses not only one's *expectancy* that desired goals can be achieved, but one's ability to imagine *avenues* for goal attainment (42).

We are uncovering evidence of the key role that dispositional hope plays in experiencing benefits from living with fibromyalgia, a syndrome of unknown origin that often combines widespread pain, unusual tenderness in multiple tender point sites, and sleep disturbance. Our study affords a test of the relative importance of dispositional optimism/pessimism and dispositional hope as measured by the LOT and Hope (43) scales respectively, in experiencing benefits in the context of fibromyalgia pain.

The results from the 89 participants in this study show that neither the LOT pessimism scale ($r = -.12$), nor the revised LOT optimism scale ($r = .15$) correlates significantly with perceived benefits from living with fibromyalgia. Instead, it is individuals with greater dispositional hope who cited more benefits from living with their chronic pain ($r = .34$, $p < .001$). In particular, those scoring higher on the Hope scale endorsed greater agreement with the IPCB items "I have learned a great deal about myself from living with my pain," and "dealing with my pain has made me a stronger person." The ability of dispositional hope to predict these facets of perceived growth, controlling for differences in the related constructs of optimism and pessimism, is strong evidence of its unique role in shaping positive appraisals of adversity. Later in this chapter we will describe how fibromyalgia patients actually *use* their conviction of personal growth as a daily cognitive coping strategy for contending with their pain.

The "Big Five" Dimensions of Personality

McCrae and Costa (44) found that individuals low in *neuroticism*, high in *extraversion*, and high in *openness to experience* tend to rely on "drawing strength from adversity" as a style of coping with threat. It is not clear why these broad dimensions of personality are associated with perceived benefits following crisis or adversity. Perhaps they provide a template for predicting the *types* of benefits people will construe from adversity.

Specific benefits attributed to misfortune could match the characteristic approaches to the self, the world, and others associated with these major dimensions of personality. For example, the typical negative self-perceptions associated with neuroticism/negative affectivity would lead to the hypothesis that individuals high on this trait would be less able to find benefits or gains in adversity. Those scoring higher on measures of extraversion, who are more gregarious, cheerful, and seekers of social contact, might be especially likely to cite positive consequences of adversity for social relationships. The individual who is more open to experience—imaginative, emotionally responsive, and intellectually curious—might be particularly likely to meet the challenge of adversity through a philosophical reorientation and a new direction in life plans.

In the only study to examine how the Big Five factors relate to specific benefits found in adversity, Tedeschi and Calhoun (25) asked more than 600 college students who reported recent major life stressors, such as the death of a parent, criminal victimization, or accidental injuries, to complete the *NEO Personality Inventory* (NEO; 45) and the *Posttraumatic Growth Inventory* (PTGI; 25), which measures characteristic forms of positive change claimed from adversity, such as the emergence of new possibilities, spiritual growth, and better relationships. NEO scores for extraversion, openness, agreeableness, and conscientiousness each correlated significantly with the total post-traumatic growth score. Although a multivariate analysis of personality predictors was not reported, it appears that extraversion is the most likely candidate to maintain an independent prediction of overall benefit-finding. It correlated highest with benefit-finding and was the only dimension to be associated significantly with each of the subscales of the PTGI. Extraversion, as might be predicted, correlated most strongly with the report of improved relationships. Openness to experience also was an expectedly strong correlate of the PTGI subscale labeled "new possibilities," which concerns the emergence of new interests and new life paths.

Other Personality Factors that Might Relate to Benefit-Finding

Tedeschi and Calhoun (4) propose several other personality factors that might set the stage for personal growth amid crisis and which would most likely be construed as a benefit of the crisis. One such factor is an *internal locus of control.* Individuals with an internal locus of control find rewards for their behavior in internal rather than external sources. This orientation might give them a sense of control in threatening circumstances that might infuse these circumstances with the sense of meaning and coherence associated with growth in adversity. Along with Moos and Schaefer (27), Bandura also proposes that *self-efficacy* or confidence in one's coping capacities (46), a *sense of coherence,* which includes a recognition that even catastrophic events are comprehensible and that life experiences are manageable and meaningful (47), and *hardiness* (48) position individuals to extract growth from personal crisis. In a fashion akin to locus of control, the posited "salutogenic" (47) effects of self-efficacy, sense of coherence, and hardiness derive from cognitive or behavioral effort. Self-efficacy leads individuals to try to master challenges. A sense of coherence promotes active search for meaning during threatening events, which in turn orients one to view these events as comprehensible and to muster the resources needed to master them. And hardiness involves active involvement, a sense of personal influence, and an inclination to actively derive meaning from stressful events. Notice that these are all strategic and effortful processes rather than unintended consequences of threatening life events.

Limitations of Current Conceptions of
Personality and Benefit-Finding

Although each of the personality traits described to this point may play a role in benefit-finding, investigators are aware that fully prospective designs are the best way to rule out the possibility that the personality characteristics associated with benefit-finding are not themselves a response to adversity. In support of retrospective designs in which both personality and an aversive event are measured some time after the event, investigators have suggested that because personality demonstrates temporal stability during adulthood, we can assume that preevent personality can be accurately inferred from postevent assessments. This simply is not so. Moderately high test-retest correlations and no mean difference for a cohort on a personality factor does *not* rule out even dramatic change for certain individuals within the cohort (49). As Pervin (50) reminds us: "overall stability, as reflected in correlation coefficients, may mask significant gains in functioning. . . . By the same token, stable means may mask significant individual differences" (p. 321).

The concerns we have raised regarding the "usual suspects" have been primarily methodological: indicators of some of these personality predictors overlap with one another; they have not been put to the rigorous requirements of fully prospective studies; and they are assumed to remain stable. Yet what may be most limiting about rolling out these same personality characteristics to explain individual differences in benefit-finding is the implication that those who are *already* well functioning are most likely to benefit further—or at least experience such benefit—from a crisis. Individuals who already experience a sense of personal control, who are optimistic about the future, who are outgoing and open to new experience, who are confident in their coping capacities, and who view the world as meaningful and its slings and arrows as manageable are, according to current theory, most likely to emerge from a crisis or traumatic experience believing that they are in some way better off than they were prior to the experience.

Implicit in this work is that paragons of mental health and personal development are the sole beneficiaries of perceived benefits following adversity, a perspective that fails to explain the most interesting and dramatic instances of positive change documented in accounts of such change, such as the heroin addicts described by Biernacki (51), who decided to give up their identity as an addict and successfully did so without treatment. These were by all accounts pessimistic, hopeless, fatalistic individuals who nonetheless managed to experience profound personal growth in the process of intentionally changing a central component of their identities. Current visions of personality characteristics associated with finding benefits in adversity also are contradicted by descriptions of perceived positive change offered by the many research participants who lacked the postulated personality characteristics prior to their traumatic experience. Miller and C'deBaca (52) and Lifton (53) described individuals who were certainly not optimistic, hardy, or extraverted. They were not particularly open to experience, and lacked a sense of coherence and meaning in life. And from all evidence, they maintained an external control orientation. Yet they reported dramatic change in the face of personal crisis. A more complete understanding of the role of personality in benefit-finding thus requires that we consider other conceptions of personality. It is to such conceptions that we now turn.

Levels of Personality, Personal Narratives, and Benefit-Finding

McAdams and his colleagues have recently offered a different personality context from which to interpret finding benefits in the face of adversity. McAdams (54) distinguishes three levels of personality: *dispositional traits*, *personal concerns*, and *life narratives*. Investigators interested in personality *correlates* of benefit-finding have relied exclusively on personality construed from the trait perspective, which is why all of the personality characteristics related to benefit-finding we have described to this point are all at McAdams's first level.

Yet this approach may be the most limited and limiting for the study of benefit-finding. Among the many critiques of trait conceptions of personality, those most relevant to our discussion have been offered by Thorne (55) and Mischel and Shoda (56), who argue convincingly that personality defined as traits leaves no room for "conditional patterns" (55) or "*if . . . then . . .* situation-behavior relations as signatures of personality" (56). These conditional relations between the person and her/his world are captured in the statements: "I lose my sense of control when I am threatened," and "Life seems to lose its meaning when someone important in my life leaves." The notion of conditional patterns may offer clues to areas in which perceived benefits might arise.

Personal concerns, McAdams's (54) second level of personality includes an individual's current life tasks (57), strivings (58), personal projects (59), and current concerns (60). Personal concerns refer to what a person wants at a particular point in life, and how s/he plans to get what s/he wants (61, 62). These concerns are neither traits nor are they epiphenomena of the trait level of personality. People are quite aware of this second level of their personalities because personal concerns guide everyday activities. Unlike Level 1, Level 2 is contextual and motivated, and McAdams (54) makes a strong case for the ebb and flow of personal concerns throughout life.

Whereas personality correlates of benefit-finding have been investigated exclusively at Level 1, the actual benefits described by research participants seem to reflect changes in this second level of personality, though as we will soon argue, McAdams's Level 3 may be even more closely related to experiences of personal growth. When a research participant states that an unforeseen benefit of having received a life-threatening diagnosis is that personal relationships have become a focus of her everyday life in a way that is new and rewarding, she is describing a benefit related to personality at Level 2. Or consider a man whose son died after a long illness. When asked whether he has experienced any benefits, he reports that despite his continuing grief he has shifted his priorities from his work to the community. He organized a community program for chronically ill children, volunteers at a local hospital, and shares freely his time and expertise with the town Little League. These generative efforts have given his life renewed purpose and reflect perceived benefits related to a change in personality at Level 2. Similarly, when we asked middle-aged heart attack victims about possible benefits from their heart attack (6), a common response was that a new found appreciation of life had led to radical lifestyle changes. This too is a benefit related to personality at Level 2.

Personality at Level 3 concerns the individual's attempt to shape an identity by finding unity and purpose in life. McAdams and colleagues (63) refer to this level as "integrative narratives of the self" and suggest that contemporary Western adults construct life stories as a way of bringing purpose to their lives (64). This third level of inquiry into personality processes has gained momentum among investigators interested in personal crisis (65), and theoreticians interested in trauma (66, 67). It is also consistent with Snyder, McDermott, Cook, and Rapoff's assertion that hope lives in the personal stories that children and adults construct about themselves (68). McAdams and others who draw on the narrative tradition to understand personality consider identity as an "evolving story that integrates a reconstructed past, perceived present, and anticipated future into a coherent and vitalizing life myth" (54, p. 306). Personal myth cannot be reduced to traits (Level 1) or personal concerns (Level 2). It is an internalized, unfolding narrative that is revised so as to give life a sense of direction, meaning, and continuity.

McAdams (64) speculates that whereas traits remain stable throughout adulthood and personal concerns change in response to circumstances and life stage, identity is continuously being shaped—both consciously and without awareness—to provide narrative coherence and a sense of meaning and purpose to life, and to fit personal experiences into this coherent account. Personal trauma or crisis (called "nuclear episodes" or "nadirs" in McAdams's scheme) provides the individual an opportunity to fit the experience into her/his life narrative and even to use the incident to affirm personal transformation. Citing Taylor's (69) concept of positive illusions, McAdams (54) describes how narrative explanations of serious illness and other forms of adversity shape and reshape personal identity. We believe that finding benefits in adversity is one way individuals reshape their life stories in an effort to bring coherence and meaning during threatening encounters.

Employing narrative methods including McAdams's (70) life-story interview, McAdams et al. (63) examined how life narratives relate to Erikson's (71) concept of generativity by comparing the narratives of highly generative and less generative adults. These investigators anticipated that "redemptive sequences in life scenes" would emerge more frequently among their highly generative participants. Redemptive sequences are narratives in which particularly bad events are subsequently redeemed or made better through some positive outcome or sequelae. Such sequences have much in common with Colby and Damon's (72) description of the narratives provided by adult moral exemplars, in which misfortune or life tragedy contains a positive aspect or leads to a positive outcome.

McAdams et al. (63) indeed found that highly generative adults described more redemption sequences in their accounts of turning points and nadir experiences in their lives. Most germane to our discussion of benefit-finding is the redemption sequence characterized by "growth." In their life stories, some participants, particularly highly generative participants, describe episodes in which adversity ultimately leads to some personal gain or benefit: a painful divorce leads a participant to develop a better relationship with his son; a father's death brings someone closer to her family; and a failed love affair produces more assertive and confident behavior.

These narrative sequences show a remarkable similarity to the perceived benefits elaborated by participants in our studies of adaptation to threatening medical conditions, and they show the same positive association to psychosocial adaptation (73). This raises a fascinating issue for those of us who study cognitive adaptation to adversity: Might interview or questionnaire responses acknowledging benefits or gains from a threatening experience reflect a narrative redemptive sequence that certain individuals are inclined to bring to all of life's slings and arrows? If so, and if McAdams (54) is correct in hinting that life stories themselves may be construed as personality constructs, then what investigators have interpreted as adaptive cognitions may actually be an aspect of personality. Whereas dispositional traits may be *correlates* of benefit-finding, and contextualized concerns may be reflected in the *content* of benefits found, integrative narratives of the self, particularly growth narratives, may be precisely what is being measured by investigators who study benefit-finding.

Benefit-Finding: An Adaptive Phenomenon in Search of a Conceptualization

We have summarized the prevalence of benefit-finding, the range of threatening events in which its role has been examined, its association with personality and emotional well-being, and its capacity to predict health outcomes months and years later, even after controlling for likely confounds. The evidence is clear: Benefit finding enhances emotional and physical adaptation in the face of adversity. But unlike the adaptational benefits of sharing one's story (see chapter 4 in this volume), of focusing on emotions (see chapter 5 in this volume), of optimism (see chapters 8 and 9 in this volume) and hope (see chapter 10 in this volume), and of rebuilding shattered assumptions (see chapter 14 in this volume), benefit-finding lacks a reliable conceptual "home." Although theorists have moved beyond blanket interpretations of benefit-finding as a form of denial or as a maladaptive reality distortion (1), and investigators have freely offered their own conceptual frameworks for benefit-finding, alternative formulations have for the most part been ignored. We now suggest five ways to understand benefit-finding among individuals in adverse circumstances.

Benefit-Finding as Cognitive Reappraisal

The most common interpretation of benefit-finding in the stress and coping literature is that it represents a "selective evaluation" (2). Along with finding a sense of order and purpose in the threatening experience, imagining "worse worlds," and making comparisons to less fortunate others, construing benefits or gains help individuals restore valued assumptions and cherished beliefs about themselves as worthy and relatively invulnerable and their world as orderly, predictable, meaningful, and benevolent or at least benign (2, 74, 75).

Implied in this constructivist interpretation of benefit-finding is that it is the *appraisal* of benefits that helps people adapt to victimization. Yet when individuals identify greater family harmony as an unexpected benefit of a crisis, might the adaptational benefits associated with this appraisal be due to their improved ability to obtain social support? If so, the inferred cognitive adaptation may be an epiphenomenon, of interest only as a marker of an influential change that has occurred (13). The working hypothesis of investigators coming from the "selective appraisal" perspective is that the accuracy of benefits construed by victims is less important to adaptation than the belief that positive changes have occurred. From this perspective, when people construe a beneficial change, true or not, they create a reality to which they then respond (13).

Benefit-Finding as a Personality Characteristic

McAdams's (64) speculation that trauma or crisis provides an opportunity to recreate one's life narrative and to structure a life story with coherence and meaning shares the constructivist perspective on benefit-finding, but places it in the context of a personality characteristic. If, in fact, there are individuals who characteristically provide narratives in which misfortune or life tragedy contains a positive aspect or leads to a positive outcome, and if highly generative people typically describe episodes in which adversity ultimately leads to some personal gain or benefit, the generative qualities interpreted by an investigator as an adaptational consequence of benefit-finding may in reality be a characteristic of those individuals who are more likely to generate "redemptive sequences" in which personal benefit or gain is an integral part.

Benefit-Finding as a Reflection of Growth or Change

An emerging literature on post-traumatic growth (4) and thriving in the midst of adversity (5) approaches the claim of benefits not as a cognitive construction designed to protect threatened assumptions, but as a potential indicator of genuine positive change. The distinction between benefit-finding as a selective appraisal and reported benefits as a veridical perception of change is critical to how we interpret research findings linking benefit-finding to adaptational outcomes. Consider the woman with breast cancer who responds to an interviewer's query about benefits or gains by claiming that her surgery and chemotherapy has made her see what is important in life. Along with her new perspective, she finds that she is far less anxious about anticipated daily hassles and is now able to accept everyday disappointments without becoming despondent. How should the investigator interpret her scores on measures of well-being? Is her positive adaptation a product of selective appraisal, for example, benefit-finding, or is her selective appraisal an accurate representation of her positive adaptation? In the only study to our knowledge that has attempted to corroborate reports of personal growth derived from negative events, Park et al. (19) found significant intrapair agreement between the reports of participants and those of close friends and relatives who served as informants. We believe that these findings present a genuine challenge to a purely constructivist view of benefit-finding.

Benefit-Finding as a Rationalization of Temperament

McCrae (personal communication, May, 13, 1996, cited in 20) has suggested that some of the benefits reported by individuals facing adversity may represent a mechanism for restoring their characteristic hedonic level (76). The well-adjusted extrovert who typically feels relatively happy regardless of her circumstances may find herself feeling happy despite her recently experienced life crisis. She may explain her continued positive emotional state by attributing it to her appreciation of life's small pleasures or what may seem like a new found capacity to feel grateful for past good fortune. When asked in a research interview if she has experienced any benefits or gains from her untoward experience, she is likely to offer her appreciation of the little things in life and her sense of gratitude. McCrae believes that she may be rationalizing her temperament. He asserts that because distressing events are incompatible with high hedonic levels, the people who are most likely to experience benefits are those who already are well functioning. Individuals who are chronically distressed (e.g., those who score higher on indicators of neuroticism) have no need for cognitive reappraisal when they face adversity because their emotional states fit their circumstances.

The notion that benefit-finding is motivated by a need to rationalize temperament poses yet another challenge to most current formulations of cognitive adaptation to adversity and underscores the need for prospective inquiry and outcome indicators that move beyond self-report.

Benefit-Finding as Coping

Finding benefits in threatening circumstances also has been construed by investigators, at least implicitly (2), as an emotion-focused coping strategy. Largely due to the influence of Richard Lazarus (77, 78), but anticipated by others (79), coping researchers have come to appreciate that "not all adaptive processes are coping. Coping is a subset of adaptational activities that *involves effort* and does not include everything that we do in relating to the environment" (77, p.132, italics added). Although not all theorists agree that coping strategies require conscious effort (80, 81), we maintain the distinction between coping and other adaptational behaviors that do not require conscious effort.

Despite Lazarus and Folkman's (77) care to focus on the effortful and strategic nature of coping, they included perceived benefits as an indicator of emotion-focused coping. The *Ways of Coping Questionnaire* (82), for example, includes the following items: *changed or grew as a person in a good way; came out of the experience better than when I went in; found new faith;* and *discovered what is important in life.* Yet coping theory, as currently formulated, distinguishes among adaptive behaviors that do not require effort, beliefs (which any of these questionnaire items may reflect), and coping strategies.

Lazarus and Folkman's widely accepted definition of coping excludes beliefs that can be held without corroborating evidence, even if they enhance emotional well-being and health. Although adaptive, these beliefs are not coping strategies as now defined. Thus, if a seriously ill individual actively searches for evidence of benefits, she is coping. If she takes the time to remind herself of these perceived benefits, she is coping. If she eventually concludes that there have indeed been benefits associated with her illness and reports this belief when provided the opportunity during an interview, she is no longer coping. That her conclusion may have been reached through selective evaluations or convoluted reasoning or is biased by objective standards is irrelevant to its status as a coping strategy. Its adaptive function is equally irrelevant to whether it is a coping strategy (83).

Consider Dunkel-Schetter, Feinstein, Taylor, and Falke's (84) factor analysis of the *Ways of Coping Questionnaire* (82) among cancer patients. One of the five strategies derived was positive focus, "characterized by *efforts* to find meaning in the experience by focusing on personal growth" (85, italics added). We can imagine someone with cancer trying to find meaning in the illness experience or trying to grow as a person from the experience. But items measuring positive focus do not measure such efforts. Rather, as we asserted above, they measure conclusions, for example, "I came out of the experience better than I went in." And to the extent that such conclusions are veridical, we should be neither surprised nor impressed if they are associated with positive psychological or health outcomes. The confusion between benefit-finding as a coping strategy and benefit-finding as a conclusion reflects a confusion in the broader coping literature that has only rarely (83, 86) been addressed.

Under what circumstances can benefit-related cognitions be effortful? Consider an individual with a chronic pain disorder facing an extended period of intense pain who may be trying to *remind* herself of some of the benefits she has found from living with this disease as a way of making her pain more bearable. This effort to savor the benefits she has construed from her illness can justifiably be called a coping strategy. It captures the intentional, strategic quality of coping and in this way "behaves" like other cognitive pain-coping strategies such as diverting attention or reinterpreting pain sensations (87).

Whereas only those who already have discovered benefits from their adversity can use this discovery to comfort themselves in difficult times, there is nothing about the admission of benefits per se which implies that benefit-related cognitions will be used as effortful coping strategies. In a recent study of fibromyalgia pain, we examined this and related questions. This investigation is unique in its measurement of benefit cognitions in a daily process design that permits within-person analysis of relations among variables over time and the combination of idiographic and nomothetic methods (see 88 and 89 for detailed discussions of the benefits of this design).

Daily Process Findings on Benefit-Reminding

Our study of 89 women with fibromyalgia uses a prospective daily design which entails time-intensive self-monitoring of daily symptoms, experiences, behaviors, emotions, and cognitions for 30 days. We describe below their effortful daily use of benefit cognitions (benefit-reminding) and its relation with benefit-finding and personality/dispositional variables, and characterize the *within-person* relations of these comparison processes with fluctuating levels of daily pain and daily mood.

The time-intensive self-monitoring methodology used in this study combines a nightly structured diary with a computer-assisted "real-time" assessment of pain intensity and mood several times each day. The hardware for the electronic diary is a PSION palmtop computer programmed to deliver auditory signals to complete an on-screen interview at randomly selected times during the mid-morning, mid-afternoon, and mid-evening. The interview responses were time-stamped and stored in the palmtop computer for subsequent uploading to a desktop system. Shiffman and colleagues (90,91) have established the feasibility of similar electronic diaries for self-monitoring studies, and we have demonstrated its many advantages over traditional paper-and-pencil methods (92,93).

One item on the nightly questionnaire measured benefit-reminding: participants used a 0 (not at all) to 6 (very much) scale to describe how much that day they had "reminded [themselves] of some of the benefits that have come from living with their chronic pain." The average daily mean for this item was .70 (SD = 1.12); the mean percentage of days the average respondent reported any benefit-reminding was 24.3% (SD = 33.1). Thirty-three participants never reminded themselves of benefits; 31 participants reported benefit-reminding on 1–9 days; 10 participants did so on 10–20 days; and 15 participants did so on 21–30 days. Clearly, there are considerable individual differences in how frequently these individuals actually reminded themselves of any benefits they had construed from their illness. Some who had cited many benefits never reminded themselves of these during a month's time span, whereas some who had cited only one or a few reported benefit-reminding on many days.

Personality Correlates of Benefit-Reminding.   As expected, individuals who had scored higher on the benefit-finding subscale of the IPCB did report more days of benefit-reminding ($r=.51$, $p<.001$). Potential confounds including participants' duration of symptoms, education, and level of daily pain intensity were unrelated to benefit-finding or benefit-reminding. Older participants did report more benefits ($r=.36$, $p<.001$) as well as more days of benefit-reminding ($r=.22$, $p<.05$), but the age-partialed relation between benefit-finding and benefit-reminding remained significant ($r=.48$, $p<.001$). Several personality measures, including scores on the NEO Personality Inventory neuroticism and extraversion scales and the LOT's pessimism and revised and original optimism scores, were unrelated to benefit-reminding frequencies.

The personality measure which did correlate with benefit-reminding was the Hope scale ($r=.28$, $p<.01$). Recall that we noted earlier that the Hope scale also correlated with benefit-finding in this sample. Because the relation between Hope and benefit-reminding became nonsignificant when benefit-finding was partialed from this association, while the relation between benefit-finding and benefit-reminding remained significant when Hope was partialed from that association, we can conclude that the relation between Hope and benefit-reminding is mediated by the tendency of hopeful individuals to find more benefits in their illness.

Within-Person Analysis of Benefit-Reminding.   The design of our study enables within-person analysis of day-to-day differences in benefit-reminding and other daily processes. To examine within-person relations across persons, independent of between-person differences in the daily data, a series of multilevel models with random subject intercepts (94) were tested using SAS proc mixed (95). One such analysis related daily benefit-reminding to daily pain intensity, measured by electronic diary entries of daily ratings of 14 areas of the body, and to daily mood scores, measured by electronic diary data on a 16-item mood adjective checklist, capturing all octants of the circumplex model of mood pleasantness and mood arousal (96): pleasant mood, unpleasant mood, aroused mood, unaroused mood, pleasant-aroused mood, pleasant-unaroused mood, unpleasant-aroused mood, and unpleasant-unaroused mood. Days characterized by more benefit-reminding did not differ in pain intensity, but were accompanied by significant differences in mood, specifically increased levels of pleasant (i.e., happy, cheerful) mood; aroused mood (active, lively); and aroused-pleasant (i.e., peppy, stimulated) mood. When all three of these mood dimension scores were examined together as correlates of benefit-reminding frequency, there remained a unique relation only with pleasant mood. Thus, on days when these chronic pain sufferers made greater efforts to remind themselves of the benefits that have come from their illness, they were especially more likely to experience pleasurable mood, regardless of how intense their pain was on these days.

This within-person analysis of efforts to remind oneself of the benefits of living with chronic pain strengthens the hypothesis that benefit-reminding can improve one's emotional well-being on more difficult days. Interested readers can consult articles that provide various multilevel data analytic strategies for modeling individual differences due to personality in stress-symptom and stress-mood relations across time (97,98).

Research Directions and Clinical Implications

If this chapter could offer only one message for investigators, it would be to underscore the need for detailed, *prospective* studies of coping with threatening events, including the role of benefit-finding and benefit-reminding in the process of adaptation to adversity. We are convinced that coping is an unfolding process, and that cross-sectional studies seeking correlations between perceived benefits and well-being at a particular moment are rarely revealing and often misleading. We are committed to studying people over time, and we have been impressed at how readily research participants let us into their lives at their darkest moments and allow us to stay with them as they face adversity, most often to better times.

If we could offer only one message for practitioners, it would be to respect the adaptational value of benefit-finding and benefit-reminding, while resisting the understandable desire to directly influence these adaptational processes. Nothing in this chapter should be construed as evidence that deliberate attempts by family, friends, or helping professionals to shape or influence the perception of benefits will be helpful. Although there may be some people who appreciate being reminded by someone else to "look at all the good that has come from this experience," and it is even possible that family, friends, or treating physicians helped shape the benefit perceptions of some individuals (2), our research participants have told us spontaneously and repeatedly that they view such efforts as insensitive and inept. They are almost always interpreted as an unwelcomed attempt to minimize the unique burdens and challenges that need to be overcome. Although clinical impressions suggest that sensitive health care professionals might be able to facilitate benefit-finding (2), the empirical literature offers few clues regarding how or when to offer such facilitating interventions. Whereas finding benefits and reminding oneself of benefits enhance emotional and health outcomes in the face of adversity, our research participants indicate that *directed, imposed,* or *suggested* benefits will almost surely fail to achieve their desired goal. Most people have a remarkable capacity to withstand and overcome threatening events without our well-intentioned efforts to provide them with a different way to interpret their plight. As provocative as the present findings on benefit-finding and benefit-reminding may be, they demand a caveat: There is a great deal more we need to know before we apply these findings to therapeutic endeavors.

Acknowledgment: The unpublished findings reported in this chapter come from a study funded by the National Institute of Arthritis, Musculoskeletal, and Skin Diseases Grant #AR-20621 to the University of Connecticut Multipurpose Arthritis Center. We appreciate Susan Urrow's and Micha Abeles's collaboration, the aid of Jeffrey Siegel of National Technology Services for programming the electronic diary described in this chapter, and the assistance of Pamela Higgins and Debra Begin with data collection and management.

References

1. Affleck, G. & Tennen, H. (1996). Construing benefits from adversity: Adaptational significance and dispositional underpinnings. *Journal of Personality, 64,* 899–922.
2. Taylor, S. (1983). Adjustment to threatening events: A theory of cognitive adaptation. *American Psychologist, 38,* 624–630.
3. Janoff-Bulman, R. (1992). *Shattered assumptions: Toward a new psychology of trauma.* New York: Free Press.
4. Tedeschi, R.G., & Calhoun, L.G. (1995). *Trauma and transformation: Growing in the aftermath of suffering.* Thousand Oaks, CA: Sage.
5. O'Leary, V.E., & Ickovics, J.R. (1995). Resilience and thriving in response to challenge: An opportunity for a paradigm shift in women's health. *Women's Health: Research on Gender, Behavior, and Policy, 1,* 121–142.
6. Affleck, G., Tennen, H., Croog, S., & Levine, S. (1987). Causal attribution, perceived benefits, and morbidity following a heart attack: An eight-year study. *Journal of Consulting and Clinical Psychology, 55,* 29–35.

7. Taylor, S.E., Lichtman, R., & Wood, J. (1984). Attributions, beliefs about control, and adjustment to breast cancer. *Journal of Personality and Social Psychology, 46,* 489–502.
8. Bulman, R., & Wortman, C. (1977). Attributions of blame and coping in the "real world": Severe accident victims react to their lot. *Journal of Personality and Social Psychology, 35,* 351–363.
9. Tennen, H., Affleck, G., & Mendola, R. (1991a). Coping with smell and taste disorders. In T. Getchell, R. Doty, L. Bartoshuk, & J. Snow (Eds.), *Smell and taste in health and disease* (pp. 787–801). New York: Raven Press.
10. Tennen, H., Affleck, G., & Mendola, R. (1991b). Causal explanations for infertility: Their relation to control appraisals and psychological adjustment. In A. Stanton & C. Dunkel-Schetter (Eds.), *Infertility: Perspectives from stress and coping research* (pp. 109–132). New York: Plenum.
11. Affleck, G., Pfeiffer, C., Tennen, H., Fifield, J. (1988). Social support and psychosocial adjustment to rheumatoid arthritis: Quantitative and qualitative findings. *Arthritis Care and Research, 1,* 71–77.
12. Thompson, S. (1991). The search for meaning following a stroke. *Basic and Applied Social Psychology, 12,* 81–96.
13. Affleck, G., Tennen, H., & Rowe, J. (1991). *Infants in crisis: How parents cope with newborn intensive care and its aftermath.* New York: Springer-Verlag.
14. Affleck, G., Allen, D., Tennen, H., McGrade, B., & Ratzan, S. (1985). Causal and control cognitions in parent coping with a chronically ill child. *Journal of Social and Clinical Psychology, 3,* 367–377.
15. Aldwin, C. (1994). *Stress, coping, and development: An integrative perspective.* New York: Guilford.
16. Calhoun, L.G. & Tedeschi, R.G. (1991). Perceiving benefits in traumatic events: Some issues for practicing psychologists. *The Journal of Training & Practice in Professional Psychology, 5,* 45–52.
17. Park, C.L. & Folkman, S. (1997). Meaning in the context of stress and coping. *Review of General Psychology, 1,* 115–144.
18. Tennen, H., Affleck, G., Urrows, S., Higgins, P., & Mendola, R. (1992). Perceiving control, construing benefits, and daily processes in rheumatoid arthritis. *Canadian Journal of Behavioral Science, 24,* 186–203.
19. Park, C., Cohen, L., & Murch, R. (1996). Assessment and prediction of stress-related growth. *Journal of Personality, 64,* 71–105.
20. Tennen, H. & Affleck, G. (1997). Personality and transformation in the face of adversity. In R.G. Tedeschi, C.L. Park, & L.G. Calhoun (Eds.), *Posttraumatic growth: Positive change in the aftermath of crisis* (pp. 65–98). Hillsdale, NJ: Erlbaum.
21. Hoorens, V. (1996). Self-favoring biases for positive and negative characteristics: Independent phenomena? *Journal of Social and Clinical Psychology, 15,* 53–67.
22. Marshall, G., Wortman, C., Kusulas, J., Hervig, L., & Vickers, R. (1992). Distinguishing optimism from pessimism: Relations to fundamental dimensions of mood and personality. *Journal of Personality and Social Psychology, 62,* 1067–1074.

300   COPING

23. Wollman, C., & Felton, B. (1983). Social supports as stress buffers for adult cancer patients. *Psychosomatic Medicine, 45*, 321–331.
24. Kiecolt-Glaser, J., & Williams, D. (1987). Self-blame, compliance, and distress among burn patients. *Journal of Personality and Social Psychology, 53*, 187–193.
25. Tedeschi, R., & Calhoun, L. (1996). The post-traumatic growth inventory: Measuring the positive legacy of trauma. *Journal of Traumatic Stress, 9*, 455–471.
26. McCrae, R.R. (1992). The five-factor model: Issues and applications. *Journal of Personality, 60* [special issue].
27. Moos, R.H., & Schaefer, J.A. (1990). Coping resources and processes: Current concepts and measures. In H.S. Friedman (Ed.), *Personality and disease* (pp. 234–257). New York: Wiley.
28. Scheier, M., & Carver, C. (1985). Optimism, coping, and health: Assessment and implications of generalized outcome expectancies. *Health Psychology, 4*, 219–247.
29. Fitzgerald, T., Tennen, H., Affleck, G., & Pransky, G. (1993). Quality of life after coronary artery bypass surgery: The importance of initial expectancies and control appraisals. *Journal of Behavioral Medicine, 16*, 25–43.
30. Carver, C., & Gaines, J. (1987). Optimism, pessimism, and post-partum depression. *Cognitive Therapy and Research, 11*, 449–462.
31. Litt, M., Tennen, H., Affleck, G., & Klock, S. (1992). Coping and cognitive factors in adaptation to in-vitro fertilization failure. *Journal of Behavioral Medicine, 15*, 119–126.
32. Taylor, S. E., Kemeny, M., Aspinwall, L., Schneider, S., Rodriguez, R., & Herbert, M. (1992). Optimism, coping, psychological distress, and high-risk sexual behavior among men at risk for AIDS. *Journal of Personality and Social Psychology, 63*, 460–473.
33. Fontaine, K., Manstead, A., & Wagner, H. (1993). Optimism, perceived control over stress, and coping. *European Journal of Personality, 27*, 267–281.
34. Curbow, B., Somerfield, M., Baker, F., Wingard, J., & Legro, M. (1993). Personal changes, dispositional optimism, and psychological adjustment to bone marrow transplantation. *Journal of Behavioral Medicine, 16*, 423–443.
35. Carver, C., Pozo, C., Harris, S., Noriega, V., Scheier, M., Robinson, D., Ketcham, A., Moffat, F., & Clark, K. (1993). How coping mediates the effect of optimism on distress: A study of women with early stage breast cancer. *Journal of Personality and Social Psychology, 65*, 375–390.
36. Mendola, R. (1990). *Coping with chronic pain: Perceptions of control and dispositional optimism as moderators of psychological distress.* Doctoral dissertation, University of Connecticut, Storrs, CT.
37. Scheier, M., Carver, C., & Bridges, M. (1994). Distinguishing optimism from neuroticism (and trait anxiety, self-mastery, and self-esteem): A reevaluation of the Life Orientation Test. *Journal of Personality and Social Psychology, 67*, 1063–1078.
38. Harvey, J. (1965). Cognitive aspects of affective arousal. In S. Tomkins & C. Izard (Eds.), *Affect, cognition, and personality: Empirical studies* (pp. 242–262). New York: Springer.

39. Linville, P. (1987). Self-complexity as a cognitive buffer against stress-related illness and depression. *Journal of Personality and Social Psychology, 52*, 663–676.
40. Morgan, H., & Janoff-Bulman, R. (1994). Positive and negative self-complexity: Patterns of adjustment following traumatic versus non-traumatic life experiences. *Journal of Social and Clinical Psychology, 13*, 63–85.
41. Schaefer, J.A., & Moos, R.H.. (1992). Making the case for coping. In B.N. Carpenter (Ed.), *Personal coping: Theory, research, and application* (pp. 149–170). Westport, CT: Praeger.
42. Snyder, C., Irving, L., & Anderson, J. (1991). Hope and health. In C.R. Snyder & D.R. Forsyth (Eds.), *Handbook of social and clinical psychology: The health perspective* (pp. 285–305). New York: Pergamon Press.
43. Snyder, C., Harris, C., Anderson, J., Holleran, S., Irving, L., Sigmon, S., et al. (1991). The will and the ways: Development and validation of an individual difference measure of hope. *Journal of Personality and Social Psychology, 60*, 570–585.
44. McCrae, R.R., & Costa, P.T., Jr. (1986). Personality, coping, and coping effectiveness. *Journal of Personality, 54*, 385–405.
45. Costa, P., & McCrae, R. (1985). *The NEO Personality Inventory manual.* Odessa, FL: Psychological Assessment Resources.
46. Bandura, A. (1982). Self-efficacy mechanism in human agency. *American Psychologist, 37*, 122–147.
47. Antonovsky, A. (1987). *Unraveling the mystery of health: How people manage stress and stay well.* San Francisco: Jossey-Bass.
48. Kobasa, S.C. (1979). Stressful life events, personality, and health: An inquiry into hardiness. *Journal of Personality and Social Psychology, 37*, 1–11.
49. Weinberger, J.L. (1994). Can personality change? In T.F. Heatherton & J.L. Weinberger (Eds.), *Can personality change?* (pp. 333–350). Washington, DC: American Psychological Association.
50. Pervin, L.A. (1994). Personality stability, personality change, and the question of process. In T.F. Heatherton & J.L. Weinberger (Eds.), *Can personality change?* (pp. 315–330). Washington, DC: American Psychological Association.
51. Biernacki, P. (1986). *Pathways from heroin addiction: Recovery without treatment.* Philadelphia: Temple University Press.
52. Miller, W.R., & C'deBaca, J. (1994). Quantum change: Toward a psychology of transformation. In T.F. Heatherton & J.L. Weinberger (Eds.), *Can personality change?* (pp. 253–280). Washington, DC: American Psychological Association.
53. Lifton, R.J. (1993). *The protean self: Human resilience in an age of fragmentation.* New York: Basic Books.
54. McAdams, D.P. (1994a). Can personality change? Levels of stability and growth in personality across the life span. In T.F. Heatherton & J.L. Weinberger (Eds.), *Can personality change?* (pp. 299–313). Washington, DC: American Psychological Association.
55. Thorne, A. (1989). Conditional patterns, transference, and the coherence of personality across time. In D.M. Buss & N. Cantor (Eds.), *Per-*

sonality psychology: Recent trends and emerging directions (pp. 149–159). New York: Springer-Verlag.

56. Mischel, W., & Shoda, Y. (1995). A cognitive-affective system theory of personality: Reconceptualizing situations, dispositions, dynamics, and invariance in personality structure. *Psychological Review, 102,* 246–268.

57. Cantor, N. (1990). From thought to behavior: "Having" and "doing" in the study of personality and cognition. *American Psychologist, 45,* 735–750.

58. Emmons, R. (1986). Personal strivings: An approach to personality and subjective well-being. *Journal of Personality and Social Psychology, 51,* 1058–1068.

59. Palys, T.S., & Little, B.R. (1983). Perceived life satisfaction and the organization of personal project systems. *Journal of Personality and Social Psychology, 44,* 1221–1230.

60. Klinger, E. (1977). *Meaning and void: Inner experience and the incentives in people's lives.* Minneapolis: University of Minnesota Press.

61. Buss, D.M., & Cantor, N. (1989). Introduction. In D.M. Buss & N. Cantor (Eds.), *Personality psychology: Recent trends and emerging directions.* (pp. 1–12). New York: Springer-Verlag.

62. McCrae, R.R., & Costa, P.T., Jr. (1996). Toward a new generation of personality theories: Theoretical contexts for the five-factor model. In J.S. Wiggins (Ed.), *The five-factor model of personality: Theoretical perspectives* (pp. 51–87). New York: Guilford Press.

63. McAdams, D.P., Diamond, A., de St. Aubin, E., & Mansfield, E. (1997). Stories of commitment: The psychosocial construction of generative lives. *Journal of Personality and Social Psychology, 72,* 678–694.

64. McAdams, D.P. (1993). *The stories we live by: Personal myths and the making of the self.* New York: William Morrow.

65. Harvey, J.H., Orbuch, T.L., Chwalisz, K.D., & Garwood, G. (1991). Coping with sexual assault: The roles of account-making and confiding. *Journal of Traumatic Stress, 4,* 515–531.

66. Herman, J.L. (1992). *Trauma and recovery: The aftermath of violence from domestic abuse to political terror.* New York: Basic Books.

67. Pearlman, L.A. & Saakvitne, K.W. (1995). *Trauma and the therapist: Countertransference and vicarious traumatization in psychotherapy with incest survivors.* New York: Norton.

68. Snyder, C.R., McDermott, D., Cook, W., & Rapoff, M.A. (1997). *Hope for the journey: Helping children through good times and bad.* Boulder, CO: Westview Press.

69. Taylor, S.E. (1989). *Positive illusions: Creative self-deception and the healthy mind.* New York: Basic Books.

70. McAdams, D.P. (1985). *Power, intimacy and the life story.* New York: Guilford Press.

71. Erikson, E.H. (1963). *Childhood and society* (2nd ed.). New York: Norton.

72. Colby, A., & Damon, W. (1992). *Some do care: Contemporary lives of moral commitment.* New York: Free Press.

73. McAdams, D.P. (August, 1997). Sequences of redemption and contam-

ination in adults' life stories. Presented at the annual meetings of the American Psychological Association, Chicago.

74. Janoff-Bulman, R., & Frieze, I. (1983). A theoretical perspective for understanding reactions to victimization. *Journal of Social Issues, 39*, 1–17.

75. Thompson, S. & Janigian, A. (1988). Life schemes: A framework for understanding the search for meaning. *Journal of Social and Clinical Psychology, 7*, 260–280.

76. Brickman, P., Coates, T., & Janoff-Bulman, R. (1978). Lottery winners and accident victims: Is happiness relative? *Journal of Personality and Social Psychology, 36*, 917–927.

77. Lazarus, R.A., & Folkman, S. (1984). *Stress, appraisal, and coping.* New York: Springer.

78. Lazarus, R.S. (1991). *Emotion and adaptation.* New York: Oxford University Press.

79. Murphy, L.B. (1974). Coping, vulnerability and resilience in childhood. In C.V. Coelho, D.A. Hamburg, & J.E. Adams (Eds.), *Coping and adaptation* (pp. 69–100). New York: Basic Books.

80. Houston, B.K. (1987). Stress and coping. In C.R. Snyder and C. Ford (Eds.), *Coping with negative life events: Clinical and social-psychological perspectives* (pp. 373–399). New York: Plenum.

81. Coyne, J.C., & Gottlieb, B.H. (1996). The mismeasure of coping by checklist. *Journal of Personality, 64*, 959–992.

82. Folkman, S., & Lazarus, R.S. (1988). *The Ways of Coping Questionnaire.* Palo Alto: Consulting Psychologists Press.

83. Tennen, H., & Affleck, G. (1997). Social comparison as a coping process. In B. Buunk & R. Gibbons (Eds.), *Health, coping and well-being* (pp. 263–298). Hillsdale, N.J.: Erlbaum.

84. Dunkel-Schetter, C., Feinstein, L., Taylor, S.E., & Falke, R. (1992). Patterns of coping with cancer and their correlates. *Health Psychology, 11*, 79–87.

85. Taylor, S.E., & Aspinwall, L.G. (1992). Coping with chronic illness. In L. Goldberger and S. Breznitz (Eds.), *Handbook of stress: Theoretical and clinical aspects* (2nd ed.; pp. 511–531). Toronto: The Free Press.

86. Aldwin, C.M., & Revenson, T.A. (1987). Does coping help? A Reexamination of the relation between coping and mental health. *Journal of Personality and Social Psychology, 53*, 337–348.

87. Rosenstiel, A.K., & Keefe, F.J. (1983). The use of coping strategies in low-back pain patients. Relationship to patient characteristics and current adjustment. *Pain, 17*, 33–40.

88. Tennen, H. & Affleck, G. (1996). Daily processes in coping with chronic pain: Methods and analytic strategies. In M. Zeidner & N. Endler (Eds.), *Handbook of coping* (pp. 151–180). New York: Wiley.

89. Larsen R., & Kasimatis, M. (1991). Day-to-day physical symptoms: Individual differences in the occurrence, duration, and emotional concomitants of minor daily illnesses. *Journal of Personality, 59*, 387–424.

90. Penner, L., Shiffman, S., Paty, J., & Fritzche, B. (1994). Individual differences in intraperson variability in mood. *Journal of Personality and Social Psychology, 66*, 712–721.

91. Stone, A., & Shiffman, S. (1994). Ecological momentary assessment (EMA) in behavioral medicine. *Annals of Behavioral Medicine, 16,* 199–202.

92. Affleck, G., Tennen, H., Urrows, S., Higgins, P., Abeles, M. et al. (1998). Fibromyalgia and the pursuit of personal goals: A daily process analysis. *Health Psychology, 17,* 40–47.

93. Carney, M.A., Tennen, H., Affleck, G., Del Boca, F., & Kranzler, H. (1998). Levels and patterns of alcohol consumption using timeline follow-back, daily diaries, and real-time "electronic interviews." *Journal of Studies on Alcohol, 59,* 447–454.

94. Jaccard, J., & Wan, C. (1993). Statistical analysis of temporal data with many observations: Issues for behavioral medicine data. *Annals of Behavioral Medicine, 15,* 41–50.

95. SAS Institute. (1996). SAS/STAT Software: Changes and enhancements through release 6.11. Cary, North Carolina.

96. Larsen, R., & Diener, E. (1992). Promises and problems with the circumplex model of emotion. In M.S. Clarke (Ed.), *Emotion* (pp. 25–59). Newbury Park, CA: Sage.

97. Affleck, G., Tennen, H., Urrows, S., & Higgins, P. (1994). Person and contextual features of stress reactivity: Individual differences in relations of undesirable daily events with mood disturbance and chronic pain intensity. *Journal of Personality and Social Psychology, 66,* 329–340.

98. Bolger, N., & Schilling, E. (1991). Personality and the problems of everyday life: The role of neuroticism in exposure and reactivity to daily stressors. *Journal of Personality, 59,* 335–386.

14

Rebuilding Shattered Assumptions after Traumatic Life Events

Coping Processes and Outcomes

Ronnie Janoff-Bulman

It is deeply disturbing to consider the tragedies that could befall us, so understandably we direct our thoughts elsewhere. Yet, debilitating accidents, criminal assault, life-threatening disease, rape, early loss of a spouse or child, and natural disasters strike nevertheless, throwing their victims into a state of profound distress and disintegration. How do these people cope? How would you cope if you were the victim of a traumatic life event?

My goal in this chapter is to provide an understanding of what is involved in coping with such experiences. What accounts for the magnitude and severity of the survivor's reaction? What psychological processes are engaged on the road to recovery? What is the prognosis for most survivors, and why? Hopefully, answers to these questions not only will be informative, but will themselves also have the potential to facilitate coping in the aftermath of extreme negative events. If survivors can make sense of their experiences—the emotional pain, the fear, the mental chaos, the detachment, the intrusions, the fault-finding, the unusual interpretations—they are apt to find it easier to move through the coping process without the added psychological burden imposed by questioning their own sanity or their ability to recover. It also may be encouraging to know that for those who successfully arrive at a state of well-being—and most survivors do—there are often unexpected gains that follow from their harrowing experience, and these too should be understood as an important piece of the recovery process.

The key to understanding coping is recognizing the role of fundamental assumptions in our lives. We are typically unaware of these basic beliefs until they have been seriously challenged by traumatic life events. It is the shattering—and ultimately the rebuilding—of these fundamental assumptions that constitute crisis and coping in the aftermath of extreme life events (1), and it is therefore to these assumptions that we turn.

Our Fundamental Assumptions

At the core of our inner world lie several assumptions that serve as automatic guides as we navigate our course through a lifetime of experiences. These basic beliefs are our internal representations or theories about ourselves, the external world, and how these interact. Variously referred to as working models (2), theories of reality (3), structures of meaning (4), or our assumptive world (5), this network of assumptions essentially represents what William James (6) would describe as "our individual way of just seeing and feeling the total push and pull of the cosmos" (p. 4).

Within this diverse network, there are some theories that are more global and basic than others. Thus, your beliefs that you are a good swimmer and a fine piano player, for example, are both less abstract and global than the beliefs that you are a good athlete and a fine musician, which are in turn less abstract and global than the beliefs that you are a competent person and a decent human being. Our assumptions are hierarchically organized (7) with our fundamental assumptions representing those theories that are most general and abstract; they are the most pervasive in their applicability and least subject to disconfirmation. If I think I am an excellent swimmer, yet almost drown when I jump into a pool, it is likely that I will alter my assumption about my swimming ability. Such direct behavioral disconfirmation is least likely to occur in the case of my broadest, most abstract theories; I can believe I am a competent person, for example, even in the face of evidence that I am a poor swimmer. Not only is the specific evidence needed to disconfirm this global theory more ambiguous, but I can overvalue the importance of other abilities or domains (e.g., intellectual, social, other sports), and undervalue the importance of swimming in my self-perception of competence.

Our fundamental assumptions constitute the very foundation of our cognitive-emotional world, and as such they are the internal representations that we are least aware of and least likely to challenge. They are the very bedrock of our inner mental world, and yet we generally are not only unaware of their existence, but also of their content. What are these fundamental assumptions?

The nucleus of our assumptive world includes our fundamental assumptions about the nature of the external world, our theories about the distributions of good and bad outcomes in this world, and our beliefs about ourselves. More specifically, we assume that the world is benevolent, the world is meaningful, and the self is worthy. Certainly, not everyone maintains these fundamental assumptions, but it appears that most people do. If you are among those who believe these assumptions do not apply to you, I would ask that you not yet discount their existence in your assumptive world and the role they play in your life. I ask this not only because what we think we believe and what we actually believe are often not one and the same, but also because 20 years of research with men and women who experienced traumatic life events has made it all too clear that an extreme negative event can readily reveal the very assumptions we are generally all too eager to discount in our lives.

Benevolence of the World

In general, people believe that the world is a good place, or rather that *their* world is a good place. The world in this context refers to both people and events, and the belief in benevolence entails the assumption that people are basically good, caring, and helpful, and that events are predominantly positive rather than negative in outcome. Yet certainly, if we open our eyes, we can all too readily see misery, need, pain, and oppression; there is no dearth of misfortune. How, then, can we maintain an assumption about the benevolence of the world? We do so by psychologically distinguishing between the world in general and the world in which we live; the people and events that touch us constitute our world, and it is these people and events that we expect to be benevolent rather than malevolent. Thus, when discussing their own lives, people are typically optimistic (8), and survey researchers have found that people generally make a distinction between their own lot and that of their nation or the larger world; even when the nation or world are perceived negatively or pessimistically, people still respond positively and optimistically regarding their own lives (9).

This belief in benevolence is powerfully captured by Maya Angelou in her discussion of the title of her book of poetry, *Just Give Me a Cool Drink of Water 'Fore I Diiie* (10). In explaining her choice, Angelou remarks on the remarkable "unconscious innocence" of human beings, who believe that even a murderer would have the compassion to grant us a final glass of sweet water before killing us (11). The phrase "unconscious innocence" is particularly apt in that it describes our assumption about benevolence and our lack of awareness regarding the role such an assumption plays in our lives.

Meaningfulness of the World

Our assumption about the meaningfulness of the world refers specifically to the distribution of good and bad outcomes; in other words, why do particular events happen to particular people? A meaningful world is one in which this distribution "makes sense," for there is a comprehensible contingency between people and their outcomes. We do not believe that misfortune is random or haphazard, but rather that there is a meaningful relationship between people and what happens to them. In science events are comprehensible if they fit certain accepted laws of physical events. In our everyday lives events are comprehensible if they fit certain accepted laws of social phenomena, and in Western culture these are most apt to involve theories of justice or control.

When we invoke justice as an explanation, we perceive outcomes as deserved. From this perspective, peoples' decency, morality, and goodness essentially determine what happens to them. As the just world theory (12) suggests, we believe that people get what they deserve and deserve what they get, and this worldview enables us to minimize the role of randomness in our lives. Misfortune is regarded as the appropriate lot of those who are morally corrupt. We seem to have a need to blame the rape victim for being sexually provocative or the car accident victim for being drunk, and we find ourselves searching for other "comprehensible" causes when these explanations are proven mistaken. When justice provides the basis of our perception of person-outcome contingencies, we view positive events as rewards and negative events as punishments. This orientation is well illustrated by Brother Juniper's conclusions about the five travelers who fell to their death in Thornton Wilder's *The Bridge of San Luis Rey* (13). "He thought he saw in the same accident, the wicked visited by destruction and the good called early to Heaven" (p. 219).

Justice explanations, which are based on our judgments about people's character, are not the only ones that render an outcome comprehensible. Sometimes we specifically turn to people's behaviors and understand outcomes more directly in terms of what people did prior to the event. We assume that we can control what happens to us by engaging in the "right" behaviors, and therefore we see a natural association between outcomes and what people did, rather than who they are (i.e., justice). From this perspective, if you drive carefully you won't be in a car accident, if you exercise and eat well you won't get sick, and if you avoid certain city streets you won't be mugged. Certainly such behaviors may decrease the likelihood of the negative outcomes, but unfortunately they will not reduce the probability to zero. Careful drivers are hit by other cars, trim runners die of heart attacks, and people who know city survival tactics still get physically assaulted on our nation's streets. Nevertheless, our exaggerated belief in control contributes to our blaming victims of extreme negative events.

This exaggeration of control is also apparent in our perceptions of control over obviously chance events. Practice, effort, and exertion are strategies that have a positive impact on outcomes that are within our control, such as performance on a fair test. Researchers have shown, however, that people believe these strategies also impact purely chance outcomes as well (14, 15, 16). The ritualized behaviors of gamblers and people's superstitious behaviors in general suggest the extent to which people believe that "right" behaviors—whether shaking the dice three times or wearing red socks—will bring about a positive outcome. In Western society, personal control is a fundamental way of understanding outcomes in our world.

Other cultures may use different social theories or laws, which nevertheless serve to explain person-outcome contingencies. Thus, when his son's boat is overturned by a hippopotamus, the Azande father, living in the Sudan, turns to witchcraft to explain the event (17). Although he is fully aware that the boy actually died by drowning, the father seeks to explain why this happened to his son. Why did the path of the hippopotamus cross his son's path? In other words, why did this happen to his son? For the Azande father a witch or sorcerer brought about the misfortune; it was not a random or haphazard event. Like our own beliefs in justice and control, witchcraft can explain the selective incidence of events, and it is this selective incidence—why given outcomes happen to particular people—that is addressed by our basic assumptions about the meaningfulness of the world.

Self-Worth

A third fundamental assumption at the foundation of our inner world is self-worth, the belief that we are good, decent, competent people. This is a global self-evaluation, and as psychological research consistently demonstrates, people generally evaluate themselves positively. Like the kids at Garrison Keillor's fabled Lake Wobegon, people's self-evaluations reflect a belief that they are above average, and researchers consistently find that scores on self-esteem scales are skewed toward the positive end of the distribution (8, 18). We regard ourselves as capable and decent because we are able to focus on the positive aspects of ourselves, overvalue our strengths, ignore our weaknesses, and exaggerate our responsibility for positive outcomes (19, 20, 21). Regarding justice, we see ourselves as the type of person who deserves good things, and regarding control, we see ourselves as the type of person who engages in the right behaviors. Our self-worth, then, provides us with further support for believing in our own comfort and security.

We believe we are good people who live in a meaningful, benevolent world. These fundamental assumptions are built and substantiated by years of experience. Originating in our earliest experiences, our theories about our self and our world grow out of our preverbal representations first established through interactions with a responsive caregiver (23, 24, 25). When caregivers respond to infants' cries, they are providing the earliest evidence of a world in which others are benevolent and there is a person-outcome contingency; throughout these interactions the seed is also planted for the infant to perceive the self as worthy of such care. To develop these positive representations, it is not necessary for the caregiving to be superb or maximally responsive, but simply "good enough" (22, 23, 24). Work with infants suggests that by the age of seven months, they have already begun to construct higher level generalizations about self and others based on their experiences (25), and these function as the preverbal foundation for our fundamental assumptions about benevolence, meaning, and self-worth.

Within the domain of research derived from attachment theory (2), it appears that a "secure" attachment style most closely parallels these positive fundamental assumptions. A secure child is one who has had responsive caretaking and thereby feels confident to explore his or her surroundings in the absence of the mother; this is the child who is also accepting of the mother following a brief separation (26). In recent work that has extended attachment styles to adulthood and, in particular, to expectations and interactions in romantic relationships, secure adults are characterized as comfortable with both intimacy and autonomy, and their experience of love is described as trusting, happy, and friendly (27). To differentiate a secure style from insecure attachment styles in adulthood, researchers have crossed positive and negative views of self with positive and negative views of others; a securely attached adult has both a positive view of self and a positive view of others, whereas different types of insecure attachment (i.e., preoccupied, dismissing, and fearful) complete the other cells in the model (28). Although this research paradigm was developed and applied only to people's thoughts and behaviors regarding adult romantic relationships, the positive self–positive other orientation surely has an impact on far more than these specific interactions. These reflect fundamental assumptions that color how we approach the world in general.

Our basic beliefs about benevolence, meaning, and self-worth afford us the sense of trust and safety necessary to tackle each new day, but they go further to provide us with a feeling of relative invulnerability. After all, an internal dialogue based on these assumptions might read as follows: "In our world, positive outcomes and good people predominate, and even if bad things happen, they happen to people who acted improperly or are bad people. I'm a good person and I do the right things, so I'm protected. Bad things can't happen to me."

There is a great deal of research demonstrating that people overestimate the likelihood of good things happening to them and underestimate the likelihood of negative outcomes. Such "unrealistic optimism" (29, 30) has been found regardless of gender, age, occupation, and education (8). This positive illusion is very robust and seems to follow directly from the fundamental assumptions that reside at the very bedrock of our inner world.

We typically move through life feeling safe and secure. Intellectually, we may acknowledge that bad things happen, but in our gut we don't believe they will happen to us. Even if we know people get into car accidents or get raped or get diagnosed with life-threatening illnesses, we feel certain that somehow we will avoid these negative experiences—if not by who we are, then by what we do. We believe we can and will take the precautions necessary to fend off misfortune. Not surprisingly, then, "I never thought it could happen to me" was the sentence I heard most often during my 20 years of research with individuals who had experienced traumatic life events in adulthood.

The Traumatic Experience:
Shattered Assumptions

The comfort and complacency provided by our positive views of the world, the self, and the relationship between the two are radically fractured by traumatic life events (1, 31, 32, 33). Victimizations ranging from physical assault to debilitating accidents and life-threatening disease strike at the core of our inner world and shatter our fundamental assumptions. Suddenly, survivors are forced to confront their own vulnerability. They come face to face with their own fragility.

In writing about the philosophy and sociology of science, Thomas Kuhn argues that most science—"normal" science—proceeds by working within the comfortable framework provided by accepted paradigms (34). These are the broadest schemas that drive scientific activity, and typically research and theory-building proceed through minor, additive adjustments of knowledge. Typically, data, even somewhat anomalous data, can be readily assimilated by the accepted paradigms. Kuhn goes on to write, however, that there are times when basic paradigms are simply stretched too far, and the paradigms themselves are called into question. These are times characterized by scientific revolutions, which are marked by periods of extreme crisis in science.

So, too, does extreme crisis characterize the profound challenge posed to accepted paradigms within the psyche of a single individual. These are times of trauma for the person, times when the fundamental assumptions that had previously served as comfortable guides to reality are recognized as powerfully inadequate and painfully false. The person's victimizing experience cannot be accounted for by theories that describe the world as good and caring, events as comprehensible, and the self as worthy and competent, and a state of psychological disintegration results. For survivors of extreme negative events, old securities and certainties are gone; they have been made intensely aware that bad things can happen to them.

Trauma is not the stuff of "normal" change. We often experience changes in our inner world, for the very process of learning involves adjustments in our theories of the world and ourselves. Yet, these changes are likely to occur in our narrower assumptions, which are most apt to be responsive to behavioral feedback. As we acquire knowledge and skills, our schemas about specific stimuli and abilities are altered. Yet these are not our fundamental assumptions, our most abstract generalizations underlying the entire conceptual system. Further, any changes are likely to be incremental—small and gradual. Such changes do not disrupt the entire system.

Thus, "normal" change occurs slowly and incrementally at the level of our narrower, more specific theories. There are life events that alter some of our broader assumptions, but these too are apt to entail gradual changes. Role transitions, for example, occur at different points in our lives—entering kindergarten, high school, college, getting a job, getting married, becoming a parent—and affect our more general views of ourselves. Still less basic than our fundamental assumptions about benevolence, meaning, and self-worth, this change process is also unlikely to involve massive disruption of the conceptual system. Typically, the transition process involves a great deal of psychological preparation by a culture interested in easing people into new roles. The young child is given preparatory information, the college student anticipates the world of work, and the pregnant woman is showered with information and stories about motherhood. Stability and coherence are the norm in such cases, whereas instability and incoherence characterize traumatic experiences.

Sudden, unexpected change at the level of our most fundamental assumptions is overwhelming. Individuals who have experienced traumatic life events know the terror of their own vulnerability. Traumatic victimization involves the perception of threat to our very survival; assaults, accidents, diseases, either involving the self or a loved one, force individuals to confront the possibility of their own annihilation. Survivors experience "a jarring awareness of the fact of death" (35, p.481) and are now all too aware of their own mortality. It is as if a serious threat to our biological integrity powerfully undermines our psychological integrity as well. We generally live in the world of symbols and take for granted our biological "creatureliness." As Kierkegaard has so aptly put it, it appears like some hoax that we can have consciousness, self-expression, deep feelings, and yet are creatures that die (36). The terror of our confrontation with our own fragility is captured by Ernest Becker (37) when he writes that seeing the world as it really is "is devastating and terrifying . . . it makes 'routine, automatic, secure, self-confident activity impossible. . . . ' It places a trembling animal at the mercy of the entire cosmos and the problem of meaning in it" (p.26).

Overwhelming life events deal victims a double dose of anxiety. Their fundamental assumptions have been shattered, and they not only perceive a frightening universe in which they are unsafe and unprotected, but their disintegrated inner world has left them without any road map for negotiating daily living. Survivors often experience hyperarousal and hyperreactivity, physiological responses that mirror their psychological state. In one fell swoop, their comfortable, secure world—internal and external—has been destroyed, to be replaced by intense fear and anxiety. The proportions of the traumatic experience are overwhelming. How, then, do such survivors cope?

Coping Processes: Rebuilding the Assumptive World

For individuals who have experienced a traumatic life event, coping involves the rebuilding of their inner world. This is an arduous task that is framed by two possibilities. At one extreme are the old, comforting assumptions that no longer seem valid, but would certainly be comfortable.

At the other extreme are the frightening assumptions implied by the victim-ization, assumptions involving malevolence, meaninglessness, and per-sonal inadequacy; these now seem valid, yet emotionally they are very dis-turbing. The old assumptions are recognized for what they are—illusions that do not describe the world or account for life outcomes. Survivors can-not simply embrace their old, comforting assumptions, for their confron-tations with mortality and human fragility now preclude embracing such seemingly naive beliefs. Yet, these same survivors also are motivated to avoid wholly accepting the new, threatening assumptions, for this would spell continuous anxiety and dread.

Coping involves navigating a course between these two extremes and ultimately creating a set of assumptions that can account for the traumatic experience, yet provide some modicum of personal solace. In essence, sur-vivors struggle to move toward their old assumptions, while developing a new worldview that allows for the real possibility of misfortune. Social support is particularly helpful following traumatic life events, for caring others provide strong, directly experienced support that the world is be-nevolent and the survivor is worthy. Support by others provides a context that in many ways reenacts the process of building positive assumptions in early childhood; at that time the positive assumptions were first con-structed through interactions with responsive caregivers, whereas now they are reconstructed through supportive interactions as well.

In the immediate aftermath of the traumatic event, survivors are aided by automatic psychological processes that help them get through each day. They also engage in a number of motivated cognitive strategies that con-tinue long after the automatic processes cease to be needed. It is via these motivated strategies that survivors implicitly attempt to revisit questions of benevolence, meaning, and self-worth, so as to create a viable assumptive world. First, however, they must get through the intense emotional crisis posed by the combination of a disintegrated inner world and a threatening external world.

Automatic Processes

Thankfully, in the days and weeks following the extreme experience, a sort of psychological detachment sets in that helps survivors go through the motions of daily life. Discussed in terms of both emotional numbing and cognitive denial, this "denial numbness" (38, 39) enables the individual to modulate the massive onslaught of the victimization. The organism largely shuts down; the survivor feels little and acknowledges little about the threatening implications of the trauma. This "psychic closing-off" (35) al-lows a slower, more incremental process of cognitive-emotional change to be implemented. The survivor's acute state of arousal needs to be somewhat dissipated in order for the "work" of integration and rebuilding to begin (40). Numbing and denial help the survivor establish some psychological equilibrium, a kind of "pseudoadjustment," in the immediate aftermath of the experience. Yet over time, as the arousal diminishes and the ability to confront the experience grows, the intensity and pervasiveness of denial and numbing decrease. Over the course of the healing process, psychological detachment and shutting down give way to psychological engagement with the traumatic experience and its implications.

Yet the need to confront the trauma, and the efforts at rebuilding that constitute the survivor's primary coping task, are not entirely absent, even during the most intense early periods of numbing and denial. The person's implicit motivation to deal with the trauma is simply too great, and there is a type of "breakthrough" effect even in the midst of the denial numbness. This is the involuntary reexperiencing of the victimizing event that is so common in the aftermath of extreme life events. Through intrusive recollections or distressing dreams, survivors relive the experience and their trauma. Their thoughts and memories are extremely disturbing, but they are symptomatic not simply of the survivor's distress, but rather of the survivor's need to process and integrate the experience. Not surprisingly, numbing and reexperiencing are regarded as the sine qua non of traumatic stress (e.g., see DSM criteria for the diagnosis of PTSD). The numbing and denial protect the survivor from excessive amounts of anxiety and arousal, whereas the intrusive reexperiencing are in the service of the crucial reconstruction process that requires directly confronting the threatening experience (38,39). In essence, the two processes work in tandem; intrusive recollections break through the barrier of detachment, and as the reexperiencing episode gets overwhelming, numbing once again takes over. There is a striking balance between approach and avoidance processes, and it is during these relatively early days of coping, which can take days, weeks, or months, that any therapeutic interventions must be extremely sensitive to the individual survivor's relative comfort in confronting the traumatic experience.

As survivors successfully move through the healing process, not only do numbing and denial decrease, but reexperiencing the trauma increases. Over time, however, control over this reexperiencing shifts, such that thoughts and images are no longer unbidden and involuntary, but consciously and intentionally considered.

Motivated Cognitive Strategies

As survivors struggle to integrate their experience, they are motivated to understand what happened in ways that are themselves minimally threatening. If their experience is perceived as wholly malevolent and meaningless, for example, it is far more difficult to create an assumptive world that is not also extremely threatening and distressing. To the extent that positive interpretations can be placed on the experience—interpretations that maximize perceptions of benevolence, meaningfulness, or self-worth—the rebuilt inner world can be both accurate and comfortable. After traumatic events, then, survivors engage in interpretive strategies that are motivated by a healthy system striving to recover. It is not that survivors consciously will these strategies; they do not say to themselves, "Okay, I need to rebuild my assumptive world and therefore need to change how I interpret my experience." Rather, the strategies are essentially natural products of a healthy organism seeking equilibrium after a crisis. Three examples of such constructive interpretations involve comparison processes, self-blame, and reevaluations of the event as beneficial. Although these may not strike the reader as necessarily constructive, they nevertheless serve survivors well in their efforts to rebuild their fundamental assumptions.

Comparison Processes.   It is a well-accepted psychological finding that people frequently evaluate their outcomes by comparing them with the outcomes of others. Based on years of social psychological research, however, it is apparent that our choice of the comparison other is quite flexible. Thus, early research suggested that we compared with similar others or with those who have done somewhat better at a task (41, 42, 43). In fact, when we seek accurate self-evaluations, we do seek similar others, whereas when we seek self-improvement, we look to those who are better off and can potentially provide us with information about how to do better—that is, we make upward comparisons. More recently, it has also become clear that there are times when we compare with those who have performed more poorly or who are worse off than we. In such cases of downward comparisons, we are motivated by self-enhancement; we want to feel better about ourselves and therefore compare with others whose outcomes are not as good as our own (43, 44, 45). We have a great deal of freedom in our choice of comparisons, and thus this is actually a creative psychological process, reflecting our own motivations at the time.

In the aftermath of traumatic events, when survivors are feeling very threatened, they often engage in downward social comparisons. As Shelley Taylor and her colleagues have illustrated in her work, survivors compare their own experience with that of real or hypothetical others as one means of feeling better about themselves and their world (44). It is not at all uncommon to hear survivors say, "It could have been worse." They are considering their outcome in light of worse possible outcomes, either real or imagined, and most people can think of a worse outcome. People think of greater losses, greater injuries. The paraplegic after the accident compares with the quadriplegic, the middle-aged mastectomy patient compares with the younger woman, the tornado victim who has lost all physical possessions compares with the victim who has lost a family member, and the assault victim who has suffered psychological degradation compares with the victim who has also experienced physical injuries. If we choose the right attribute or dimension, we generally can imagine ourselves better off than somebody.

When working with survivors, it is always somewhat surprising to hear someone say, "I was lucky. It could have been a lot worse." True, it probably could have been worse, but of course to nonvictims, the relevant comparison when thinking about the survivor's experience is the experience of no victimization. There seems to be little that might be deemed fortunate about the survivor's lot. Yet, to the individual who has experienced the traumatic event, the possibility of a worse outcome—a "hypothetical worse world" (44)—provides a psychologically more useful comparison, one that minimizes threat and facilitates coping.

Self-Blame.   Whether victimized by assault, rape, life-threatening disease, disabling accident, or unexpected loss of a loved one, survivors engage in considerable self-blame after the traumatic experience (for a review, see 46). They engage in far more self-blame than would appear warranted by outsiders or observers. What accounts for the pervasiveness of this response?

Survivors are motivated by recovery, not accuracy. If they can perceive or impose some person-outcome contingency, some comprehensible relationship between themselves and what happened to them, then they can minimize the perceived randomness of the world. So survivors reevaluate their own role in the traumatic experience. They search for their own possible contribution to the outcome, and as such maximize the meaningfulness of their experience.

Past research has suggested that there are at least two types of self-blame, both of which satisfy the search for person-outcome contingency (47). Characterological self-blame reflects assessments about the decency or goodness of a person, and as such focuses on the person's enduring qualities or character. Behavioral self-blame, on the other hand, is a less global evaluation and instead focuses on specific behaviors, the acts or omissions that are perceived as having contributed to the traumatic event. Thus, a rape victim who says she is a bad person or the type of person who cannot be trusted is engaging in characterological self-blame, while a rape victim who says that she should not have hitchhiked or should not have gone back to a man's apartment is engaging in behavioral self-blame; the former is esteem-related, whereas the latter is control-related. Although both self-attributions provide a person-outcome contingency and minimize randomness, there are certainly more costs associated with characterological self-blame, including decrements in self-esteem and the possible perception of oneself as a chronic victim. With its more specific, narrow attributional focus, behavioral self-blame is more likely to protect against loss of self-esteem; it is a particular behavior rather than the more global self that is deemed blameworthy. Further, behavioral self-blame also provides for a decreased sense of future vulnerability, because survivors can believe that by altering particular behaviors (presumably far easier than changing basic character) they can minimize the probability of future victimizations. Behavioral self-blame is particularly common following traumatic life events.

Survivors play and replay their experience, looking for ways that they could have contributed to the outcome. Researchers who have focused on crime victims report that these survivors often seem eager to take responsibility by pointing to specific behaviors for which they fault themselves (48, 49); it might be leaving a window open or walking on a particular street. "If you have been raped and are still alive, you will forever ask yourself why you didn't fight harder, why you didn't think of some trick to break away, or why you didn't engage in some act—obvious to you now—which would have prevented rape" (50, p. 95). Parents of terminally ill children look for something they did or failed to do that could have altered the devastating outcome, and victims of life-threatening diseases blame themselves for eating the wrong foods, working too hard, and not taking care of themselves (51, 52, 53). These do not necessarily represent accurate assessments, but probably rather reflect the survivor's need to minimize threat by imposing a comprehensible, reassuring appraisal onto the event.

Positive Reevaluations of the Traumatic Event.   Self-blame is an early, virtually knee-jerk response to survivors' newfound anxiety about meaninglessness and malevolence. Over time, efforts to move closer to old, comfortable assumptions increasingly take the form of reevaluations of the traumatic event itself. Survivors essentially transform the experience through interpretations that focus on benefits, thereby emphasizing benevolence over malevolence, meaning over meaninglessness, and self-worth over self-abasement. Long after the traumatizing experience, survivors' confrontations with their victimization is no longer wholly threatening, but rather includes new, far more consoling evaluations framed primarily in terms of suffering for a purpose.

Many survivors come to perceive their victimization as providing benefits to others. Although at times their interpretations may not be readily comprehensible to observers, they nevertheless make sense when understood within the context of the need to rebuild fundamental assumptions. I still vividly recall a young man, paraplegic as a result of a car accident, telling me that everything was fine because God needed his legs for someone else. Concentration camp survivors speak of the significance of bearing witness for others so that future evils might be avoided. Rape victims, AIDS victims, and Vietnam veterans have often used their experience to help others directly through outreach projects and crisis centers. Their victimization is now perceived as the source of a new altruistic orientation in their lives.

Survivors more readily transform their victimization by perceiving benefits to the self, particularly in terms of important lessons learned. Their suffering now has redeeming value, for they are somehow better people for having gone through it. Many survivors discuss a newfound sense of their own strengths and possibilities. Not only are they more caring and compassionate, but they are also far stronger. They recognize their ability to handle "just about anything"; after all, they "went through hell" and have come through with a renewed appreciation for themselves. They are more confident that regardless of what life has in store for them, they will be able to manage successfully. Apparently, what doesn't kill you may truly make you stronger.

The traumatic experience is perceived as a great teacher, not only of one's own strengths, but also of life's value. And it is this aspect of victimization—its ability to transform how survivors perceive their lives—that is one of the most powerful and persistent outcomes of the traumatic experience. Motivated largely by a healthy organism seeking to cope with the terrifying losses associated with trauma—the loss of a safe, secure external world and the loss of a workable, comfortable inner world—survivors understand not only that bad things can happen, but also that good things are to be appreciated.

The Legacy of Traumatic Experiences: Tempered Disillusionment and Appreciation

Even years after traumatic life events, survivors' fundamental assumptions are less positive than they had been previctimization (1). No longer do they reflect absolute beliefs in benevolence, meaningfulness, and self-worth. Rather, survivors have been stripped of illusions and know that tragedy can strike at any time. Yet their new assumptive worlds, reconstructed over time, are typically not wholly negative and threatening. Instead, they are generally positive, but allow for the real possibility of misfortune. Surely, there are survivors who are not so successful, who overgeneralize from their traumatic experience and now hold wholly negative, threatening assumptions about the world and themselves; intense anxiety and despair define their lives. Yet this is not the lot of the majority of survivors, who instead incorporate their experience within a more benign set of assumptions. For them, the world is benevolent and meaningful, *but not always*; the self is competent and worthy and can make a real difference, *but not always*. With the help of other people, automatic processes, and motivated strategies, most survivors successfully rebuild an inner world that is comfortable, yet reflects their experience.

Survivors have been changed by their traumatic experience. Their world is forever altered, but not simply for the worse. In fact, increasingly studies suggest that there are both positive and negative consequences of victimization, and that these changes are reported by the same survivors (1, 54, 55). They know the pain of shattered assumptions and the jarring awareness of their own vulnerability; they know human outcomes can be random and meaningless. Yet, they also experience the pleasure of a newfound appreciation of life and sense of value in their daily existence (1, 31, 53, 54, 55, 56, 57, 58, 59, 60, 61). These positive reappraisals of their life do not occur in spite of the negative consequences of their victimization, but rather because of them. It is through knowing the fragility of human existence and the real possibility of loss that survivors arrive at a new understanding of life's value.

The traumatic experience forever resides in the minds of survivors, easily imagined and accessible (62). It is always there as a reminder of what was and could be—loss and pain. This provides a new context for evaluating their daily experiences, and whether considered from the psychological perspective of simulation processes (63,64), adaptation level theory (65, 66), anchoring and adjustment (62), or norm theory (67), the traumatic experience provides a potent contrast against which to positively compare elements of daily living. This salient event is always there to endow previously underappreciated elements of the survivor's life with pleasure and value.

Uniformly positive assumptions, such as those that largely define the inner world of nonvictims, are less likely to foster attitudes of appreciation. Good fortune is certainly no guarantee of appreciative attitudes. Most of us take our lives, or important aspects of our lives, for granted, expecting positive outcomes and failing to notice what we have. As Thornton Wilder's Emily in *Our Town* (68) remarks when she returns to Grover's Corners after her death, "I didn't realize. So all that was going on and we never noticed? . . . Oh, earth, you're too wonderful for anybody to realize you" (p. 138). And as another deceased character notes, to be alive is to "move about in a cloud of ignorance. . . . To spend and waste time as though you had a million years" (68, p. 140). Survivors of traumatic events are now all too aware that they don't have a million years; awareness of their mortality is ever-present in their minds.

Suddenly living is precious, and survivors strive to create value and worth in their daily existence. Now that life has been stripped to its essentials, they reconsider what is important to them and engage in a reordering of priorities. Survivors report that they now know what really matters; they now live their lives more fully and are not "just existing." Many remark that they now spend time on "the important things." For most, these "important things" include people they care about—close family and friends— although social causes and some form of spirituality are also often mentioned; survivors seem to particularly value connection with others (69), whether those close to them, the larger community that could benefit from their efforts, or something they define as far greater than themselves in understanding their relation to the world.

Survivors actively consider what is important to them. They do not live life on the surface, but make choices and commitments. In the more immediate aftermath of their victimization, their efforts were largely devoted to coming to terms with a world that seemed malevolent and meaningless, in the sense that there was no comprehensible relationship between people and what happened to them. Yet over time this concern with meaning "out there" appears to give way to a concern with a different sort of meaning, that associated with significance and worth rather than comprehensibility

(70). Survivors establish their own meaning in life, as if aware that they must, as Sartre (71) argues, create their own values out of nothingness. Survivors know life cannot be taken for granted; they know that misfortune can occur when least expected, and so they recognize the preciousness of existence.

Survivors often say that they would never have chosen their victimization, but they recognize that it has had its invaluable lessons and benefits. They possess a special sort of wisdom, aware of the greatest threats and deepest gifts of human existence. Life is simultaneously terrifying and wonderful. Their traumatic experience was undeniably agonizing, and yet, having successfully struggled to rebuild their inner world, survivors emerge profoundly and gratefully aware of the extraordinary value of life in the face of the ever-present possibility of loss.

References

1. Janoff-Bulman, R. (1992). *Shattered assumptions: Towards a new psychology of trauma.* New York: Free Press.
2. Bowlby, J. (1969). *Attachment and loss* (Vol. 1): *Attachment.* London: Hogarth.
3. Epstein, S. (1973). The self-concept revisited, or a theory of a theory. *American Psychologist, 28,* 404–416.
4. Marris, P. (1975). *Loss and change.* Garden City, New York: Anchor/ Doubleday.
5. Parkes, C. M. (1975). What becomes of redundant world models? A contribution to the study of adaptation to change. *British Journal of Medical Psychology, 48,* 131–37.
6. James, W. (1907). *Pragmatism.* NY: Longmans, Green, & Co.
7. Epstein, S. (1980). The self-concept: A review and the proposal of an integrated theory of personality. In E. Staub (Ed.), *Personality: Basic issues and current research.* Englewood Cliffs, NJ: Prentice-Hall.
8. Taylor, S. E. (1990). *Positive illusions: Creative self-deception and the healthy mind.* New York: Basic Books.
9. Watts, W., & Free, L. A. (1978). *State of the nation III.* Lexington, MA: Lexington Books.
10. Angelou, M. (1971). *Just give me a cool drink of water 'fore I diiie.* New York: Random House.
11. Weller, S. (1973). Work in progress: Maya Angelou. *Intellectual Digest,* June 1973, 11–12, 14.
12. Lerner, M. J. (1980). *The belief in a just world.* New York: Plenum.
13. Wilder, T. (1927). *The bridge of San Luis Rey.* New York: Grosset & Dunlap.
14. Langer, E. J. (1975). The illusion of control. *Journal of Personality and Social Psychology, 32,* 311–328.
15. Wortman, C. B. (1975). Some determinants of perceived control. *Journal of Personality and Social Psychology, 31,* 282–294.
16. Henslin, J. M. (1967). Craps and magic. *American Journal of Sociology, 73,* 316–330.

17. Gluckman, M. (1944). The logic of African science and witchcraft: An appreciation of Evans-Pritchard's "Witchcraft Oracles and Magic among the Azande" of the Sudan. *The Rhodes-Livingstone Institute Journal*, June 1944, 61–71.
18. Taylor, S. E., & Brown, J. D. (1988). Illusion and well-being: A social-psychological perspective on mental health. *Psychological Bulletin, 103*, 193–210.
19. Greenwald, A. G. (1980). The totalitarian ego: Fabrication and revision of personal history. *American Psychologist, 35*, 603–618.
20. Brown, J. D. (1986). Evaluations of self and others: Self-enhancement biases in social judgments. *Social Cognition, 4*, 353–376.
21. Snyder, C. R., Higgins, R. L., & Stucky, R. J. (1983). *Excuses: The masquerade solution*. New York: Wiley.
22. Fairbairn, W. R. D. (1952). *An object-relations theory of the personality*. New York: Basic Books.
23. Winnecott, D. W. (1965). *The maturational process and the facilitating environment*. New York: International Universities Press.
24. Greenberg, J. R., & Mitchell, S. A. (1983). *Object relations in psychoanalytic theory*. Cambridge, MA: Harvard University Press.
25. Stern, D. N. (1985). *The interpersonal world of the infant: A view from psychoanalysis and developmental psychology*. New York: Basic Books.
26. Ainsworth, M. D. S., Blehar, M. C., Waters, E., & Wall, S. (1978). *Patterns of attachment*. Hillsdale, NJ: Erlbaum.
27. Hazan, C., & Shaver, P. (1987). Romantic love conceptualized as an attachment process. *Journal of Personality and Social Psychology, 52*, 511–524.
28. Bartholomew, K., & Horowitz, L. M. (1991). Attachment styles among young adults: A test of a four-category model. *Journal of Personality and Social Psychology, 61*, 226–244.
29. Weinstein, N. D. (1980). Unrealistic optimism about future life events. *Journal of Personality and Social Psychology, 39*, 806–820.
30. Weinstein, N. D. (1989). Optimistic biases about personal risks. *Science, 246*, 1232–1233.
31. Janoff-Bulman, R. (1985). The aftermath of victimization: Rebuilding shattered assumptions. In C. Figley (Ed.), *Trauma and its wake: The study and treatment of post-traumatic stress disorder*. New York: Brunner/Mazel.
32. Epstein, S. (1991). The self-concept, the traumatic neurosis, and the structure of personality. In D. Ozer, J. M. Healy, Jr., & A. J. Stewart (Eds.), *Perspectives on personality* (Vol. 3). London: Jessica Kingsley.
33. McCann, I. L., & Pearlman, L. A. (1990). *Psychological trauma and the adult survivor: Theory, therapy, and transformation*. New York: Brunner/Mazel.
34. Kuhn, T. S. (1962). *The structure of scientific revolutions*. Chicago: The University of Chicago Press.
35. Lifton, R. J. (1967). *Death in life: Survivors of Hiroshima*. New York: Simon and Schuster.
36. Kierkegaard, S. (1944). *The concept of dread*. Princeton, NJ: Princeton University Press.

37. Becker, E. (1973). *The denial of death*. New York: Free Press.
38. Horowitz, M. (1976). *Stress response syndromes*. New York: Aronson.
39. Horowitz, M. (1982). Stress response syndromes and their *treatment*. In L. Goldberger and S. Bresnitz (Eds.), *Handbook of stress*. New York: Free Press.
40. Epstein, S. (1967). Toward a unified theory of anxiety. In B. A. Maher (Ed.), *Progress in experimental personality research* (Vol. 4). New York: Academic Press.
41. Festinger, L. (1954). A theory of social comparison processes. *Human relations, 40,* 427–428.
42. Suls, J. M., & Miller, L. M., Eds. (1977). *Social comparison processes: Theoretical and empirical perspectives*. New York: Wiley.
43. Wood, J. V. (1989). Theory and research concerning social comparisons of personal attributes. *Psychological Bulletin, 106,* 231–248.
44. Taylor, S. E., Wood, J. V., & Lichtman, R. R. (1983). It could be worse: Selective evaluation as a response to victimization. *Journal of Social Issues, 39(2),* 19–40.
45. Wills, T. A. (1981). Downward comparison principles in social psychology. *Psychological Bulletin, 90,* 245–271.
46. Janoff-Bulman, R., & Lang-Gunn, L. (1989). Coping with disease and accidents: The role of self-blame attributions. In L. Y. Abramson (Ed.), *Social-personal inference in clinical psychology*. New York: Guilford.
47. Janoff-Bulman, R. (1979). Characterological versus behavioral self-blame: Inquiries into depression and rape. *Journal of Personality and Social Psychology, 37,* 1798–1809.
48. Bard, M., & Sangrey, D. (1979). *The crime victim's book*. New York: Basic Books.
49. Medea, A., & Thompson, K. (1974). *Against rape*. New York: Farrar, Straus, & Giroux.
50. Hursch, C. J. (1977). *The trouble with rape*. Chicago: Nelson-Hall.
51. Bard, M., & Dyk, R. B. (1956). The psychodynamic significance of beliefs regarding the cause of serious illness. *Psychoanalytic Review, 43,* 146–162.
52. Chodoff, P., Friedman, S. B., & Hamburg, D. A. (1964). Stress, defense, and coping behavior: Observations in parents of children with malignant disease. *American Journal of Psychiatry, 120,* 743–749.
53. Taylor, S. E. (1983). Adjustment to threatening events: A theory of cognitive adaptation. *American Psychologist, 38,* 1161–1173.
54. Collins, R. L., Taylor, S. E., & Skokan, L. A. (1990). A better world or a shattered vision: Changes in life perspectives following victimization. *Social Cognition, 8,* 263–285.
55. Lehman, D. R., Davis, C. G., DeLongis, A., Wortman, C. B., Bluck, S., Mandel, D. R., & Ellard, J. (1993). Positive and negative life changes following bereavement and their relations to adjustment. *Journal of Social and Clinical Psychology, 12,* 90–112.
56. Affleck, G., Tennen, H., & Gershman, K. (1985). Cognitive adaptations to high-risk infants: The search for mastery, meaning, and protection from future harm. *American Journal of Mental Deficiency, 89,* 653–656.
57. Schwartzberg, S. S. (1996). *A crisis of meaning: How gay men are making sense of AIDS*. New York: Oxford University Press.

58. Silver, R. L., & Wortman, C. B. (1980). Coping with undesirable life events. In J. Garber & M. E. P. Seligman (Eds.), *Human helplessness: Theory and application.* New York: Academic Press.
59. Tedeschi, R. G., & Calhoun, L. G. (1996). The posttraumatic growth inventory: Measuring the positive legacy of trauma. *Journal of Traumatic Stress, 9,* 455–471.
60. Thompson, S. C. (1991). The search for meaning following a stroke. *Basic and Applied Social Psychology, 12,* 81–96.
61. Thompson, S. C., & Janigian, A. S. (1988). Life schemes: A framework for understanding the search for meaning. *Journal of Social and Clinical Psychology, 7,* 260–280.
62. Kahneman, D., & Tversky, A. (1973). On the psychology of prediction. *Psychological Review, 80,* 237–251.
63. Kahneman, D., & Tversky, A. (1982). The simulation heuristic. In D. Kahneman, P. Slovic, and A. Tversky (Eds.), *Judgment under uncertainty: Heuristics and biases.* New York: Cambridge University Press.
64. Taylor, S. E., & Schneider, S. K. (1989). Coping and the simulation of events. *Social Cognition, 7,* 176–196.
65. Brickman, P., Coates, D., & Janoff-Bulman, R. (1978). Lottery winners and accident victims: Is happiness relative? *Journal of Personality and Social Psychology, 36,* 917–927.
66. Helson, H. (1964). Adaptation level theory: An experimental and systematic approach to behavior. New York: Harper.
67. Kahneman, D., & Miller, D. T. (1986). Norm theory: Comparing reality to its alternatives. *Psychological Review, 93,* 136–153.
68. Wilder, T. (1975). *Our town.* New York: Avon Books.
69. Herman, J. L. (1992). *Trauma and recovery.* New York: Basic Books.
70. Janoff-Bulman, R., & Frantz, C. M. (1997). The impact of trauma on meaning: From meaningless world to meaningful life. In M. Power & C. Brewin (Eds.), *The transformation of meaning in psychological therapies: Integrating theory and practice.* Sussex, England: Wiley & Sons.
71. Sartre, J. P. (1966). *Being and nothingness: A phenomenological study of ontology.* New York: Washington Square Press.

15

Coping

Where Are You Going?

C. R. Snyder

As we turn the corner into the next millennium, coping will help to define the agenda of our civilization. Already, we find the popular literature addressing various topics that fall under the rubric of coping. We are urged to think about those things in our lives that are unwanted stressors, and we are given tips about how to deal with them. Those who do research on coping increasingly are called upon to comment on a variety of events that are occurring in society. Whether it is the print or video media, coping fascinates us and preoccupies our collective attention.

The very goals that we set for ourselves will be influenced, in part, by our coping armamentarium. How we have handled our life stressors previously will impact the tasks that we will select to stretch our capacities in the future. For the most part, we humans prefer things the way they have been, perhaps with a slight increase in difficulty (1). The psychological literature of years past makes this latter point (e.g., the achievement motivation research), as does more recent literature (e.g., the hope research). Some challenge is needed, and this premise helps to understand how we select environments that pull us beyond the comfort of relatively easy goal attainment. The same is the case for coping, as we reconstruct our environs to provide a stimulating mix of old and certain goal attainment, along with the new and less certain. In this sense, there is a dialectic between coping and the challenges that we set for ourselves.

In the present volume, the authors attend to the processes of facilitating adaptive functioning. There is yet another less explored approach, however, that focuses more on the barriers to adaptive functioning. Elsewhere, I have described these as "problems of passion" (2), which are related to the processes by which people do or do not constrain themselves. There are three general categories for these passions. One involves the social problems of constraint that yield such disorders as drug and alcohol abuse, along with associated crimes and losses in productivity. A second set of social problems of constraint involves people who are "lost"; included here are such examples as teenage pregnancy, school drop-outs, voter absenteeism, and so on. A third social problem of constraint is related to health issues, and it includes unsafe sexual practices, unhealthy eating habits, not using seatbelts, and so on. As a means of tackling these problems, I would suggest that scholars in the coping area should spend more time on those processes that block or constrain people from adopting the healthy or adaptive patterns of behavior. Such behaviors impact millions of people, and their costs are enormous in terms of money and, more important, talents and life satisfactions lost.

Just as coping researchers are well qualified to explore ways of increasing adaptive functioning, these scholars also are very well qualified to explore these constraint-related problems of passion. If we do not, we can be assured that others who probably are less skilled at addressing these thorny issues will tackle them. As I have written elsewhere, "At times it seems that we are like gardeners cleaning the leaves of a social plant that is ill, when we should be attending to the roots that feed the problem. Our viability . . . will not depend on our willingness to undertake small, highly circumscribed problems. Rather, our chance at a grander viability will relate to our willingness to grapple with these larger social questions" (2, p. 240). On this point, I know that we can do better.

Why have we not addressed these "problems of passion"? My guess is that they are extremely difficult and complex, and they necessitate long-term approaches to our research. This means that the young scholars who are immigrating into the coping field will need new incentives to attract them to these topics. Likewise, middle-career and beyond scholars who do not have to face the uncertainties of the tenure process need to turn their considerable talents to these "problems of passion."

To some degree, of course, the coping area will be led by the interests of relevant granting agencies. As such, coping researchers would be well advised to advocate the systematic study of these "problems of passion," as well as other topics that will enable the field to grapple with truly important societal questions. I recently had the pleasure of listening to Martin Seligman give an impassioned speech about the important role of psychology in taking a proactive stance in investigating the ways to make the lives of people better, happier, and more productive (3). After Dr. Seligman ended his talk, Sir John Templeton, the founder of the Templeton Philanthropic Foundation, asked him what we could do to help in his "glorious crusade." Seligman answered that much of the support for this new research initiative would need to come from granting agencies that would embrace such priorities for funding. I applaud such entrepreneurial talk and generally perceive that those of us in the field have not done enough to publicly promote the worth of our work. I believe that we can rise to this challenge.

Another dialectic that defines the activities of coping scholars relates to the relative emphasis on theory or empiricism as the guiding framework. The writers in the present volume generally advocate the theoretical approach in which a lucid model drives the subsequent empirical investigations. The reader may be misled by the present sampling of authors, however, and assume that most coping researchers advocate such theory-driven research. On the contrary, my sense is that the majority of research is undergirded by an empiricism in which the researchers "just see what happens." With this attitude, correlational research appears to be rampant.

As the editor of a journal in which most of the incoming manuscripts relate to health and coping issues (i.e., the *Journal of Social and Clinical Psychology*), I have witnessed firsthand this onslaught of correlational research. I certainly believe that such correlational research plays a valuable role, but oftentimes I have found myself urging authors to generate new theories that could explain the relationships obtained in their studies. Although there seemingly is an attributional pull, if you will, to answer the fundamental "why" questions about correlational relationships per se, I am surprised at the high proportion of authors who are content merely to report the relationships. Such relationships are as sterile as the numbers on which they are based, unless we develop cogent theories to understand the processes that underlie them. To state the obvious, new theories certainly are needed as we turn the corner into the twenty-first century.

I have asked colleagues about this dearth of new theory in the area of coping. One answer I have gotten is that we simply are not teaching theory and its importance in graduate school. Although we are producing waves of new coping researchers who are armed with the latest in sophisticated procedures for analyzing questions, my sense is that far less attention is being given to the important role of inventing theoretical frameworks onto which these data can be hung. This is a troubling paradox for the field, and I would encourage those who are involved in the graduate education of coping researchers to attend to this deficiency. We may have the most advanced statistical procedures imaginable, but these will remain as barren mathematical calculations without the theories that bring the data to life.

What can be said about the typical methodologies that we bring to bear on the topics of coping? Generally, most investigators have focused upon self-report indices, both as predictors and criterion variables. As noted previously, a common approach is the simple correlational one in which one predictor variable (or set of variables) is examined in relation to another target criterion variable that pertains to coping. The target criterion variable may be taken in close temporal proximity, or, less frequently, several days or weeks later. Relatedly, we frequently have employed cross-sectional methodologies in which we compare several groups at the same time, rather than a longitudinal approach in which we track one or more groups over time. Finally, coping researchers have followed the nomothetic (group) tradition of trying to make inferences that will generalize to a category of people, rather than utilizing the in-depth ideographic approach that attempts to thoroughly map the psychological terrain of one individual. In regard to the aforementioned approaches, it is probably accurate to assert that coping researchers merely have borrowed from the prevailing research paradigms that form the zeitgeist in clinical, social, and personality psychology more generally. This status quo mentality about our methods, however, will not suffice as we address the complex and grand coping questions in the twenty-first century.

What changes can be made in this typical approach in order to expand what we know about coping? Generally, it is probably fair to suggest that we often have employed a snapshot methodology that misses many of the deeper and enduring aspects of each topic of inquiry. To increase our understanding of coping phenomena, therefore, more long-term longitudinal studies are warranted. Although this issue is rarely discussed in the following manner, it strikes me that this is a sampling issue as much as a methodological one. That is to say, if we sample only once with our research participant, we rightfully should be left wondering about how that one instance relates to many other earlier and later instances in regard to understanding coping more generally.

Granting agencies can help to facilitate increases in the longitudinal approach by making this a requisite part of the methodologies that they fund. One of the reasons that this snapshot approach has proliferated is that this is the typical paradigm taught in graduate education. Those who are responsible for the graduate educations of coping researchers need to place a greater emphasis on longitudinal methodologies. Likewise, the snapshot approach is seductive in that it begets the multiple publications that are demanded of our young assistant professors in order to attain tenure. Again, those among us who are in academia can join together to change the promotion criteria away from sheer numbers, to an emphasis on more labor intensive longitudinal approaches.

Though there certainly are reasons to be upbeat about the short-term benefits of coping on psychological well-being and health, we really know very little about the long-term implications of coping for health. It will be difficult to achieve profound changes in long-term health via coping because health is influenced by many forces over which we have little influence (accidents, genetics, etc.), and to compound matters, health is relatively stable over the life span (4). Nevertheless, while these factors may serve to cap the impact of coping on long-term health, there still remains the possibility of meaningfully improving the general health of our population.

Another change already under way is that coping researchers increasingly are examining markers other than self-report. Actual behaviors are being tapped, as are physiological indices. Greater strides need to be made in this area, however, in order to more fully understand the nature of coping. Perhaps an applied example would help to clarify this point. For years, I have seen people in psychotherapy, with clients in the more recent years having health-related challenges. The core process for transacting such treatment, of course, is the mode of talking. Whenever possible, however, I also try *to get information from other sources so as to gain a more elaborated view of the issues being addressed.* In a recent case, for example, my client's presenting problem was that she was feeling tense and her facial muscles seemed to hurt especially whenever she had to give a talk. Further, she believed that her public speeches had become ineffective because of this pain, and this self-insight was extremely distressful for her. My first strategy was to check out how her presentations actually were being received. To do this, I asked her to give short "teacher evaluation" surveys at the end of her talks. She was reluctant to do this because she felt the outcome would be "painfully obvious" (her pun). Nevertheless, she agreed to give it a try for her next three talks. To her surprise, she was rated as a fine speaker, and there was no clue anywhere in the audience responses about manifestations of her pain. Therefore, she apparently had adopted an overly self-critical stance about her talks. This exercise helped to reduce this pattern of self-criticism and worry. Although my client wanted to believe that her pain and tense facial muscles surely were related to giving bad talks, this no longer seemed tenable when the pain remained *while* she was giving talks that were well received.

Another approach that I employed later with this same client was to encourage her to see an oral surgeon, on the hunch that there might be a physical basis for her pain. This indeed proved to be the case. She had severe protrusion of the upper jaw, which was corrected surgically. Subsequently, her facial pain improved and, over time, disappeared. This one case example shows how gaining information from others (i.e., the evaluations from her audience members) rather than relying on the self-report of the client, as well as checking the physical and mechanical bases of the problem, both provide useful information that elaborated the understanding of this person's problem in coping. Although this is an applied example, it shows how researchers examining coping may profit by exploring the coping issues via several indices. Borrowing from the "The Psychology of What Works" subtitle of this book, coping is best examined from several differing perspectives in order to find out those things that may be most helpful.

Many of the authors in the coping field are fascinated with individual differences models and measurements. What does this mean, and what are the strengths and weaknesses of such an approach? The individual differences approach rests upon the assumption that there is some underlying dimension upon which people can be measured, and that differing scores on that dimension of interest can contribute to the understanding of one or more coping responses. The "understanding" in this sense is based on the predictions that the individual differences indices yield. This approach has the advantage that the individual differences dimension is inherently built upon a theory of some sort. Another advantage is that the score on the individual differences dimension allows the researcher or clinician to obtain a measure of where any one person stands. This score, in turn, may have utility.

The individual differences approach is not without drawbacks, however. One difficulty with this approach is that the proponents of one viewpoint can champion their individual differences approach to the exclusion of other dimensions. Equally problematic is the fact that the person may be reduced to, or equated with, his or her score, and as such the richness of the many facets of the person and environment interaction are missed. Another weakness of this highly popular approach is that it tends to pull the investigator or clinician *into* focusing on the person (i.e., the intrapersonal perspective), and it does not emphasize the importance of situational factors in the coping process (see 5). Indeed, as the name denotes, the *individual* differences approach sharply focuses the attention on the individual, and this perspective matches the predilections of the Western society in which it is studied (6). Further, the individual differences approach often does not readily translate to directions for making interventions. Also, individual difference approaches neglect the more communal strategies for understanding the coping processes from a larger, interactive, and systemic perspective. Certainly, more attention needs to be given to the communal aspects of the coping process in future theory and research. Likewise, studies taking a dyadic approach to coping are largely lacking at present, and this also is an important focus for future activities.

The topic of coping is explored in a multitude of research populations. Wherever people encounter stressors, coping can be studied. Coping researchers, like their counterpart colleagues in the psychology subfields of social, clinical, and personality, can be admonished at times for an over-emphasis on the sample of convenience—the college psychology student who is participating in research as part of course requirements. Coping researchers, however, also should be praised for their willingness to recruit a wider range of people beyond the aforementioned college sophomore psychology student. My sense is that there has been more attention paid to males than females, however, and this bias should be remedied in future research. Likewise, there are few studies focusing on the coping of persons other than Caucasians. Further, there appears to be a bit of an age bias in coping research in that younger people typically are examined. (This latter phenomenon probably is related to reliance upon college students as research participants.) The gender, age, and race issues can be remediated by an emphasis on these samples in the graduate education of future coping researchers. Likewise, a standard part of almost any grant application these days involves how the particular coping process will be explored in samples of men *and* women, as well as Caucasian *and* other races; likewise, for the appropriate study of certain chronic health issues, granting agencies may require samples of older persons. Perhaps the issue of addressing older persons in the study of coping will increase by necessity with the aging of the baby boomers in America. In this latter regard, certainly the researchers and a sizable portion of the population are getting older.

Although the authors in the present volume are psychologists, the topic of coping obviously is not solely their turf. If one examines the contents of journals in the fields of social work, sociology, anthropology, epidemiology, and psychiatry in particular and medicine more generally, as well as government, law, business, and speech and communication, coping is a common topic. As we note in the first chapter, the numbers of citations to coping are skyrocketing, and a variety of professionals are addressing this topic. Indeed, as the twenty-first century unfolds, coping may be one of the central scholarly topics across all academic fields. This comes as no surprise to those of us who have been drawn to this fascinating area previously. No one scholarly discipline, however, can or should lay claim to the sole rights for studying coping. On the contrary, it may well be the collaborative work by scholars from varying disciplines that produces the most important advances on the topic of coping.

Another suggestion that I would make for the future of the coping area is that there be better bridges built between those who do psychotherapy outcome research and those who do coping research. Both groups can gain by a cross-fertilization of theorization, research, and applications. I believe that these two groups of researchers may come to build their work on similar frameworks. Previously, such cooperative work may have been difficult because the psychotherapy researchers typically were utilizing pathology models of human behavior, whereas the psychologists exploring health and coping were embracing models that emphasized the strengths in people. More recently, however, the psychotherapy researchers have been shifting out of their time-honored pathology models, and they have been examining the assets that people have for positive change. Relatedly, the role of narrative is increasingly gaining attention as an important vehicle for psychotherapeutic change (see 7). In this regard, the new coping research paradigm of writing about one's traumatic experiences that has been advanced by Jamie Pennebaker and his colleagues may share important principles with the psychotherapy and narrative approach. Whatever can be done to facilitate the interaction of the psychotherapy and coping researchers will aid both perspectives. In this regard, symposia at conventions, conventions with this bridge as the theme, books with this interface perspective, and joint research teams, to name but a few examples, would be productive.

Another point worth noting is that the reality-negotiation processes may apply to all coping activities. That is to say, whatever a person does in terms of coping, she or he must then place that activity within the context of how it preserves the underlying personal theory. Many of these self-theories appear to enable people to maintain attachments to positive self-referential input and to distance themselves from negative input. The revised helplessness model fits here, but so do hope and optimism, as well as benefit-finding, mastery thinking, and so on. Indeed, my sense is that the clinicians and researchers who apply the various coping strategies must understand how the given approaches may fit into the client's conceptualization of his or her world. Similarly, I believe that future coping theoreticians and researchers will embrace social constructivist assumptions in order to better understand the coping process. Social constructivist views already have made strong inroads into the study of psychotherapy (5), and it follows that the appraisal processes that have been at the core of recent coping thought will be amenable to such constructivist views. My sense is that we only have scratched the surface in our understanding of the contribution that appraisal plays in the coping process. As such, I believe that it is incumbent upon each proponent of a new coping theory to explicate the nature of the appraisal process, as well as the constructivist context.

To what extent are our coping ideas a by-product of our Western society? Certainly, the teleology of hope, optimism, and mastery are, as is the emphasis on the individualistic self in the ego-depletion model, and the attributional roots of the revised helplessness approach. My point is not that this lessens the importance or usefulness of these coping constructs, but rather that we should always keep an eye on the societal context in which our models live. In the degree to which we entertain a social constructivist perspective, as I have advocated in the previous paragraph, then we will look at the underlying roots of our coping theories. If our societal values shift as we move into the next century, then coping researchers should keep their hands on the pulse of this changing society.

As the reader may recall from my comments about the history of coping in the first chapter, the earliest zeitgeist for studying coping was a pathology model. That approach explored the weaknesses of people, and it has begun to give way to a more positive, healthful approach in recent years. Indeed, coping researchers, many of whom identified themselves as being members of the new and growing health psychology movement, accentuate the strengths of people. My sense is that this movement toward a positive, adaptive view about people is still evolving, and that there still are many negative, pathological assumptive networks being applied to the understanding of the coping process. To some extent, this latter focus is understandable because the study of coping occurs in those circumstances in which people are truly provoked and pushed to their limits. Indeed, the eliciting stimulus of coping, the *stressor*, evokes images of the person being pummeled by the bad in life. Surely, then, the bad and the negative are by necessity best understood by focusing on the weaknesses? *I think not*, but one of the problems here is the fundamental negative bias, in which the negative label tends to seduce our attention and offer a powerful model for understanding humans (see 5). What future coping theorists and researchers must be certain to emphasize, in order to counteract this fundamental negative bias, is how people can bring their considerable strengths to bear upon the stressors. This will mean that we must consciously look for the positives that any given person brings to the stressor situation. Indeed, the authors of the chapters in this volume can be praised for focusing on adaptive coping. Further, we must search for these coping strengths in both the intrapersonal makeup *and*, perhaps more important, in the surrounding environment. Finally, as I noted earlier in this chapter, we need to explore the processes that constrain people.

In my perusal of the articles appearing in professional journals, I do not perceive that much attention is being given to the issue of prevention as it relates to the coping processes. Notable exceptions here include the work of Breznitz (8) and Folkman and Lazarus (9) on "anticipatory coping," as well as the "proactive coping" framework presented by Aspinwall and Taylor (10). In the degree to which persons can anticipate and react so as to lessen or negate subsequent stressors in their lives, however, they then rightfully can be said to be engaging in anticipatory coping. The stressor in such a circumstance is imagined, but this does not lessen its importance. Indeed, one of the powerful virtues of Homo sapiens is our intellectual capacity to anticipate those things that portend to stress us. Surely, therefore, such preventive coping is a very legitimate area of inquiry, and one to which we should turn our future attention as we study coping in the twenty-first century.

Yet another exciting frontier that is related to appraisal processes involves the role of imagined activities or mental simulations in the production of adaptive coping strategies (see 11, 12). Likewise, the degree to which we can help people to coordinate their mental coping simulations with their actual behavioral practices should take on important implications for research and interventions. These and related questions strike me as fundamental to many of the processes that have been discussed in the chapters in the present volume.

What would the person who is unfamiliar with the coping literature learn from this book? Overall, there are two broad "take-home" messages worth highlighting. First, coping has taken on a primacy in our society. Whereas our ancestors probably went about their daily toils without even thinking much about coping per se, today we actually may analyze how well we are coping. With the rise in interest in coping, the average person, by necessity, thinks more about those stressors in modern life that demand coping. Stressors and their associated coping probably make up a large part of our daily conversations, as well as the entertainment that we enjoy. To illustrate an example of this latter point, consider the inherent stress and coping content of popular songs (from country to rock). The protagonists in such lyrics are caught in the throes of some stressor that has necessitated heartfelt coping actions.

As a second general theme that emerges in this book, the chapters make the case that there are some among us who are better at dealing with the stressors—that is to say, there are some people who are better copers. Painting a quick sketch of such a person, she or he probably is optimistic, has a sense of mastery, is hopeful, can ward off negative events via the explanations made about those events, finds a silver lining in adversity, understands and effectively uses emotions, and so on.

The concept of coping occupies an important place within the psyche of cultures more generally, and with people specifically. To answer the rhetorical question that forms the "Coping: Where Are You Going?" title of this final chapter, the link between now and the future will be written as a saga of coping in which, individually and communally, we will strive to deal successfully with the stressors that come our way. This volume offers a partial road map of our travels on this coping journey so far, as well as what lies ahead. Wherever coping goes, so too will our civilization . . . and vice versa.

References

1. Snyder, C. R. (1994). *The psychology of hope: You can get there from here.* New York: Free Press.
2. Snyder, C. R. (1997). State of the interface between clinical and social psychology. *Journal of Social and Clinical Psychology, 16(3),* 231–242.
3. Seligman, M. E. P. (1998, February 10). *Optimism, hope, and ending the epidemic of depression.* Paper presented at the Science of Optimism and Hope: A Research Symposium. Philadelphia.
4. Lazarus, R. S. (1991). Evaluating psychosocial factors in health. In C. R. Snyder & D. R. Forsyth (Eds.), *Handbook of social and clinical psychology: The health perspective* (p. 798). Elmsford, NY: Pergamon.
5. Wright, B. A. (1991). Labeling: The need for greater person-environment individuation. In C. R. Snyder & D. R Forsyth (Eds.), *Handbook of social and clinical psychology: The health perspective* (pp. 469–487). Elmsford, NY: Pergamon.
6. Snyder, C. R. , & Fromkin, H. L. (1980). *Uniqueness: The human pursuit of difference.* New York: Plenum.
7. Neimeyer, R. A., & Mahoney, M. J. (Eds.) (1995). *Constructivism in psychotherapy.* Washington, DC: American Psychological Association.
8. Breznitz, S. (1983). Anticipatory stress and denial. In S. Breznitz (Ed.), *The denial of stress* (pp. 225–255). New York: International Universities Press.
9. Folkman, S., & Lazarus, R. S. (1985). If it changes, it must be a process: Study of emotion and coping during three stages of a college examination. *Journal of Personality and Social Psychology, 48,* 150–170.
10. Aspinwall, L. G., & Taylor, S. E. (1997). A stitch in time: Self-regulation and proactive coping. *Psychological Bulletin, 121,* 417–436.
11. Taylor, S. E., & Pham, L. B. (1996). Mental simulation, motivation, and action. In P. E. Gollwitzer & J. A. Bargh (Eds.), *The psychology of action: Linking cognition and motivation to behavior* (pp. 219–235). New York: Guilford.
12. Taylor, S. E., & Schneider, S. K. (1989). Coping and the simulation of events. *Social Cognition, 7,* 174–194.

Index

environment
  external, 7, 13–14
  internal, 7
  social, 106, 175–76, 248–49
Epictetus, 35
Epstein, S., 12, 24
Erikson, E. H., 186, 290
Ersek, M., 37
Esterling, B., 73
ethnicity, 218–19, 329
excuse-making, 20, 23–25, 27–28,
    33, 38
executive function, of self, 52, 57,
    58, 63, 64–65
expectancy-value motivation
    models, 182–86, 190
explanatory style, 184–85, 258–60
  catastrophizing and, 258–60, 264–
    69
  in children, 167–69, 170–71, 177–
    78, 272
exposure-based therapy, 104
external environment, Adlerian, 7,
    13–14
extraversion
  benefit-finding and, 279, 286, 287
  as catastrophe predictor, 255
  optimism and, 186
  as personality trait, 119, 121–35
Eysenck, Hans, 121

failure
  mastery vs. helpless views of, 232–
    35, 238, 242–43, 244, 246, 248
  stressful aspects of, 58
Falke, R., 294
Fanshel, D., 83
fatalism, 256, 259
fatigue, 255
Faustian bargains, 60
fear, 104, 107, 122
feedback-loop theory, 51
Feinstein, L., 294
fibromyalgia, 215, 286, 295
Fisler, R., 80
Foa, E. B., 79, 104, 105, 272
Folie à Deux. See shared psychotic
    disorder
Folkman, Susan, 9–11, 53, 97, 110,
    257, 280, 294, 332

folk wisdom, 182
Fontaine, K., 283
Ford, C. E., 24
Fowles, D. C., 134
Framingham Type A Scale, 11
Francis, M. E., 73, 80, 81
Frank, Jerome, 206
Fresco, D. M., 272
Freud, Anna, 7, 8
Freud, Sigmund, 6–7, 8, 13
Friedman, L. N., 56
Friedman, Meyer, 11
Frijda, N. H., 105
functionalism, 90, 91–96
fundamental assumptions. See
    assumptions, fundamental
Funder, D., 12–13

Gardner, Howard, 143
Garvey, A. J., 57
gender
  children's emotion-focused coping
    and, 107
  hope and, 218
  research bias, 329
  See also men; women
general adaptation syndrome, 53
generativity, 290–91, 292
genetic factors, 186, 199
gestalt therapy, 94
Gidron, Y., 77
Giuliano, T. A., 149–50
Glaser, R., 73
Glass, D. C., 55, 56
Glass, G., 76
goals
  emotions as signals of, 105, 108
  in expectancy-value models, 183,
    200
  hope and, 207–8, 214, 216, 218,
    221–22, 285–86
  mastery vs. helpless orientation,
    233, 237–39, 241, 244, 247
Goldman, S. L., 146
Goleman, D., 159
Gompertz models, 265
Goodman, E., 198
goodness, children's views of, 242–
    43
Gordon, J. R., 57

Gottman, J. M., 153
Gough, H. G., 121
Greenberg, L. S., 94–95, 105
Greenberg, M. A., 72, 78, 257
Greening, L., 263–64
grief, 77, 85, 148
growth, personal, 291, 293
guilt, 122

Haan, N., 7–8
habit, 60
habituation, stressor, 104–5
Hage, J. N., 55
Hagstrom, R., 256
Halpern, P. L., 55
Hamilton Depression Rating Scale, 216
Hammen, C. L., 30
Hammer, A. L., 53
happiness, 144–45
hardiness, 287
Harris, S., 283
Harvey, A. G., 257
Harvey, J., 285
hassles, 254, 260
health problems
  benefit-finding and, 279–84, 290, 294–95
  coping research on, 325, 327
  disclosure therapies, 70–86, 94
  emotion-focused coping and, 10
  explanatory style as factor, 258–60, 266
  hope and, 214–16, 220, 222
  hope-related cures, 206
  optimistic-pessimistic views of, 188–89, 191–96, 283
  personal-disclosure effects, 70–86, 96, 105, 154, 155
  reality-negotiation strategies, 20, 29, 32–39
  relaxation therapy, 70
  social support benefits, 151–52
  Type A behavior factors, 11–12
  See also pain; specific conditions
health psychology, 14, 70, 331
Hearst-Ikeda, D., 272
heart disease
  benefit-finding by patients, 35, 281–82, 290

optimism-pessimism factors, 168, 191–92, 195
  social support benefits, 152
  Type A behavior and, 11–12
Heath, A. C., 133
Heatherton, T. F., 51
Hegel, Georg Wilhelm, 23
helpless coping style, 233–49, 258–59
helplessness, learned, 55, 57–58, 330
  characterization of, 57
  and childhood depression, 165, 166–67, 171, 175, 178
  and reactions to failure, 233–35
Henderson, A. S., 133
Henderson, V., 239–40
heritability, of optimism, 186, 199
Herman, C. P., 57
Hervig, L. K., 126
Higgins, P., 283
Higgins, R. L., 20, 26, 30, 31, 33, 34
HIV virus, 192, 195–96, 198
Hodgins, D. C., 57
Hofball, S. E., 53
Hogan, Robert, 13
Holleran, S., 213
Holmes, T. H., 253
Hooker, K., 126
hope, 205–22, 330
  benefit-finding and, 279, 285–86
  bias impediments and, 217–19
  definitions of, 207–8
  in emotion-focused coping, 100
  future research issues, 219–22
  historical perspectives, 205–6
  individual differences in, 211–16
  intervention research, 216–17, 219–21
  measurement of, 209–10
  reality negotiation and, 23–24, 25, 26
  resource replenishment role, 61–62
hopelessness, 166, 174, 259, 260
hope-reminding, 220
Hope Scale, 26, 286, 296
Hostile Automatic Thoughts Scale, 12
hostility
  as catastrophe predictor, 255

as disclosure impact factor, 75
learned optimism and, 176
as negative affect, 122, 124
as Type A behavior component, 12
Houston, B. Kent, 12
Hoza, B., 210
Hubbard, B., 126, 127
Hull, J. G., 56
Hume, David, 30
humor, 193, 194
hypochondriasis, 28

Ickovics, J. R., 283
illness. *See* health problems
illusion-based coping, 8, 29, 36–38, 39
illusions, positive, 29, 39, 212, 258, 290, 310
immune system functioning, 33, 73, 95, 152, 154
impulse control, 52, 59, 60
incremental theory of intelligence, 238–42, 248, 249
individual differences
    as coping theory approach, 12–13, 328–29
    as disclosure impact factor, 75
    emotional intelligence and, 148–49
    emotion-focused coping and, 101–2
    in hoping, 210–16
    reality-negotiation role, 24–26
    See also personality
infertility, 189
information-processing styles, 144–45
inhibition
    autonomic effects of, 78
    model of psychosomatics, 154
intelligence
    emotional, 93, 141–60
    entity and incremental theories, 238–42, 247–49
    mastery vs. helpless orientation and, 232, 233, 234–35, 238–48
intentional trauma, 254
internal environment, Freudian, 7
internal explanation, 258–59

internal locus of control, 287
intrapersonal intelligences, 143
introversion, 121
Inventory of Perceived Control Beliefs, 283, 296
in vitro fertilization, 189, 192
Iowa Basic Test of Skill, 212
IPCB. *See* Inventory of Perceived Control Beliefs
ironic processes, 154–55
Irrational Beliefs Test, 258
irrationality, 258

James, William, 23, 306
Janoff-Bulman, R., 62, 256, 285
Jardine, R., 133
Jenkins Activity Survey, 11
Jouriles, E., 56
Journal of Personality and Social Psychology, 13
joviality, 122, 123
judgmental criticism, 244–45
justice, 308–9
just world theory, 308

Kahen, V., 152
Kaiser, C. F., 57
Kant, Immanuel, 23
Keillor, Garrison, 309
Kelley, H. H., 27–28
Kendler, K. S., 133
Kendrick, D. T., 12–13
Kessler, R. C., 133
kidney failure, 33
Kiecolt-Glaser, J., 73
Kierkegaard, S., 312
Kinnunen, T., 57
Klausner, E. J., 216
Kleck, R. E., 103
Kolar, D. W., 126
Koons, A. N., 272
Kozak, M. J., 104
Kozlowski, L. T., 57
Kraemer, D. T., 146
Kuhn, Thomas, 311
Kumar, M., 73

Labov, W., 83
Laird, S. P., 215
Larsen, R. J., 264

problem solving, 235
 emotions' role in, 144
 hope as factor in, 210, 213–14
 learned optimism and, 169, 172,
   173, 175
process-experiential therapy, 94–95
psychic closing-off, 313
psychodynamic model, 6–8, 12, 13–
 14
psychological adjustment, hope and,
 210–12
psychology, 142, 330
 coping concept development, 6–13
 emotion portrayals, 90, 142–43
 health psychology movement, 14,
   331
psychopathology, 331
 emotion-focused coping and, 10,
   97, 98–99
 personality trait factors, 124, 132
psychosomatic medicine, 70
psychotherapy, 76, 82, 93–94, 166,
 330
psychoticism, 121
PTGI. See Posttraumatic Growth
 Inventory
PTSD. See post-traumatic stress
 disorder
Publilius Syrus, 142

RA. See rheumatoid arthritis
racism, 218–19
Rahe, R. H., 253
Rapoff, M. A., 290
rational-emotive therapy, 258, 272–
 73
rationalization, 293–94
Ratzan, S., 38
Rauch, S., 80
reality negotiation, 20–39, 330
 as coping mechanism, 29–32
 definition of, 20–22
 historical context, 23–24
 individual differences role, 24–26
 strategy overview, 26–29
reappraisal, 105, 191, 194, 200, 292
reason, 142
reasoning, 144–45
reattribution, 169, 170–73, 178, 199–
 200

reciprocity, social support, 35–36
recovery from coping. See ego depletion
redemptive sequences, 291, 292
Reeve, Christopher, 36
reexperiencing of traumatic events,
 314
regulation of emotions, 144, 146,
 150–51, 153, 155–56
relapse, stress and, 56–57, 59
relaxation therapies, 70
religion, as coping mechanism, 127,
 130, 215
repression, 155
resignation, 195
resolution rituals, 94
resources, coping, 50–65
response styles theory, 147
responsibility-diminishing, in
 excuse-making, 23
rest, replenishing effects of, 59–60,
 63, 65
restraint, 130
Revised NEO Personality Inventory,
 122, 127, 128
revolving self-images, 23, 32
rheumatoid arthritis, 35, 77, 85, 215,
 283–84
Richards, J. M., 72
Riggs, D., 79
risk homeostasis theory, 270
risk-taking, 255, 270
Robinson, D., 283
Rogers, Carl, 23, 94
role models, 23, 153
role playing, 94
Rosenman, Ray, 11
Rothbaum, F., 54
Rowe, J., 281, 283
ruminative coping, 147–51, 156, 257

Saarni, C., 92–93, 107
sadness, 107, 122, 144–45
Safran, J. D., 94–95
Salovey, P., 93
Sampson, W. S., 272
Samuelson, B. E. A., 25–26
Sartre, Jean-Paul, 320
Sattler, D. N., 57
Schachter, S., 57